MW01517893

Short Story Theories

A Twenty-First-Century Perspective

49 DQR STUDIES IN LITERATURE

Series Editors

C.C. Barfoot - A.J. Hoenselaars
W.M. Verhoeven

Short Story
Theories
A Twenty-First-Century Perspective

Edited by
Viorica Patea

Amsterdam - New York, NY 2012

Cover image: Acrylic on handmade paper, 53 x 43 cm, 2007
Wolfgang Hunecke (born 1950, Bonn), painter, sculptor and engraver is one of
the foremost German contemporary artists.

Cover design: Aart Jan Bergshoeff and Carlos Fortes, www.carlosfortes.es

The paper on which this book is printed meets the requirements of
'ISO 9706: 1994, Information and documentation - Paper for documents -
Requirements for permanence'.

ISBN: 978-90-420-3564-5
E-Book ISBN: 978-94-012-0839-0
©Editions Rodopi B.V., Amsterdam - New York, NY 2012
Printed in The Netherlands

To the memory of Per Winther
(1947-2012)

CONTENTS

III. Borders, Postcolonialism, Orality, and Gender

IV. Postmodernism and the Twenty-first Century: Intertextuality, Minifiction, Serial Narration

ACKNOWLEDGEMENTS

The idea of putting together a collection of essays on the short story and short story theories originated in two research projects funded by grants from the Regional Ministry of Culture of the Regional Autonomous Government of Castile and Leon (ref. number SA012A10-1) and the Spanish Ministry of Science and Innovation (ref. number FFI2010-15063). This research developed into a larger project that outgrew its initial scope and included new scholars who contributed to this subject.

Other friends and colleagues have also assisted by contributing their ideas and encouragement. The editor wishes to thank Consuelo Montes-Granado, Ana María Manzanas, Antonio López Santos and Pepe Mayo for their generous supply of friendship, kindness and humor over these last few years. Special thanks go to Santiago Vaquera, who graciously volunteered to translate Lauro Zavala's essay from Spanish into English, and to Carlos Fortes for his constantly generous help regarding artistic matters. The editor is indebted in various ways to Ileana and Adrian Parvulescu for their willingness to locate important bibliographical material unavailable in Spanish libraries.

Last but not least, I wish to thank all of the contributors, who have made this book possible through their patience with and enthusiasm for a project that I hope will offer new insights into the short story genre and further the vitality of the current critical debate.

THE SHORT STORY: AN OVERVIEW OF THE HISTORY AND EVOLUTION OF THE GENRE

VIORICA PATEA

> A story is a way to say something that can't be said any other way, and it takes every word in the story to say what the meaning is. You tell a story because a statement would be inadequate. When anybody asks what a story is about, the only proper thing is to tell him to read the story. The meaning of fiction is not abstract meaning but experienced meaning, and the purpose of making statements about the meaning of the story is only to help you to experience that meaning more fully.[1]

Theory and history of the form

As early as 1937 Elizabeth Bowen claimed, "The short story is a young art ... the child of this century", which developed at the same time as the cinema and photography.[2] According to Mary Rohrberger, one of the first theorizers of the genre, "short narrative fiction is as old

This study is part of two research projects funded by grants from the Regional Ministry of Culture of the Autonomous Government of Castile and Leon (ref. number SA012A10-1) and the Spanish Ministry of Science and Innovation (ref. number FFI2010-15063).

[1] Flannery O'Connor, "Writing Short Stories", in *Mystery and Manners*, eds Sally and Robert Fitzgerald, New York: Farrar, Straus and Giroux, 1969, 96.

[2] Elizabeth Bowen, "The Faber Book of Modern Short Stories" (1937), in *The New Short Story Theories*, ed. Charles E. May, Athens: Ohio University Press, 1994, 152. See also Julio Cortázar, "Some Aspects of the Short Story", in *ibid.*, 246-47.

as the history of literature .... But the short story, as we know it today, is the newest of literary genres."[3]

The origins of the short form go back to myth and biblical verse narratives, medieval sermons and romance, fables, folktales, ballads and the rise of the German Gothic in the eighteenth century. But its mythic origins, filtered through the Romantic influence, had to come to terms with the conventions of mimesis and *vraisemblance* of eighteenth- and nineteenth-century realism.[4] Charles May observes that "the short story has from its beginning been a hybrid form combining both the metaphoric mode of the old romance and the metonymic mode of the new realism".[5]

Although the short story constitutes a form in its own right, it has suffered a theoretical neglect in comparison with other genres such as poetry, drama, the epic, or the novel. As May argues, "a genre only truly comes into being when the conventions that constitute it are articulated within the larger conceptual context of literature as a whole".[6] In the case of the short story this was a long-deferred process. Until half a century ago those who theorized about the genre were not literary critics but practitioners of the form themselves: Edgar Allan Poe, Herman Melville and Anton Chekhov in the nineteenth century; and Henry James, Flannery O'Connor, Julio Cortázar and Eudora Welty, among others, in the twentieth. But interest in the short story has been growing continuously since the

---

[3] Mary Rohrberger, "The Short Story: A Proposed Definition", in *Short Story Theories,* ed. Charles May, Athens OH: Ohio University Press, 1976, 80.

[4] Charles May believes the short story is "the structural core of all fiction in its derivation from folktale and myth" ("The Metaphoric Motivation in Short Fiction: 'In the Beginning Was the Story'", in *Short Story Theory at a Crossroads,* eds Susan Lohafer and Jo Ellyn Clarey, Baton Rouge: Louisiana State University Press, 1989, 64). He persuasively observes that the main challenge the short form poses to its practitioners is how to integrate the tension of the mythic with the realistic modality, a reconciliation that is finally projected in the aesthetic ("Why Short Stories Are Essential and Why They Are Seldom Read", in *The Art of Brevity: Excursions in Short Fiction Theory and Analysis,* eds Per Winther *et al.*, Columbia: University of South Carolina Press, 2004, 22). On this issue, see also Charles May, *The Short Story: The Reality of Artifice* (1995) rpt. New York: Routledge, 2002, 1-42; May, "The Nature of Knowledge in Short Fiction", in May, *The New Short Story Theories,* 138-43; Warren Walker, "From Raconteur to Writer: Oral Roots and Printed Leaves of Short Fiction", in *The Teller and the Tale: Aspects of the Short Story,* ed. Wendell M. Aycock, Lubbock: Texas Tech Press, 1982, 13-26.

[5] May, *The Short Story: The Reality of Artifice,* 72.

[6] *Ibid.*, 108.

Sixties; critical and theoretical studies of the form have been flourishing since the last decades of the twentieth century.

Poe's critical comments towards the middle of the nineteenth century are responsible for the birth of the short story as a unique genre.[7] As the first short story theorist, he brought into discussion issues of form, style, length, design, authorial goals, and reader affect, developing the framework within which the short story is discussed even today. Evaluating the status of the short story as a genre, he ranked it very high in the pantheon of arts, second only to the lyric form. His major contribution was to invest the short story with tension and thus to impregnate it with the defining attributes of poetry. Its compact and unified form, which it shares with the lyric, allows the short story to achieve effects unattainable in the novel. He also observed that its brevity and intensity created a strong "undercurrent of suggestion".[8] Poe was the first to consider endings as crucial elements in compositional strategies and defined the short story in terms of reading experience.

A traditional view of the short story is that it is a compressed, unified, and plotted form. Theoretical discussions of the genre explore notions such as totality, brevity, intensity, suggestiveness, unity of effect, closure, and design. Attention to the formal structure of the short story is mainly a twentieth-century critical enterprise. The aesthetics of the genre's form attracted the interest of critics and narrative theorists in the Sixties – the period of the international dissemination of Russian Formalist writings of the 1920s (Boris Éjxenbaum, Viktor Shklovsky), the emergence of structuralism (Vladimir Propp) and anthropology (Claude Lévi-Strauss), and the philosophy of culture (Ernest Cassirer). The rise of the short theory then also further developed in parallel with the growth of interest in narratology, reader-response criticism, and discourse analysis and cognitive science.

---

[7] See Poe's review of *Zinzendorff, and Other Stories* by L.H. Sigourney, *Southern Literary Messenger*, January 1836; his review of *Night and Morning: A Novel* by Edward Bulwer-Lytton, *Graham's Magazine*, April 1841; his review of *Twice Told-Tales* by Nathaniel Hawthorne, *Graham's Magazine*, May 1842, are all to be found in Edgar Allan Poe, *Essays and Reviews*, ed. G.R. Thompson, New York: Library of America, 1984, 874-91, 146-60, 568-69. Poe's articles and passages of his aesthetic pronouncements on the short story excerpted from his lesser-known reviews are conveniently collected in May, *The New Short Story Theories*, 59-72.

[8] Poe, review of Hawthorne's *Twice-Told Tales*, 571.

Pioneering work on the theoretical analysis of short stories goes back to Frank O'Connor's *A Lonely Voice* (1963) and Mary Rohrberger's *Hawthorne and the Modern Short Story: A Study of Genre* (1966), both of which owed debts to Brander Matthews' early *The Philosophy of the Short-Story* (1901).[9]

The establishment of a field of short story theory, though, is largely due to Charles May's groundbreaking study *Short Story Theories* (1976), a collection of essays that summed up various perspectives on the short story and opened up new avenues for future research within the genre. His *New Short Story Theories* (1994) soon became a sourcebook for studies of the form and a compendium of frameworks within which the short story is currently being analyzed. May's *The Reality of Artifice* (1995) was a further step toward providing a firm critical history to the form, tracing the origins, shape, influences, and evolution of the short story from its beginnings to the present day.

Efforts to recognize the short story as a valid subject for discussion were furthered by Susan Lohafer's theoretically challenging collection *Coming to Terms with the Short Story* (1983) and her co-edited volumes, *Short Story Theories at a Crossroads* (1989) and *The Tales We Tell: Perspectives on the Short Story* (1998),[10] which make an effort to ground the short story in cognitive patterns. More than any other set of components, Lohafer relates storyness to closural elements and analyzes the reader's perception of storyness and preclosure (those instances in which the reader senses that the story might end although it does not). Within the same line, John Gerlach's *Toward the End: Closure and Structure in the American Short Story* (1985)[11] builds a comprehensive system of narrative closural categories for the short story, based on the assumption that endings condition our reading of the entire text as well as the endings themselves.

---

[9] Frank O'Connor, *The Lonely Voice*, Cleveland, OH: World, 1963; Mary Rohrberger, *Hawthorne and the Modern Short Story: A Study in Genre*, The Hague: Mouton, 1966; Brander Matthews, *The Philosophy of the Short-Story*, New York: Longmans, Green, 1901.

[10] Susan Lohafer, *Coming to Terms with the Short Story*, Baton Rouge: Louisiana State University Press, 1983; *The Tales We Tell: Perspectives on the Short Story*, eds Barbara Lounsberry, Susan Lohafer *et al.*, Westport, CT: Greenwood Press, 1998.

[11] John Gerlach, *Toward the End: Closure and Structure in the American Short Story*, Tuscaloosa: University of Alabama Press, 1985.

Studies of autonomous short stories that highlighted various interconnections between works within the same volume introduced a new genre for theoretical analysis, successively called the "short story cycle" (Forrest Ingram, 1971), the "short story sequence" (Luscher, 1989) and the "short story composite" (Lundén, 1999).[12] As Rolf Lundén argues, short story composites go back to Boccaccio's *Decameron*, or Chaucer's *The Canterbury Tales*, and draw on independent yet interrelated stories and episodes that articulated the oldest sagas and epics. Their modern counterparts can be found in the short story composites developed by James Joyce in *Dubliners* (1914), Sherwood Anderson in *Winesburg, Ohio* (1919), Ernest Hemingway in *In Our Time* (1925), William Faulkner in *Go Down Moses* (1942), or Eudora Welty in *Golden Apples* (1949), to mention only a few. The generic specificity of the composite expresses the underlying tension between "variety and unity, separateness and interconnectedness, fragmentation and continuity, openness and closure".[13] Studies of the short story composite focus on the existing variety of textual strategies, networks of association, and underlying patterns, themes, characters and motives that bridge the apparent gaps between the individual stories. These strategies suggest the form's close alliance with sonnet sequences, music, and lyric poetry, which similarly feature recurrent patterns and the progressive development of themes and motifs.[14]

Beginning in the Eighties, a series of studies examined the short fiction belonging to different schools and artistic time periods – such as modernism or postmodernism. Clare Hanson's *Short Stories and Short Fictions, 1880-1980* (1985), as well as her collection *Re-reading the Short Story* (1989) and Dominic Head's *The Modernist Short Story* (1992), analyze the many ways in which modernism changed the shape of modern fiction, supplanting plot with mood,

---

[12] Forrest Ingram, *Representative Short Story Cycles of the Twentieth Century: Studies in a Literary Genre*, The Hague: Mouton, 1971; Robert Luscher, "The Short Story Sequence: An Open Book", in *Short Story Theory at a Crossroads*, 148-67; Rolf Lundén, *The United Stories of America: Studies in the Short Story Composite*, Amsterdam: Rodopi, 1999.
[13] Lundén, *The United Stories of America*, 12.
[14] See Adrian Hunter, *The Cambridge Introduction to the Short Story in English*, Cambridge: Cambridge University Press, 2007.

impressions and moments of awareness.[15] Similarly, Farhat
Iftekharrudin's co-edited collection *The Postmodern Short Story:
Forms and Issues* (2003) pursued the subsequent evolution of the
genre in its postmodern instantiations, which tend to explore the
illusions of the real and make artistic devices and conventions the
subject of their fiction.[16] W.H. New's *Dreams of Speech and
Violence: The Art of the Short Story in Canada and New Zealand*
(1987), followed by Gerald Lynch's *The One and the Many: English-
Canadian Short Story Cycles* (2001), were among the first to explore
genre developments from a postcolonial perspective.[17]

In the Eighties the publishing house Twayne inaugurated two
series, one on studies of short fiction and one on the critical history of
the short story; special issues on the form were published by *Modern
Fiction Studies* (1982), and the Dutch journal *Poetics* (1988); the
Journal of the Short Story in English was founded in 1983, the First
International Conference, which was to become a biannual event, was
initiated in 1989; and by 1994, the date that marks the foundation of
the journal *Short Story*, the genre already constituted an autonomous
field of study.[18]

The architecture of the short story: aspects of structure and form
Theories about the short story as a genre tend to be "interdisciplinary
and gender-bending".[19] Discussions of the short story relate the form
to myth, folklore, romance, genre theory, cognitive science,
narratology, discourse analysis, and visual arts. From its very

---

[15] Clare Hanson, *Short Stories and Short Fictions, 1880-1980*, London: Macmillan,
1985; *Re-reading the Short Story*, ed. Clare Hanson, New York: St Martin's, 1989;
Dominic Head, *The Modernist Short Story*, Cambridge: Cambridge University Press,
1992.
[16] *The Postmodern Short Story*, eds Farhat Iftekharrudin *et al.*, Westport, CT: Praeger,
2003. Among recent interdisciplinary contributions to the field, see *Contemporary
Debates on the Short Story*, eds José R. Ibáñez, José Francisco Fernández and Carmen
M. Bretones, Bern: Peter Lang 2007.
[17] W.H. New's *Dreams of Speech and Violence: The Art of the Short Story in Canada
and New Zealand*, Toronto: Toronto University Press, 1987; Gerald Lynch's *The One
and the Many: English-Canadian Short Story Cycles* (1987), rpt. Toronto: Toronto
University Press, 2001; *Telling Stories: Postcolonial Short Fiction in English*, ed.
Jacqueline Bardolph, Amsterdam: Rodopi, 2001.
[18] For the most recent studies, see Paul Russell, *The Short Story: An Introduction*,
Edinburgh: Edinburgh University Press, 2009.
[19] Susan Lohafer, Introduction to *The Tales We Tell*, xi.

beginnings the short story was considered a form that mediated between the lyric and the novel, yet within its space it came to exhibit a protean variety.[20] As Penn affirms, the short story "has genres of its own invention".[21] Besides the novel and the lyric form, the short story is close cousins with the essay (Hesse), the letter (Pasco), cinema (Bowen, Bates), and photography (Cortázar), as well as painting and the visual arts (Hanson).[22]

Its long-standing theoretical neglect, though, made the short story appear to be "a form at the margins".[23] Seen as ex-centric and at the low end of the hierarchy of arts – contrary to Poe's earlier vision – the short story began to be invested with the vindicating powers of the wronged and the underrated. The first to attribute subversive powers to the genre was the Irish writer Frank O'Connor, who defined the short story as the "lonely voice" of "outlawed figures wandering about the fringes of society". In his view, the short story is a genre that "never had a hero", and its protagonists have been collective groups of submerged populations.[24] In the same line, Marie Louise Pratt links the short story with regional, gender, and political marginalization. In her opinion, the form flourishes in regions in which new groups seek to affirm their voice within emerging national literatures or in the process of decolonization.[25] Clare Hanson endowed the form with the capacity of expressing the repressed knowledge of a dominant culture.[26] These critics argue that the short story thrives in societies with no fixed cultural framework, especially in colonial contexts, and

[20] Hanson, Short Stories and Short Fictions, 9.
[21] W.S. Penn, "The Tale as Genre in Short Fiction", in May, The New Short Story Theories, 44.
[22] See Douglas Hesse, "A Boundary Zone: First-Person Short Stories and Narrative Essays", in Lohafer and Clarey, Short Story Theory at a Crossroads, 85-105; Allan H. Pasco, "On Defining Short Stories", in May, The New Short Story Theories, 114-30; Bowen, "The Faber Book of Modern Short Stories", 256. For H.E. Bates the short story and film resort to the same technique that consists of gestures, shift shots, moments of suggestion: "The Modern Short Story: A Retrospect", in May, The New Short Story Theories, 76. Cortázar, "Some Aspects of the Short Story", 246. Clare Hanson, Introduction to Re-reading the Short Story, 6.
[23] Hanson, Introduction to Re-reading the Short Story, 3.
[24] Frank O'Connor, "The Lonely Voice", in May, The New Short Story Theories, 87 and 86, respectively.
[25] Marie Louise Pratt, "The Short Story: The Short and the Long of It", in May, The New Short Story Theories, 104. See also O'Connor, "The Lonely Voice", 83-93.
[26] Hanson, Re-reading the Short Story, 1-8.

is linked to marginal people, women, or outsiders, all of whom are plagued by a sense of exile and existential isolation.[27] For them the volatility of class structure accounts for the genre's experimental nature.

Because the short story is situated at varying crossroads, defining the short story genre has proved problematic.[28] Attempts at definition have been highly diverse: short stories have been approached in terms of unity (Poe, Brander Matthews), brevity, intensity and tension (Oates, Bader, Friedman, Cortázar),[29] lyricism (Lukács, Moravia),[30] theme (O'Connor's "human loneliness"),[31] insight, vision and mystery (Éjxenbaum, May, Rohrberger), hybridity (May, Pratt),[32] fractals (Leslie Marmon Silko),[33] and closure (Lohafer, Gerlach). Nevertheless, it is still difficult to determine which features distinguish it from other genres and account for its unique nature. A range of different issues and perspectives also informs the discourse on genre: the short story's origin in myth and oral storytelling (May); its focus on the ineffable (Rohrberger); issues of length in the form of contemporary attraction to minimalism (Zavala);[34] concern with fragments, closure or frames (Reid,[35] Winther); or the generic affinities the short story shares with the novel, the lyric, autobiography, letter-writing, music, and so on. As Charles May aptly observes, among the most challenging generic issues remain the relationship between sequence and significance, mystery and pattern,

---

[27] See Pasco, "On Defining Short Stories", 119; Pratt, "The Short Story", 104.

[28] Gerald Gillespie, "Novella, Nouvelle, Novela, Short Novel: A Review of Terms", *Neophilologus*, LI/1 (January 1967), 117-27; Charles May, "Prolegomenon to a Generic Study of the Short Story", *Studies in Short Fiction*, XXXIII/4 (Fall 1996), 461-73. For definitions based on generic expectations, see André Jolles, *Formes Simples* (1930), rpt. Paris: Seuil, 1972.

[29] See Joyce Carol Oates, "The Beginnings: Origins and Art of the Short Story", in *The Tales We Tell*, 46-52; A.L. Bader, "The Structure of the Modern Short Story", and Norman Friedman, "What Makes the Short Story Short?", in May, *The New Short Story Theories*, 107-15 and 131-46.

[30] Georg Lukács, *The Theory of the Novel*, Cambridge, MA: MIT Press, 1971, 51-52; Alberto Moravia, "The Short Story and the Novel", in May, *The New Short Story Theories*, 147-51.

[31] O'Connor, "The Lonely Voice", 87.

[32] May, *The Reality of Artifice*, 72.

[33] Leslie Marmon Silko, "Earth, Air, Water, Mind", in *The Tales We Tell*, 92.

[34] Lauro Zavala, "De la Teoría Literaria a la Minificción Posmoderna", *Ciências Sociais Unisinos*, XLIII/1 (January-April 2007), 86-96.

[35] Ian Reid, "Generic Variations on a Colonial Topos", in *The Tales We Tell*, 83-90.

the fusion of the trivial and the significant, and the eschewal of explications.[36]

In the 1980s, some critics doubted that a definition of the short story was possible. But while Mary Louise Pratt considered this an hopeless enterprise,[37] Charles May hoped to provide a possible definition of the discipline through Wittgensteinian family resemblance theories, which assume existing clusters of qualities, family traits and dominant characteristics.[38] According to the Russian Formalist Boris Éjxenbaum, the short story is a primary elemental form which maintains its strong ties to myth and whose characteristics are compression and concentration: "The story is a riddle." In his view, the novel and short story are "not only different in kind but also inherently at odds". While the short story "is a fundamental, elementary form", the novel remains "synchretic". The discrepancy between the two is marked by the essential disparity between short and long forms: "the story is a problem in posing a single equation with one unknown; the novel a problem involving various rules and soluble with a whole system of equations with various unknowns in which the intermediary steps are more important than the final answer."[39]

Generic considerations of the short story focus on its split allegiances to the narrative and the lyric.[40] The short story shares with the novel the medium of prose, yet it also makes use of poetry's metaphorical language, its strategies of indirection and suggestion. So although the novel and the short story resort to the same prose medium, their artistic methods are different.[41] The short form possesses both the peculiarities of storyness and narrativity and the intensity, tension, compression and suggestion of the lyric mode. The short story blends the brevity and intensity of the lyric with narrative

---

[36] May, "Why Short Stories Are Essential", 14-25.

[37] Pratt, "The Short Story", 91-113; May, "The Nature of Knowledge in Short Fiction", 138-43.

[38] May, "Prolegomenon to a Generic Study of the Short Story", 461-73.

[39] Boris M. Éjxenbaum, "O. Henry and the Theory of the Short Story", in May, *The New Short Story Theories*, 81-82.

[40] See Gerlach, *Toward the End*, 7; Oates, "The Beginnings", 46-52; Helmut Bonheim, "The 200 Genres of the Short Story", *Miscelánea: A Journal of English and American Studies*, XXIV (2001), 39-52.

[41] Valerie Shaw, *The Short Story: A Critical Introduction* (1983), rpt. London: Longman, 1995, 3.

features such as plot, denouement, character, and events. It shares to a certain degree the characteristics of poetic language and metaphor, since it operates through oblique telling, ellipsis and implication, shunning the more explicit statements and causal effects that characterize longer works of prose. The short story emphasizes tone and imagery. Its maximum economy targets intensity, suggestiveness and lyricism.

The fusion of these antagonistic traits accounts for the singular effects of the short story, which Poe defined as a unique narrative form. In *The Theory of the Novel*, Georg Lukács argues that the lyric nature of the short story results from a process of selection, a "form-giving, structuring, delimiting act" that emphasizes the "strangeness and ambiguity of life".[42] The lyric element is inherent in the short story's compact form. And it is through selection that the trivial detail becomes charged with meaning. More stylized than the novel, the short story tends to distort everyday reality more than long-form narratives do and operates through intuition and lyric effects. In fact, lyricism is an inherent feature that derives from the tension and intensity of the short form and is present even in the most realistic short stories. Unlike the novel, which basically has a more "public" vocation, the short story remains "romantic, individualistic and intransigent", the affair of a lonely voice.[43]

Poe argued that, like the lyric poem, the short story should be read at one sitting. Because of its compressed structure, the short form lends itself to pictorial perceptions and can be perceived in spatial terms by the reader.[44] The form's brevity invites an analogy between the short story and the spatial dimension of visual arts – such as painting and photography – which differentiates the short form from the temporality of the novel, which more clearly unfolds in time. While the novel operates on the assumption that it presents "a full and authentic report of human experience",[45] the short story deals only with a fragment, an incident, a single small-scale event. In contrast to the novel, which focuses on the interconnectedness of things and on events that take place over a longer period of time, the short story

---

[42] Lukács, *The Theory of the Novel*, 51-52.
[43] O'Connor, "The Lonely Voice", 88.
[44] See Hanson, *Short Stories and Short Fictions*, 67-68; May, *The Reality of Artifice*, 89; Pasco, "On Defining Short Stories", 119.
[45] Rohrberger, *Hawthorne and the Modern Short Story*, 125.

depicts only a fragment. It centers on a scene, a person cut off from a larger social, historical or existential continuum,[46] and concentrates on a moment of awareness rather than a completed action. Unlike the novel, the short story does not attempt to embrace the whole of experience with its complex fabric of causal processes or elaborate temporal durations; instead it presents "slices" or "snapshots" of reality. Raymond Carver argues that the short story offers only a glimpse that, "given life, turn[s] into something that illuminates the moment" and so acquires "further-ranging consequences and meaning". The short story writer's task consists precisely in "invest[ing] the glimpse with all that is in his power".[47] Moreover, this moment plucked out of the flow of time seeks meaning beyond the contingent and the particular. This "glimpse" or "flash", to use Nadine Gordimer's terms, strives towards something more general and universal, something that is left unstated and appears to be incommunicable.[48]

Julio Cortázar discusses the difference between the novel and the short story through the metaphoric comparison of photography and motion pictures. Whereas the novel, like a film, constitutes "an open order", the short story resembles the photograph, which isolates a fragment from the whole, circumscribes it, and paradoxically uses its limitations in order to open it up to a much more ample reality, presenting "a dynamic vision that spiritually transcends the space reached by the camera".[49]

Charles May convincingly observes that the problem of the short story writer is how to transform a story, which is a series of events, into something significant, something that transcends mere sequence.[50] The solution to this dilemma lies in the two defining attributes of the short story: intensity and tension. Both result from the compactness of the form, its cultivation of economy and the adoption of an oblique, elliptical and concise style. Carver contends that for a story to exist "there has to be tension, a sense that something is

---

[46] Pratt, "The Short Story", 99-101. See also Pasco, "On Defining Short Stories", 124-26; Wendell Harris, "Vision and Form: The English Novel and the Emergence of the Short Story", in May, *The New Short Story Theories*, 182-94.

[47] Raymond Carver, "On Writing", in *ibid.*, 277.

[48] See also *Sudden Fiction: American Short Stories*, eds Robert Shapard and James Thomas, Salt Lake City, UT: Gibbs Smith, 1986.

[49] Cortázar, "Some Aspects of the Short Story", 246.

[50] May, "Why Short Stories Are Essential", 14.

imminent, that certain things are in relentless motion". He draws attention to the fact that this tension in fiction is created not only by "the way concrete words are linked together to make up the visible action of the story", but also by "the things that are left out, that are implied, the landscape just under the smooth (but sometimes broken and unsettled) surface of things".[51]

The aesthetics of brevity imposes limitations that directly affect the short story's epistemology and style. Brevity prevents the short story from being cumulative and does not allow for extended explanations. The aesthetics of economy accounts for the genre's cryptic and elliptical nature. Given the confinement and limitations of the short form, the writer cannot indulge in details. Compactness and conciseness are responsible for the short story's proclivity to fragmentariness, its tendency to describe moments instead of processes, its preference for the outline of events instead of events in their detailed wholeness. The very shortness of the form requires a style that goes against literary conventions based on mimetic artistic principles, that eludes the trivial or the merely decorative, and that avoids causal relationships or sequences of events.

Short fiction makes room for commonplace things and events, yet the ordinary or the uneventful are never allowed to remain so. Raymond Carver observes that the prosaic elements –"[a] chair, [a] window curtain, [a] fork, [a] stone, a woman's earring"– that appear in the short story have to be endowed "with immense, even startling power".[52] In a short story, as in a poem, particulars cannot remain such; they need to be invested with implication, suggestiveness. Details need be "concrete and convey meaning", and "the particular must be given general significance".[53] The effect of brevity is relevance, intensity, and tension. Since the short story writer cannot resort to elaborate statements, the challenge consists, as Flannery O'Connor points out, in making "the concrete work double time".[54]

Brevity deforms the real and imposes a greater need for stylization, which in turn requires a greater need for design.[55] In *The*

---

[51] Carver, "On Writing", 277.
[52] *Ibid.*, 275.
[53] *Ibid.*, 277; Bowen, "The Faber Book of Modern Short Stories", 259. See also May, "Why Short Stories Are Essential", 17-18.
[54] O'Connor, "Writing Short Stories", 98.
[55] Hanson, *Short Stories and Short Fictions*, 6.

Dehumanization of Art, the Spanish philosopher José Ortega y Gasset argues that artistic technique involves a distortion and defamiliarization of everyday reality.[56] With its elliptical, metaphoric and metonymic discourse, the short story's brevity generates a heightened sense of concentration, compression and intensity that counters mimetic conceptions of art, leading to an increased emphasis on aesthetic stylization. Strategies of brevity and concentration, then, are responsible for the highly formalized style of the short story. Since tension and intensity are its constitutive traits, the short story, including work written in its most realistic vein, does not imitate external reality but presents a highly patterned and stylized representation of experience. As May observes, "Even the most realistic style emphasizes the difference between everyday reality and the reality of fiction itself, which is the only way to penetrate into the real".[57]

Chekhov's dictum – "In the short stories it is better to say not enough than to say too much" [58] – anticipates by several decades the modernist aesthetic agenda and Hemingway's famous iceberg theory, inspired, in turn, by Pound's imagist principles. A century later the postmodernist John Barth observed that, unlike the novel, which tends towards inclusion, the short story inclines towards exclusion: "Short story writers as a class, from Poe to Paley, incline to see how much they can leave out, and novelists as a class, from Petronius to Pynchon, how much they can leave in."[59] The elimination of intermediary links, situations, and ideas as well as the tightly wrought unity of the form invite the reader to go on a quest for something that is hinted at, obscured or hidden behind the texture of words.

---

[56] José Ortega y Gasset, *The Dehumanization of Art and Other Writings on Art and Culture*, New York: Doubleday Anchor Books, 1956, 23. See also May, "Chekhov and the Modern Short Story", in May, *The New Short Story Theories*, 214-16.

[57] May, "Chekhov and the Modern Short Story", 211.

[58] Anton Chekhov, "The Short Story", in May, *The New Short Story Theories*, 198. Ernest Hemingway formulated his omission theory thus: "If a writer of a prose knows enough about what he is writing about he may omit things that he knows and the reader, if the writer is writing truly enough, will have a feeling of those things as strongly as though the writer had stated them. The dignity of movement of the iceberg is due to only one-eighth of it being above water. The writer who omits things because he does not know them only makes hollow places in his writing" (Ernest Hemingway, *Death in the Afternoon*, New York: Scribner, 1932, 192; also in *Ernest Hemingway on Writing*, ed. Larry Phillips, New York: Scribner, 1984, 77).

[59] John Barth, "A Novel Perspective: 'It's a Short Story'", in *The Tales We Tell*, 2.

14   *Viorica Patea*

The short form yearns towards a quintessential reality that lies beyond the particulars of everyday life or the appearance of the extensional world.[60] Relying on intensity and tension, the short story also aspires to transpose the incommunicable into aesthetic forms. As Cortázar aptly remarks, whether the short story depicts a real or imaginary happening, it always possesses "that mysterious property of illuminating something beyond itself, to the extent that a common domestic occurrence ... is converted into an implacable summary of a certain human condition or the burning symbol of a social or historical order".[61]

Critics and short story writers agree that the short story is concerned with an exceptional, mysterious, strange, unexpected or unusual experience. Walter Benjamin argues that the short story dwells on the mysteries of human experience that go against our logico-rational frame of mind, contradicting the laws of plausibility and verisimilitude.[62] Writers such as Eudora Welty, Flannery O'Connor, and Julio Cortázar emphasize the mystery that lies at the heart of the short story. The dynamics of the form rest on the clash between common everyday experiences and a hidden, unconscious, strange reality that deeply unsettles our logico-rational certainties and the conventions of the ordinary. The philosophy of the short story seems to imply, as Rohrberger suggests, "the metaphysical assumption that the idea and the real merge at the moment of revelation, a moment as profound as epiphany".[63]

Critics have noted that the short story has the potential to challenge notions of conventional truth and to dwell on moments of breakup in the experience of everyday reality.[64] The short story conflates time and upsets Cartesian categories and our empirical certainties.

---

[60] May, "The Nature of Knowledge in Short Fiction", 138-43; May, *The Reality of Artifice*, 1-2.
[61] Cortázar, "Some Aspects of the Short Story", 247.
[62] Walter Benjamin, "The Storyteller", in *Illuminations*, New York: Schocken Books, 1968, 83-109.
[63] Mary Rohrberger, "Where Do We Go from Here?", in *The Tales We Tell*, 205. See also Valerie Shaw, *The Short Story: A Critical Introduction* (1983), rpt. London: Longman, 1995, 193; May, "Why Short Stories Are Essential", 16-18.
[64] In "The Nature of Knowledge in Short Fiction", May rightly observes that "the short story is closer to the nature of reality as we experience it in moments when we are made aware of the inauthenticity of everyday life, those moments when we sense the inadequacy of our categories of conceptual reality" (May, *The New Short Story Theories*, 141). See also May, *The Reality of Artifice*, 52.

Paraphrasing T.S. Eliot, Maurice Shadbolt contends that the short story attempts to produce a "hallucinatory point in which time past and time future seem to coexist in time present".[65] To Cortázar the short story offers "a live synthesis ... something like the shimmering water in a glass, the fleeting within the permanent".[66]

For Flannery O'Connor, the challenge for the short story writer consists in "how to make the action he describes reveal as much of the mystery of existence as possible".[67] Along the same lines, Welty confirms that "we can't really see the solid outlines" of a short story, that "it seems bathed in something of its own ... wrapped in an atmosphere".[68] Mystery is the effect of brevity and the form's reliance on pattern and structure.[69] The mystery of the short story proceeds, then, not only from its mythical or romantic affinities but also from the compactness, intensity and economy of its short form. The mysterious is provoked by the readers' intuitions of an unresolved and unstated reality, which become amplified in the absence of explanatory elements.

The short story probes the nature of the real, which proves to be more complex than the reality of mere appearances. Melville associated Hawthorne's tales with the art of telling the truth.[70] To him the actual world was a mere façade, an illusion. The fictive world led to truth, although, paradoxically, the way to it led from the surface of reality to the core of meaning.

Theorists agree that the epistemology of the short story is one of revelation, vision or insight. The fundamental element of the short form resides not in narrative structure but in "the moment of truth" or of crisis conducive to a heightened awareness, a momentary realization that marks the passage from ignorance to knowledge.[71] As

---

[65] Maurice Shadbolt, "The Hallucinatory Point", in May, *The New Short Story Theories*, 269.

[66] Cortázar, "Some Aspects of the Short Story", 246.

[67] O'Connor, "Writing Short Stories", 90.

[68] Eudora Welty, "The Reading and Writing of Short Stories", in May, *The New Short Story Theories*, 163.

[69] May, "Why Short Stories Are Essential", 16.

[70] Herman Melville, "Hawthorne and His Mosses" (1850), in *Melville: Pierre, Israel Potter, The Piazza Tales, The Confidence Man, Uncollected Prose, Billy Budd*, ed. Harrison Hayford, New York: Library of America, 1962, 1154-71.

[71] Pratt, "The Short Story", 99; Robert F. Marler, "From Tale to Short Story: The Emergence of a New Genre in the 1850s", in May, *The New Short Story Theories*, 172.

Cortázar remarks, "A story is meaningful when it ruptures its own limits with that explosion of spiritual energy, which suddenly illuminates something far beyond that small and sometimes sordid anecdote which is being told".[72] This formulation seems to be a recasting of Pound's famous postulations on the effects of imagist poetics, his conception of the poem as a "delightful psychic experience" in which the poem tries to record "the precise instant when a thing outward and objective transforms itself, or darts into a thing inward and subjective".[73] The short story also shares this mysterious property of bringing a fragment to the point of translucency. It renders a moment "whose intensity makes it seem outside the ordinary stream of time" and "whose significance lies outside the ordinary range of experience".[74] The dramatization of this moment of awareness can equally belong to the marvelous, the psychological, or the hidden aspects of everyday life.

Flannery O'Connor remarks that short story writers make "alive some experience which we are not accustomed to observe everyday, or which ordinary man may never experience in his ordinary life".[75] The short story deals with dreams or fears or psychological obsessions, the marvelous, the fantastic, the absurd.[76]

Whether fantastic or realistic, modernist or postmodernist, focusing on imaginary happenings or realistic everyday accounts, the short story strives towards something unstated yet hinted at in the text, which accounts for its intensity. One could say it has a liminal quality, constantly attempting to dissolve the boundary between the known and the unknown, the visible and the invisible, the surface and the inner secret of things.

The evolution of the short form
Although old in literary lineage, the short story took shape as a modern form only in the nineteenth century. Thanks to Poe, who articulated its conventions into a larger conceptual framework, it became America's most identifiable homegrown literary genre and

---

[72] Cortázar, "Some Aspects of the Short Story", 247.
[73] Ezra Pound, *A Memoir of Gaudier Brzeska*, New York: New Directions, 1970, 89.
[74] Harris, "Vision and Form", 188.
[75] Flannery O'Connor, "The Grotesque in Southern Fiction", in *Mystery and Manners*, 40.
[76] May, "Why Short Stories Are Essential", 17.

contribution to world literature.[77] In the nineteenth century the allegoric and symbolic language of Irving, Poe and Hawthorne shaped the short story as a Romantic form, while Melville initiated the transition to realism.[78] These two legacies, the mythico-Romantic tradition and the modern realistic one, then coexisted in a tense balance throughout the twentieth century in the works of Anderson, Hemingway, Joyce, Faulkner, and Welty and in the short fictions of postmodern writers.[79]

If the nineteenth-century short story was mainly dramatic and relied heavily on plot, the modernist short story came to renounce narrative structure. Even more than work in the mode of the fantastic, such modernist forms tend to frustrate realistic expectations of cause-and-effect logic. Influenced by Chekhovian techniques that combine realistic detail with a Romantic poetic lyricism, the modernist story interiorized and subjectivized notions such as plot and design.

It was "in or about December 1910", to use Virginia Woolf's[80] famous commemoration of the post-Impressionist exhibition of Cézanne, van Gogh, and Matisse in England, that a drastic change in contemporary sensibility took place that was to affect not only the visual arts, but also the conception of poetry, the novel and the short story. In these disciplines, conventional discourse or narrative was abandoned in favor of a style that registered fleeting impressions, moods, feelings and atmosphere. The new shift in sensibility was also marked by the influence of impressionism, which fuses a Romantic subjectivity with the objectivity of realism in order to "fix the last fine shade"[81] of mood and feeling. The short story becomes, then, the appropriate medium in which to discriminate feeling and render the nuances of emotions of *le moi profond*. As Suzanne Ferguson remarks, in this period "imitation of how things feel or seem to

---

[77] May, "The Metaphoric Motivation in Short Fiction", 62.

[78] *Ibid.*, 65. Santiago Guerrero Rodríguez-Strachan, "Récit, story, tale, novella", in *Romantic Prose Fiction*, eds G. Gillespie *et al.*, Amsterdam: Benjamins, 2008, 364-82.

[79] May, "The Metaphoric Motivation in Short Fiction", 67. See also May, *The Reality of Artifice*, 18-22.

[80] Virginia Woolf, "Mr Bennett and Mrs Brown", in *Collected Essays*, London: Chatto and Windus, 1966, I, 320.

[81] Arthur Symons, "The Decadent Movement in Literature", *Harper's New Monthly Magazine*, XXVI, November 1893: http://homepage.mac.com/brendanking/huysmans.org/criticism/harpers.htm

characters is preferred [to] ... the imitation of what things are in the real world".[82]

With the rise of impressionism, reliance on traditional elements of plot or on temporal sequences of cause and effect gives way to the presentation of sensations and inner experience. The modernist narrative thus develops as a mosaic of feelings, moods and impressions rather than a sequential narrative. Privileging "objective correlatives for abstract states of mind and feeling",[83] the modernist short story becomes bound by images, symbols and themes. Intensity derives not from plot but, rather, from strategies of point of view, effects of imagery and tone, or formal and stylistic economy. Mood and atmosphere supplant events and articulate the structure of the story. Plot, conventional narrative strategies or marvelous occurrences are replaced by moments of heightened awareness.

Joyce's most important contribution to the theory and technique of the modern narrative is his notion of epiphany,[84] a variation on the Romantic moment of insight into the nature of reality and experience, Wordsworth's passionate desire to "see into the life of things".[85] Robert Langbaum defines the Romantic epiphany as a "manifestation in and through the visible world of an invisible life".[86] In its modernist instantiation, this moment of insight still unveils the hidden structures of the real, but its spiritual affinities and secret intimations induce wonder without necessarily being otherworldly. The epiphany becomes the focus and the structural device of a modernist story form that distrusts plot and elements of narrative sequence.[87]

Fragmentary, static, capturing a fleeting moment, a mood or a nuance, the modern short story thus turns into a story without a

---

[82] Suzanne Ferguson, "Defining the Short Story, Impressionism and Form", in May, *The New Short Story Theories*, 220.

[83] Hanson, *Short Stories and Short Fictions*, 4.

[84] Joyce defined the epiphany as "a sudden spiritual manifestation, whether in the vulgarity of speech or of gesture or in a memorable phase of the mind itself" (James Joyce, *Stephen Hero*, ed. Theodore Spencer, New York: New Directions, 1944, 51).

[85] William Wordsworth, "Lines Composed a Few Lines above Tintern Abbey, on Revisiting the Banks of the Wye during a Tour. July 13, 1798" (ll. 46-48): "While with an eye of made quiet by the power / Of harmony, and the deep power of joy, / We see into the life of things" (William Wordsworth, *The Poems*, ed. John Hayden, New Haven, CT: Yale University Press, 1977, I, 359).

[86] Robert Langbaum, *Poetry of Experience*, Chicago: University of Chicago Press, 1957, 46.

[87] Ferguson, "Defining the Short Story", 225.

story.[88] It becomes a site for recognitions of states of consciousness and impressionistic perceptions of reality, reflecting a multiplicity of points of view, with characters conceived mainly as registers of different, changing moods. The short story reflects the spirit of contemporary relativism. Its emphasis on both single moments of awareness and the fragment marks a mentality in which fixed, stable concepts are abandoned in favor of the vision of a modern world in which "all that is solid melts into air".[89] This modest aspiration for the short story, which renounces overarching structures in favor of momentary impressions, results from an increasing epistemological skepticism and relativism in twentieth-century authors, many of whom are deeply troubled about the human capacity to apprehend the truth. It expresses an awareness that, in a fragmented and splintered world, wholeness is no longer possible.

With its brief, fragmentary, inconclusive form, the modernist short story expresses the limits of human knowledge in a world that holds no absolutes. Reflecting our restrained processes of cognition, the short form renders perception in a mode close to the way in which we experience and know the world: occasionally, in fragments, through glimpses, or, as Gordimer writes, in "a flash of fireflies, in and out, now here, now there, in darkness". In the modernist period, human cognition is seen to stop short of absolute truths and to take place only in momentary, spontaneous flashes, in "discrete moment[s] of truth".[90] In this the modern short story resembles modern poetry, which, in its attempt to offer a "momentary stay against confusion", also represents, to use Robert Frost's words, only a provisional "clarification of life".[91]

With their play with intertextuality, collage, and issues of originality and authorship, postmodern short stories have become, even more than their modernist models, plotless antistories. Postmodern writers are conscious that short stories are verbally constructed artifacts that focus on the reality of illusions of the real.

---

[88] Bader, "The Structure of the Modern Short Story", 105.

[89] In his analysis of modernity, Marshall Berman, *All That Is Solid Melts into Air: The Experience of Modernity* (1982), rpt. London: Penguin, 1988, paraphrases Marx's expression in the *Communist Manifesto* (1848).

[90] Nadine Gordimer, "The Flash of Fireflies", in May, *The New Short Story Theories*, 179.

[91] Robert Frost, "The Figure the Poem Makes", in *Selected Prose of Robert Frost*, eds Hyde Cox and Edward Connery Lathem, New York: Collier Books, 1956, 18.

They thus make artistic conventions and artistic devices the subject of their fiction. Writers such as the postmodernists John Barth and Donald Barthelme, or the minimalists Raymond Carver, Robert Coover, or Tobias Wolff, among many others, brought about a revival of the short story genre in the eighties. One of the newest and most interesting twenty-first-century manifestations of the short story comes with the emergence of minifiction and minifiction sequences, which expand even further the original hybridity of the genre. Oscillating between modernist forms of writing and postmodernist ones, minifictions mark a new phase in the evolution of the short story. Flash fiction, sudden fiction, microfiction, micro-story, short short, postcard fiction, prosetry and short short story are new forms that distinguish themselves by extreme brevity proliferate.[92] Situated at the boundary between the literary and the nonliterary, narration and essay, narration and poetry, and essay and poetry, minifictions also integrate extraliterary elements and so demand a reformulation of canonical genre boundaries and definitions. Hybrid, protean and fragmentary, minifictions introduce a new simultaneity of genres and have been read alternatively as prose poems, essays, chronicles, allegories or short stories.

Minifictions represent, as Lauro Zavala observes, "a new form of writing and reading the world" and mark "the beginning of a new sensitivity". Distinct from the tradition of the short story, minifiction is at the same time the latest expression of the genre. Its most notable development is occurring in the Spanish American context, which presents a vigorous and flourishing literary tradition of genre experimentation related to serialization and fragmentation suggesting new ways in which it may go in the future.

Looking ahead into the twenty-first century
This present collection of articles provides significant theoretical foundations for a re-evaluation of the short story as well as reconsiderations of accomplishments of short story writers and their artistic legacy. Its aim is to explore the main theoretical issues raised

---

[92] Thomas James, Introduction, *Sudden Fiction: American Short Stories*, 11-14; *Flash Fiction: 72 Very Short Stories*, eds Tom Hazuka, Denise Thomas, James Thomas, New York: W.W. Norton, 1992; *Micro Fiction: An Anthology of Fifty Really Short Stories*, ed. Jerome Stern, New York: W.W. Norton, 1996.

by the short story as a genre. This volume deals with historical considerations, problems of definition, issues of form and technique, and aspects of the contemporary short story. It includes critical surveys on the development of the short story and discussions of various types of short stories.

The book brings together theoretical investigations and text-based direct analysis of the different literary works under scrutiny, which are examined in the light of different theoretical perspectives that project short story writing into a wider cultural, literary, and theoretical context. Theories about genre take place in the form of historical and aesthetic considerations, ideas about gender and genre, reader-response experiments, cognitive patterns, sociolinguistics, discourse analysis, postmodern techniques, and contemporary use of short forms such as minifictions.

The volume presents cross-generational approaches to the short story form, combining new work by some of the founders of short story theory, including Charles May, Farhat Iftekharuddin, Per Winther, and Lauro Zavala, with essays by a younger generation of scholars who enthusiastically further and amplify the study of the genre, offering fresh perceptions on the theory and writing of short fiction.

The authors explored – Poe, Charlotte Perkins Gilman, Katherine Mansfield, Bernard Malamud, John Updike, Leslie Marmon Silko, Sandra Cisneros, Donald Barthelme, Tobias Wolff, Margaret Atwood, and Isabel Allende, among many others – already occupy a central position in the history of the short story. At the same time this collection also discusses the work of contemporary short story writers who are less well known but whose compositions have contributed to the latest developments of the genre or help to illustrate different aspects of short story theory: the American, David Leavitt; Canadians such as Douglas Glover, Guy Vandergaeghe, Katherine Govier, and Barbara Gowdy; and Luís Bernardo Honwana, António Jacinto, Baltasar Lopes, three postcolonial writers in Portuguese-speaking countries.

This volume is composed of sixteen different essays that debate theoretical issues related to a wide range of short story practices. They trace the evolution of the short story from Chaucer through the Romantic writings of Poe and on to postmodern developments and emerging tendencies of the twenty-first century.

The articles are divided into four sections. The first group includes
essays concerned with the "The Beginnings of the Short Story and the
Legacy of Poe". Antonio López Santos analyzes Chaucer's narrative
formulas and structural elements in "The Nun's Priest's Tale" and
"The Wife of Bath's Prologue and Tale" that pave the way for the
structure of the modern short story. Erik van Achter considers the
problems of genre definition of the short story and goes back to Poe's
seminal paradigm, which remains an inescapable mainstay in
theorizing about the genre, despite the changing fashions and schools
of critical theory. Peter Gibian traces Poe's legacy as a foundational
model in the development of European aestheticism and decadence,
showing how the peculiar dynamics of reading and reception that are
played out in the American writer's stories shaped the way these later
authors read Poe, influencing their vision of the process of aesthetic
transmission.

The second section, "The Linguistic Turn", presents essays that set
short story criticism in relation to cognitive theory, discourse analysis
and linguistics. Pilar Alonso explores the cognitive connections
between the novel and the short story, interpreting the existing
differences and similarities between the two genres in terms of
variations of goals, decisions, focus, scope, and degrees of
elaboration. Per Winther applies notions of discourse analysis to the
processes at work in the writing and reading of short fiction texts and
examines how the concept of framing (circumtextual, intertextual, and
extratextual) can achieve narrative and hermeneutic closure in short
stories. Drawing on considerations of reader-oriented criticism,
Consuelo Montes-Granado analyzes the mixed linguistic identity of
Chicano writing from a literary, sociolinguistic perspective. She
examines Sandra Cisneros' symbolically charged use of code-
switching and narrative skill within the confines of the short story as a
literary genre.

The third section of this volume, "Borders, Postcolonialism,
Orality, and Gender", addresses issues of gender and genre, orality,
hybridity, brevity and testimony literature. Carolina Nuñez-Puente
looks at short stories from a feminist and Bakhtinian perspective and
hails Charlotte Perkins Gilman as the creator of a new genre, "the
dialogical feminist short story". Rebeca Hernández argues that in
postcolonial literature, the letter, irrespective of the form it adopts,
whether that of an autonomous narrative unit or poem, takes on the

defining features of the short story, such as orality, marginality, and short-storyness. María Jesús Hernáez Lerena expands the generic considerations of the short story through the prism of witness or testimony literature, a comparison she illustrates by looking at recent Canadian short fiction. Teresa Gibert provides new insight into the way in which Margaret Atwood challenges the conventions of the short story genre and exploits stories' narrative potential through a strikingly innovative usage of metaphorical conceptualization.

Just as Chekhov and Guy de Maupassant had a crucial bearing on the evolution of the modernist short story at the beginning of the twentieth century, in recent years the short story's development has been powerfully influenced by Latin American writers. Hence, this volume includes two essays on Spanish American short story writers. Farhat Iftekharuddin's analysis (located in part 3) of Isabel Allende's *The Stories of Eva Luna* focuses on gender and genre issues based on the complexity involved in female/male dynamics and argues that the lyrical and enigmatic nature of the short story reflects the equally mysterious nature of the feminine. It is followed (in Part 4) by a survey by Lauro Zavala, who deepens our understanding of minifiction in the Spanish American tradition, a trend that marks the literary dawn of the twenty-first century.

The fourth section of this book, "Postmodernism and the Twenty-first Century: Intertextuality, Minification, Serial Narration", examines the aesthetics of postmodern short stories and maps the horizon of the twenty-first century. Luisa María González Rodríguez explores the techniques of postmodern short fiction. Taking as a case in point Donald Barthelme's short stories, she analyzes various postmodern strategies of subversion of conventional forms of representation, such as collage and intertextuality. Santiago Rodríguez Guerrero-Strachan throws new light on the rise of minimalism in the works of Tobias Wolff and considers the strategies of narrative voice that fuse inner reality with realistic description. The avant-garde of these new forms is to be found in the Spanish American tradition. Lauro Zavala furthers the study of minifictions, minifiction cycles, and dispersed short stories, which are new postmodern instantiations of the genre. He addresses fundamental problems of theory and literary criticism and makes an appeal for a new theory of literary genres that relativize the conventional boundaries of textual unity and generic diversity.

Just as he has thrown light into the origins and evolution of the genre which he has helped conceptualize, Charles May, in his essay here, surveys the present state of the art and adumbrates the contours of the future. He sketches the map of the contemporary horizon of American short fiction and considers the works of recent short story writers such as T.C. Boyle, George Saunders, Rick Bass, Eric Puchner, Ryan Harty, Julie Orringer, ZZ Packer, Joan Silber, David Means, Joy Williams, Charles D'Ambrosio, Andrea Barrett, and Deborah Eisenberg.

The various authors of this volume, scholars from several different continents, have reflected on wide-ranging aspects of the short story from multiple perspectives that relate to varying traditions: European, American, Native American, Canadian, South American, and African. Looking back to the origins of the short story, the articles in this volume also throw new light on the future in an attempt to sketch the emerging panorama of the most recent short story writers and short story theories.

THE PARATACTIC STRUCTURE IN THE *CANTERBURY TALES*: TWO ANTECEDENTS OF THE MODERN SHORT STORY

ANTONIO LÓPEZ SANTOS

Although the first theories about the short story originate with Poe's "The Philosophy of Composition" (1846), historically the first forms of the genre go back to the emergence of the medieval tale. Some scholars acknowledge in passing that the medieval tale lies at the origins of the short story, yet very few critics have explored these connections further. As W.S. Penn aptly remarks:

> Historically, the earliest genre of the story ... is the tale .... The description of the tale as a genre of the story is only a beginning; yet, as long as we are able to describe the genre, structure, enunciative and narrative postures, mode and tropical convention, the beginning is a valid one.[1]

This is an old, complex controversy[2] whose full elucidation lies beyond the scope of the present study, which takes Penn's affirmation

This study is part of a research project funded by a grant from the Regional Ministry of Culture of the Regional Autonomous Government of Castile and Leon (ref. number SA012A10-1)

[1] W.S. Penn, "The Tale as Genre in Short Fiction", in *The New Short Story Theories*, ed. Charles May, Athens: Ohio University Press, 1994, 54.

[2] See Ian Reid, *The Short Story*, London: Methuen, 1977, 15-27; *The Teller and the Tale: Aspects of the Short Story*, ed. Wendell M. Aycock, Lubbock: Texas Tech Press, 1982; Frances Newman, *The Short Story's Mutations: From Petronius to Paul Morand*, New York: B.W. Huebsch, 1924; Charles May, *The Reality of Artifice*, New York: Routledge, 2002, 1-20; Joyce Carol Oates, "Beginnings: The Origins and Art of the Short Story", in *The Tales We Tell: Perspectives on the Short Story*, eds Barbara Lounsberry, Susan Lohafer *et al.*, Westport, CT: Greenwood Press, 1998, 47-52; Gerald Kennedy, "The American Short Story Sequence: Definitions and Implications", in *Modern American Short Story Sequences*, ed. Gerald Kennedy, Cambridge: Cambridge University Press, 1995, vii-xv.

as a point of departure and attempts to demonstrate that the examination of medieval tales offers interesting approximations to the study of the modern short story. At present only a few studies have considered the relationship between the short story and the medieval tale, and even then they have done so only briefly.[3] This study aims to fill the gap in the literature in this field.

Especially interesting for our purposes are those medieval tales that deliberately fuse the popular oral tradition (in which moral trials and individuals' triumphs over desire are predominant) with the literary tradition (which attempts to capture the world's unique, inexplicable or mysterious aspects). Destined to become one of the most successful and surprising genres of the twentieth century, and predictably one of the predominant artistic forms of the twenty-first, the short narrative underwent several developmental phases before emerging as a new genre in the nineteenth century. The short story is indebted to the medieval literary tale, which represents one of the most fruitful phases of its evolution.

This essay argues that some of the *Canterbury Tales* announce the ulterior evolution of the modern short story. It focuses on Chaucer's new narrative techniques, which center on the manipulation of the most important narrative elements, such as time, space, characters, narrators, and endings that prefigure the dynamics of the modern short story and modify the final meaning of the tale.

Critics have regarded the fourteenth century as the culminating moment of collections of "popular tales",[4] which had existed for more than three thousand years. Translations and adaptations of collections

---

[3] See Barry Sanders, "They All Laughed When I Sat Down to Write: Chaucer, Jokes, and the Short Story", in *The Tales We Tell*, 53-62; Robert Luscher, "The Short Story Sequence: An Open Book", in *Short Story Theory at a Crossroads*, eds Susan Lohafer and Jo Ellyn Clarey, Baton Rouge: Louisiana State University Press, 1989, 153; Rolf Lundén, *The United Stories of America: Studies in the Short Story Composite*, Amsterdam: Rodopi, 1999, 1; Suzanne Ferguson, "The Rise of the Short Story in the Hierarchy of Genres", in *Short Story Theory at a Crossroads*, 179-83; John Gerlach, *Toward the End: Closure and Structure in the American Short Story*, Tuscaloosa: University of Alabama Press, 1985, 17-23; Valerie Shaw, *The Short Story: A Critical Introduction*, London and New York: Longman, 1995, 214-15.

[4] I am using the term "popular tales" in Robinson's technical sense of anonymous tales written by successive writers. See F.N. Robinson, "Popular Prose Fiction", in *Lectures on the Harvard Classics*, eds William Allan Neilson *et al.*, The Harvard Classics, New York: P.F. Collier and Son, 1914, 227-28, also available at http://www.bartleby.com/60/162.html.

of oriental and classical stories were popularized by Christian preachers and flourished in the works of authors such as Boccaccio, Chaucer and Gower. Scholars commonly agree on the division of these collections into three main groups according to their organizing structure: unframed tales, tales with an introduction and tales with a fully developed frame.[5]

The first group consists of unframed tales – loose stories without any kind of organizational criteria. Probably the most famous collection of unframed tales is the *Gesta Romanorum* (towards the end of the thirteenth century and the beginning of the fourteenth), a compilation of more than 180 stories, all of which end with a moral exemplification. There is no link among these stories, and in some cases there even seems to be no correspondence between the story and its moral.

The second group comprises tales with an introduction. These are collections of unrelated tales preceded by an introduction or a prologue that instructs the reader as to the content and the aims envisaged by their publication. Miracles and the lives of saints generally belong to this category. A good example is the *South English Legendary*, compiled during the late thirteenth century, or the Aesopets, a collection of animal fables, compiled during the twelfth and thirteenth centuries.

Tales with a fully developed frame form the third group. Preceded by an introduction, these tales show explicit links to each other that are meant to give an overall meaning to the story. An example of this group is the *Historia Regum Britanniae* (*c.* 1136) by Geoffrey of Monmouth. Although the *Historia* may at first glance seem to be a story of real events, it is in fact a product of pure imagination. The same applies to John Gower's *Confessio Amantis* (*c.* 1386), which resorts to stories in order to illustrate moral beliefs.

Chaucer, however, surpasses these classifications, since he sets in motion two simultaneous processes: first, he relates his tales to the concrete situations and circumstances of the journey; and second, he adapts the tale to each narrator's personality. Consequently, the tales and the narrators are not interchangeable anymore. In this way, an oral narration, of universal values and truths, addresses specific values

---

[5] See Piero Boitani, *English Medieval Narrative in the 13th and 14th Centuries*, Cambridge: Cambridge University Press, 1982, 114ff; Helen Cooper, *The Structure of the Canterbury Tales*, London: Duckworth, 1983, 8-41.

related to specific historical moments. Thus, Chaucer dramatizes a traditional and widely known story, investing it with specific relevance to the concrete reality of the fourteenth century. Chaucer's narrative approach is unique and is not paralleled by any other collections of tales of the period, not even by the most innovative ones, such as Giovanni Boccaccio's *The Decameron* (1353), or Gower's *Confessio Amantis*.

Gower's tales do have some similarities with Chaucer's, however.[6] In his *Confessio Amantis*, Gower establishes an indissoluble link between the narration and the narrator, who in this case is the lover. The narrator introduces his personal experience into the tale by means of his own confession of the sins he has committed against love. However, his confession has a general universalizing dimension and is not that of an individual character; it can be Everyman's tale, the confession of anyone in a similar situation. Gower's *Confessio* maintains the universal characteristic of the oral tale. In the *Decameron* each narrator sets his or her story in accordance with a plan designed by Boccaccio, but there is no personal and untransferable relationship between the narrator and the tale he or she tells. If the tales were attributed to other young narrators, the message would remain intact. Neither of these suppositions is true for the *Canterbury Tales*: the moral is not universal and cannot be applied to any character in a similar situation, and the tale of one narrator cannot be attributed to another pilgrim. This assertion is supported by analysis of the contextualizing backstory and by the use of certain narrative devices that break the supposedly indissoluble unity of the tale. From the standpoint of traditional definitions, the tale attempts to produce a unique intellectual and emotional response in the reader by using the least possible means to achieve the greatest possible emphasis.

In narratology, the backstory is conceived as a literary device that contextualizes and sets into motion the main story.[7] The backstory typically includes descriptions of characters, objects, places or other materials needed to add color, provide verisimilitude or complete the overall meaning of the main story by means of juxtapositions of

---

[6] See B.W. Lindeboom, *Venus' Owne Clerk: Chaucer's Debt to the Confessio Amantis*, Amsterdam: Rodopi, 2007.
[7] See Robert Kernen, *Building Better Plots*, Cincinnati, OH: Writer's Digest Books, 1999.

situations and attitudes. Moreover, according to traditional definitions, the tale's essential elements or its narrative techniques have the fundamental role of creating unity while making the tale gravitate towards a single adventure and a rapid denouement and avoiding any type of digression that might distract the reader's attention. Some of Chaucer's tales clearly illustrate the way in which traditional forms can be transgressed without breaking the narrative thread, thereby becoming unequivocal precursors of the modern short story. This critical assumption, advanced at the beginning of the twentieth century by George W. Gerwig and now generally accepted,[8] has not been fully applied to the analysis of concrete tales. In this essay we will focus exclusively on two of Chaucer's tales, "The Nun's Priest's Tale" and "The Wife of Bath's Prologue and Tale". Thanks to their complex structure and numerous narrative levels, these two tales serve as the best illustrations for my argument.

Both "The Nun's Priest's Tale" and "The Wife of Bath's Prologue and Tale" have their origins in the oral storytelling tradition. The former's connections with the Aesopian animal fables and the latter's links to the chivalrous romance are clear. "The Nun's Priest's Tale" draws on an ancient fable in which animals take on human behavior. The protagonist, a cock called Chauntecleer, lives together with seven hens in a poor widow's yard. One morning he wakes up horrified by a nightmare. He has dreamed that he was almost killed by a fox. His pride and lechery prevent him from perceiving the same danger in real life. Thus he almost becomes prey to an astute canid but manages to get free by means of his ingenious arguments. "The Wife of Bath's Prologue and Tale" is composed of two different tales: the Prologue narrates the wife's story of her five marriages, while the tale recounts the adventures of a knight at King Arthur's court who is sentenced to death because he has raped a maiden. He can be saved from hanging if he is able to answer the queen's question as to what women desire most. He can think of many answers, but the true answer is provided by a witch to whom he will have to submit and marry in return for her help.

Chaucer does not produce a new version of these tales, nor does he adapt them to new social, historical or mental realities in the fourteenth century. Instead he construes a new meta-representational

---

[8] George W. Gerwig, *The Art of the Short Story*, Akron, OH: Werner Company, 1909, 13-15.

story, the representation of a representation, which he invests with new literary value and a new original message. One of the most effective techniques he uses is time shifting: the narrative moves from the present back to the past and forwards to the future through either analeptic (flashback) strategies or proleptic (flash-forward) techniques, such as memories, dreamlike visions or premonitions. This implies an alteration of the meaning of the linguistic signs and involves the incorporation of new points of view in the development of the narrative action. Thus, listeners and readers are forced to contrast their perspective with that of the main character or that of secondary characters or even with the voice of the narrator who controls the entire process. This narrative shift can produce several effects, such as the delayed delivery of certain information, a change in feelings towards a certain character or characters, and alterations in the power relationships among the characters. In short, the author resorts to these techniques in an attempt to control the information that is transmitted.

A detailed examination of some of the essential elements of these two tales – time, space, characters, narrators and endings – following Lauro Zavala's categorization[9] may indicate the extent to which Chaucer merely collects and reforms original sources and the degree to which these sources serve as launch pads for his new concept of storytelling.

Time
In the classic tale, time is structured sequentially from the beginning of a story to a predictable and inevitable end. In both "The Nun's Priest's Tale" and in "The Wife of Bath's Prologue and Tale," Chaucer basically follows a sequential pattern, but time is reorganized from the psychological perspective of the protagonists and does not alter the narrative logic.[10] Chaucer narrates two parallel stories that become two simultaneous stories in the mind of the reader.

In "The Nun's Priest's Tale", the story of the poor widow in whose yard the proud rooster camps at his leisure has generally been

---

[9] Lauro Zavala, "De la teoría literaria a la minificción posmoderna", *Ciências Sociais Unisinos*, XLIV/1 (January-April 2007), 86-96, and *Cartografía del cuento y la metaficción*, Seville: Renacimiento, 2004, 15-65.
[10] Joseph Frank, "Spatial Form in Modern Literature", *The Sewanee Review*, LIII/2 (Spring 1945), 221-40.

considered by critics as a simple element of contextualization of the main narration, or as a means of contrasting two lifestyles that are different not only visually but also morally.[11] Actually, however, they introduce two different moments in time that are nevertheless simultaneous. One could say that the widow's life story is inscribed in real time, while Chauntecleer's belongs to a mythic time. The mythical element links Chaucer to a line of poets that goes back to Aesop's fable "The Fox and the Crow", the anonymous *Gallus et Vulpes* (12th century) or "The Fox and the Wolf" (13th century), and some other texts[12] that have transmitted the story of the self-important cock from generation to generation.

By "real time" I mean the time in which the widow has to survive hour by hour and day by day and which reflects the hardships of medieval life, especially the tribulations of the lower classes. The mythical time introduces the reveries and the most intimate dreams harbored by the inhabitants of an unhappy world. It is sufficient to draw a brief comparison of the lexicon (mainly adjectives, nouns and verbs) used to describe the widow's and Chauntecleer's world in order to illustrate the contrast between the two characters:[13]

Widow's real world	Chauntecleer's mythic world
— **povre** wydwe (1.2821)	— His voys was **murier** than the murie orgon (1.2851)
— **narwe** cotage (1.2822)	
— **symple** lyf (1.2826)	— coomb redder than the **fyn coral** (1.2859)
— **litel** was hir catel and hir rente (1.2827)	— his byle ... as the jeet it **shoon** (1.2861)
— **sooty** was hire bour (1.2832)	— **asure** were his legges and his toon (1.2862)
— **sklendre** meel (1.2833)	— nayles whitter than the lylye flour (1.2863)
— **repleccioun ne made** hire nevere sik (1.2837)	— **gentil** cok (1.2865)
— **attempree diete** was al hir phisik (1.2838)	— al his **plesaunce** (1.2866)

[11] David Bland, "Chaucer and the Art of Narrative Verse", *English* VII/41 (Summer 1949) 216-20; David Holbrook, "The Nonne Preestes Tale", in *The Pelican Guide to English Literature*, ed. B. Ford, *The Age of Chaucer*, Harmondsworth: Penguin, 1975, I, 116-26.

[12] See *Sources and Analogues of the Canterbury Tales*, eds Robert M. Correale and Mary Hamel, Cambridge: D.S. Brewer, 2002, I, 449-89.

[13] Excerpts from the text and the numbering of the verses are from *The Riverside Chaucer*, 3rd edn, ed. Larry Benson, Boston: Houghton Mifflin, 1987.

| – **no wyn** ne drank she (l.2842) | – **curteys** she was (l.2871) |
| – **whit and blak** (l.2843) | – **brighte** sonne (l.2878) |

Although it may seem unlikely, in "The Wife of Bath's Prologue and Tale" Chaucer presents two simultaneous stories if we consider the prologue and the tale as a unified narrative. The story of the five marriages narrated in the prologue (beginning at "Experience", l. 1) and the story of the lecherous knight (beginning at "in the olde dayes of Kyng Arthour", l. 857) embedded in the tale are in fact one and the same narration, viewed from two different perspectives and from two different temporal dimensions. In the real world, the widow will never be able to marry the young and good husband she longs for and will never find the solution she is looking for. She invariably associates goodness with wealth and old age, because her old husbands gave her everything she desired and let her be in control of their marriage. However, her young husbands have no tolerance for her whims and do not allow her to have the upper hand. Yet, in the mythical realm, the widow is able to resolve this dichotomy that she could never work out in real life. There she can reconcile the irreconcilable: youth and goodness. Only in mythical time does she find a solution to this equation. In real time, the widow describes her various husbands as good or bad according to their docility. Their obedience is linked to their age: "I shal seye sooth; tho housbondes that I hadde, / As thre of hem were goode, and two were badde" (ll. 195-96). In the mythical time, the young husband submits, although not without some reluctance, to her fantasy and desires: "My lady and my love, and wyf so deere, / I put me in youre wise governance" (ll. 1230-31). However, Chaucer does not insert real time into mythical time, as is usual in these types of stories. The mythical dimension does not serve merely as a framework: on the contrary, it incorporates the central story.

The story of the widow's life does not really have an end: she makes her young husband believe she is on the brink of death and asks him to kiss her for the last time. She interprets his kiss as a sign of acquiescence. Thus this solution hardly corresponds to the harsh realities of the medieval period, which were even harder for women; rather, it belongs to the realm of her desires.

Space

In Chaucer's tales, space does not conform to the conventions of *vraisemblance*, but is distorted by the narrator or the characters' needs and fantasies. In "The Nun's Priest's Tale" there are two distinct realms: the courtyard of the old lady and the paradise of the rooster. The two spaces are physically the same, but socially and literarily different.[14] The real space is delimited, filled with real objects and real animals. Its description is so specific and true to reality that we could accurately draw it on paper: "A yeerd she hadde, enclosed al aboute / With stikkes, and a drye dych withoute" (ll. 2847-48). By contrast, mythical space is vague, general and similar to that of any other oral tale. It exists in broad strokes of strong chromatic tones and variegated colors: "By nature he crew eche ascencioun / Of the equynoxial in thilke toun" (ll. 2855-56). Real objects coexist with fantastic elements such as plants endowed with magical and miraculous powers:

> Though in this toun is noon apothecarie,
> Shal myself to herbes techen yow,
> That shul been for youre hele and for youre prow.
> And in oure yeerd tho herbes shal I fynde,
> The whiche han of hir propretee by kynd
> To purge yow bynethe and eek above.
>
> (ll. 2948-53)

In "The Wife of Bath's Prologue and Tale" these two types of spaces differ even more from each other. The widow's real world is circumscribed by concrete things and events, such as the presents she has received ("gaye thynges fro the fayre", l. 221), or the exact age of her lover: "He was, I trowe, a twenty wynter oold, / And I was fourty, if I shal seye sooth" (ll. 600-601). She does not talk about ideal love and goes so far as to make references to her own sexual organs: "I hadde the beste *quoniam* myghte be" (l. 608).

The real space is qualified by concrete, specific geographic names. References are made to "Londoun" (l. 550), "Essex at Dunmowe" (l. 218) and "a clerk of Oxenford" (l. 527), and range "from Denmark unto Ynde" (l. 824). Furthermore, the landscape is individualized and becomes the setting of the characters' precise actions. Thus, the widow reduces her relationships with her various husbands to mere

---

[14] See the comparative chart of these examples above.

sexual intercourse or fakes love in order to obtain material rewards. Examples abound throughout the Prologue, but it will suffice to mention only a few. One husband gives her land, authority and physical pleasure: "And sith they hadde me yeven al hir lond" (l. 212); "Be maister of my body and of my good" (l. 314); "But in oure bed he was so fressh and gay" (l. 508). The wife expresses thus her pragmatic outlook on life: "With empty hand men may none haukes lure. / For wynnyng wolde I al his lust endure" (ll. 415-16). She falls in love with her fifth husband because of his attractive physical appearance: "me thoughte he hadde a paire / Of legges and of feet so clene and faire / That al myn herte I yaf unto his hoold" (ll. 597-99). By contrast, the fantastic world is full of stereotypes: characters and events characteristic of traditional narratives are interchangeable and do not alter the meaning of the story. In the widow's narrative the geographic setting gives way to a magical space, "this land fulfild of fayerye" (l. 859). Its inhabitants, therefore, are also mythical beings: "The elf-queene, with hir joly compaignye, / Daunced ful ofte in many a grene mede" (ll. 860-61).

Thus, space determines the actions that will take place and that will inevitably submit to the laws of this fantasy world. Unexpected appearances and disappearances occur, altering the course of the knight's quest. During the first days of his quest for answers, the knight meets only real characters of the real world who provide him with commonsense solutions: they tell him that women desire riches, marriage, happiness, and so on. The farther the knight penetrates into the magical world, the vaguer the answers become. Finally the witch gives him the key that expresses in fact the wife's desire. She tells him that women's utmost desire is to exert power over their husbands:

> But certeinly, er he cam fully there,
> Vanysshed was this daunce, he nyste where.
> No creature saugh he that bar lyf,
> Save on the grene he saugh sittynge a wyf –
> A fouler wight ther may no man devyse.

> (ll. 995-99)

In this context it is not strange that the knight not only finds an answer he has been looking for – or, rather, an answer the narrator, in this case the wife, has been looking for – but he also surprisingly achieves happiness in the end: "And thys they lyve unto hir lyves ende / In parfit joye" (ll. 1257-58).

Characters

According to E.M. Forster's classification, characters of traditional tales tend to be "flat" rather than "rounded".[15] In "The Nun's Priest's Tale" and "The Wife of Bath's Prologue and Tale" this is true of the secondary characters, but not of the protagonists.

In "The Nun's Priest's Tale", the widow or the hen, Pertelote, are undoubtedly flat characters and display a univocal archetypal personality: "A povre wydwe, somdeel stape in age" (l. 2821), or "Curteys she was, discreet, and debonaire, / And compaignable" (ll. 2871-72). Yet neither the rooster, Chauntecleer, nor the fox fits this definition. They are certainly metaphorical characters who form part of an allegory of the medieval world. However, their personality reflects their inner conflicts. They are not mere puppets who illustrate the priest's moral discourse. The rooster doubts, argues, looks for answers in philosophy books. The variety of linguistic registers in his language – his tones range from the courtly to the confidential – clearly undermines stereotypical representations.

The first description of the rooster reflects his patently complex personality:

> His coomb was redder than the fyn coral,
> And batailled as it were a castel wal;
> His byle was blak, and as the jeet it shoon;
> Lyk asure were his legges and his toon;
> His nayles whitter than the lylye flour,
> And lyk the burned gold was his colour.

(ll. 2859-64)

The rooster's psychological depth is especially evident in his behaviour and in his conversation with the fox. In these passages his discourse features contradictory nuances and mixed emotions, expressing his rich and exuberant personality. Sometimes he is fearful and worried about the future, as when, trembling tearfully, he evokes the vision of the fox that terrifies him:

---

[15] E.M. Forster, *Aspects of the Novel* (1927), rpt. Harmondsworth: Penguin, 1985, 54-84.

> And tipped was his tayl and bothe his eeris
> With blak, unlyk the remenant of his heeris;
> His snowte smal, with glowynge eyen tweye.
> Yet of his look for feere almoost I deye.
>
> (ll. 2903-6)

In other cases, he is defiant: prospects of a pleasant encounter with his beloved Pertelote make him forget all the bad omens, and he imagines himself a majestic and vital creature:

> Real he was, he was namoore aferd.
> He fethered Pertelote twenty tyme,
> And trad hire eke as ofte, er it was pryme.
> He looketh as it were a grym leoun,
> And on his toos he rometh up and doun.
>
> (ll. 3176-80)

And finally, on other occasions he experiences a whole range of contradictory feelings that transport him from joy to fear:

> … and Chauntecleer so free
> Soong murier than the mermayde in the see; …
> And so bifel that, as he caste his ye
> Among the wortes on a boterflye,
> He was war of this fox, that lay ful lowe.
> Nothyng ne liste hym thanne for to crowe,
> But cride anon, Cok! cok! and up he sterte
> As man that was affrayed in his herte.
>
> (ll. 3269-78)

Yet fear can rapidly turn into confidence, especially when the fox's flattery boosts his pride, which is an eloquent example of the different personalities of these two characters:

> This Chauntecleer his wynges gan to bete,
> As man that koude his traysoun nat espie,
> So was he ravysshed with his flaterie.
>
> (ll. 3322-24)

The linguistic manipulations the fox uses to secure his ambitions are equally complex. In his interventions the fox displays his most amiable side, with the secret intention of destroying the bad image that the medieval world has of him:

> Seyde, gentil sire, allas! wher wol ye gon?
> Be ye affrayed of me that am youre freend?
> Now, certes, I were worse than a feend,
> If I to yow wolde harm or vileynye!
> I am nat come youre conseil for t'espye,
> But trewely, the cause of my comynge
> Was oonly for to herkne how that ye synge.
>
> (ll. 3284-90)

As soon as the fox achieves his goal, he takes off his mask and shows the true face of a predatory animal:

> And daun Russell the fox stirte up atones,
> And by the gargat hente Chauntecleer,
> And on his bak toward the wode hym beer,
> For yet ne was ther no man that hym sewed.
>
> (ll. 3334-37)

His personality becomes even more complex once he has lost his prey and, forced to reconsider his actions, scrutinizes his failure in order to come up with a strategy that may prevent him from failing a second time:

> Nay, quod the fox, but God yeve hym meschaunce,
> That is so undiscreet of governaunce
> That jangleth whan he sholde holde his pees.
>
> (ll. 3433-35)

The narrator himself seems to be aware of this situation, and he intentionally emphasizes the role of the characters over the tale's moral: "My tale is of a cok, as you may heere" (1. 3252). He avoids any temptation to advance a universal, generic or moral interpretation. Thus he conveys his message through a particular character, whose actions and strategies refer to a particular moment and circumstance for which the author alone is responsible.

In "The Wife of Bath's Prologue and Tale" the widow, the witch and the young husband are also defined by their own actions. Although she would not admit it, the widow is what her previous

marriages have made of her. She cannot escape the reality of the
medieval world, where a woman occupies the role assigned to her by
her parents or husbands, or both. She bears the marks of her five
marriages and of the demolishing effects of time:

> But age, allas! that al wole envenyme,
> Hath me biraft my beautee and my pith.
> Lat go, farewel! the devel go therwith!

(ll. 474-76)

The wife is the victim of male domination and physical abuse, which
were quite frequent in that period. Her relationship with her fifth
husband proves this:

> And yet was he to me the mooste shrewe;
> That feele I on my ribbes al by rewe,
> And evere shal unto myn endyng day.

(ll. 505-507)

In a burst of sincerity, she avows the real situation:

> And he up stirte as dooth a wood leoun,
> And with his fest he smoot me on the heed,
> That in the floor I lay as I were deed.

(ll. 794-96)

However, this is not the image she wants to project of herself, so she
tries to touch it up and presents herself as the real winner, as the one
with the upper hand:

> And neer he cam and kneled faire adoun,
> And seyde, – deere suster Alisoun,
> As help me god! I shal thee nevere smyte.

(ll. 803-805)

In this way, the Prologue, which was apparently intended as a
conventional "confession", with its stereotyped messages of
repentance, the author's admission of possible guilt, and, above all,
his traditional submission to a higher authority (whether divine or
human), has become a fictional narrative of the many adventures of a
woman who rebels against the social and cultural constraints of her

time. Thus the character of Alisoun takes on a different personality depending on who her husband is and the circumstances of her life. In her story she mixes fact and fiction to her convenience.

For her part, the witch seems to be the perennial flat character of popular literature, the character of an unreal world towards which she lures the knight. But in reality it is she who, through her arguments, rehabilitates the young man and obliges him to accept the fact that he has to earn his position in the world by his own deeds. The witch's complexity is manifested in her two roles, that of an ugly sorceress and that of a beautiful maiden. Not only is she capable of quoting the great sages of the philosophical and literary tradition, such as Seneca, Boethius, Dante and Valerius, but she also starts a judicious argumentation on the notion of "true nobility", which reminds us of other later Renaissance writers, such as John Rastell or John Heywood.

The knight insists that nobility is determined by old possessions, yet the witch rebuts this notion:

> Looke who that is moost vertuous alway,
> Pryvee and apert, and moost entendeth ay
> To do the gentil dedes that he kan;
> Taak hym for the grettest gentil man.
>
> (ll. 1113-16)

As a witch, she has the discursive capacities to disarm the young knight when he tries to eschew his commitment. Furthermore, she is very good at manipulating discourse and using almost irrefutable, quasi-sophistic arguments, easily defeating her interlocutors. When the young knight objects to marrying her because of her ugliness, which he believes might make him feel unhappy for the rest of his life, she replies:

> "Chese now", quod she, "oon of thise thynges tweye:
> To han me foul and old til that I deye,
> And be to yow a trewe, humble wyf,
> And nevere yow displese in al my lyf;
> Or elles ye wol han me yong and fair,
> And take youre aventure of the repair
> That shal be to youre hous by cause of me,
> Or in som oother place, may wel be.
> Now chese yourselven, whiether that yow liketh." (ll. 1219-27)

As soon as he admits his verbal defeat, she becomes a beautiful maiden who is able to satisfy his wildest desires:

> Kys me, quod she, we be no lenger wrothe;
> For, by my trouthe, I wol be to yow bothe,
> This is to seyn, ye, bothe fair and good.

(ll. 1239-41)

The knight also blends two personalities: that of the lusty heir who believes that everything he sees is his and the submissive convict sentenced to death who, after being pardoned, will have to come to terms with the fact that his merits in life are only the results of his actions: "That he is gentil that dooth gentil dedis"(l. 1170).

In sum, the characters in these tales exceed convention and behave as complex, even inconsistent human beings, who think, are plagued by doubts and devise strategies for overcoming their own predicaments. They are therefore dynamic characters who change as their situation changes and who, despite their apparent universality, gradually acquire individualized traits, especially through their flaws and inconsistencies.

The narrators

The narrators of these two tales – "The Wife of Bath" and "The Nun's Priest's" – are basically omniscient, like the narrators of traditional tales, yet they introduce several other narrative levels and points of view. Their narration contradicts their ideas, their unconscious personal attitudes and their behavior. Thus, the story acquires more than one meaning, especially at the end, when it becomes an ironic commentary that undermines its manifest intention. That is to say, the narrators are not conscious of how they portray themselves, and much less of the effect of their disclosures, through which they present an undesirable image of themselves. This happens in practically all of the *Canterbury Tales*, but most openly in "The Wife's Prologue" and "The Nun's Priest's Tale", as well as in the "The Pardoner's Tale".

Chaucer makes no comments on the personality of the Nun's Priest. He is not even listed among the characters he portrays in the General Prologue, where he provides descriptions of most of his characters-narrators. The tale is thus the only source of information about the priest's personality. The host's commentary in the Epilogue of the story has become the official portrait of the priest. Chaucer's technique involves mixing external appearance (*effictio*) with moral qualities (*notatio*).[16] The narrator turns out to be a strong man – "See, whiche braunes hath this gentil preest / So gret a nekke, and swich a large breest!" (ll. 3455-56) – and an exceptionally powerful and virile male:

> But by my trouthe, if thou were seculer,
> Thou woldest ben a trede-foul aright.
> For if thou have corage as thou hast myght,
> Thee were nede of hennes, as I wene,
> Ya, moo than seven tymes seventene.
>
> (ll.3450-54)

This description might seem somewhat exaggerated, even irrelevant, if it were not preceded by the narrator's incursions in his own narrative, which turn him into as fictional a character as the other characters in his story. The priest, who is also the narrator, begins to tell his story in third person, but cannot avoid getting involved in the adventures of his characters. He takes sides and eventually turns the story into a first-person narration. On occasions, the host assumes the role of a commentator; nevertheless, his interventions as a literary critic do not consider the artistic skills of the priest's story but focus instead on his physical qualities: "'Sire Nonnes Preest,' oure Hooste seide anoon, / I-blessed be thy breche, and every stoon!" (ll. 3447-48).

It is evident that the narrator is not a character in the story, but at times he has the ability to hold up the story, to fragment it in order to manipulate the message or emphasize certain moments: "Leve I this Chauntecleer in his pasture, / And after wol I telle his aventure" (ll. 3185-86). On other occasions, he becomes distracted by digressions through which he tries to convince his listeners of the veracity of his story, then he feels constrained to go back to his tale: "Now wol I torne agayn to my sentence" (l. 3214).

Above all, the narrator cannot help showing his enthusiasm – he does so in the first person – in the culminating moments of the action, and it is on these occasions that he expresses his own wishes and his own ideas about the relationships between men and women. He even experiences a certain fascination with the sins he so zealously

---

[16] See *Rethorica ad Herennium*, ed. and trans. Salvador Núñez, Madrid: Bibliotéca Clásica Gredos, IV, 1997.

criticizes in his sermon. On such occasions, his discourse adopts the
fashionable rhetoric of the period, based on *Poetria Nova* by Geoffrey
of Vinsauf.[17] According to the prevailing rhetorical conventions, the
preacher reveals his true discursive skills, his real fears or his sensual
appetites by means of satire or through a figurative rhetoric replete
with interjections.

In order to suppress his sinful desires, Chaucer's narrator returns to
his role as moralizing preacher and informs his fellow travelers of the
fatal consequences that such temptations have caused throughout
history, since Adam's expulsion from Paradise. However, he skillfully
places these claims in the mouth of the rooster: "Thise been the
cokkes wordes, and nat myne; / I kan noon harm of no womman
divyne" (ll. 3265-66). At this point in the narrative, the reader has
already realized that the narrator (the priest) and the protagonist
(Chauntecleer) share similar impulses. Thus his warning directed to
his fellow pilgrims to remain alert to any kind of flattery, and by
extension to any kind of temptation, is in fact a piece of advice to
himself, and he himself is its first addressee:

> Lo, swich it is for to be recchelees
> And necligent, and truste on flaterye.
> But ye that holden this tale a folye,
> As of a fox, or of a cok and hen,
> Taketh the moralite, goode men.
> For seint paul seith that al that writen is,
> To oure doctrine it is ywrite, ywis;
> Taketh the fruyt, and lat the chaf be stille.
> Now, goode god, if that it be thy wille,
> As seith my lord, so make us alle goode men,
> And brynge us to his heighe blisse! Amen.

(ll. 3436-46)

The tale that began as a third-person narration ends as a first-
person narration. This technique helps merge the personalities of the
protagonist and the narrator into the same person, while actions can be
easily transferred from one character to another. The Nun's Priest,

---

[17] In his youth, Chaucer was a fan of Geoffrey of Vinsauf's *Poetria Nova* (*c.* 1200), a
treatise on rhetoric that all preachers used in the Middle Ages. In later years Chaucer
adopted an ironic stance towards these rhetorical precepts. Geoffrey of Vinsauf
appears under the name Gaufred in verse 3347.

combining the use of "I" and "him", has assumed the role of "the narrator with a face", in Anderson Imbert's words,[18] and has become yet another character in his own narrative. But one cannot affirm that he is a narrator-protagonist who narrates his adventures in first person. Nor is he a totally omniscient narrator, although he is in control of his characters' thoughts. The priest is a mixture of the two narrators: pretending to be omniscient, he unwittingly becomes the protagonist.

In "The Wife of Bath's Prologue and Tale" the fusion of the narrator (the Wife of Bath) with the witch, the protagonist of the tale, is even more evident. The tale is a third-person narration throughout, except in places where Chaucer wants to clarify the wife's opinions, especially towards the end, when the widow cannot contain her enthusiasm over the happy ending of the witch and knight's story. By using the plural "us" she assigns to herself the protagonist's good luck:

> And thys they lyve unto hir lyves ende
> In parfit joye; and jhesu crist us sende
> Housbondes meeke, yonge, and fressh abedde,
> And grace t' overbyde hem that we wedde.
>
> (ll. 1257-60)

However, in her next prayer, by using the singular pronoun "I", the narrator takes upon herself the curse of all those who do not accept women's rule as a universal norm. Thus she merges the fantasy of the tale with the reality of the Prologue, which has been narrated from beginning to end in the first person. In the Prologue the narrator and the protagonist are one and the same person, the wife, while in the tale the narrator is the wife and the protagonist is the witch. At the end of the Prologue the wife claims to have achieved control over her fifth husband. She explains that he has accepted her power and entrusted her with the reins of their marriage by the kiss he gave her. Yet the final curse on all those not "governed by their wives" implies that she has doubts concerning the authenticity of her power and in fact envies the witch's situation:

> And eek I praye jhesu shorte hir lyves
> That wol nat be governed by hir wyves;

---

[18] Enrique Anderson Imbert, *Teoría y técnica del cuento*, Barcelona: Ariel, 1978, 45.

And olde and angry nygardes of dispence,
God sende hem soone verray pestilence!

(ll. 1261-64)

Yet this confusion between desire and reality that becomes evident
in the end has operated throughout the tale. Whereas Alisoun believes
she is achieving the one obsessive goal she has set for herself – that is,
exercising control over her current husband – reality proves that her
aims are unattainable. The first sign of this confusion lies in the
question the knight has to answer, "What thing it is that women most
desire" (1. 905): because the question has so many possible answers,
it cannot be answered correctly in a conventional way. Undoubtedly,
the question has been chosen by the narrator, who is the wife, but the
selection of the right answer is completely conditioned by her:

Wommen desiren to have sovereynetee
As wel over hir housbond as hir love,
And for to been in maistrie hym above.

(ll. 1038-40)

During his quest, the knight has received many other possible
answers to this fateful question – "richesse", "honour", "jolynesse",
"riche array", "lust abedde", "to be wydwe and wedde", "flattery", or
"bisynesse" – yet the wife in her role as narrator rejects them because
they do not wholly satisfy her desires. Yet many of these tangible and
intangible solutions are more reasonable than the one he chooses in
the end, "sovereynetee". Using the first-person plural "we", Alisoun
refuses to accept this entire series of apparently reasonable answers in
the name of all women and their supposedly indiscreet nature. Her
rejection does not correspond to an objective truth but only reflects
her personal criteria: "But that tale is nat worth a rake-stele" (1. 949).

Since she cannot find a satisfactory solution in the real world, the
wife opts for the world of fantasy and assumes the personality of the
witch who is the protagonist of her story. Each utterance and victory
of the witch will be the utterance and victory of the wife as narrator.
The witch's final happiness, which she achieves once her lover
accepts her conditions – "My lady and my love, and wyf so deere, / I
put me in youre wise governance" (ll. 1230-31) – is interpreted by
Alisoun as her own happiness. The witch's demand, "Kys me" (1.
1239), duplicates Alisoun's demand to her fifth husband in the

Prologue (l. 802), which she interprets as his acquiescence to her supremacy. Once again it is difficult to distinguish fantasy from reality. The narrator has found the solution to her dilemma through her character, or at least this is what she believes. While the wife is getting older – "But age, allas! that al wole envenyme, / Hath me biraft my beautee and my pith" (ll. 474-75) – the witch has become a beautiful maiden: "That she so fair was, and so yong therto, / For joye he hente hire in his armes two" (ll. 1251-52). Rejuvenation seems to be the necessary requirement for controlling one's husband, a fact the wife experienced for herself when she was young.

In this way, Chaucer's continuous change of points of view manipulates the reader's sympathy towards some of his characters. Merging the characters of the tale with the narrators ultimately makes for a complex characterological construction, which usually shows the characters as different from the image they have created of themselves.

Endings

As Lauro Zavala[19] aptly remarks, in order to achieve a true representation of a narrative reality the classic tale tends to be circular, gravitating towards a central truth; epiphanic, seeking a final revelation; sequential, maintaining a single structure from beginning to end; hypotactic, presenting an embedded structure in which every episode depends upon the preceding one; and realistic, abiding by conventions of the genre. In contrast, the modern tale possesses a treelike structure open to many possible interpretations, allowing the inclusion of cross-references between different elements, such as characters or episodes within the narrative texture. Gauged by these parameters, the *Canterbury Tales* seem closer to the modern short story than to the classic tale.

The treelike structure is obvious in both "The Nun's Priest's Tale" and "The Wife of Bath's Prologue and Tale", since both tales integrate different episodes into what appears to be a narrative unity. In "The Nun's Priest's Tale" the main story, that of the rooster and the fox, vanishes or acquires final meaning only within a continuous cycle of narratives, debates, sermons, or rhetorical commentaries. Taken out of its specific context, the meaning of Chauntecleer's story would be different. Yet as it proceeds through various scenes and digressions –

---

[19] See *Cartografía del cuento y la metaficción*, 15-65.

the old woman's yard, the interpretations of dreams, Boethius' philosophy, the eroticism of Venus, the biblical motif of the crucifixion, the rhetorical strategies established by *Poetria Nova*, and the moral disorder discernable behind the virtuous mask of the priest and his indictment of pride and lust – the rooster's tale acquires new valences and different perspectives. In fact, each episode takes on a life of its own and becomes an autonomous narration that could be separated from the rest of the text but achieves full meaning only in relation to the other episodes.

This ramified structure is probably most evident in "The Wife of Bath's Prologue and Tale", since it relates two completely different stories (the story of the wife's five husbands in the Prologue, and the story of the knight and the witch). These two stories differ even in time and space. The wife's story and that of her five husbands unfold in the present and in England; the knight's story is located in the past, in the time of King Arthur, in a vague and imprecise mythical world. However, the different tales complement each other so neatly that their ultimate meaning emerges from the unification of the two tales. If each story were narrated separately, the final conclusion would be different. Whereas the prologue appears to be an objective and realistic narration, the tale is a highly subjective story, designed to end according to the wife's desires. This may seem paradoxical in view of the narrative techniques that are employed: the Prologue is told in first person, and the tale is mainly in third person. The encounter between the knight and the witch is marked by a series of digressions on poverty, old age, and nobility, which have a surprising effect on the reader and which modulate the end of the tale according to the narrator's wishes.

All this creates an open-ended story, very different from the traditional tales. The Priest proclaims the triumph of virtue – a victory that is doubtful, since his own behavior does not meet these moral standards. Neither is the wife of Bath's domination over her fifth husband entirely clear, even though she wants to convince us of this by means of the happy ending she imposes on the tale. The final result is therefore ambiguous: the author leaves room for different interpretations.

The narrative layout of "The Nun's Priest's Tale" and "The Wife of Bath's Prologue and Tale" corresponds to Chaucer's specific strategy to manipulate meaning, which prefigures by several centuries

Bakhtin's concept of "dialogism". The *Canterbury Tales* become a polyphony of different voices, all of which can convey a legitimate final meaning that differs from the narrator's overtly declared intentions, unlike in the oral storytelling tradition. The polysemic effect is achieved by means of the author's manipulation of time, space, characters, narrators and endings. In this way language creates semantic possibilities beyond the unequivocal affirmation of the linguistic object and produces a distancing effect.[20] If we apply to these tales the axial concepts that Ferdinand de Saussure applied to language, we discover that in both "The Nun's Priest's Tale" and "The Wife of Bath's Prologue and Tale", Chaucer emphasizes the vertical axis more than the horizontal one, a practice that goes against the conventional definitions of the tale, which privilege stories that proceed rapidly to their end without digressions that may delay the process. Chaucer's narrative approach is more paradigmatic than syntagmatic, more associative than contiguous, more metaphoric than metonymic. For Northrop Frye this vertical axis goes beyond the associative function and includes "the mythological line of descent from previous poets back to Homer".[21] In the same vein, Suzanne Ferguson insists on the connection between the modern short story and the literary tradition of ancient fables and tales: "our knowledge of Aesop and a fairy tale or Scott's tale – or any of the stories we heard as children or read in adolescence, no matter how crude or cheap – provides us with the basic knowledge of the fictional codes that we need to begin reading sophisticated modern short stories and their longer relatives."[22] This study of "The Nun's Priests's Tale" and "The Wife of Bath's Prologue and Tale" has showed that Chaucer, who is a crucial link in this "mythological line of descent", prepared the road towards the modern short story and confirms the belief that

---

[20] This manipulation technique presents a resemblance to what Helen Phillips calls "free indirect discourse", in *An Introduction to the Canterbury Tales*, New York: St Martin's, 2000, 19-45. This concept was already used by Monika Fludernik, *The Fictions of Language and the Languages of Fiction*, London: Routledge, 1993. For a more general theoretical approach, see Helmut Bonheim, *The Narrative Modes: Techniques of the Short Story*, Cambridge: D.S. Brewer, 1982.

[21] "The horizontal bar forms the social and ideological conditioning that made him intelligible to his contemporaries, and in fact to himself. The vertical bar is the mythological line of descent from previous poets back to Homer" (Northrop Frye, *Words with Power*, Toronto: Penguin Books, 1990, 47).

[22] Suzanne Ferguson, "Defining the Short Story: Impressionism and Form", in *The New Short Story Theories*, 229.

the beginnings of the short form go back at least to the origins of the
literary tale in the Middle Ages.

ANTICIPATING AESTHETICISM:
THE DYNAMICS OF READING AND RECEPTION IN POE

PETER GIBIAN

"The Oval Portrait" and "The Fall of the House of Usher", two of
Edgar Allan Poe's best-known and most paradigmatic short stories,
can serve as key case studies helping us both to understand his
peculiar vision of aestheticism and also to begin to explore the
peculiar dynamics involved in the international transmission and
circulation of this aesthetic vision through the nineteenth century.

A haunted brotherhood: the reception and transmission of aesthetic vision

Despite its surface celebrations of idiosyncrasy, eccentricity, or
expressive originality, aestheticism developed as a curiously
international phenomenon, re-emerging in strikingly similar form in
the works and lives of authors across a wide range of nations, cultures,
and historical periods. One of the defining aspects of this international
movement, then, involves its focus on the mystery of this pattern of
aesthetic influence or transmission. The aesthetic vision seems, in
fact, to center less on the production of unique, powerful, compelling
works of art than on their reception – where reception is seen as a
complex, half-creative, semi-involuntary process by which a pre-
existing form or voice or mode of expression becomes internalized
and repeated across distances of time or space. Not direct or simply
passive, this aesthetic mode of absorbed and absorptive reading
operates through projection as much as through reception, and through
distancing as well as identification. For late-nineteenth-century French
Decadents as for writers associated with British Aestheticism, this
process is frequently described as one of textual contagion – where
the transmission of an aesthetic vision or stance is understood by
analogy to the communication of an infectious disease. In the earlier,

foundational works of Poe, as in his followers, aesthetic influence is often imagined as a form of haunting – a return of something that had been repressed. And to be powerfully haunted in this way is to accede to a place in the line of a timeless, international aesthetic brotherhood.

Examining Poe's role as a founding figure whose works haunted the leading writers and artists in several successive waves of nineteenth-century aestheticism, this essay is framed by a simple, general recognition of the lines of dissemination by which his influence was transmitted across cultures and periods. But its primary emphasis is on analysis of one specific aspect of this transmitted vision: many of Poe's most influential short stories are about the dynamics of aesthetic reception, playing out in their plots and narrative structure a complex vision of the process of reading, transmission, or influence that would be taken up by a line of later artists and writers. This new look at some key elements in Poe's aesthetic and critical theory highlights the uncanny combination of foreignness and familiarity in what Poe's model offered first to his antebellum American contemporaries (notably Nathaniel Hawthorne); then to later European definers of aestheticism (notably Charles Baudelaire and Joris-Karl Huysmans in France, and Oscar Wilde in England); and finally to leading figures in the movements of Aestheticism and Decadence that emerged in America at the turn of the twentieth century.

In a 1904 essay, Henry James described aestheticism to Americans as "a queer high-flavored fruit from overseas, grown under another sun than ours, passed round and solemnly partaken of at banquets organized to try it, but not found on the whole really to agree with us".[1] As the editor of the *Atlantic Monthly*, William Dean Howells wrote of aestheticism along similar lines – picturing it as a threat to native ways of writing and thinking, taken up only by a "sickly colony, transplanted from the mother asphalt of Paris".[2] And this defensive vision quickly coalesced into the standard literary-historical account: Aestheticism and Decadence, related movements that insisted on the autonomy of art, reveling in the bizarre, the artificial,

---

[1] Henry James, *Literary Criticism: French Writers, Other European Writers, the Prefaces to the New York Edition*, eds Leon Edel and Mark Wilson, New York: Library of America, 1984, II, 908.
[2] William Dean Howells, *Literary Friends and Acquaintance: A Personal Retrospect of American Authorship*, New York: Harper and Brothers, 1900, 68.

the perverse, and the arcane, came to be viewed as distinctly European phenomena speaking for anxieties of degeneracy very much specific to the cultural moment in *fin-de-siècle* England and France. Even when it is noted that, from the late 1870s through the 1890s, America experienced a widespread aesthetic craze in the sphere of consumer culture, and that turn-of-the-century America saw an explosion of ambitious, avant-garde art work on the Aesthetic model, with the formation of numerous aesthetic societies and the launching of over two-hundred-and-fifty little magazines in the Decadent vein, these American developments are nonetheless usually portrayed as pale, belated, inauthentic, sickly echoes of European forms – and sad signs of the success of a dangerous foreign invasion of American cultural space.[3]

But is this story in fact that of a one-way movement? Is it a story of passive reception? And is it the story of a response to something threatening and foreign – a queer fruit or a germ arriving fully-formed from overseas, from the corrupt, declining, "decadent" Old World, from England or from France? This essay explores an alternative, opposed story of the transatlantic transmission of Aestheticism and Decadence from Europe to America – now not so much a story of passive reception and foreign invasion but a more gothic plot of ghosts and haunting: the story of a homeland haunted by the uncanny return of the familiar in a strange new form. If French Aestheticism and Decadence largely developed as self-conscious movements out of Baudelaire's response to Poe, and key works of British Aestheticism – writings by Wilde, or paintings by James McNeill Whistler, for

---

[3] On the enthusiastic reception of Aestheticism in American consumer culture and popular culture, see Jonathan Freedman, *Professions of Taste: Henry James, British Aestheticism, and Commodity Culture*, Stanford, CA: Stanford University Press, 1990, xxiii-xxiv, 13-14, 79-81, 107-108; Roger B. Stein, "Artifact as Ideology: The Aesthetic Movement in Its American Cultural Context", in *In Pursuit of Beauty: Americans and the Aesthetic Movement*, ed. Doreen B. Burke, New York: Rizzoli, 1986, 22-51; Michèle Mendelssohn, *Henry James, Oscar Wilde and Aesthetic Culture*, Edinburgh: Edinburgh University Press, 2007, 1-3, 12-15. On more high-cultural, literary movements of Aestheticism in America, see David Weir, *Decadent Culture in the United States: Art and Literature Against the American Grain*, Albany: State University of New York Press, 2008; Kirsten MacLeod, "'Art for America's Sake': Decadence and the Making of American Literary Culture in the Little Magazines of the 1890s", *Prospects*, XXX (2005), 309-38; Jonathan Freedman, "An Aestheticism of Our Own: American Writers and the Aesthetic Movement", in *In Pursuit of Beauty*, 385-99.

example – were powerfully shaped by Poe's vision as it was embedded within and foregrounded as foundational to the influential writings of Baudelaire and Huysmans, then it is intriguing to see the late-nineteenth-century transmission of European Aestheticism to America as a return to his native land of crucial elements in Poe's vision – a return of the repressed.

The horror of aestheticism in antebellum America: Poe in dialogue with Hawthorne

Even in his own day, in antebellum America, Poe was received by other leading authors as a deeply troubling presence, a "negative image" embedded with the local culture, both eerily like and fearfully unlike his contemporaries. As Shawn Rosenheim and Stephen Rachman observe

> It is precisely Poe's syncopated relation to American culture, at once both in and out of step, that gives his writing its unique power to clarify the American tradition …. Poe's work invites the reader into a dialectical process of identification and differentiation that is one of his foundational accomplishments.[4]

In this way, Poe's aesthetic experiments made him a "double" figure, or dark twin, always haunting the vision of Ralph Waldo Emerson and Walt Whitman. And negotiating this sort of ambivalent response to Poe was certainly central to Nathaniel Hawthorne's early development – as several of Hawthorne's short fictions play out both fascinated recognitions of intimate association with Poe and also crucial efforts to turn away, to establish some standpoint for critical detachment.

This complex, multi-leveled ambivalence is nowhere so vivid as in Hawthorne's 1843 story "The Birth-mark" – a key work written in dialogic response to Poe's "The Oval Portrait" of 1842. "The Oval Portrait" is a highly wrought miniature recognized by many as an epitome of Poe's Aesthetic vision. Baudelaire placed it last, as the summary story, in one of his volumes of Poe translations; Jean Epstein and his assistant Luis Buñuel, in their 1928 Poe film *La Chute de la maison Usher*, merged the plots of "The Fall of the House of

---

[4] Shawn Rosenheim and Stephen Rachman, "Introduction: Beyond 'The Problem of Poe'", in *The American Face of Edgar Allan Poe*, eds Shawn Rosenheim and Stephen Rachman, Baltimore, MD: Johns Hopkins University Press, 1995, xii-xiii.

Usher" and "The Oval Portrait" to make this cinematic work a paradigmatic Poe experience; and this mini-tale, centering on the powerful, over-determining life-force seen to be immanent within a painting, is (along with Hawthorne's related story, "The Prophetic Pictures") a key precursor to a line of later-nineteenth-century fiction leading from Henry James' "The Story of a Masterpiece" and "The Liar" to Wilde's *The Picture of Dorian Gray*. So it seems fitting that Poe's American contemporary Nathaniel Hawthorne made "The Oval Portrait" the locus of a telling public dialogue with Poe in 1842-43.

Through a series of paired tales and reviews in the early 1840s, these two prime shapers of the modern short story form used each other as sounding boards as they worked to establish their literary careers, testing opposed impulses as part of a shared exploration of questions fundamental to their literary project – questions about the aesthetic and psychological implications of a fixation on the image, and about both the power and the danger in a proto-Aesthetic conception of visionary art. In April and May of 1842, Poe initiated the textual interchange when he published in *Graham's Magazine* both his now-famous, celebratory review of Hawthorne's *Twice-Told Tales* and a key story, the first version of "The Oval Portrait" (under its initial title "Life in Death") – written as a commentary on and corrective to the aesthetic vision implied in Hawthorne's "The Prophetic Pictures" (1837). This self-reflexive Hawthorne tale explores the story of an artist (here characteristically figured as a painter) endowed with a quasi-divine ability to produce aesthetic representations that have the visionary power not only to reflect natural, temporal reality but also to transfigure it, to form it or control it, to penetrate its soul, to take over its spirit, its life.

But while Hawthorne's fable begins by evoking the dream of an iconic art of miraculous agency, in the end the self-divided tale registers Hawthorne's deep ambivalence about this aesthetic ideal, finally turning away from this dream as his narration raises ethical questions about the dangers of such an urge to dominance. Here, as in many works in this line, successful aesthetic figuration is seen to tear apart the fabric of intimate social life, leading to the prideful alienation of the artist and the shattered marriage of his subjects. And though his portraits give the painter a magical, God-like power to regulate human destinies, the tale finally seems to renounce what is described as the "spell of evil influence" in such dark arts.[5] But Poe's revision of the tale in "Life in Death" intervenes to make the counter-argument. According to Richard Fusco, Poe, both "inspired" and "inflamed" by Hawthorne's vision, decided to "respond in kind, ... that is, to retaliate by mocking Hawthorne's aesthetic".[6] If Hawthorne was too timorous to see his plot through to the end, to face up to its full implications, and thus in the end trivialized the powerful potential of the aesthetic imagination, Poe would produce a short fable unambiguously embracing the power of ambitious art to transfigure life and celebrating the artist as a god-like creator.

Poe's work called out for a response, and the response came in "The Birth-mark" (1843), Hawthorne's revisionary reading of Poe's "Life in Death", produced as a fascinated and worried meditation on the bases of Poe's aesthetic vision – and on the closeness of that vision to Hawthorne's own. Finally, in 1845, the intertextual exchange took a further turn when Poe published a new version of "Life in Death", now titled "The Oval Portrait", significantly revised at least in part as an answer to "The Birth-mark" – an attempt, once again, to recognize and to counter its vision of art and aesthetic figuration.[7]

"A modern Pygmalion": anticipating Aestheticism in "The Oval Portrait" and "The Birth-mark"

Both "The Oval Portrait" and "The Birth-mark" take up a modified version of the Pygmalion story – actually an inversion of the classic Pygmalion story – as a way of exploring a shared sense of the founding dynamics of aestheticism.[8] Each tale conjures the vision of a

---

[5] Nathaniel Hawthorne, *Tales and Sketches*, ed. Roy Harvey Pearce, New York: Library of America, 1982, 468.

[6] Richard Fusco, "Poe's 'Life' and Hawthorne's 'Death': A Literary Debate", *Poe Studies/Dark Romanticism*, XXXV/1-2 (2002), 33.

[7] D.M. McKeithan suggests that the major revisions Poe made before this republication can be seen to have been inspired, in large part, by his careful reading of "The Birth-mark": "Poe and the Second Edition of Hawthorne's *Twice-Told Tales*", *Nathaniel Hawthorne Journal*, (1974), 258.

[8] In "The Birth-mark", Aylmer directly compares his project to that of Pygmalion: "Even Pygmalion, when his sculptured woman assumed life, felt not greater ecstasy than mine will be" (Hawthorne, *Tales and Sketches*, 768). The fact that the Pygmalion myth was very much on Hawthorne's mind as he wrestled with questions about his own aesthetic vision is also made clear in "Drowne's Wooden Image", a closely related work written in this same period, which develops as a conscious, over-obvious reworking of the classic plot. Here the painter John Singleton Copley, visiting the

mode of aesthetic creation that rivals natural creation; an Art separate
from and a rival to Nature; an Art forged through the sublimation or
rechanneling of *Eros*; Art as a form of Idolatry. Developing as an
enactment of aesthetic theory, both plots follow an isolated, male
artist figure as he becomes obsessively fixated on hard, unchanging
fetish objects that trouble his natural relation with an inspiring female
figure of desire. The dialogic relation between these two stories of
Hawthorne and Poe then raises questions not only about the combined
fascination and horror of aestheticism in antebellum America, but also
about the gendering of this aesthetic theory – about the place of
women in the vision of aestheticism.

The classical Pygmalion story follows the development of a male
sculptor who has no interest in worldly women but then falls in love
with the ideal beauty of his own sculpture of a woman. At first this
seems to involve a narcissistic or introverted worship of his own
work, of his own creation, of something he can wall in and completely
control – more than he could any more differentiated, exterior,
imperfect, independent entity created by God or Nature. And early on
this dead-end position is expressed in kinky, perverted, and silly forms
of fetishism and idolatry – as the artist clothes and bejewels the
sculpture, caresses it, gives it a name, and so on. But finally, when he
gets his wish and the sculpture does come to life, the sculptor finds
himself humbled and admonished by his artwork, realizing that he
should never have shunned living women. So he learns from his
artwork to turn from art back to life. And, in the process of this turn,
he also humbles himself before Aphrodite – a female goddess with
great creative powers.

But if the classical myth thus in the end works as a challenge to the
doctrine of art for art's sake – the artist here breaks from his idol, and
wishes his art could have life – in both Hawthorne and Poe things
move in just the opposite direction. These narratives are not about art
coming to life, but about art coming to have a life of its own. The
central artist figures here will put up with a loss of physical life as a

---

workshop of a humble Boston wood-carver who seems to have become involved in
idolatrous worship of a bejeweled female figure he has sculpted, sees how this
craftsman's passion for the "mysterious image" gives it a miraculous physical and
spiritual "life" that is absent in the "stolid", hard, cold "abortions" of his other
carvings, and marvels at the transformation in both artist and art work that has made
the rude Yankee artisan, for at least one moment, into "a modern Pygmalion" (*ibid.*,
937).

sort of collateral damage necessary to the pursuit of art: in each case, the artist transfers his affections and his visual gaze from the "living object of desire" to the inanimate aesthetic image of that love object. Becoming married to his art, the creator begins to love his perfect, ideal representation of that love object's life (or of his love for that life) more than he loves the living figure herself. Rechanneling *Eros* into art, the artist finds that the art object he produces then preserves his love for eternity, even if the mortal, temporal, fleshly female object of that love falls by the wayside. Indeed, in both plots, the life of art is seen to be founded upon the death of the female subject of representation, and the male artist's creation is seen to develop out of a rivalry with the creative powers of a female Mother Nature. Women can create life; men can create art.

In their basic outlining of this proto-Aesthetic version of the Pygmalion story, Hawthorne and Poe are registering and playing out a strong mid-century American fascination with and anxiety about aesthetic representation, the uses of symbols, or graven images – perhaps even (especially in Poe) anticipating more twentieth-century, Benjaminian concerns about aesthetic reproduction and the decline of "aura", about "simulacra" and a crisis in representation brought to the fore by the advent of photography, panoramas, and other extensions of realist art.[9] The perfect portrait-replica destroys the original object through its power to make possible infinite replication of that object's form.

"The Oval Portrait" follows the results of an artist's compulsive portraiture of his wife, "a maiden of rarest beauty". A prototypical Aesthetic type, he lives austerely in and for his art. In fact he has pushed this aesthetic devotion to the point of Decadence – he has a "bride in his Art" – and in the service of Beauty he will live the truth of Poe's own dictum: the "death of a beautiful woman is, unquestionably, the most poetical subject in the world".[10] When he walls his fleshly wife into his workshop space, turning his gaze

---

[9] Walter Benjamin, "The Work of Art in the Age of Its Technological Reproducibility: Third Version", in *Selected Writings: Volume 4, 1938-40*, trans. Edmund Jephcott *et al.*, eds Howard Eiland and Michael W. Jennings, Cambridge, MA: Harvard University Press, 2003, 251-83. Poe's "Oval Portrait" is read in this light in Michael Rothberg, "The Prostitution of Paris: Late Capital of the Twentieth Century", *Found Object*, I (Fall 1992), 2-22.

[10] *The Selected Writings of Edgar Allan Poe*, ed. G.R. Thompson, New York: W.W. Norton, 2004, 298, 680.

resolutely from the woman to the portrait emerging on the canvas, the interminable sittings destroy her health and her spirit, with each brush stroke seeming to transfer another drop of blood and vitality from her body to her effigy on the canvas. The tale ends as the artist's triumph – his monstrous completed painting is "indeed *Life* itself!" – reduces his wife to a corpse: "She was dead!"[11]

"The Birth-mark": Hawthorne's response to his uncanny double
In Hawthorne's "The Birth-mark" the central artist figure, Aylmer, also enters the story attempting to negotiate a balance between his marriage to his scientific/aesthetic studies and his love for his new bride, Georgiana. And he too soon turns away from his wife to fixate his visual gaze and his emotional life on a fetish image of her – in this case a synechdochic figure of his own creation: the birthmark. Although he is initially presented as more a scientist/philosopher than an artist, then, Aylmer's relation to his wife comes to center on the workings of his symbolist arts. His cold, inhuman, scientific stare is what first brings the mark out on his shocked wife's suddenly pale face; seizing upon this naturally-occurring mark, his blinkered vision then removes it from the flow of everyday life, converting it into an hieratic visual icon invested with magical potency and significance. Fastening on this image as the sole object of his further studies, he moves Georgiana out of their home to a new place inside the controlling walls of his laboratory – and thus (in a move typical of many Hawthorne characters) transforms an intimate human relationship into an intellectual experiment. Repelled by this figure that in his eyes disfigures his wife, he nonetheless soon finds that the birthmark comes to dominate any vision of her. But a heightened focus on this image also seems to be the only means to respond to its power. Channeling all his energies into work on this mark, Aylmer then discovers that it takes over his inner life; he too, along with Georgiana, becomes a victim of the powerful image he has constructed.

The birthmark provokes this artist, most fundamentally, as a symbol of the woman's fleshly mortality; to him it is the mark that she was born, and so will die. Its physical form also comes to represent, more generally, her physical existence – the fact that, like all humans, she is grounded on this earth as well as potentially angelic; the fact

---

[11] *Ibid.*, 299.

that her life involves bodily form as well as spiritual idea. In manipulating and attacking the bodily mark, Aylmer then is working to eradicate Georgiana's ties to material, bodily existence – to eradicate her physicality (including, it seems, the threat of her sexuality). Paradoxically, he uses this physical form – a mark in the flesh – to express his idealist vision. But if the birthmark is a sign that Georgiana was born into the natural creation, Aylmer will work to take her out of that creation (clearly marked in the story as the realm of a female Mother Nature), to erase this mark of the original creator – and thus to produce a perfect image of her that is fully his own creation. The final goal of such an experiment with the birthmark would be to see Georgiana erased from the book of life and written into Aylmer's great book – the lab journal and testament that records all of the attempts of this artist/creator to triumph over Nature, to capture or recreate life in a perfect, non-temporal, non-physical form.

But if "The Birth-mark" thus shares foundational impulses with Poe's "The Oval Portrait", Hawthorne develops these shared premises into a very different narrative – finally implying an opposed response to the aesthetic vision played out in these paired plots. First, his scientist/artist figure produces no object; no thing is created that will remain after the woman is gone. While in Poe the painter does succeed in passing down the art object that he produced, the male artist in Hawthorne, here more of an idealist philosophical seeker than a physical creator, uses his symbolist arts not only to construct and manipulate the image that enthralls him but also, finally, to destroy that image. Working to erase a physical mark rather than to create one, Aylmer is seeking to sever his wife's ties to flesh and physicality, to take her out of mortal creation so that she could take a place in his own disembodied, perfectionist vision. At the story's conclusion, then, when perfecting her turns out to take her out of earthly life, Aylmer is left alone with his philosophical ideal.

Secondly, and crucially, Hawthorne's tale approaches the central artist's actions through the point of view of a detached, moralizing, judgmental narrator, while in Poe's tale readers follow (and identify with) the much-less-detached progress of a viewer-within-the-tale as he is drawn into absorbed enthrallment before the artist's painting. If "The Birth-mark" develops through a singular focus on the psychology of the artist/scientist Aylmer, Poe's tale divides its focus to follow two plots associated with two main characters. And although

"The Oval Portrait" concludes with a vision of one of these characters, the painter, recreating the dramatic scene of his completion of the portrait, the story begins with an extended, first-person introduction to the point of view and psychology of the narrator – who is also given a key role in Poe's work as the character who views the portrait, reads critical literature about it, and responds to it. The emphasis on the experience of this model reader-within-the-tale is what fundamentally distinguishes Poe's vision from Hawthorne's.

In "The Oval Portrait", this narrator/viewer is a prototypical Poe character – a relative of Roderick Usher and many others: a highly educated, last-of-the-line aristocrat stranded inside a ruined chateau full of bizarre art. Sick, wounded, hypersensitive, delirious, he is hardly presented as an objective or neutral observer. In fact, in the first published version of the story, "Life in Death" (of 1842), where Poe places an even greater stress on this character's role and perspective, his experiments with pain-killing opium have left him with "reeling senses" and marked boundary problems, so that he struggles to distinguish external sense perceptions from internal dreams, projections, or feverish hallucinations.[12] This narrator-reader, then, expresses himself less through action than through intense personal reaction to a host of exotic stimuli – a stance that leaves him especially susceptible to the shock of a first viewing of the oval portrait. Thus, while Hawthorne's narrative structure leaves his readers detached from Aylmer and his fraught interactions with the birthmark, Poe's narrator, when he encounters the portrait, does not judge it in terms of its moral or ethical effects, or speculate about multiple possible responses to it, but instead finds himself immediately carried away by it. He relives it. Ravished by a compelling emotional connection with the painted figure, he re-experiences the artist's complex, multi-leveled affective response at the moment of the painting's completion – feeling again a combination of wonder and horror at this triumph of art. The painted simulacrum here thus makes possible a reproduction or repetition, across the ages, not only of a sense of the "life" of the female subject but also of the love of the painter – his aesthetic response to that life.

While in the Hawthorne story the focus is on the husband-wife relation, and then on the loss of the potential of that relational life along with the life of the young bride, in Poe's version the woman's

[12] *Ibid.*, 296.

role is minimal. She remains mainly the initial object of the gaze, the raw material to be objectified in art. The Poe story's emphasis is much more clearly on the mystery of the bizarre moment of shared feeling – bridging a separation of space and time – that the painting has made possible between the tale's two central male characters. In Poe's allegory of aesthetic process, the dying woman is the necessary subject or material for art, the painter is the producer of art, and the narrator models the process of the reception of art. The woman's death is mainly valued as it makes possible the production of the visual representation of her, which in turn makes possible the intimate sharing of love and life between the artist and his specially attuned audience – through the mediation of the work of art.

While Hawthorne's narrative becomes a horror story about a self-divided aesthetic impulse combining fascination with, fixation on, and fear of the visual image that leads to ethical failure and human loss – placing the accent on the life that has been lost in the present – Poe's parallel narrative centers on evocation in his readers of the titillating horror seen to be foundational to the making of the aesthetic image – and thus to the success of the timeless work of art that lives on in the enthralled, affective responses of future readers. In its plot about the painter's production of a work of art, "The Oval Portrait" plays out Poe's poetics of aestheticism. But with its central emphasis on the mystery of the reception and recreation of such a work of art through the narrator's haunted absorption in the painting and its story, as the aesthetic object makes possible a powerful sharing of experience between the absent artist and his audience, Poe's story models his dream of the reception and transmission of his poetics by a long line of future readers.

"Hypocrite lecteur, – mon semblable, – mon frère!": reading as doubling in Poe and Baudelaire

One representative example of the complex, mixed, ambivalent response to Poe in antebellum America, Hawthorne felt compelled to face Poe's work head on in order finally to be able to turn away from his perverse example. Europe at mid-century, on the contrary, seemed primed to welcome Poe with open arms, making him perhaps the key figure shaping the course of European Aestheticism and Decadence. But these diametrically opposed responses might in some ways be seen as mirror images of one another: if Hawthorne's relation to Poe's work always involved more than simple detachment, the reception by many mid-century authors both in England and on the Continent was more complex than might be suggested by easy surface expressions of homage and identification.

In England the most immediate relations would be with Dante Gabriel Rossetti, Algernon Swinburne, Ernest Dowson, and Robert Louis Stevenson, as well as Wilde. But Poe's major, and initial, mark was within French traditions – of Symbolism, Aestheticism, Decadence, and later modernist and Surrealist work. Patrick Quinn's broad 1957 study, *The French Face of Edgar Poe*, still provides a most useful overview of the pervasiveness of the American author's works and ideas in France.[13] But to review "the French face of Poe" is also to begin to bring out what we might term the American Face of European Aestheticism and Decadence.

Examining how Poe became the "pivot on which for the past century French literature has turned", Quinn observes that "there is scarcely one French writer from the time of Baudelaire to the present who has not in one way or another paid his respects to Poe .... For this interest became something very like a religious cult."[14] For over a hundred years (1847 to 1945), Poe's poetic theory served as the point of origin for the work of three great French poets: Baudelaire, Stéphane Mallarmé, and Paul Valéry – "the beginning, the middle, and the end of a particular tradition in poetry" – each of whom sang the praises of a different aspect of the American's *oeuvre*: Baudelaire stressing the biography and psychology of the writer of tales; Mallarmé the mind and craft of the poet; and Valéry the critical and aesthetic theory of the philosopher. Following the impetus of these poets, many successive generations of French writers, painters, film-makers, and theater people (not to mention psychoanalysts, philosophers, and literary theorists in later eras) continued in this line – not only taking Poe as a revered model, but, in putting on his mask, coming to identify fully with him.

This process of idolization and internalization of Poe was initiated in the first stages of Poe's reception in France. Baudelaire, the first major French writer to take up Poe, did not respond to him as one influence among others. Describing what has become a legendary

---

[13] Patrick F. Quinn, *The French Face of Edgar Poe*, Carbondale: Southern Illinois University Press, 1957.
[14] *Ibid.*, 12-13.

moment in the study of literary transmission, he writes that he experienced a "singular shock" on first coming across Poe poems and stories – sensing that these writings were somehow playing his own thoughts back to him. He felt he was here reading works that he himself had sketched out as vague, confused story-ideas in his own notebooks – but now he found that Poe had already brought these inklings to "perfection".[15] Laying the foundation for the future French response to Poe – and, in the process, introducing Poe to a worldwide audience – Baudelaire made it a lifelong project to discover and translate his American mentor's works. Working obsessively on this project from 1847 to 1863, he reportedly would spend the first five hours of each workday on Poe before turning for three hours to his own poetry.[16]

The resulting Poe translations finally make up five volumes of Baudelaire's *Complete Works*. But the intensity of these efforts at explication, interpretation, and imitation also meant that Baudelaire came to internalize Poe – identifying with his life and psychological experience, and incorporating Poe's words and literary stance into almost every aspect of his own writing. "Do you know why I so patiently translated Poe?" he wrote:

> Because he resembled me. The first time I opened one of his books I saw, to my amazement and delight, not only certain subjects that I had dreamed about but SENTENCES that I had thought of and that he had written down twenty years before.

In reading Poe he felt he was discovering himself; translating Poe's work became, in some ways, then, for Baudelaire, as Quinn puts it, "an avenue for his own self-expression". To this avid disciple, Poe appeared from foreign shores as his uncanny alter ego, his "semblable", his double – something like a cousin, or a brother, separated at birth.[17]

And one major result or symptom of this internalization of Poe is that Baudelaire adopted Poe's peculiar vision of the dynamics of reading. Marked especially by Poe critical essays, like "The

---

[15] Lois Davis Vines, "Charles Baudelaire", in *Poe Abroad: Influence, Reputation, Reception*, ed. Lois D. Vines, Iowa City: University of Iowa Press, 1999, 165.

[16] Quinn, *The French Face of Edgar Poe*, 102.

[17] Baudelaire cited in Quinn, 135-36, 15.

Philosophy of Composition", in which aesthetic production is seen to be founded in a dream of direct, precise, and powerful communication of emotional affect to the reader, Baudelaire was also well aware through his own reading of Poe stories that such communication is most powerful when most indirect. In Poe, contagion or haunting is most likely to occur where it is resisted, denied, or unconscious. The full story of the process of literary influence or transmission, then, involves more than a simple, univocal, willed process of imitation and identification – following footsteps, copying gestures, mouthing lines, learning a part.

In fact, beginning with Baudelaire, French readers of Poe tended to focus their attention on stories of morbid psychology that, like "The Oval Portrait", center on the complexities of the reading process, foregrounding and playing out the vexed dynamics involved in aesthetic reception and transmission. Tracing the trajectories of readers-within-the-tale in Poe's works, we are introduced to a form of reading that involves not only the simple assimilation of an imposed pattern of externalities but also a divided, internalized response oscillating between attraction and repulsion, identification and detachment. The narrator in "The Oval Portrait", for example, does not easily and immediately mirror the painter's own experience of the compelling painting on his wall. His first response, on the contrary, is to try to stop the process, to shut out this stimulus – "I glanced at the painting hurriedly, and then closed my eyes .... It was an impulsive movement to gain time for thought" – only to find that this leads to an even more powerful, internalized, and unwilled repetition of the aesthetic affect.[18]

The canon of Poe fictions elevated to a central place by Baudelaire includes, in addition to "The Oval Portrait" and "The Fall of the House of Usher", two key narratives of crime and detection in the interdependent setting of urban life: "The Man of the Crowd" and "The Purloined Letter". In each of these characteristic works, readers are invited to model their response to the story matter on the response of a character who is figured, again, as a reader-within-the-tale. Whether he is conscious of it or not, this reader-within-the-tale finds that complete detachment from the plot or crime analyzed in the tale is impossible; the process of his reading leads, in fact, to repetition of the central matter of the story. But this implication in the story matter

---

[18] *The Selected Writings of Edgar Allan Poe*, 297.

is not advocated, sought out, or celebrated; rather, it is denied, parried, screened. What we follow in the central drama of interpretation, then, are the traces of an involuntary or unconscious repetition of the crime. In these classic Poe tales, the central story matter or story atmosphere is seen to be infectious, and Poe's model readers enact a process of reading in which transmission of the story is imagined on analogy to the transmission (or communication) of a disease.

"The Fall of the House of Usher" can serve as an introductory example of this process. If Roderick Usher was taken up as a key figure in the transmission of Aestheticism, a full reading of his story is not grounded in simple, direct response to this character's bizarre gestures and predicament; rather, our response is modeled by an intermediary character, a reader-within-the-text, the first-person narrator who enters the story scene from outside and begins to try to interpret it. Although this narrator is initially detached from the disintegrating home and family members, the buried plot of the tale comes to center on dramatic, if covert, signs of this reader's progressive implication in what he narrates. The process of trying to understand his friend's predicament leads the narrator, over the course of the story's plot, to become an unconscious "double" of Usher. Rather than solving the mystery of the house's "atmosphere" or of Usher's disease, he becomes infected by it or absorbed into it; rather than preventing Roderick's crime – the live burial of his sister-muse – he becomes complicit in it, a catalyst for the plot's actions. (His arrival at the manse coincides with the eruption of the sister's illness; he quickly takes over her place as intimate counselor at Usher's side. Then, he provides the active helping hand making possible the closing of the coffin for the live burial. Though a trained doctor, he ignores the physiological signs that she is alive, and later explains away the sounds of the sister's attempts to explode out of the closed casket.) By the story's end, the narrator-reader's divided relation to the story matter has become the key to its mystery; we realize that the exaggerated rationality of his interpretations and explanations is largely a cover, a vain attempt to mark and maintain a false distance from the irrational horror of the story events that absorb him.

"The Purloined Letter" works along similar lines, as, within this story plot, a master reader, Dupin, solves a crime by repeating it, internalizing it, becoming the double of the criminal. What distinguishes Dupin from other reader figures in Poe is his articulation of a conscious theory of this mode of reading as doubling. Moving away from the Prefect's laboratory model, Dupin describes reading or analysis not as the detached observation of an object by a separate, disinterested subject but as an experimental process of interaction between subjectivities that begins with the investigating subject putting himself in the place of the subject to be studied. Referring to the children's game of "even and odd", he stresses that a successful solution depends upon getting inside the thinking processes of a rival – and that this involves not simply guessing at mental patterns but in fact taking on the physical existence of the other, becoming the double of the other to the point of mirroring his facial features and repeating his bodily behaviors.[19]

In "The Murders in the Rue Morgue", it is the narrator, Dupin's uncanny twin – a reader-within-the-tale who undergoes his own version of the process of quasi-absorption in the example of his powerful friend – who provides the summary definition of the dynamic of doubling fundamental to the detective's interpretive method: an investigator with an especially acute "analytical" mind, he says, will be able to "throw himself into" and "identify himself" with the person being investigated.[20] And Dupin's solution of the case of the purloined letter shows even more clearly than these examples from game theory how this reading method breaks down the boundaries between investigator and investigated, policeman and outlaw, science and poetry, monarchy and revolution, respectable and "odd", and, most crucial here: subject and object. The motivations that lead Dupin to throw himself into this case, though, are not clear but mixed, confusing: he enters into the Minister's crime partly out of reverent homage, and partly out of bitter revulsion. After the application of his investigative method has solved the surface crime, defused the power of the letter, and restored social order, readers are left to meditate on the true mystery here that cannot be solved or clarified: the dark, irrational, unconscious urges of love and rivalry that lead to the curious, brotherly intimacy between the detective and Minister D--. The shared process of reading (and, in the end, rewriting) of the purloined letter finally makes it a vehicle that exposes and strengthens the closeness of communication between the detective and Minister D--.

---

[19] *Ibid.*, 374.
[20] *Ibid.*, 240-42.

But perhaps "The Man of the Crowd", with its minimalist plot, provides the most clarifying case study of Poe's vision of reading as a dynamic process of psychological doubling between reader and author, or reader and read. Beginning and ending with the refrain "*er lasst sich nicht lesen*" ("it does not permit itself to be read"),[21] "The Man of the Crowd" presents the paradigmatic story of a master reader and his final crisis of reading, a failure to read based in a failure to comprehend the implications of this new reading situation. Swept away by the uncanny foreignness-and-familiarity in the figure of an old man endlessly wandering city streets, this narrator cannot bring himself to recognize that in his attempts to read or understand this figure he has himself become a "man of the crowd". No longer self-contained, self-centered, or independent, he becomes strangely dependent upon the motive force of the homeless wanderer that he follows, or stalks, in an obsessive attempt at comprehension. During the twenty-four hours of this joint wandering, this narrator-reader becomes the double of the man he so desperately hopes to read. A third party (or a reader) observing the joint movements of this odd couple during their meandering voyage through the city might see them as mirror-images of one another – both dazed, manic wanderers with the same "wild and vacant stare",[22] impelled forward by an intense, internal, psychological fixation on something outside of themselves.

After this experience, the narrator's vain effort in the last paragraph suddenly to return to his prior mode of detached reading only highlights the extent of his interpretive crisis. This is not successful closure but the symptom of a crisis of closure; we end not with a triumph of reading but with an admission of failure: "it does not permit itself to be read." The narrator now works hard to point to the wanderer as a separate, exteriorized entity whose existence can be summed up and whose meanings can be fixed in the neat typological labels of the physiognomist's cabinet:

> This old man is the type and the genius of deep crime. He refuses to be alone. *He is the man of the crowd.*[23]

---

[21] *Ibid.*, 232, 239 (italics in the original).

[22] *Ibid.*, 237.

[23] *Ibid.*, 239 (italics in the original).

But this last-ditch effort at closure, pointing the finger of judgment at the old man as a figure of "deep crime", simply highlights the narrator's crisis of reading in the face of the flux of city crowds. Seeking to separate himself from the "crime" of this scene, he finds this horror "cannot be read"; thinking his goal is a reading of that "man of the crowd", he has failed to read himself – and his own experience of alienated, interdependent crowd movement; more precisely, his failure to read the crowd is based in a failure to comprehend his own entanglement with what he wishes to read. With these last efforts to avoid being infected by the contagious city scene, to summon up a detached judgment of the "man of the crowd" as an epitome of all the crimes of modern city life, the narrator stands as a classic example of the "hypocrite lecteur" in Baudelaire's famous invocation to *Les Fleurs du mal* – "Hypocrite lecteur, – mon semblable, – mon frère!" – who does not recognize that he is a "double" and "brother" of that which he would condemn, deeply if unconsciously implicated in what he reads.[24]

The "deep crime" evoked here is not simply that of the old man; he is more precisely seen as the "genius" or dark muse who triggers the narrator's enthralled response – which develops as an involuntary repetition of the crime. Baudelaire could find here, in "The Man of the Crowd", a model enactment of one possible relation between French mid-century writers and the genius of Poe. Indeed, when Walter Benjamin points to "The Man of the Crowd" as "the classic example" of a literary work revealing the "hidden depths" and "shocks" of the experience of the crowd, the element that he highlights as most "decisive" for Baudelaire is precisely the profound "ambivalence" of Poe's *flâneur*-narrator in relation to the old man, and to the other passers-by on city streets. In final gestures combining implication and self-protective repression, complicity and forced detachment, the deeply divided narrator of "The Man of the Crowd", like Baudelaire's poetic persona, becomes most fully a "man of the crowd" at the moment of his attempted rejection of the crowd: "If he succumbed to the force that attracted him to them and that made him, as a *flâneur*, one of them", writes Benjamin, "he was nevertheless unable to rid himself of a sense of their essentially inhuman character":

---

[24] Charles Baudelaire, "Au lecteur", in *Oeuvres*, ed. Yves-Gérard Le Dantec, Paris: Bibliothèque de la Pléiade, 1931-32, I, 18.

> He becomes their accomplice even as he dissociates himself from
> them. He becomes deeply involved with them, only to relegate them
> to oblivion with a single glance of contempt.[25]

Reading under the influence: from Des Esseintes to Dorian Gray
As a self-conscious movement, French Aestheticism was developed
out of (and codified by) Baudelaire's response to Poe – with a special
emphasis on Poe's claim (in "The Poetic Principle" of 1850) that the
supreme art work is a "poem *per se*", a "poem written solely for the
poem's sake".[26] This and related Poe pronouncements of an art-for-
art's-sake ideal – the vision of Art as separate from and a rival to
Nature; the stress on the autonomy or self-sufficiency of the work of
art, on the priority of Form over Content, and on the formal and
rational craft of the artist – were extended further, becoming a quasi-
religious doctrine, in the writings of Mallarmé, Valéry, and others.

    In the later nineteenth century, however, some French proponents
of Aestheticism, again following Baudelaire, also began to follow up
on another set of concerns in Poe – the exploration of abnormal or
perverse psychological states and dynamics, the psychopathology of
modern life – and this led to a movement more specifically termed
"Décadence". Decadence, as a literary movement, found its source in
Baudelaire's translations of Poe – and most especially in "The Fall of
the House of Usher". The totemic text for the Decadent movement in
France, as well as for the related Aesthetic movement in England,
Poe's self-reflexive tale spoke powerfully not only to low-brow,
juvenile lovers of Gothic machinery but also to the most advanced
European artists with its sensational portrait of Roderick Usher as an
elite, effete artist-figure, walling himself off from the life of Nature to
experiment with new forms of unworldly aesthetic pleasure,
wallowing in a religion of art that also becomes a sort of cult of death
– both for himself and for his sister/muse, who lives out Poe's
gendered definition of the "poetical": the most poetical topic being, as
Poe had written in "The Philosophy of Composition", the "death of a
beautiful woman".[27] Once again, here, the proto-Aesthetic vision of an
art for art's sake that makes nothing happen is allied with a sense of

[25] Benjamin, "On Some Motifs in Baudelaire", in *Selected Writings: Volume 4, 1938-
40*, 326.
[26] *The Selected Writings of Edgar Allan Poe*, 700.
[27] *Ibid.*, 680.

the artist less as a producer of beautiful objects than as a hyper-sensitive receiver and transmitter of beauty. A reactor rather than an actor, Usher explores waves of aesthetic sensation as stimuli wash over him amidst last-of-the-line decline and decay. Passive before the impulses of his delirious, drugged, and feverish imagination as well as his sense perceptions, Usher shows how an obsession with the aesthetic can merge with the decadence of a sort of hyper-esthesia.

Poe's "Usher" became most fully and directly paradigmatic in France when it was taken up by J.-K. Huysmans to define the plot, the scene, the atmosphere, the imagery, and the static, mesmerizing, florid narrative form of his classic 1884 novel of Decadence, *A Rebours* (*Against the Grain*). From the beginning of Huysmans' work, the hero, Des Esseintes, follows the model in life and art of Roderick Usher.

Because Des Esseintes is, like Usher, mainly a reader – whose whole existence revolves around analysis of his own aesthetic appreciation of objects and art works – his life story takes the form of a logbook of stimuli and sensations: a sort of reading list. And, as a list of suggested reading, this "breviary of the Decadence" (as Arthur Symons memorably called *A Rebours*) expands to advertise and advocate for its foundation not only on the story of Usher but on the entire oeuvre of Poe.[28] The survey of Des Esseintes' literary tastes begins and ends with works of the American proto-Aesthete. In the second chapter, we learn that he has singled out one book to be placed on an altar-like side table that "dominates" the interior space of his cloistered everyday life: a richly-printed special edition of Poe's *Narrative of Arthur Gordon Pym*.[29] And in its last chapters, *A Rebours* culminates in an ecstatic, extended celebration of his further readings in the works of "the wise and wonderful Edgar Allan Poe" – purveyor of "these terrible philtres imported from America" – and of a conception of the dramatic, immersive, unsettling process of reading that is seen to have its source in the dynamics of Poe's fiction.[30]

Today it may be hard to imagine the strange, inert *A Rebours* in itself as the site of this sort of intense reading experience, but in its

---

[28] Symons cited in G.A. Cevasco, *The Breviary of Decadence: J.-K. Huysmans's A Rebours and English Literature*, New York: AMS Press, 2001, ix.

[29] Joris-Karl Huysmans, *Against Nature*, trans. Robert Baldick, New York: Penguin, 1959, 34.

[30] *Ibid.*, 190, 192.

own day the novel played a remarkable role as a nexus in the international dissemination of Aesthetic vision. If Poe's words spoke powerfully and intimately to Des Esseintes, Huysmans' report of these private experiments in the reading of Poe seemed to speak in the same way to an entire generation of artists and writers – exploding as a literary sensation across Europe and England. In France the novel was immediately received as a "bible", a "breviary", or a "bedside book" that captivated Mallarmé, Verlaine, the Gourmont brothers, Valéry, Guy de Maupassant, and Paul Bourget, among others. And its influence also quickly spread across the channel, as key artists associated with the Aesthetic Movement – notably Whistler, Symons, and George Moore – fell under the spell of Des Esseintes in the same way.[31] Swinburne hailed *A Rebours* as the "Golden Book" of the later, decadent phases in British Aestheticism.[32] But perhaps the most crucial reception of Huysmans' work came with Oscar Wilde, who made *A Rebours* a key text figuring centrally in the plot of *The Picture of Dorian Gray* – as the "golden book" given to Dorian by Lord Henry to initiate the process of his recruitment to Aestheticism.[33] So, just as Poe's books became models of life for Des Esseintes, Des Esseintes' book becomes the life-altering, life-determining model for the *Bildung* of Dorian Gray.

Along the lines of Poe's "The Oval Portrait", Wilde in *Dorian Gray* divides two aspects of the Aesthetic impulse into the projects of two central male characters: Basil, the solitary producer of the visual art work, plays out the role of the painter in Poe's plot (and in Hawthorne's related tale, "The Prophetic Pictures") as he tends to divert life and *Eros* into painted effigies and wants to make Dorian over into a fixed, beautiful aesthetic object;[34] Lord Henry, the

---

[31] Cevasco, *The Breviary of Decadence*, ix-xii.

[32] Freedman, *Professions of Taste*, 36.

[33] Oscar Wilde, *The Picture of Dorian Gray*, ed. Camille Cauti, New York: Barnes and Noble, 2003, 127-30. On Wilde's notion of the "golden book", see Camille Cauti, "Introduction", in *ibid.*, xvii. On the probability that the "golden book" in *Dorian Gray* is closely based on *A Rebours*, see Freedman, *Professions of Taste*, 36; Cevasco, *The Breviary of Decadence*, xii, 67-68, 71; Cauti, "Introduction", in *The Picture of Dorian Gray*, xvii-xix.

[34] For critical suggestions that Wilde's painting plot in *Dorian Gray* was at least partly modeled on these Poe and Hawthorne stories, see Cevasco, *The Breviary of Decadence*, 75; Kerry Powell, "Hawthorne, Arlo Bates, and *The Picture of Dorian Gray*", *Papers on Language and Literature*, XVI/4 (Fall 1980), 403-16; Karl

sociable, highly verbal critic/viewer, concentrates on the reception of art, and wants to make Dorian into a beautiful person, an appreciator of life *as* art – an Aesthete like himself. And, like Poe's story, Wilde's novel gives its most extended treatment to the latter impulse, tracing in detail the drama of aesthetic influence enacted in Dorian's reception of art – exploring the power of Lord Henry's voice or of Des Esseintes' text to enthrall, to haunt, to infect, or, in the repeated words of Lord Henry, to "dominate".[35]

The dynamics of this haunting operate in Dorian's case just as they did in Baudelaire's, or later Des Esseintes', reading of Poe – as a form of textual contagion in which internal appropriation can become at the same time a mode of external domination, and a voice from without is received as speaking strangely from within. This is how Dorian first responds to Lord Henry's spoken wit – "He was dimly conscious that entirely fresh influences were at work within him. Yet they seemed to him to have come really from himself" – and it is also how he responds when he first picks up the "poisonous book".[36] Wilde's narrator observes, of Lord Henry's gift book,

> For years Dorian Gray could not free himself from the influence of this book; or perhaps it would be more accurate to say that he never sought to free himself from it .... Indeed, the whole book seemed to him to contain the story of his life, written before he had lived it.[37]

Like Baudelaire and Des Esseintes before him, Dorian is bewitched here by the reading of a book from foreign shores that is, at the same time, uncannily familiar – seeming to anticipate and prefigure the patterns of his innermost life. But he also finds that the process of internalizing and reproducing such a textual model is not simply voluntary, easy, or free. He soon discovers that the shaping power of such a "poisonous book" can insinuate itself in ways that make its influence fearful.

When Wilde takes up Huysmans' Poe-saturated novel centering on the drama of aesthetic reading, placing it at the center of his own novel, it is seen to trigger in Dorian just the sort of anxious, nervous

---

Beckson, *Oscar Wilde: The Critical Heritage*, London: Routledge, 1970, 77; Jeffrey Meyers, *Edgar Allan Poe: The Life and Legacy*, New York: Scribner's, 1992, 290.
[35] Wilde, *The Picture of Dorian Gray*, 14, 117, 119.
[36] *Ibid.*, 21, 129.
[37] *Ibid.*, 130.

mode of psychological response experienced earlier by Des Esseintes in responding to Poe: it "troubles the brain" and provokes "a malady of dreaming". And these dynamics of influence in Dorian's life are then repeated at another stage in the process when we see that, as a result of his incorporation of the patterns of the "golden book" into his own life, Dorian becomes a life-altering model himself, an "evil influence" shaping the next, emerging generation of young aesthetes who now want to copy and imitate him – trying to reproduce his style as he has reproduced the styles and voices of Lord Henry and of the "golden book" that has taken over his life.[38] In the same way that Lord Henry passed the baton to him, so Dorian will pass the baton to a new generation of enthusiastic recruits – who will learn once again to receive and repeat the aesthetic vision. In the paradigmatic plot of *Dorian Gray*, this is how the aesthetic tradition is transmitted.

Poe's return in the 1890s: the buried genius of American Aestheticism and Decadence

Imagining our way into Hawthorne's ambivalent response to Poe in the 1840s, and keeping in mind the responses of Des Esseintes and Baudelaire to the dividedness built into the dynamics of aesthetic reception played out in Poe's tales, may help us to begin to understand the nature of the broad-based cultural response to Poe's aesthetic theory in the later nineteenth century as that vision returned from overseas to American shores – having been translated and internalized in the works of European followers in the line of Baudelaire. If Poe's vision was uncannily familiar-yet-strange to Hawthorne in the 1840s, compelling a protective, distancing response, the uncanny effect would be even more pronounced for American artists by the 1890s.

Like the narrator of Poe's "The Oval Portrait" in his first encounter with the painting, many American artists and writers at the turn of the century described an initially enthralled response to new European art forms that seemed to speak to them with an eerie intimacy. And often that voice was clearly marked as emanating from Poe. In Boston, Ralph Cram seemed to be channeling the author of "Usher" in stories that combined British Decadence with the Gothic/supernatural plots and imagery of Poe. In Chicago, Herbert Stone and Ingalls Kimball, publishers of the most successful American little magazine of the 1890s, *The Chap-Book* (an American *Yellow Book*), included a ten-

---

[38] *Ibid.*, 129, 225.

volume edition of Poe's works (originally planned to be illustrated by Aubrey Beardsley) as the center-piece of their Carnation series meant to present "the best of the decadent writings".[39] In San Francisco, Ambrose Bierce derived the key principle in his aesthetic theory – "Art has nothing to do with reality" – from Poe, and produced a long line of Poe-like tales of the fantastic.[40]

But the most remarkably direct, self-conscious *fin-de-siècle* response comes with Vance Thompson and James Huneker of the New York little magazine *M'lle New York*, who (counter to James and Howells) promoted Decadence not as a foreign invasion but rather as the means for revival of a specifically American literary culture, celebrating Whitman's seminal role in the emergence of French *vers libre* and Poe's foundational role as a model for the long line of "modern French literature" to outline a reconfigured literary history in which Whitman and Poe are recognized as the "fathers of Decadence".[41] *M'lle New York*, then, suggests that in opening themselves to Continental (and especially French) influences American artists were reclaiming a tradition of American expressive possibilities that had been "disowned" or neglected since the Civil War. Still, for these 1890s aesthetic experimentalists, as for Hawthorne, the connection to Poe was certainly never direct or simple. The strangely familiar voice was also calling to them across great gaps of space and time, in a resolutely foreign guise – in some ways returning as the expression of an American urge that had been long forgotten, or repressed.

---

[39] Weir, *Decadent Culture in the United States*, 110. See also Kirsten MacLeod, "'Art for America's Sake': Decadence and the Making of American Literary Culture in the Little Magazines of the 1890s", 309-38.

[40] Bierce cited in Weir, *Decadent Culture in the United States*, 124.

[41] Thompson and Huneker cited in Macleod, "'Art for America's Sake': Decadence and the Making of American Literary Culture in the Little Magazines of the 1890s", 331. See also Weir, *Decadent Culture in the United States*, 42-49.

REVISING THEORY: POE'S LEGACY IN SHORT STORY CRITICISM

ERIK VAN ACHTER

The "Splintering Frame"

In his essay in *Short Story Theory at a Crossroads*, Norman Friedman calls for a critical consensus to ensure the future of short story theory:

> In discussing short story theory, we have a tendency to talk at cross-purposes. I do not mean simply a tendency to disagree; I mean, rather, an apparent difficulty in agreeing on what it is we are disagreeing about.[1]

For better or for worse, Friedman's plea appeared at a time when literary theory, particularly in the United States, was undergoing a process of fragmentation along the fault lines of modern identity politics, in which the identity categories and identifications of the writer, reader and theorist came to serve as categories that were not only political but also theoretical.[2] The ascendancy of identity politics in the wake of the rise of post-structuralist and post-modern theories increasingly demanded what might be called a poetics of identity: it was as though political identity categories necessitated the formulation of corresponding critical theories. Literary scholars were

---

[1] Norman Friedman, "Recent Short Story Theories, Problems in Definition", in *Short Story Theory at a Crossroads*, eds Susan Lohafer and Jo Ellyn Clarey, Baton Rouge: Louisiana University Press, 1989, 13.

[2] This is particularly true in post-colonial theory, in which an essential distinction is made between the identity categories of the colonizer and the colonized, who purportedly have radically different frames of reference. Moreover, the rise of identity politics in literary theory has been facilitated by the admission of the extra-textual to theory: that is, the acknowledgment of historicity, culture and the role of the reader, a dominant trend in the latter half of the twentieth century.

thus compelled to take part in the politics of identity[3] and to constitute increasingly circumscribed, politically charged sub-fields of literary research, at the very moment that Friedman was advocating the inverse of this fragmentation – for consensus, agreement and cooperation – in the field of short story theory.

In the face of this "splintering frame" of literary studies, short story theory was forced to abandon or at least call into question the unifying, universalizing critical framework defined by the tripartite "author, text, reader" structure that had been introduced and reinforced by short story theorists of the preceding era, beginning with Edgar Allan Poe and his disciple Brander Matthews. The very idea of a determinate textual form that could be defined in terms of intra-textual, immanent characteristics and relations had itself become untenable with the decline of formalistic literary methods in the period we now call post-modern, and the rise of methods that admit and refer to the extra-textual (post-structuralism, post-colonialism) or emphasize textual autonomy and indeterminacy (deconstruction). The splintering frame[4] of post-modern literary studies questioned whether the "short story as form" was merely an illusion produced by a particular, historical cognitive frame that no longer had any real existence. The historical and literary evidence suggests an affirmative answer to this question, for the differences between the short story and the novel, like the former's purported affinities with the poem, were rather numinous and indefinable. For example, an article by John Gerlach explicitly addressed the indeterminacy of the short story's relationships with poetry and longer prose forms.[5] Yet even without having been rigorously and exclusively defined before the advent of post-modernism, the short story had already achieved acceptance as a specific genre of prose fiction. The relationships between the short

---

[3] I say "compelled" because developments in post-structuralist and post-modern theory emphasized the importance of the extra-textual and the role of the process of interpretation itself. Thus, the identifications and political preferences of the theorist come explicitly into play.

[4] Here we may add to our understanding of the term "the splintering frame" the observation that this process of splintering, or fragmentation, has been aided and accelerated dramatically by the emphasis on indeterminacy in deconstruction (Derrida) and on cultural, historical and other extra-textual elements in post-structuralism (Foucault).

[5] John Gerlach, "The Margins of Narrative: The Very Short Story, the Prose Poem, and the Lyric", in *Short Story Theory at a Crossroads*, 75-84.

story, the poem and the novel had proved, to a degree, both ineffable and enduring. The dependence upon these comparisons (as well as the indisputable critical presence of the reader) in the articulation of the short story genre has resulted in a degree of critical stasis: even in the wake of post-modernism, short story theory continues to be defined in relation to these other genres; the genre of the short story continues to resist or elude definition as an independently defined, closed and unique literary form. In other words, the fundamental problematic of short story criticism – that of genre definition – continues to be posed in the same or similar terms to what it has been since Poe. The present article will trace this critical problematic in reverse by demonstrating the continuing endurance and pervasive influence of Poe's seminal contributions to short story theory.

The sterile position in Poe's Legacy

Even after the processes of fragmentation had run their course in post-modernism, the skeletal framework of a unified genre still remained for the short story: it was still accepted that the short story was neither novel nor poem and that it somehow produced an effect in the reader. Yet the persistent analogy to poetry and contrast with prose that defined the theoretical arena left no possible avenue leading toward a unified, universal and free-standing definition for the short story genre. The sterile and ultimately static position that endures in short story theory in the post-modern era is the direct legacy of the particular critical position that was first introduced and elaborated by Poe and, some decades later, was recapitulated and formalized by Brander Matthews. The influence of Poe and Matthews' original critical works has continued through the two waves of Anglo-American short story theory to inform a contemporary theoretical framework.

In what is now known as the first wave of short story theory, extending from the time of Matthews (around 1900) to the end of the era in which New Criticism was dominant, short story theory scarcely departed from Poe's theoretical framework in setting forth a prescriptive definition, often in the form of manuals purporting to teach one "how to write" a short story. In the second wave of short story theory, which generally denotes much of the theoretical work conducted since the 1970s (when short story poetics again came to the foreground), Poe's influence can be seen less as an authoritative formulation than as an influence, properly speaking, and increasingly as an obstacle to be surmounted. However, even in explicitly grappling with Poe's legacy, short story theory usually preserved much of his theoretical frame.

Second-generation short story critics, too, perpetuated the practice of comparing short prose with poetry as well as longer prose forms. We can see this practice at work in any number of theoretical texts concerned with the short story: to cite a few specific examples, drawing only on the collection *Short Story Theories*, we may point to articles such as "The Short Story and the Novel", by Alberto Moravia; "The Lyric Short Story", by Eileen Baldeshwiler; and an earlier article by Norman Friedman, entitled "What Makes the Short Story Short?".[6] However, it immediately becomes clear that such a method, which is tantamount to an attempt to bring the short story into a central position in the literary canon, has never produced a comprehensive study of the short story. To wit, there can be no definitional comparison without a known second term: for example, to compare the short story to poetry presupposes an adequate definition of poetry; and given that debates over the nature of poetry have raged for far longer than those regarding the short story, it is evident that its nature and definition are to some extent historically contingent. In other words, throughout the debates concerning the nature of poetry, dating to times immemorial, different definitions of the genre have been developed and accepted at various historical junctures. Poetry is scarcely defined today in the same manner as it was in a past age; each historical period has had a particular, contingent definition of the poetic genre. Likewise, any term that is defined in relation to such a historically contingent definition will of logical necessity be similarly defined – contingently and particularly. Given that the known term is always contingent and historical, comparative methods can thus only yield a similarly contingent and historical definition for the short story.

As a direct result of Poe's legacy, the logically contingent and historical nature of a definition arrived at by such a method has until recently tended to go unremarked. According to Poe, a suitable genre definition for the short story must necessarily be universal and timeless, and critics have mostly followed suit, with some notable exceptions (the genre-mode debate between Charles May and Suzanne

---

[6] See *Short Story Theories*, ed. Charles May, Athens: Ohio University Press, 1976, 147-51, 202-13, 131-46.

Ferguson in articles published in *The New Short Story Theories* is one such exception).[7]

If there has been any one point of consensus in short story criticism, it has been the necessity of discerning the generic difference between the short story and the novel – this is a point of consensus rooted firmly in the ultimately sterile, comparative stance taken by Poe. Although the numerous theories that have been developed diverge widely regarding the specific difference at stake, two distinct issues have given this question its central position within the paradigm that emerged from the fallout of first-wave short story poetics.

The first issue is the historical fact that the short story did not emerge as a distinct genre or specific narrative mode until the first half of the nineteenth century, just as the novel did not appear as a genre until the early seventeenth century, with Cervantes' *Don Quixote*. It is unsurprising that the short story is often defined through contrast with its predecessor, the novel, for centuries ago the latter had to be distinguished by comparing it with its narrative forebears, including verse fiction, folk tales, myths and the epic. The second issue is that those seeking to define the short story generally agree that the nature of the short story does not inhere solely in its relative brevity; the generic difference is irreducible to a quantitative difference in terms of the sheer volume of text. Consequently, a great number of the critical articles in May's *Short Story Theories* concern the question of a specifically qualitative difference.

The quantitative difference, we shall see, is little more than a consequence of accepting a qualitative criterion. Short story criticism, which seeks to determine this generic difference, has always found itself faced with the novel's relative, if not absolute, prestige in the hierarchy of genres – an uphill battle once waged long before to establish the novel as a genre. Following Poe, short story theory has

---

[7] May argued that the short story is a genre on the basis of one dominant single feature, namely, the nature of the knowledge the genre transmits to the attentive reader, whereas Suzanne Ferguson was convinced that both short story and novel belonged to the realistic mode and had the same features in common. The natural consequence was that the short story was able to present fewer of those features than the novel. Both articles appeared elsewhere, but for didactic purposes May juxtaposed his and Ferguson's view in the same volume. See Charles May, "The Nature of Knowledge in Short Fiction", in *The New Short Story Theories*, ed. Charles May, Athens: Ohio University Press, 1994, 138-43, and Suzanne Ferguson, "Defining the Short Story, Impressionism and Form", in *ibid.*, 218-30.

attempted to ascribe to the short story the prestige of poetry, a prestige that would lend the short story a status at least comparable to that of the novel within the hierarchy of genres. It is noteworthy that even as short story criticism, in the decades following the publication of May's book, has attempted to shed every "fossil survivor of Poe's aesthetic",[8] it has continued to build on the basis of earlier generations of short story criticism. To this day, aspects of Poe's aesthetics continue to haunt short story criticism. Specifically, we can find Poe at the source both of the tradition that defines the short story in terms of its relations to other literary forms, whether to other prose forms or to poetry, and of the prestige ascribed to it.

The influence of Poe's aesthetic is evident in both quantitative and qualitative definitions of the short story and, furthermore, in the search for a distinction between a story that is merely short and a work that may properly be called a "short story". Most importantly, the aesthetic criteria handed down by Poe can be clearly seen in the qualitative aspect, which is, at once, the source of the prestige ascribed to the short story in relation to other genres, and the factor that determines the economy of prose – specifically, the short story's capacity to provoke a given effect in the reader. Thus, the turn taken by reader-response criticism, away from the text itself and toward the real reader of the text, is not in itself a turn away from Poe: Poe's emphasis on the intrinsic qualities of the written text is focused on a unity of effect, which is produced by the reader's experience of the text, in which this turn lay immanent. The qualitative dimension of the short story is thus clearly secondary to a specific, immanent quality – the capacity of the short story to produce a unitary effect in the reader.[9] Furthermore, if the analogy to poetry is a relatively unproductive aspect of Poe's paradigm, the imperative exhibited in much short story criticism – that is, to define the short story in terms of a generic form or discursive mode in relation to and in distinction from the novel – acquires greater importance.

It should thus come as no great surprise that as formalism and structuralism diminished in influence, short story theory came to draw upon the newly influential theories of *Rezeptionsästhetik* and reader-

---

[8] Friedman, "Recent Short Story Theories", 13-31.
[9] Quantitative constraints and prose economy thus follow from the necessity of the text being read in a particular manner (that is, in one sitting, *per* Poe's theory) and being of a length that makes such a reading possible.

oriented criticism. Decades of short story theory and criticism had looked for text-immanent characteristics of the short story (whether genre or mode) that would make it possible to define the genre in an objective manner. Nevertheless, this quest for an objective definition (which, as shall be seen, was not at all set back by the reintroduction of the reader) that could be obtained by means of contrast was ultimately unsuccessful; and while they retained this technique from Poe's methodology, critics thought they had eluded the larger portion of Poe's aesthetic by turning to text-immanent, objective criteria for a definition of the genre.

Reader-oriented criticism in Anglo-American scholarship, which stemmed from the rise to prominence of *Rezeptionsästhetik* in Germany during the 1960s and 1970s (and differs from it primarily by having a less theoretical and more pragmatic orientation), explicitly acknowledged, and indeed placed heavy emphasis on, the reader-text relationship. Then, as it were, the reader stepped out from the periphery and into the center of theory. A mere decade after *Rezeptionsästhetik* emerged in Germany with the publication by Wolfgang Iser of *Der Akt des Lesens*,[10] Anglo-American reader-oriented criticism began in earnest, with articles published in a special issue of *Modern Fiction Studies* titled "The Modern Short Story" (1982). Several critics who would later make important contributions to reader-oriented criticism published articles in this volume, but two articles in particular can be seen as inaugural works of Anglo-American reader-oriented criticism: an experimental piece by Suzanne Hunter Brown, and an essay by John Gerlach, "Closure in Modern Short Fiction: Cheever's 'The Enormous Radio' and 'Artemis, the Honest Well Digger'", that, appropriately enough, concluded the volume.[11]

Both reader-oriented and comparative definitions of the short story highlight the enduring importance of Poe and Matthews. The comparative or differential method clearly has its origin in Poe's positioning the short story between two already extant genres: the novel and the lyrical poem. As for the reader-oriented approach, the aesthetics of reception uses methods that aim to extract the qualitative characteristics of the text by reference to the hermeneutic activity of a

---

[10] Wolfang Iser, *Der Akt des Lesens*, Munich: Fink, 1976.
[11] John Gerlach, "Closure in Modern Fiction", *Modern Fiction Studies*, XXVIII/1 (Spring 1982), 145-52.

real or idealized reader: the reader who was already present in Poe. Both methods are, at most, elaborations and extensions of Poe's original aesthetic paradigm.

Poe ... und kein Ende?

The framework for the short story genre that has survived after the splintering frame – the claim that the short story was neither novel nor poem, and that it somehow produced an effect in the reader – consists of two elements drawn directly from the legacy of Poe's critical work.

It is important to highlight the failure of short story criticism to emancipate itself from the particular aesthetic paradigm set by Poe, Matthews and their successors. Until the advent of the "poetics of identity" in the wake of post-structuralism and deconstruction, the short story continued to be defined positively by analogy to poetry and negatively by contrast with the novel. This is an aesthetic framework that was first introduced by Poe in three essays: these are, in decreasing order of importance relative to our understanding of the short story, his "Review of Hawthorne's *Twice-Told Tales*", "The Philosophy of Composition" and "The Poetic Principle". The latter two articles focus almost entirely on poetry, covering poetry criticism and poetic composition in both descriptive and prescriptive terms, while the first is an article that was ostensibly a review of Nathaniel Hawthorne's *Twice-Told Tales*. In other words, none of these documents were deliberately intended to constitute studies on the nature of the short story or short fiction.

Throughout both "The Philosophy of Composition" (1846) and the "Review of Hawthorne's *Twice-Told Tales*" (1842),[12] Poe insists that fiction writing proceeds optimally from a deliberate choice of an overall "effect" the author wishes to create. The following citation is the *locus classicus* of short story theory:

> A skilful artist has constructed a tale. He has not fashioned his thoughts to accommodate his incidents, but having deliberately conceived a certain single effect to be wrought, he then invents such

---

[12] From the vantage point of short story theory, Poe's articles did not very much impress readers when they were first published. They started their way into modernity and into the hard core of short story studies through the mediation of the already-mentioned Brander Matthews, whose booklet *The Philosophy of the Short-Story*, New York: Longmans, Green, 1901, was a retake and in a sense a fusion of the ideas exposed in Poe's reviews and articles.

incidents, he then combines such events, and discusses them in such tone as may best serve him in establishing the preconceived effect.

While Poe clearly operates from the presupposition that a single author actively constructs a narrative, he also allows for and even demands that a hypothetical reader should play a determining role in the author's choices.

Poe's assumption of a reader introduces particular demands and limitations that the author must take into consideration in the construction of the short story: "If any literary work is too long to be read at one sitting, we must be content to dispense with the immensely important effect derivable from unity of impression – for, if two be required, the affairs of the world interfere, and everything like totality is at once destroyed."[13] By specifying a particular amount of time in which the poem should be read, Poe implies a specific reader with assumed limitations, interests and needs – this implicit construction of a general reading audience is one of the most prominent features of Poe's theory.[14] In Poe's theoretical framework, during the hour of perusal, the reader should also fall under the writer's control.[15] It is this reader who returns, a century later, in the *Rezeptionsästhetik* and other reader-oriented critical apparatuses. (Naturally, this later reader plays a more determining and autonomous role than Poe's hypothesized reader.)

---

[13] Edgar Allan Poe, "The Philosophy of Composition", in *Essays and Reviews*, ed. G.R. Thompson, New York: Literary Classics of the United States, 1984, 15.

[14] Umberto Eco and others will later designate this feature as the constitution of a "Model Reader", which may or may not coincide with the actual reader. See Umberto Eco, "*Intentio Lectoris*: The State of the Art", in *The Limits of Interpretation*, Bloomington: Indiana University Press, 1994, 44-63.

[15] In the terminology adopted by Umberto Eco in "*Intentio Lectoris*", the reader's *intentio lectoris* must precisely double the *intentio auctoris* – that is, through the work, the perspective of the reader becomes the perspective intended by the author. Consequently, the third *intentio*, that of the work itself, must be the same for both the writer and the reader of the short story. In the framework constructed by M.H. Abrams in the Introduction to *The Mirror and the Lamp*, Poe's theory clearly falls under the rubric of the expressive orientation – the short story expresses the effect, which the author intends, and reproduces it in the reader (M.H. Abrams, *The Mirror and the Lamp*, Oxford: Oxford University Press, 1953, 6-29). On the other hand (and this may be due to the fact that Abrams' study does not extend through Poe's time), this quintessentially Romantic aesthetic orientation does not fully capture the whole of Poe's theory: it places relatively greater emphasis on the role of the writer than on the reader or the work itself.

On the pivot of this enduring reading figure, Poe begins positioning the short story above the novel within a comparative hierarchy of genres. In his review of *Twice-Told Tales* Poe explicitly identifies the short "prose tale" or "narrative" as one that can be read in a single sitting, all the better to convey without mitigation the intended effect:

> The ordinary novel is objectionable, from its length as it cannot be read at one sitting, it deprives itself, of course, of the immense force derivable from totality .... In the brief tale, however, the author is enabled to carry out the fullness of his intention, be it what it may. During the hour of perusal the soul of the reader is at the writer's control.[16]

In addition to qualifying how the short prose tale should be created and received, Poe grants the genre a privileged position in the hierarchy of literary forms, subordinate only to the poem.[17] In his theory, the novel is of low rank because it is so long that it cannot be read in one sitting.[18] Indeed, when Poe compares the tale to the poem, the tale's more elusive, almost unfathomable qualities are underlined, whereas in his second comparison – the contrast between the novel with the tale – the tale's greater economy of prose is underscored, which frequently results in quantitative descriptions. What quantitative descriptions miss, however, is the determining importance of the qualitative, unitary effect – absent in the novel by virtue (or vice) of its length, but present, in some form, in the poem.

In the five decades following Poe's critical statements on short fiction, no vocal proponents of his ideas were to emerge, at least in the United States.[19] As critics such as Charles May have observed, it was Brander Matthews who ensconced Poe's ideas in the canon of literary criticism during the twentieth century.[20] In *The Philosophy of the Short-Story*, published in 1901, Matthews built on Poe's premises,

---

[16] Poe, "Review of *Twice-Told Tales*, by Nathaniel Hawthorne", in *Poetry and Tales*, ed. Patrick F. Quinn, New York: Literary Classics of the United States, 1984, 586.
[17] *Ibid.*, 585.
[18] *Ibid.*, 586.
[19] In France, by contrast, Charles Baudelaire emerged as a rather aggressive promoter of Poe's writings even during the last years of Poe's life.
[20] Charles May, *The Short Story: The Reality of Artifice*, New York: Prentice Hall, 1994, 107, 109.

giving Western literary criticism what would arguably be its first
poetics of the genre that would commonly become known as the
"short story". Matthews constructed his theoretical framework on the
basis of Poe's ideas, while expanding and elaborating a relatively new
genre category.

Matthews reinforces the essential hierarchical contrast between the
short story and the novel, attributing an originality to the short story
that is comparatively absent from the novel. In the tone of his
argument here we find confirmation that his project in approaching
the short story genre is not mere objective description but rather the
promotion and defense of a new American genre: "The novelist may
be commonplace, he may bend his best energies to the photographic
reproduction of the actual; if he shows us a cross-section of real life
we are content; but the writer of Short-stories must have originality
and ingenuity."[21] Notably, Matthews follows Poe in privileging the
tale over longer forms such as the novel, albeit by means of a three-
part strategy of his own design. In the first case, he differentiates the
"Short-story" from the novel in order to highlight the story's
essentially superior qualities. Of these, the most important is the
story's totality of effect: "a Short-story has unity as a Novel cannot
have it."[22]

Critics, generally speaking, recognize Poe rather than Matthews
(despite Matthews' more specifically theoretical articulation) as the
progenitor of modern short fiction criticism, although with regard to
the literary form itself, some might grant greater credit to Guy de
Maupassant or Anton Chekhov. In terms of critical influence,
however, Poe still retains precedence (if only for chronological
reasons): his two central critical texts on the subject are to this day
frequently cited in studies of the short story and its origins. Matthews
served primarily to cement Poe's place in the canon of short story
theory.

The enduring genius of Poe, as well as the originality of his critical
writings on the topic of the short story, or the "tale proper", lies
precisely in the perfect integration of what Umberto Eco has called
the *intentio auctoris*, the *intentio operis* and the *intentio lectoris*.[23]

---

[21] Matthews, *The Philosophy of the Short-Story*, 23.
[22] *Ibid.*, 15.
[23] Eco, "*Intentio Lectoris*", 50-54, 57-62.

These terms, featured in Eco's essay, denote three specific interpretive stances that may be taken by the reader of a given text: first, "interpretation as research of the *intentio auctoris*", that is, the attempt to divine the author's intended meaning; second, "interpretation as the research of the *intentio operis*", that is, the New Critical attempt to discern the text-immanent meaning, independent of both author and reader; and finally, "interpretation as imposition of the *intentio lectoris*", that is, the reader-oriented, or hermeneutic, position, in which the reader imposes his or her own "intentions", which are always, as in all literary hermeneutics, interpretive presuppositions whether they concern methodology or the contents of the text. Generally, one of the three is categorically excluded in favor of another (in structuralism, the *intentio auctoris* is excluded in favor of the *intentio lectoris*;[24] in New Criticism, the *intentio auctoris* is excluded in favor of the *intentio operis*; in traditional authorial-intent theories, the *intentio lectoris* is devalued in favor of the *intentio auctoris*, etc.).

Poe's theory, by contrast, finds its enduring strength in its reliance upon the objectivity of the *intentio operis* and its insistence on certain transcendent criteria. At the same time, its very aim and criterion of success can be seen in bringing about, from the *intentio operis*, the perfect coincidence and reproduction of the *intentio auctoris* in the *intentio lectoris*. In Poe's theory of the short story, the author is also the reader and ought to be able to judge, as a reader, the effect of the text. The reproduction of the intended effect in the reader, according to Poe's theory, effects this coincidence in the short story; moreover, the necessity of this reproduction and coincidence implies the necessity of a reader without whom the short story would not be what it is. In effect, the inclusion of the reader becomes an essential characteristic of the short story as a genre.

Still, in Poe's theory the *intentio auctoris* was never completely understood in the same way that we customarily understand the term, particularly in the context of nineteenth-century French criticism. Rather, it was more an *intentio operis*, in the sense of an Aristotelian act of *poeein*, of the production of a self-subsistent object. And how

---

[24] We may note in passing that this is due to the emphasis structuralists place on language and its impact on the reading process. It is worthy of note that the *intentio operis* is also relatively privileged by structuralism, for language and its structures are already at stake in the text-immanent structures of the work itself.

could it not be so? For in his theoretical writings Poe played the role of both of the critic and the writer, critically engaging his own texts, and he could (as both author and critic of the same works) thus readily superimpose the *intentio auctoris* upon the *intentio lectoris*, resulting in an approximation of a pure *intentio operis*. Drawing upon the elegant, utilitarian theoretical framework described in M.H. Abrams' Introduction to *The Mirror and the Lamp*,[25] one might say that Poe's theory can be understood not as fitting cleanly within the expressive orientation but, rather, as a composite orientation that, in the end, is closer to an "objective orientation" than it would initially appear. This coincidence of productive and authoritative intentions resulted in a well-balanced theory and perhaps explains why Poe remains perched, raven-like, casting the authoritative shadow of a primal source upon the theoretical work of new critics and reader-response theorists alike. Poe's texts thus approximate the New Critical ideal of a self-contained text in which the *intentio lectoris* and *intentio auctoris* vanish. However, at the same time, Poe's texts fulfill the ideal textual model for reader-oriented theorists, in that these two *intentios* balance one another, or cancel each other out, as opposed to being absent. In other words, by virtue of the privileged status they granted to and the explicit emphasis they placed upon the reader, Poe's texts already undermined the ideology of the New Critics.

It is perhaps this precarious, yet perfectly harmonious, balancing of the *intentio auctoris* and the *intentio lectoris*, and the corresponding illusion of a pure *intentio operis*, which has preserved the authority of Poe's critical writings. Moreover, whether it is an accident of literary history or the product of a careful brilliance, this has also allowed Poe to outlive his epigones, untainted by the commodity that the short story had become in the early twentieth century, to influence the theory of short fiction to this very day.

Nevertheless, as noted earlier, this balance could not be sustained indefinitely. Furthermore, no shift in focus could satisfactorily resolve every latent difficulty of short story theory. Developments in recent decades have thus been able to introduce new theoretical concepts and constructs, suggesting alternative paradigms to the one first set out by Poe. What is important in these developments is not their success or failure, but the possibilities they hold for the future of theory. In any case, attempts to define the specific nature and qualities of the short

---

[25] Abrams, *The Mirror and the Lamp*, 21-26.

story, whether as a distinct genre or otherwise, have dominated the research and polemics of specialists in short story theory to this day.[26] The overriding emphasis on this question and the means by which an answer has traditionally been sought clearly follow in the footsteps of Poe and Matthews. And, as if this were not sufficient to highlight the importance of Poe, the theoretical turn taken toward the reception of the reader points in the same direction, for the qualitative, aesthetic dimensions of Poe's theory center around the role of the reader. It is thus clear that, according to this theoretical orientation, the quantitative dimension is clearly secondary, a mere consequence of the qualitative, aesthetic and reader-oriented criteria first established in Poe's theoretical works: the facile definition of the short story as "a story that is short" has already been proscribed at the outset by his inclusion of the reader.

---

[26] Ann Charters writes about Poe's legacy in yet another way. According to her, not only Poe's critical texts but also his legacy as such – the short story writer's work as an editor and a critic – are of foremost importance for the future of the short story as a genre. In her essay "Writers as Critics on the Short Story", Charters lists two good reasons why Poe's legacy as a writer and as a critic is important: it gives students permission to think critically and independently about what they have read, and it gives students the feeling of direct transmission of a literary tradition (Ann Charters, "Poe's Legacy: The Short Story Writer as Editor and Critic", in *The Tales We Tell: Perspectives on the Short Story*, eds Barbara Lounsberry, Susan Lohafer *et al.*, Westport, CT: Greenwood Press, 1998, 97-98).

FRAMES SPEAKING: MALAMUD, SILKO, AND THE READER

PER WINTHER

One area that short story criticism has moved into in recent decades is discourse analysis, which I believe has most to offer on the level of the sentence and the paragraph. Its analytical procedures frequently seem too detailed to be of great help in dealing with overall narrative structure, which presupposes taking in larger chunks of text than discourse analysis will normally address. The rather elaborate terminological apparatus it employs in describing the interrelationships between words in sentences and between sequences of sentences with a view to depicting minute steps in the processing (the receiving and producing) of text will normally appeal more to the linguist than to the literary critic. In relation to short fiction, many of the communicative processes described amount to a belaboring of the obvious and/or trivial, processes which, if they are at all found interesting or relevant by the literary scholar, can often be described much more economically using the terminology already established in his/her own field.

Some of the conceptual models of discourse analysis, however, undoubtedly do offer useful assistance in systematizing and giving names to the processes at work in the production and reading of short fiction texts. The study of narrative closure frequently involves taking stock of minute textual modulations, and here discourse analysis procedures may be quite useful. For instance, the notion of framing has proved itself analytically fruitful in the hands of a number of short story critics.[1] In this essay I examine how the concept of framing may

---

[1] See, for instance, Suzanne Hunter Brown's "Discourse Analysis and the Short Story", in *Short Story Theory at a Crossroads*, eds Susan Lohafer and Jo Ellyn Clarey, Baton Rouge: Louisiana State University Press, 1989, 217-48, and "Reframing Stories", *ibid.*, 311-27; Susan Lohafer's "Preclosure and Story

serve to systematically order a discussion of a set of ways in which
short fiction texts achieve narrative and hermeneutic closure.[2]

The concept of frames has been variously defined. As used here it
denotes certain central aspects of the knowledge a user of the
language depends on in order to make sense of linguistic
communications. Notions like "frames" and "scripts" have been
developed to describe how we make use of our prototypical
knowledge of the world in discourse comprehension. Frames,
according to Teun A. van Dijk, denote *"prototypical situations,
backgrounds, environments,* or *contexts* in which events and actions
may take place .... A room, a library, a restaurant, the street, the
beach, a bus, and a university are such frames." Scripts denote
"prototypical *episodes,* that is, sequences of events and actions taking
place in frames". Scripts, then, *"are embedded in frames*; that is, the
subsequent interactions are, among other things, defined in terms of
objects, persons, properties, and relations of a frame".[3]

In reading – or processing, as discourse analysts normally put it –
any kind of text, including fiction, one obviously activates a large
number of frames and scripts. Equally obvious, establishing closure
involves testing a given text against our knowledge of the prototypical
possibilities of the relevant frames or scripts; we would not be able to
recognize a closural signal[4] unless it somehow called into play Susan

Processing", in *ibid.*, 249-75; and Ian Reid, "Destabilizing Frames for Story", in *ibid.*,
299-310.
[2] Narrative closure I understand as that point in the text where either narrative
expectations created by the story are fulfilled, or the impossibility of fulfilling them is
somehow demonstrated (see John Gerlach, *Toward the End: Closure and Structure in
the American Short Story*, Tuscaloosa: University of Alabama Press, 1985, Chapter
1); hermeneutic closure occurs when the reader – after sifting all of the story's
components, not just the story elements associated with narrative closure – "closes"
the story, e.g., with regard to theme, ideational structure, aesthetic design, and mood
(See Per Winther, "Closure and Preclosure as Narrative Grid in Short Story
Analysis", in *The Art of Brevity: Excursions in Short Fiction Theory and Analysis*,
eds Per Winther *et al.*, Columbia: University of South Carolina Press, 2004, 63-64).
[3] Teun A. van Dijk, *Macrostructures: An Interdisciplinary Study of Global Structures
in Discourse, Interaction, and Cognition*, Hillsdale, NJ: Erlbaum, 1980, 233 and 235
(emphases in the text).
[4] In the following I use the term "closural signal" to identify a textual element that
anticipates or promises narrative closure (i.e., a narrative motif that signals closural
potential), whereas I use the term "closural marker" to describe a narrative element
that delivers on that promise. An example of a closural signal is the early mention in
Hemingway's "Hills Like White Elephants" that the train to Madrid is due in forty

Lohafer's notion of "grammar of expectation".[5] To know the world verbally is to tell stories about it. Most of the stories we tell are universal, understood by anyone irrespective of creed, color, or culture. Every sentient human being is aware that when he gets out of bed in the morning, he/she will in all probability return to that bed after a certain number of hours; every birth bespeaks a death, and so on. However, a number of the stories we tell in our efforts at cognition are cultural, instilled in us by the civilization to which we belong, and therefore the frames and scripts activated in a narrative may lead to pivotal differences in signification for people of different cultural backgrounds. Administering holy water during a burial will mean one thing to a Catholic minister but may carry a quite different meaning for a Pueblo Indian, as illustrated by a short story that I will address towards the end of this essay, Leslie Silko's "The Man to Send Rain Clouds".

Fictional texts will of necessity mobilize a number of frames and scripts that are part of everyday communication, universal as well as cultural. In addition, literariness as such has developed its own set of frames and scripts. In the words of Menakhem Perry: "Any reading of a text is a process of constructing a system of hypotheses or frames which can create maximal relevancy among the various data of the text – which can motivate their "co-presence" in the text according to models derived from reality, from literary or cultural conventions, and the like."[6] In his essay "Destabilizing Frames for Story", Ian Reid has developed a set of categories that usefully identifies four different kinds of frames employed in Daudet's *Letters from a Windmill*:

---

minutes; the arrival of that train at the end of the story is a closural marker, of the type that John Gerlach has labelled "natural termination" (for a further discussion of the difference between closural signals and markers, see Winther, "Closure and Preclosure as Narrative Grid in Short Story Analysis", 64-65). In his study, John Gerlach identifies five types of closural signals/markers: solution of the central problem; natural termination; completion of antithesis; manifestation of a moral; and encapsulation. In my essay "Closure and Preclosure" I add two further signals/markers of closure: "emotional and/or cognitive reversal" and "evaluation".

[5] Susan Lohafer, *Coming to Terms with the Short Story*, Baton Rouge: Louisiana State University Press, 1983, 50.

[6] Menakhem Perry, "Literary Dynamics: How the Order of a Text Creates Its Meanings", *Poetics Today*, I/1 (Autumn 1970) 43 (quoted in Brown, "Discourse Analysis and the Short Story", 224).

circumtextual, intertextual, extratextual and intratextual frames.[7]
Primarily Reid is out to show that the often presumed generic stability
of the short story is frequently destabilized through subtle interplay
with other generic types. Even though Reid's essay does not aim at a
conclusive survey of the distributional possibilities of frames in short
stories, I feel that in terms of the existing systematic possibilities, the
four categories he discusses in this particular case also seem to cover
quite well the more general conceptual terrain with regard to framing.
Since closure in short fiction of necessity depends on the activating of
frames, understanding the different functions played by these frames
also helps to further clarify some of the systematic ways in which
closure is achieved – an abiding interest in the charting of systematic
ways of reading short fiction. In this essay, I focus on the first three
types of frames that Reid addresses.[8]

Circumtextual frames
"The most palpable reading frame", Reid suggests, "is constituted by
the material borders of a text. These will include details of its physical
format, cover and prefatory information, title, opening and closing
formulas, authorial ascriptions, and other such circumtextual (or
paratextual) markers."[9] In the context of closural analysis it would
seem that some of the circumtextual frames that Reid identifies tend
to be of very little interest: For example, the back cover of a particular
edition of *Letters from a Windmill* offers a few passing remarks on the
author, the status of the translation, and the book illustrations. Only in
exceptional cases will frames of this kind serve to establish either
narrative or hermeneutic closure. But for some of the other
circumtextual frames identified by Reid, such as prefatory information
and authorial ascriptions, the hermeneutic closural potential is
obviously higher.

---

[7] Ian Reid, "Destabilizing Frames for Story", in *Short Story Theory at a Crossroads*,
299-309. Although he is aware of the distinction that van Dijk and others make
between frames and scripts, Reid uses the term "frame" to denote both concepts; see
his n. 2 (299-300). Since observing the distinction between scripts and frames yields
very little extra in terms of the analysis of closure, I too generally adopt this
terminological practice.
[8] For extended analyses of how Reid's fourth type, intratextual frames, come into play
in relation to narrative closure, see the studies by John Gerlach, Susan Lohafer,
Suzanne Hunter Brown, and myself cited above.
[9] Reid, "Destabilizing Frames for Story", 300-301.

Titles frequently serve as circumtextual frames. However, titles that introduce a particular story work differently than those that serve as titles for collections of stories. Individual story titles will usually establish a frame that serves as a closural signal for the story in question, to be filled by the narrative proper; the title prepares the reader for certain semantic eventualities that are then closed through text elements that serve as more or less explicit markers of closure. Once that frame is filled with the semantic content provided by the story, it may serve as an overall frame for the whole collection, but then usually in a general sense, one less dependent on direct textual reference. An example is Bernard Malamud's *The Magic Barrel*, where one of the stories in the collection carries the same title as the collection itself.

In the titular short story we meet the rabbinical student Leo Finkle, who is in search of a wife. He mistrusts his own ability to find one and requests the assistance of the matchmaker, Pinye Salzman. After various reversals, Leo persuades Salzman to introduce him to the matchmaker's prostitute daughter, Stella, and the story ends with this curious romantic meeting between rabbinical student and prostitute. The barrel mentioned in the title refers to Salzman's packet of client cards, wherein Leo spots Stella's picture. The matchmaker's packet is a "magic barrel" in that it brings redemption to all the central characters in mysterious and totally unexpected ways. In declaring his love for Stella, Leo saves himself and her ("He pictured, in her, his own redemption");[10] Christ-like, he asks her father, "Put me in touch with her, Salzman .... Perhaps I can be of service."[11] By declaring himself ready to lose himself (planning to marry a prostitute makes for poor career-planning for a rabbi), he hopes to find himself, and his God. Stella shares Leo's thirst for eventual redemption; we learn that "her eyes – clearly her father's – were filled with desperate innocence".[12]

The text never shows us Leo's and Stella's redemption – we are not told how their lives turn out after Salzman brings them together – but the narrator clearly wants us to believe that this is a strong possibility. And if Stella is redeemed through Leo's intervention, so is

---

[10] Bernard Malamud, *The Magic Barrel*, New York: Farrar, Straus and Giroux, 1958, 214.
[11] *Ibid.*, 213.
[12] *Ibid.*, 214.

Salzman, the "commercial cupid". In flat contradiction to the cultural logic of his profession, Salzman in the end accepts Leo's non-orthodox position that love must come before and not after matchmaking. Earlier he had insisted, in keeping with the orthodox faith on which his profession is based, that love "comes with the right person, not before".[13] Matching a rabbi and a prostitute hardly agrees with the cultural dictates of the matchmaking institution, and the fact that in the end Salzman agrees to the meeting between Leo and Stella is an expression of his personal change. Christians might identify this redemptive turn of events as manifestations of God's grace; Malamud's title provides a frame, or closural signal, for equating them with magic.

In the short story that gave the collection its name, then, the title has a specified referent in the narrative itself (Salzman's "barrel" of client cards). As a title for the whole collection, however, it serves less as a referent for Salzman's barrel of "discards" than as a circumtextual frame for all the stories. As the titular story is placed last in the collection, the semantic suggestiveness of the title will be stronger on a second reading than a first, but all along there will be an invitation for the readers of this collection to view the texts of the volume in a "magical" light.

A more conventional – and, in terms of frames, semantically weak – way of entitling short story collections is to add the noncommittal phrase "and Other Stories", as in Ethel Wilson's *Mrs Golightly and Other Stories*.[14] In this collection, Wilson experiments with a variety of themes and short fictional forms, so that to read individual texts in the light of the other texts would seem contrary to the artistic plan behind the collection; the closural, or framing, potential of the overall title with regard to particular stories would in this case seem to be close to nil.

Intertextual frames
Text elements often have a dual framing capacity. Like the title of Sherwood Anderson's *Winesburg, Ohio*, Daudet's title, *Letters from a Windmill*, is a circumtextual frame in that it promises a certain setting for the whole volume. However, the title also identifies the book as a

---

[13] *Ibid.*, 198.
[14] Ethel Wilson, *Mrs Golightly and Other Stories* (1961), rpt. Toronto: McClelland and Stewart, 1990.

collection of "Letters": Daudet thereby invites his readers to consider the hermeneutic relevance of the collection's generic status. In other words, the title sets up an intertextual frame as well as a circumtextual one. Intertextuality, in Reid's use of the term, "comprises devices by which a text signals how its very structure of meanings depends on both its similarity to and its difference from certain other texts or text types".[15]

Merging different generic traditions in one text, whether long or short, obviously provides a wealth of aesthetic possibilities for the artist. Malamud, for example, puts elements from the fairy tale tradition to marvelous artistic use in what is otherwise an unmistakably contemporary story. Failure to recognize the presence of this intertextual frame in "The Magic Barrel" would in fact lead one to miss two important early closural signals: the title and the "once-upon-a-time" echo in the opening sentence: "Not long ago there lived in uptown New York."[16] The instantiating of the fairy tale frame here seems very innocent and almost whimsical, to the point where one would be tempted to deny its relevance at all. The fairy tale tradition requires a setting distant in time and place, whereas Malamud's story puts us in uptown New York in the twentieth century. Furthermore, the story dramatizes cultural and psychological conflicts in a manner partaking of traditionally mimetic social realism. Orthodox Jewish beliefs concerning both matter and spirit, as represented by Salzman, clash fundamentally with the modern views of the younger generation. For Stella, "to be poor was a sin", complains Salzman;[17] Leo grows into the realization that the orthodox views of love as represented by the matchmaking institution (for Salzman both a religious conviction and the source of his livelihood) do not adequately address his deepest human needs.

In this light it would be tempting to see the title as an ironic frame. Salzman's decidedly threadbare appearance and comical manner, his name and salesman-like approach to his business (Lily Hirschorn, he assures Leo, is a "wonderful opportunity"[18]), as well as his kosher habits, which always cause him to reek of fish, could easily make him seem the butt of the author's joke. However, tracing the closural

---

[15] Reid, "Destabilizing Frames for Story", 304.
[16] Malamud, *The Magic Barrel*, 193.
[17] *Ibid.*, 212.
[18] *Ibid.*, 196.

signals connected with the fairy tale frame of the short story shifts the
emphasis away from a narrow socio-psychological reading focusing
on cultural conflict and yields a more timeless story, almost biblical in
shape and intention. Leo achieves his redemption, and love, by
engaging in the archetypal form of sacrifice associated with Malamud
characters like Frank Alpine and Sid Levine; in fact, the titles of the
novels in which they appear outline the method and ambition of Leo
Finkle's quest: by becoming an assistant he hopes to achieve a new
life.

The fairy tale echoes in the story are multiple; Leo's fantasies
about sensing Salzman's disguised presence (imagining him as a
"cloven-hoofed Pan, piping nuptial ditties as he danced his invisible
way before them"[19]) during his interview with Lily Hirschorn, as well
as the unresolved puzzle of whether Salzman planted Stella's picture
in the "barrel", help contribute to an air of unreality. So do Leo's
repeated "visions": first "a profusion of loaves of bread [goes] flying
like ducks high over his head" as he is confessing to Lily that he
"came to God not because [he] loved Him, but because [he] did
not";[20] then, as he is rushing forward to meet Stella, "flowers
outthrust", he has a Chagall-inspired vision of "violins and lit candles
[revolving] in the sky".[21] The repeated depictions of Salzman as
someone gradually disappearing before our eyes – the last two times
we meet him he is described as a "skeleton with haunted eyes" and
"haggard, and transparent to the point of vanishing"[22] – not only serve
as symbols reminding the reader of the diminishing role of religious
orthodoxy in his life but also contribute to the story's effort to portray
him as a spirit, working magic in spite of himself, as it were.

When earlier I characterized the story as "almost biblical", I did so
because despite the parable-like logic of the narrative articulations of
the story, which climaxes with Leo and Stella meeting on a spring
night to start their new life together, the text also contains a playful,
decidedly non-biblical humor that undermines somewhat – or
"destabilizes", to use Reid's phrase – the tone of somber morality that
controls large parts of the story. An important vehicle for that humor
is the fairy tale frame, but through ironic modulations rather than

---

[19] *Ibid.*, 202.
[20] *Ibid.*, 204.
[21] *Ibid.*, 214.
[22] *Ibid.*, 206, 213.

through straightforward import of traditional generic features. Some of the closural markers support the traditional morality of the story. We find markers of natural termination and solution of a central problem (wooing leads to matching; Leo gets wife) and, more marginally, the manifestation of a moral ("He pictured, in her, his own redemption"). Alongside these, however, there is a less obvious but thematically significant marker of circularity in response to the two early closural signals, the title and opening formula. Rabbi getting prostitute in the end is a humorous inversion of that fairy tale convention that routinely allows clever Ashlad to win the princess and half a kingdom; part of the purpose behind Leo's seeking the help of the matchmaker in the first place, we are informed early on, was to make it "easier to win himself a congregation",[23] and then he ends up possibly marrying a prostitute.

Malamud's seemingly whimsical use of clichéd color symbolism in the final scene dovetails nicely with this almost vaudevillian inversion. We learn that Leo is relieved to find Stella wearing "white with red shoes, which fitted his expectations, although in a troubled moment he had imagined the dress red, and only the shoes white". The rabbinical student's impulse to "convert [Stella] to goodness" [24] has a distinct Messianic ring to it. However, the author brings him down a notch or two, and thereby humanizes the character for the reader, by giving Leo these comical doubts as regards his own moral stamina in dealing with the social complications of reforming Salzman's prostitute daughter; presumably he is thinking that a red dress would be indicative of greater sinfulness, which would have made his job of saving Stella a tougher one. The humor arising from the ironic play on the fairy tale frame in that final tableau helps to make the story more persuasive to a contemporary audience skeptical of the moral exemplum tradition.[25]

---

[23] *Ibid.*, 193.

[24] *Ibid.*, 213-14.

[25] An elaborate form of intertextual framing occurs in the genre variously called "short story cycles" (Forrest Ingram, *Representative Short Story Cycles of the Twentieth Century: Studies in a Literary Genre*, The Hague: Mouton, 1971), "sequences" (Luscher), and "composites" (Lundén). By short story sequence Robert M. Luscher means "a volume of stories, collected and organized by their author, in which the reader successively realizes underlying patterns of coherence by continual modifications of his perceptions of pattern and theme". As Luscher points out, generically speaking these works "should be viewed, not as failed novels, but as

Extratextual frames
Extratextual frames are in many ways both the easiest and the hardest
to address in terms of closure. Examples are legion because it is the
form of closure most closely tied to the general laws of perception and
cognition; the necessary profusion of extratextual frames in any text
makes it difficult to talk about them in a systematic fashion. Frames
and scripts, then, give us prototypical situations, backgrounds,
environments, or contexts where prototypical events or sequences
may take place. At numerous junctions in a short story the text will
activate some extratextual frame or other: characters enter police
stations, dental offices, classrooms, city streets, or, say, an Indian
reservation, and immediately the reader will anticipate, or enscript, a
set of events normally connected with that location, such as bringing
charges, filling a tooth, learning a lesson, and so on. Frames and
scripts like these form the necessary cognitive and semantic building
blocks of mimetic fictions at large. The cognitive processing of these
will be of such an elementary nature that from the point of view of
literary analysis a careful inspection will frequently prove
tautological. This point seems so obvious that it needs no further
elaboration here.[26] However, as reception theory has demonstrated, it
makes a considerable difference which "horizon of expectations"
("*Erwartungshorizont*")[27] controls a particular reading.

How frames are filled depends on a variety of factors. For one
thing, the meaning of a given frame is likely to change with the
passing of time. For example, the birth of a child out of wedlock was
censured by Western society in the nineteenth century, but it will not
raise many eyebrows today. The question of what constitutes the

unique hybrids" (Robert M. Luscher, "The Short Story Sequence: An Open Book", in
Short Story Theory at a Crossroads, 148, 149-50). Since the focus of the present
essay is on the individual story as an art form, I leave the matter unexplored here, as
the study of short story cycles generally foregrounds the intertextual patterns of short
story collections. For a full introduction to the study of the short story
cycle/sequence/composite as a field of investigation in its own right, in addition to
Luscher's discussion and survey, consult Rolf Lundén's *The United Stories of
America: Studies in the Short Story Composite*, Amsterdam: Rodopi, 1999.
[26] For a concise summary of discourse analysis theory addressing how frames of this
kind are activated, see Susan Lohafer's "Preclosure and Processing", especially 262-
67; Lohafer is obviously right that "the number and complexity of such frames defy
any kind of exhaustive listing or study" (267).
[27] Hans Robert Jauss, *Literaturgeschichte als Provokation*, Frankfurt an Main:
Suhrkamp Verlag, 1970, 173.

prototypical content of frames and scripts is thus frequently a matter of historical change, and also of cultural belonging. One writer who expertly draws on cultural difference for artistic effect is Leslie Marmon Silko. For instance, in the frequently anthologized short story "Lullaby" she invokes the frame "signing of paper" to set in motion a thematically significant plot development. Readers brought up in a literate culture, where a written contract is binding, will immediately sense danger when white doctors in khaki uniforms wave papers and a black ballpoint pen in front of Ayah, the Navajo female protagonist of the story, asking her to sign the documents they have brought with them. For Ayah, a product of Navajo culture through and through, and unfamiliar with Western legal thinking, the frame suggests a different script. Knowing only her own native language and orally based culture, and hoping they will stop looking at her children if she complies, Ayah gives them her signature, thereby unwittingly authorizing these representatives of white health authorities to take her children away.

The overall deployment of closural signals and markers in this story further foregrounds the centrality of cultural difference. Interestingly, all closural signals linked with the majority culture are followed up by preclosural rather than closural markers.[28] In other words, the issues of colonial exploitation and social displacement – which obviously are of great historical importance and of inherent thematic interest in the story – are taken care of early, established as a given, as it were, shifting the focus of the story to the existentially more important question for Silko: how to deal with such historical circumstances as meaningfully as possible. Thus the ending is dominated by a set of closural markers that presuppose the activating of frames rooted in Amerindian culture. This closural strategy on Silko's part allows "Lullaby" to transcend social protest, making it more than anything else a story celebrating a set of values inherent in her own culture.

The ending of "Lullaby" is prepared for in the opening tableau of the story, which provides a strong signal of natural termination: old Ayah is sitting down in the snow with her back against a cottonwood

---

[28] Here I follow Susan Lohafer in distinguishing between preclosure (i.e., closure that happens along the way, somewhere before the endpoint) and closure that fulfills a narrative expectation at the end of the story (see Lohafer "Preclosure and Story Processing").

tree. In her mind she goes over the many defeats she has suffered in her life, particularly the death of her son Jimmie, the abduction of little Ella and Danny by the health authorities, and her husband Chato's sudden loss of job as a ranch hand after an accident, resulting in the loss of the family house. This difficult background, and the fact that Ayah allows herself to be covered up by snow, produces the expectation that this story will retrospectively outline the causes that have brought the old Navajo woman to her self-inflicted death. Had this anticipated closural pattern been allowed to run its natural course, the thematic impact of the text would have been that of unmitigated social protest. But the early closural signal (sitting down in the snow) is temporarily followed up by a preclosural rather than a closural marker: Ayah gets up and walks back to find Chato, who has gone to get his weekly fill of cheap wine.

This in itself is an act of affirmation. Ayah had hated her husband for what she considered his complicity in the abduction of the children, and until he grew ill and weak, she stayed away from him. Now she assumes total responsibility for him with a natural authority derived from Navajo culture: responsibility for his life, in that she decides to renew their marriage in the face of difficulty, as well as for his death. Administering his death in the fashion rendered in that final tableau is an act that moves beyond euthanasia; sitting down with Chato to die in the cold is a redemptive act, an effort to become reunited with the elements in keeping with Navajo religion. A signal of this closural resolution is provided through a cultural frame identified by Ayah as she sits down the first time, presumably to die on her own, before deciding also to help Chato to a meaningful death; the wind and snow, she thinks to herself, sing a Yeibechei song – a song of healing.[29] As she sits there, she feels "peaceful remembering";[30] she thinks of pain but also of the curative continuity of Navajo culture: the example of mother and grandmother, who had taught her to weave. As she sits down the second time, now with Chato, she experiences the coming death by the elements as a process of healing. Chato is lying on his side, as in rebirth: "with his knees pulled up near his belly for warmth ... and in the light from the stars and the moon, he looked young again." The freezing "came gradually,

---

[29] Editor's note, in *Heath Anthology of American Literature*, eds Paul Lauter *et al*., Lexington, MA: Houghton Mifflin, 1990, II, 2169.
[30] Leslie Silko, "Lullaby", in *Storyteller*, New York: Seaver Books, 1981, 43-51.

sinking snowflake by snowflake until the crust was heavy and deep. It had the strength of the stars in Orion, and its journey was endless."

Had the social and historical extratextual frames been invoked at this point in the story, the death scene might have been read merely as a dramatization of self-imposed annihilation in response to social degradation. Through the author's foregrounding of Navajo frames, however, the scene is contextualized as an emblem of regeneration and cosmic healing. There is a strong sense of cultural continuity, rooted in a cosmic vision tied to nature, suggesting that celebration is possible despite social circumstance. The lullaby Ayah sings for Chato (and, surely, for herself) is another thing she has learned from her mother and grandmother. The song affirms the eternal cosmic unity of man and nature in life as well as in death: "*There never was a time / when this / was not so*".[31] The resounding finality of the ending, established by a unique concentration of a wide range of closural markers, lends it a quiet dignity, in keeping with the stoic nature of Navajo religion: natural termination (death), solution of a central problem (how to cope with social and cultural desolation), emotional reversal (from bitterness to affirmation), circularity (duplication of opening scene as well as the singing of the lullaby promised in the title), and, finally, evaluation (lullaby again). Of these markers, all but the first derive their closural force from extratextual frames with a basis in Navajo culture and religion.

Culturally specific extratextual frames appear to have a particularly high potential for dramatic irony, something that, for instance, ethnic writers may turn to their own artistic advantage. In "Lullaby" we have an isolated case of dramatic irony when readers immediately see the mistake Ayah is making in signing official forms, whereas she on her part regards this as a means of escaping a problem. An excellent example of a sustained use of culturally determined extratextual frames for ironic purposes is Silko's "The Man to Send Rain Clouds", in which irony once again involves celebration where one might have expected a story of lament. The text achieves this by activating two partly contradictory sets of extratextual frames rooted in two different cultures: Christianity (Catholicism) and Pueblo Indian religion. When the old Pueblo shepherd Teofilo has died, the village missionary priest, Father Paul, expects a Christian funeral, but his Amerindian parishioners have their own ideas about life, death, and funeral rites.

---

[31] *Ibid.*, 51 (emphases in the text).

They want to bury Teofilo in accordance with Pueblo tradition, which at significant points is at odds with the theological frames established by the Catholic funeral tradition.

Through a flexible handling of point of view, where the author alternates between the perspective of the third person narrator (not identified, but clearly sympathetic towards the Indian characters) and that of the central characters, including (towards the end) Father Paul, Silko creates tonal modulations with absorbing closural implications. The tone of the opening passage, where Leon and Ken find Teofilo, is not one that a non-Amerindian reader is likely to expect, given the subject matter. The tone is matter-of-fact, rather casual. The first two sentences of the story read:

> They found him under a big cottonwood tree. His Levi jacket and pants were faded light-blue so that he had been easy to find.

The focalizers of that second sentence are presumably Leon and/or Ken. The early off-hand reference to the practicalities of finding the dead man might suggest to Christian readers an absence of sorrow or mourning, an impression likely to be strengthened by an even more casual remark a few lines further down: "[Leon] squinted up at the sun and unzipped his jacket – it sure was hot for this time of year."[32]

This matter-of-fact depiction of the scene indicates that the two young Pueblos feel a relaxed self-assuredness that is likely to surprise readers who approach the text with a Christian set of extratextual frames. Without speaking, obviously knowing perfectly well what to do, the two men calmly go through a series of symbolic actions in a manner which, even if one knows very little about Amerindian religion, suggests a natural and practical view of life and death. A small feather is tied to the old man's hair; stripes of white, blue, yellow, and green are painted on his face; pinches of corn meal and pollen are thrown into the air. Smiling, Leon concludes the brief ceremony with the theologically and culturally significant admonition "Send us rain clouds, Grandfather".[33] Even though the text does not provide a detailed explanation concerning the relevance of these actions, the context suggests a view of life's end where the dead come back and help the living, in this case by bringing salutary rain.

---

[32] Leslie Silko, "The Man to Send Rain Clouds", in *Storyteller*, 182.
[33] *Ibid.*, 183.

Whereas the Christian frame dictates a linear view, seeing death as a clear break between life on earth and afterlife, the view implied in Leon and Ken's proceedings is cyclical. This difference also produces a significant variation in emotional response: Christians mourn their departed, while Amerindian vegetation myths accommodate the notion of death as cause for celebration of the life cycle.[34]

Awareness of these conflicting frames sets the stage for a rich play of dramatic irony in the first encounter in the story between Father Paul and his theologically unruly parishioners. Driving back to the pueblo with Teofilo bundled up in a blanket in the back of their pickup, they meet the priest, and the following exchange takes place:

> "Did you find old Teofilo?" he asked loudly.
> Leon stopped the truck. "Good morning, Father. We were just out to the sheep camp. Everything is O.K. now."
> "Thank God for that. Teofilo is a very old man. You really shouldn't allow him to stay at the sheep camp alone."
> "No, he won't do that any more now."
> "Well, I'm glad you understand. I hope I'll be seeing you at Mass this week – we missed you last Sunday. See if you can get old Teofilo to come with you." The priest smiled and waved at them as they drove away.[35]

The most obvious source of dramatic irony here is Leon's expert way of misleading Father Paul, elegantly avoiding direct lies. But irony also results from the clash between extratextual frames. Father Paul's worldview would not allow him to see the truth about Teofilo as "O.K." and to the extent that things are in order, a Christian God is not to be credited.

This conversation also helps to set up frames for further ironies later on. There is, for instance, an implicit play on cultural difference through the contradictory frames activated by the reference to Sunday Mass. Sunday originally meant "the day of the sun", a notion congenial to natural religions, but Christianity has appropriated it, turned it into "the day of the Son", by making it the principal day of worship of Christ, the Shepherd. The opening scene has made it abundantly clear that the Amerindians are little inclined to comply

[34] For a fuller discussion of these religious differences, see Per Seyersted, *Leslie Marmon Silko*, Boise, ID: Boise State University, 1980, 17-18.
[35] Silko, "The Man to Send Rain Clouds", 183.

with Father Paul's request and bring Teofilo to a funeral Mass and burial in Christian soil. Further deepening the irony, it is the view of Christ as Son, Savior, and Shepherd that motivates Father Paul's missionary agenda. Silko deftly establishes an antithetical opposition between the two cultures by carefully choosing which Catholic frames to include as signifiers of the semantic space occupied by the priest in the Amerindian community. As Teofilo's relatives talk in very practical terms about the details of Teofilo's death and sit down to a casual meal of beans and hot bread, they know it is noon "because the church bells rang the Angelus".[36]

In a Christian context the Angelus is a devotion in celebration of the Incarnation, or the Word made flesh in Christ. To the Pueblo community, the Angelus is a practical arrangement by which they can tell time. A direct linking of Christ to the notion of Savior/Shepherd is provided later when we learn that Father Paul's church has an "old door ... symbols of the Lamb". It is hardly accidental that Silko makes Teofilo a shepherd also, but of real sheep rather than metaphorical ones. Like Jesus, Teofilo is also cast as a savior, but in a far more concrete way than his Christian counterpart – his grandchildren are convinced that Teofilo will bring them the rain they so sorely need in the dust-filled American Southwest.

Even though the number of culturally defined extratextual frames in the story having to do with religion is quite high, religion is not the most crucial issue. Were that the case, one would have expected the Pueblo funeral ceremony to be rendered in some detail. This is not what we are given, however. The only mention of the funeral is the following: "The funeral was over, and the old men had taken their candles and medicine bags and were gone." Given the detailed nature of the early scene when Teofilo is found, this extreme foreshortening comes as a surprise. However, that early scene suffices to show the anchor points of the Amerindian view and sets up the necessary cognitive frames for the final scene, where the focus definitely shifts from theology to cultural psychology. The religious apparatus thus provides a system of closural signals that will allow a sense of overall hermeneutic closure that is only indirectly connected with religion.

After the funeral ceremony, as Teofilo's relatives are getting ready to take him to the graveyard, one of them voices an idea that helps reveal the system of closural signals casually deployed throughout the

---

[36] *Ibid.*, 183.

story: the girl, Louise, "with her hands in the pockets of Leon's green army jacket that was too big for her", wonders if they should ask Father Paul to come and sprinkle holy water for Teofilo so "he won't be thirsty".[37] Just as the significance of the Angelus is reduced to a practical rather than a ceremonial point, here a central Catholic rite is viewed as a useful practical supplement to age-old Pueblo customs. For one thing, this implies an ecumenical tolerance, which is placed in hermeneutically significant opposition to Father Paul's automatic list of items necessary for a Christian funeral. Once again extratextual frames are explored to ironic effect. A culturally conditioned grammar of expectation will predispose most non-Amerindian readers (and perhaps some Amerindian ones as well) to assume that a short story about a missionary priest and members of a Native tribe living on a reservation will of necessity be a story of social protest, focusing on the facts of colonization and cultural theft.

However, closural signals having to do not only with religious attitudes but also with less prominent aspects of culture, such as dress and everyday paraphernalia, prepare for a closure indicative of victory rather than defeat. Even the second sentence of the story, identifying Teofilo by his Levi jacket and pants, bears witness to a relaxed attitude to the acculturalization processes on the part of the story's Pueblo characters. They unsentimentally adopt the white man's clothes but combine these with traditional native emblems, like paint and feathers. Even when they dress Teofilo for the funeral, they put him in a new flannel shirt and a pair of stiff new Levis. And for Louisa to attend the funeral in Leon's army jacket is apparently not seen as a breach of decorum. After the funeral ceremony the relaxed and matter-of-fact approach continues. Teofilo is brought to the graveyard not in a hearse but in the back of Leon's pickup truck; as they lower the bundle containing Teofilo's body into the ground, "they [don't] bother to untie the stiff pieces of new rope that were tied around the ends of the blanket".[38] Seen in isolation, these many details of dress, practical solutions, and carefree attitude would appear to be almost too insignificant to be signaled out for individual attention, but when taken together, they establish a powerful frame for the final scene at the side of Teofilo's grave.

---

[37] *Ibid.*, 184.
[38] *Ibid.*, 186.

Despite his misgivings, thinking that perhaps the whole burial was
"some perverse Indian trick",[39] Father Paul agrees to bring the holy
water that Teofilo's relatives had requested, presumably from an old
habit of humoring his unpredictable parishioners. The narrator allows
him the perspective for a brief time, so that his petulant and skeptical
reflections may serve as a contrast to the untroubled cultural self-
assuredness of the Indian characters. One narrative closural marker is
natural termination (burial); another is circularity, in that Leon's final
thoughts reinvoke the title: "He felt good because it was finished, and
he was happy about the sprinkling of the holy water; now the old man
could send them big thunderclouds for sure."[40] In addition, Leon's
reflections, which give us his emotional response to the proceedings,
function as a marker of evaluation. However, hermeneutic closure
depends not so much on these narrative closural markers as on the
cumulative weight of the extratextual frames preparing for the ironic
ending. The expected situation of white exploiter and suppressed
Indian victim is turned on its head. Liberally helping themselves to
whichever aspects of the majority culture they find useful and
congenial to their own sense of tradition, these Indians prove
themselves to be the true masters of their own minds and values.

Intratextual closure
Intratextual framing, according to Reid, "operates within the terms on
the page".[41] Intratextual closure, then, is closure achieved by
activating frames principally established by a given story, as opposed
to closure that depends on the activation of circumtextual frames (for
example, the author's preface, the title of the collection in which the
story occurs) or intertextual frames (for instance, generic frames, like
that of the fairy tale or mythical allusions). These two latter frames,
and extratextual frames as well, also live a life outside the target text,
but intratextual frames do not. Rabbinical students, matchmakers, and
fairy tales exist in the world at large, whereas Leo Finkle's problems
and Salzman's particular brand of magic are interlocked in a closural
dynamism that is uniquely the product of the artistic choices Malamud
made when he wrote "The Magic Barrel".

---

[39] *Ibid.*, 185.
[40] *Ibid.*, 186.
[41] Reid, "Destabilizing Frames for Story", 302.

Such workings of intratextual framing and closure will be familiar to any student of literature and are too legion to allow systematic presentation here. By way of conclusion it should be noted that seldom will any of the four forms of closure under discussion operate in isolation. Obviously, intratextual closure also necessitates the instantiating of extratextual frames, since these form the conceptual basis of any type of discourse. In fact, it might be argued that extratextual framing is largely a tautological category in that hardly a sentence is conceivable without the activating of some extratextual frame or other. For this reason, the borderline between intratextual and extratextual frames is often blurred, and in most cases analytical clarity is not served by rigid categorization on this score. As a rule, the recognition that a given intratextual frame is also an extratextual one offers little help in interpreting the text. Harry Street's gangrene in "The Snows of Kilimanjaro" is a closural signal by virtue of the fact that readers will instantly form certain prototypical extratextual expectations concerning this illness: unless it is operated on, it will kill the patient. When the text eventually closes this signal through Harry's death, extratextual and intratextual closure coincide.

When in my own approach to short story analysis I still wish to preserve the distinction between the two, I do so because in a number of cases such a distinction allows for greater economy of expression, and also for greater analytical precision. The early mention of the Navajo Yeibeichi song in "Lullaby" serves as a signal of intratextual closure of the circularity type in that it sets up a frame for the lullaby sung at the end of the story. Analyzing it also as a signal of extratextual closure permits a foregrounding of the cultural dimension of the story's closural structure. As we have seen, hermeneutic closure in "Lullaby" in large measure actually depends on the activating of culturally specific extratextual frames not intuitively known by readers who have grown up with a different set of cultural frames.

A COGNITIVE APPROACH TO SHORT STORY WRITING

PILAR ALONSO

Reading through some of the short stories in David Leavitt's collection *Family Dancing* (1984) – "Territory", "Counting Months", "Radiation" or "Dedicated", to mention just a few – is not a very different experience from reading his novel *Equal Affections* (1989). Themes related to sickness, gay relations, and infidelity populate all examples of his short and long fiction, and the anguish and malaise they convey is comparable in substance and intensity. It is in fact quite reasonable to say that, with very few exceptions, practically all of the subjects tackled in the stories are re-created and combined into one single narration in the novel in a way that allows us to state with Friedman that "the difference is more of degree than of kind: the novel advances and develops its theme, while the story just shows it".[1] What happens in Leavitt's case, however, is not confined to a one-to-one relation between story and novel, since a succession of themes that seem independently constructed in each individual story are suddenly perceived as a fragmentary kaleidoscopic decomposition when they are re-encountered as semantically interrelated parts of a whole in the longer narrative.

A classic example of these thematically interactive exchanges between genres in literary creations is Katherine Mansfield's "Prelude", an exquisite story that often serves as a paradigmatic example of the intricacies shared by the shorter and longer versions of a single narrative work. As is widely known, this short story was a rewriting of Mansfield's longest narration, *The Aloe*, a piece which

Research for this article has been financed by the Junta de Castilla y León, grant SA012A09.
[1] Norman Friedman, "Recent Short Story Theories: Problems in Definition", in *Short Story Theory at a Crossroads*, eds Susan Lohafer and Jo Ellyn Clarey, Baton Rouge: Louisiana State University Press, 1989, 28.

she started in 1915 and which, according to O'Sullivan, was "her one successful attempt at something she believed was more or less of novel length".[2] Unfortunately for readers, and unlike Leavitt's novel *Equal Affections*, Mansfield's *The Aloe* never achieved the status of completeness, although a month after she had started what she called her "book", she already spoke of conclusion ("My work is finished ... it's already accompli"), as O'Sullivan points out.[3] It is impossible, therefore, for the theoretician to trace with precision the distance a fully developed novel might have imposed on its shorter narrative counterpart, although the opposite approach – that is, analyzing the process of conversion of the longer work into a short story – is a perfectly viable and rewarding course of action that has often been undertaken by biographers and critics alike.[4]

In consonance with Tomalin,[5] Ferguson considers not only "Prelude" but also "At the Bay" sequences of the family chronicle initiated in *The Aloe*. She believes that those portions of text that Mansfield decided to suppress from *The Aloe* when reshaping it as "Prelude" represent "all the material [that] would have 'fit' perfectly well into a novel, had Mansfield ever chosen to or been able to finish it".[6] The conversion of the novel scheme into a more feasible story (creatively more manageable and easier to publish) was done practically on demand, as Alpers, one of Mansfield's biographers, reports:

> It was in April, soon after a printing press had been unpacked on the dining-room table at Hogarth House, that Virginia Woolf had told her

---

[2] Vincent O'Sullivan, Introduction to Katherine Mansfield's *The Aloe*, London: Virago Press, 1985, v.

[3] *Ibid.*, ix.

[4] See Antony Alpers, *The Life of Katherine Mansfield*, Oxford: Oxford University Press, 1982; Claire Tomalin, *Katherine Mansfield: A Secret Life*, Harmondsworth: Penguin, 1988; Janet Kaplan, *Katherine Mansfield and the Origins of Modernist Fiction*, Ithaca, NY: Cornell University Press, 1991; Dominic Head, *The Modernist Short Story*, Cambridge: Cambridge University Press, 1992; Suzanne Ferguson, "Genre and the Work of Reading in Mansfield's 'Prelude' and 'At the Bay'", in *Postmodern Approaches to the Short Story*, eds Farhat Iftekharrudin *et al.*, Westport, CT: Praeger, 2003, 25-38, among others.

[5] Claire Tomalin, Introduction to Katherine Mansfield's *Short Stories*, London: Dent, 1983, xxiii.

[6] Ferguson, "Genre and the Work of Reading in Mansfield's 'Prelude' and 'At the Bay'", 32.

sister she was going to see Katherine Mansfield, "to get a story from her perhaps." The only manuscript suitable for that occasion was of course *The Aloe*, hitherto thought of as the opening chapters of a "novel". It was now treated for the first time as an independent story.[7]

In Alpers' words, "the whole work was sharpened and tightened, diffuseness noticed and removed, slack dialogue condensed or cut".[8] Alpers' description of the changes introduced in the narrative is in fact a rather straightforward way of referring to the conscientious cognitive decisions and operations which undoubtedly must have assisted the transformation process that helped to convert the embryonic novel into a deeply innovative and highly celebrated story. Mansfield always manifested strong convictions about the precision and watchfulness with which she wrote her stories, as can be inferred from the words she sent to her husband, the editor John Middleton Murry, regarding another story of hers, "The Young Girl":

> I send the story. As usual I am in a foolish panic about it. But I know I can trust you. You know how I *choose* my words; they can't be changed. And if you don't like it or think it is wrong *just as it is* I'd rather you didn't print it. I'll try and do another.[9]

Certainly, different writers establish different sorts of relations between their shorter and longer fictional works. For example, Bernard Malamud believes that "writing the short story, if one has that gift, is a good way to begin writing seriously".[10] In fact, his view of the short story as a good exercise preliminary to the writing of longer prose actually conceals a definition of genre:

> I love the pleasures of the short story. One of them is the fast payoff. Whatever happens happens quickly .... Somewhere I've said that a short story packs a self in a few pages predicating a lifetime. The drama is tense, happens fast, and is more often than not outlandish. In

---

[7] Alpers, *The Life of Katherine Mansfield*, 244.

[8] *Ibid.*, 245.

[9] Katherine Mansfield, *Letters and Journals*, Harmondsworth: Penguin, 1977, 184, (emphases in the original).

[10] Bernard Malamud, *The Stories of Bernard Malamud*, New York: Farrar, Straus and Giroux, 1983, x.

a few pages a good story portrays the complexity of a life while producing the surprise and effect of knowledge – not a bad payoff.[11]

But neither the differences in length and method nor the sharing of thematic content, cast of characters and/or linguistic material suffices to offer a whole picture of the many potential connections between a writer's shorter production and his or her novels or between the parts and the wholes contained in them.

Luscher talks of fiction as "a continuum" that ranges "from the miscellaneous collection, on one end, to the traditional novel on the other".[12] In the middle of this gradable phenomenon, he identifies "the short story sequence", which he defines as "a volume of stories, collected and organized by their author, in which the reader successively realizes patterns of coherence by continual modifications of his perceptions of pattern and theme".[13] Luscher sees in this type of collections "a network of associations that binds the stories together and lends them cumulative thematic impact".[14] In an earlier article, Gullason called attention to the fact that these dismembered-novel-like collections of short stories were, "ironically, the most talked about short stories in recent years" and described them as "those which are grouped like novels, and connected into a oneness by hero, theme, or mood". He cites among them "things like Sherwood Anderson's *Winesburg, Ohio*; James Joyce's *Dubliners*; and Hemingway's *In Our Time*",[15] all of them examples of "volumes that despite their more relaxed organization often cohere thematically".[16]

But the sense of unity projected by sequential stories may actually work both ways: that is, it may integrate short stories to form a whole, as in the works mentioned above by Gullason (some of which are also analyzed by Luscher[17]), or it may disintegrate a novel into virtually independent pieces, as in Soledad Puértolas' novel *Historia de un*

[11] *Ibid.*, xii.
[12] Robert M. Luscher, "The Short Story Sequence: An Open Book", in *Short Story Theory at a Crossroads*, 163.
[13] *Ibid.*, 148.
[14] *Ibid.*, 149.
[15] Thomas Gullason, "The Short Story: An Underrated Art", in *Short Story Theories*, ed. Charles May, Athens: Ohio University Press, 1976, 17.
[16] Gerald J. Kennedy, Introduction to *Modern American Short Story Sequences*, ed. Gerald J. Kennedy, Cambridge: Cambridge University Press, 1995, x.
[17] Luscher, "The Short Story Sequence: An Open Book", 148-67.

abrigo. The apparently autonomous stories in this novel are neatly and tightly interwoven by a dense network of interconnected characters; their interrelationships, though sometimes difficult to track, form the only thread that converts their single experiences into a whole.

That the composition and decomposition of literary works is susceptible to variations and can be altered at will is proven by Updike's *Olinger Stories* (1964), also discussed by Luscher.[18] The writer's foreword to the collection (which was once more prepared following editorial suggestions: "My publishers were agreeable but I hesitated"[19]) is revealing in two ways. First, it forces the reader to dwell on the unstable status of short fiction units, which, though conceived as separate pieces at different time spans, can nevertheless be gathered together to construct the single story of a multifaceted character:

> Three of these stories are from my collection *The Same Door*; seven
> are from *Pigeon Feathers and Other Stories*; and one, the last, has not
> previously been included in any book. All were first printed in the
> *New Yorker*. They have been arranged here in the order of the hero's
> age; in the beginning he is ten, in the middle stories he is an
> adolescent, in the end he has reached manhood. He wears different
> names and his circumstances vary, but he is at bottom the same boy, a
> local boy – this selection could be called *A Local Boy*. The locality is
> that of Olinger, Pennsylvania.

Second, Updike's words speak of a highly personal fictional universe, one that exists in the writer's mind – "Olinger is a state of mind, of my mind, and belongs entirely to me"[20] – and is presented to the reader in whichever form the author or other intermediate agents (for instance, the editor) choose.

Eudora Welty, too, stresses the private, individualistic approach and answers the key question "How do we write a story?" by saying, "Our own way. Beyond that, I think it is hard to assign a process to it."[21] In her refusal to think of story writing as process, Welty may

---

[18] *Ibid.*; and Robert Luscher, "John Updike's Olinger Stories", in *Modern American Short Story Sequences*, 151-69.
[19] John Updike, *The Olinger Stories*, New York: Vintage Books, 1964, vi.
[20] *Ibid.*, v.
[21] Eudora Welty, "The Reading and Writing of Short Stories", in *Short Story Theories*, 161.

have been picturing the difficulties involved in either tracing or identifying a general process broad enough to account for all writing experiences, which are distinctively linked to the creative use authors make of traditional or groundbreaking literary conventions and of linguistic resources whose capacity for potential combinations is infinite. As it happens, she considers "the act of writing ... subjective" and declares that "it is not an imitative process".[22] But the long-standing fruitful applications of discourse analysis and cognitive linguistics to literary criticism in general, and to short story theorizing in particular,[23] make it rather odd for the analyst to want to disconnect the action of writing from the idea of process, which is in fact consubstantial to all types of human interaction from a broad communicative perspective. Welty herself depicts her own perception of the writing practice as a temporal, purposeful process that involves cognitive moves, communicative goals, linguistic elaboration and interpretive independence:

> During the writing of a story, all the energy I have is put to pressure and reaches a changed-over state – so as to act for the sole and concentrated purpose of making our work excellent and to the pattern of some preconceived idea we have of beauty. The diffusion of this energy will, in the long run, prevent our story from communicating, in the degree that it prevents it from being our own.[24]

The unique quality that both Updike and Welty claim for their imagined worlds and their creative processes, respectively, resides more exactly, as cognitive theoreticians have pointed out,[25] in the

---

[22] *Ibid.*, 160.
[23] See, for example, Teun van Dijk, *Discourse and Literature*, Amsterdam: John Benjamins, 1980; Mark Turner, *Death Is the Mother of Beauty*, Chicago: University of Chicago Press, 1987; Mark Turner, "Backstage Cognition in Reason and Choice", in *Elements of Reasoning: Cognition, Choice, and the Bounds of Rationality*, eds Arthur Lupia, Mathew McCubbins and Samuel Popkin, Cambridge: Cambridge University Press, 2000, 264-86; George Lakoff and Mark Turner, *More Than Cool Reason*, Chicago: University of Chicago Press, 1989; Susan Lohafer, *Coming to Terms with the Short Story*, Baton Rouge: Louisiana State University Press, 1983; Susan Lohafer, *Reading for Storyness*, Baltimore: John Hopkins University Press, 2003; Suzanne Hunter Brown, "Discourse Analysis and the Short Story", in *Short Story Theory at a Crossroads*, 217-48.
[24] Welty, "The Reading and Writing of Short Stories", 160.
[25] Lakoff and Turner, *More Than Cool Reason*, xi-xii. See also Gilles Fauconnier and Mark Turner, "Conceptual Projection and Middle Spaces", La Jolla, CA: Cognitive

skillful way they obtain exceptional artistic results by performing the same cognitive operations and employing the same linguistic tools that the rest of us use in everyday communication. The skeletal ideational and elaborating equipment brought into play by authors is that which belongs to the human cognitive system and has been systematically raised to the level of conscious analysis by cognitive scientists, who use a wide variety of texts, including specific examples from classic and modern literary works of art, to show the universality of their claim.

Within the field of short story studies, this assertion can also be founded on the close correspondence that can be drawn between the operations and projections theoretically described as pertaining to the human cognitive system at both the production and the reception level, and the actual moves that critics, even those who do not explicitly take a cognitive or discourse standpoint, use and/or identify in their literary appreciations. A good example of how the noncognitive approaches to literary texts can serve as excellent illustrations of cognitive theories and methodologies is provided, for instance, in Hanson's words on short stories:

> The short story can approach the art of painting more nearly than the novel. An analogy with visual art highlights some of the distinctions between the short story and novel forms. The painterly analogy for the novel must, ultimately, break down, for in our response to a painting we are predominantly involved with space: our response to the novel involves us primarily with time. However, the analogy between a short story and a painting is much closer, because, as Poe remarked, the short story is read over a relatively short period of time and can therefore more readily be grasped as an aesthetic whole. Its "spatial" and structural elements can be exploited for aesthetic effect in ways not possible over the long-time course of the novel.[26]

In order to set up categorical distinctions between short stories and novels, Hanson resorts to an analogy between two frequently

---

science technical report 9401, 1994, available online at http://www.inform.umd.edu/ EdRes/Colleges/ARHU/Depts/English/englfac/Mturner/; Gilles Fauconnier and Mark Turner, "Conceptual Integration Networks", 2001, available online at http://www. inform.umd.edu/EdRes/Colleges/ARHU/Depts/English/englfac/MTurner/cin.web/cin. html.
[26] Clare Hanson, *Short Stories and Short Fictions, 1880-1980*, London: Macmillan, 1985, 68.

compared artistic domains: painting and writing. Analogy is, as cognitive theoreticians claim,[27] one of the multiple cognitive principles operating at all levels of human behavior, whether linguistic or nonlinguistic. As is demonstrated in the literature, analogical mappings help in the processes of both category formation and category extension, for they project partial meaning structure from the source domain to the target domain and induce the creation of new meaning in the cognitive schema of the target as a result of this semantic exchange.

In her analogy, Hanson activates the basic space/time metaphorical mapping amply described in the literature.[28] She assigns properties from the source domain, painting – a spatial domain – to the target domain, writing, whose nature is basically temporal and consequently more difficult to grasp and comprehend, as it lacks the visual unity characteristic of pictorial representations. That is, in Hanson's reasoning, the spatially self-contained properties of a painting, which can be visualized in one piece, are found to be compatible with the self-contained temporal disposition of the short story, but not with the longer temporal extension of the novel. Therefore, Hanson uses the analogy "like/unlike a painting" as a conceptualizing tool to produce an online category reinterpretation of the conventional concept "short story". By mapping onto the short story the spatial properties that belong to the "painting" domain, Hanson redefines it and states that it is more "author directed than the novel", as "there is less potential, during the time taken over its reading, for the imagination of the reader to play unforeseen tricks with the text". She thus conceives of the story in terms of space, wholeness and immediacy, as opposed to the novel, which is seen as extending through longer spans of time and thus having more of a tendency to be externally enriched and modified during the reading process.[29]

---

[27] See, for example, Gilles Fauconnier, "Analogical Counterfactuals", in *Spaces, Worlds and Grammar*, eds Gilles Fauconnier and Eve Swetser, Chicago: University of Chicago Press, 1996, 57-90; Gilles Fauconnier and Mark Turner, *The Way We Think: Conceptual Blending and the Mind's Hidden Complexities*, New York: Basic Books, 2002, 106, 384.

[28] See George Lakoff and Mark Johnson, *Metaphors We Live By*, Chicago: University of Chicago Press, 1981, 126-35; George Lakoff, "The Contemporary Theory of Metaphor", in *Metaphor and Thought*, ed. Andrew Ortony, Cambridge: Cambridge University Press, 1993, 202-51.

[29] Hanson, *Short Stories and Short Fictions, 1880-1980*, 68.

Raising unconscious cognitive operations to the level of consciousness in the analysis of literary discourse is productive because it helps to establish a dialogue between the writing and reading processes at the authorial and critical levels. Moreover, it also helps to reveal the strong cognitive connections between genres, which, from a nontheoretical perspective, may even appear, in some cases, to be different realizations of a given idea by a given author. As we have been able to observe, authors often talk about genres in terms of selection as part of their writing practice, sometimes obeying their personal literary preferences, sometimes following external cues such as editorial advice or demand. Seen from this perspective, the frontier between the two modes of writing that are being considered here, short stories and novels, may not be as sharp and clear-cut as would first appear.

Another piece of evidence that supports talking about short and long fiction as interacting realities is the fact that critics frequently use the term "episode" in their discussions of short stories. For example, Ferguson argues that Mansfield's original contributions to short story writing could be summarized under "the general principle of presenting episodes that can be read as the traces of a larger theme or plot".[30] May lists as one of the defining traits of modernist short stories the fact that they abandon "highly plotted stories in favor of seemingly static episodes and 'slices' of reality".[31] For Friedman, "the episode is even a more commonly found size in the short story – indeed, its frequency may warrant our calling it the typical sort of action dealt with by this art".[32] In discourse theory, episodes are defined as "a topically coherent part of discourse" introducing "different agents, places, times, objects, or possible worlds".[33] Within the global macrostructure of the text, therefore, the episode is a fairly independent semantic unit consisting of a sequence of propositions dominated by a macroproposition.

---

[30] Ferguson, "Genre and the Work of Reading in Mansfield's 'Prelude' and 'At the Bay'", 35.

[31] Charles May, *The Short Story: The Reality of Artifice*, New York: Routledge, 1995, 16.

[32] Norman Friedman, "What Makes a Short Story Short?", in *Short Story Theories*, 137.

[33] Teun van Dijk and Walter Kintch, *Strategies of Discourse Comprehension*, New York: Academic Press, 1983, 204.

In the fictional world constructed by authors, there are times when it is possible to describe a two-way thematic and/or formal relation between the role episodes play in novels and the one they play in short stories. In novels, episodes are abundant, successive and by necessity rather peripheral, given the customary length and complexity of the genre; but in short stories episodes may become central to the plot, because of the concentration and conciseness of this narrative mode. In this sense, it is possible to say that in a novel, episodes constitute an infinitesimal part of the semantic macrostructure, while in a short story, an episode may even be the macrostructure.

As I mentioned at the beginning of this essay, this is the situation with some of the stories in David Leavitt's *Family Dancing*, whose full content often invites the reader to regard them as episodic parts of his novel *Equal Affections*. If we focus, for example, on the contents of "Counting Months", there is the feeling that the protagonist's experience with cancer, the description of the different stages of her illness, her agonized thoughts, and her strong fight for survival may be read as a series of episodes preliminary to that which opens *Equal Affections*: "The first time Louise thought she was dying she called Danny and April to the side of her hospital bed."[34] The similarity between the two texts is so strong that a reader could actually work out one single mental image for the protagonists of both stories, Mrs Harrington in "Counting Months" and Louise in *Equal Affections*, fusing them together into one single character, regardless of the differing details in their stories and the peculiarities of their problems. Furthermore, the impression of thematic concurrence and continuity not only encourages the building of an image for the two female protagonists in the reader's mind; it also extends to the mental representation projected by their respective children, their families and their social background, thus making the two stories converge into a unique fictional model and encouraging the construction of a mental or idealized cognitive model,[35] which blends the separate contents of the two narrations.

When viewed from a cognitive perspective, the portion of Leavitt's fictional world dealing with illness, suffering and human relations that is captured in the stories and the novel becomes a unit, a semantic

---

[34] David Leavitt, *Equal Affections*, New York: Harper and Row, 1989, 3.
[35] See George Lakoff, *Women, Fire, and Dangerous Things: What Categories Reveal about the Mind*, Chicago: University of Chicago Press, 1987.

macroproposition; in turn, choice of genre becomes an option, a decision about which kind of narrative schema or superstructure will better suit the writer's goal and the scope of his or her narration. Superstructures were defined by van Dijk[36] as the conventionalized culturally fixed schemata that work for certain types of discourse, such as stories. Van Dijk and Kintsch see episodes as bridging the gap between global content macrostructures (that is, concerning plot, agents, action, etc.) and formal schematic superstructures (that is, the nonsemantic surface indicators of the discourse type). They say that "episodes function as psychological units in story comprehension" and claim that they "can usually be formed both on the basis of narrative categories ... and on the basis of the content of the story".[37]

I will use a couple of examples from a novel and a short story by John Updike to illustrate that episodes are pivotal cognitive units in narrative discourse whose prominence depends on the length and involvement of the text of which they form a part: (non)essential in novels, central in short stories. In Updike's novel *Bech at Bay* (1998), the last volume of his trilogy about the Jewish-American writer Henry Bech, there is a very short episode (eleven lines in a 237-page-long novel) when the protagonist, already a septuagenarian respectably retiring author who has been elected president of "The Forty", a honorary artistic organization in Manhattan that took its name from the number of its members in "wistful imitation of the French Academy",[38] questions his haughtily accepted role and panics after a "heady session of presiding":

> Bech felt the floor under him tip, the long dark desktop curve downward at both edges, and the emptying wing chairs defy perspective. The president was somehow on a slippery slope. Wasn't the Forty from its turn-of-the-century founding based on a false belief that art naturally kept company with gentility, both gracefully attendant on money – that money and power could be easily transmuted into truth and beauty, and that a club of the favored could exist, ten brownstone steps up from the pitted, filthy, sorely trafficked street? What was he doing here, presiding?[39]

---

[36] Teun van Dijk, *Macrostructures*, Hillsdale, NJ: Lawrence Erlbaum, 1980, 107 ff.
[37] Van Dijk and Kintch, *Strategies of Discourse Comprehension*, 57.
[38] John Updike, *Bech at Bay*, New York: Fawcett Crest, 1998, 49.
[39] *Ibid.*, 61.

As with Leavitt's stories and characters, from a reader's perspective
the impression this episode produces is very similar to the spirit
animating Updike's "The Wallet", a thirteen-page story in his
collection *Trust Me*. In "The Wallet", the protagonist, Fulham, a
middle-class grandfather retired from a moderately successful career
in business, is also in his seventies and, like his novelistic counterpart,
questions his position in life. Throughout the story he is repeatedly
seized by an intense and irrational sense of fear that invariably takes
the form of inexplicable foolishness. His panic rises from the depths
of his heart and develops through an elaborate network of preciously
built metaphorical mappings and extensions.[40] In one of the several
times the protagonist's sense of panic is described, it takes the image
of a floor sinking under the character's fragile feet, in a way that
closely resembles the passage from *Bech at Bay* just quoted:

> Sitting between small heads [his grandchildren] in the flickering light
> [of the movie theater] Fulham would be visited by terror: the walls of
> the theater would fall away, the sticky floor become a chasm beneath
> his feet. His true situation in time and space would be revealed to him:
> a speck of consciousness now into its seventh decade, a mortal body
> poised to rejoin the minerals, a member of a lost civilization that once
> existed in a sliding continent. The curvature of the immense Earth
> beneath his chair and the solidity of the piece of earth that would
> cover Fulham's grave would become suffocatingly real to him all in
> an instant; he would begin to sweat.[41]

"The Wallet" consists of four episodes whose cognitive
construction has been studied in detail elsewhere.[42] All of them
picture an old man terrified by the approaching end of a lifetime. This
thematic concentration is not so clearly found in *Bech at Bay*, whose
length provides for further emotional complexities, such as desire and
vanity intermingled with anxiety. But once again the reader
experiences the recounting of both occurrences with a sense of *déjà*

---

[40] For a thorough study of these issues, see Pilar Alonso, "El Alcance de las
Proyecciones Metafóricas en el Discurso Narrativo Complejo. Estudio de un Caso:
'The Wallet' de John Updike", in *Estudios de Lingüística Cognitiva*, ed. José Luis
Cifuentes Honrubia, Alicante: Publicaciones de la Universidad de Alicante, 1998, I,
29-40; Pilar Alonso, "The Conceptual Integration Network Model as a Paradigm for
Analysis of Complex Narrative Discourse", *Mosaic*, II/ 37 (June 2004), 161-81.
[41] John Updike, "The Wallet", in *Trust Me*, Harmondsworth: Penguin, 1988, 185.
[42] See n.40 above.

vu, as if the two texts were co-referential and induced a single mental image. At the writer's end, the close interconnection between episodes from apparently unrelated pieces of fiction takes us back to the way Updike talks of his imagined world in terms of "a state of mind".[43] If fiction is thus seen as the expression and formulation of a writer's mental state, then it is possible to think of the differences and similarities between his or her short stories and novels in terms of variations in the writing process, with regard to goals, decisions, focus, scope and degrees of elaboration.

Lohafer defines storying as "a form of cognitive management",[44] as do Fauconnier and Turner,[45] who include narrative structure among the multiple cognitive activities performed by the human mind. In general, Fauconnier and Turner see the construction of complex mental representations (such as those laid out by narration) as a succession of integrated cognitive operations that help in the establishment of new semantic structure by combining and blending information obtained from different knowledge or experiential domains or inputs. Among many others, they identify three creative cognitive activities: "composition", "completion" and "elaboration".[46] We consider all these operations central to the process of literary creation. At the producer's end, these operations are concerned with the conceptualization process involved in the construction of texts and discourse and with the formal expression they finally acquire. Composition is in charge of furnishing, reshaping and/or creating semantic content for the emerging cognitive structure (in our case, the literary work) by fusing, in a more or less innovative way, data obtained from other realities. Completion makes use of pre-existing background knowledge to fill with meaning the newly built mental construction. And elaboration adds the creative load of imagination to the blended construct, thus expanding its semantic contents to any extent desired. Combining all three operations allows for a high degree of intricacy in the production of texts, so much so that even if one core idea is used as the point of departure, the text may become extremely complex, as tends to be the case with fictional narrations.

---

[43] Updike, *Olinger Stories*, v.
[44] Lohafer, *Reading for Storyness*, 55.
[45] Fauconnier and Turner, "Conceptual Integration Networks", n.p.
[46] *Ibid.*, 6, 11; Fauconnier and Turner, *The Way We Think: Conceptual Blending and the Mind's Hidden Complexities*, 48-49.

Fauconnier and Turner say that "composition, completion and elaboration all recruit selectively from our most favored patterns of knowing and thinking" and that they "operate for the most part automatically and below the horizon of conscious observation".[47]

The validity of Fauconnier and Turner's systematic description of the cognitive operations underlying the construction and interpretation of texts is easily proved when the three cognitive operations (composition, completion and elaboration) are contrasted with our own unconscious processes of discourse production and reception. Applying this course of reasoning, it is possible to establish once again a close link between the procedures followed by cognitive approaches to literary discourse and noncognitive lines of criticism, even the more traditional ones, as the unconscious investigation of cognitive moves can often be traced within the works of writers and critics alike when they tackle aspects of literary creation.

For example, in his classic essay "The Philosophy of Composition",[48] Poe defends consciousness of the writing process as a counterpart of the typically claimed conception of writing as impulse and inspiration in terms that are quite similar to those used by cognitive and discourse analysts:

> I have often thought how interesting a magazine paper might be written by any author who would – that is to say, who could – detail, step by step, the processes by which any one of his compositions attained its ultimate point of completion. Why such a paper has never been given to the world, I am much at a loss to say – but, perhaps, the authorial vanity has had more to do with the omission than any one other cause. Most writers – poets in especial – prefer having it understood that they compose by a species of fine frenzy – an ecstatic intuition – and would positively shudder at letting the public take a peep behind the scenes, at the elaborate and vacillating crudities of thought – at the true purposes seized only at the last moment – at the innumerable glimpses of idea that arrived not at the maturity in full view – at the fully matured fancies discarded in despair as unmanageable – at the cautious selections and rejections – at the painful erasures and interpolations ...

---

[47] Fauconnier and Turner, "Conceptual Integration Networks", 20.
[48] See Edgar Allan Poe, "The Philosophy of Composition", in *The New Short Story Theories*, ed. Charles May, Athens: Ohio University Press, 1994, 67-69.

The difficulties in explicitly outlining one's own writing process – a sometimes automatic and often circuitous path – is also tackled by Poe when he admits that an author may not be "at all in condition to retrace the steps by which his conclusions have been attained", as "in general, suggestions, having arisen pell-mell, are pursued and forgotten in a similar manner". He states, however, that he has not "the least difficulty in recalling to mind the progressive steps of any of [his] compositions",[49] and he chooses "The Raven" to illustrate his own writing process.

Curiously enough, Poe also conceives of literary units of a given length as "merely a succession of brief ones",[50] a point that strengthens the idea of episode as a measuring unit in the process of literary creation, as well as the fact that episodes can be made central or peripheral (in relation to the global macrostructure), expanded or condensed by using strategies of composition and elaboration to suit the writer's will or needs. This is also the stand taken by Friedman when he talks of the interaction between short stories and novels as natural and subject to variations in the writing process, ruled by cognitive decisions and pragmatic purposes:

> I can think of no empirical or logical reason why an action of a smaller size cannot be expanded into a work of novel length, so long as there seems to be some formal or artistic reason for doing so, or why an action of larger magnitude cannot be condensed down to the length of a short story, so long as it seems to serve some formal and artistic purpose.[51]

To return to practical case that makes explicit the idea of narrative development as based on the gradual addition of episodes, I will briefly reconsider Soledad Puértolas' *Historia de un abrigo*. Puertolas' novel contains fifteen chapters; each of them has a distinctive title and independently recounts a consistent story. Within the novel, all chapters work as episodes, and each of them could also be divided into other sub-episodes of variable length and rhetorical weight. The cohesion that exists among them is brought about by the relations of mutual knowledge between the various characters, a

---

[49] *Ibid.*, 68.
[50] *Ibid.*, 69.
[51] Friedman, "Recent Short Story Theories: Problems in Definition", 23.

relation that is painstakingly built throughout the narration and progressively made noticeable to the reader. The writer has chosen the novel frame for her work by making episodes fit together instead of organizing and publishing them as separate independent units, which would have been an equally acceptable option. As Updike claimed in relation to the editorial decision of collecting his Olinger-based stories into one single volume, it is the writer's personal mental universe that originally gives a literary piece any potential dimension of sense, unity, and/or difference. This basic assumption involves essential and formal aspects that may be said to entail decisions which turn out to be crucial in the final consideration of genre variations.

From a general perspective, I thus argue that the application of certain cognitive operations and the structuring of semantic content into episodes of gradable prevalence (as concerns both centrality and number) are key factors in the construction and development of narrative genres. Studying the noncognitive use of these notions in literary discourse and literary criticism helps us to comprehend in a systematic way the *modus operandi* governing the process of literary creation. It also helps us to establish a direct relation between the development and accumulation of semantically interconnected episodes and the acquisition and predominance of certain features associated with genre distinctions and the classification of literary works. The number, length and degree of elaboration of episodes serve as a practical tool for distinguishing between, for example, qualities characteristic of short stories and those characteristic of novels, especially when they are derived from their intrinsically differentiating values of shortness versus lengthiness. Viewed from a cognitive perspective, with an emphasis on the construction of a unified mental model through the creation and/or evocation of episodic macropropositions and mental images, novels and short stories are not in fact so distant from one another, especially when the dense network of underlying cognitive paths that connect their respective archetypical configurations is taken into account.

CODE-SWITCHING AS A STRATEGY OF BREVITY IN SANDRA CISNEROS' *WOMAN HOLLERING CREEK AND OTHER STORIES*

CONSUELO MONTES-GRANADO

The increasing interest of linguists in English-Spanish code-switching (language alternation) in the North American Southwest, which can be considered a contact zone,[1] coincides with an increase in the publication and study of US Hispanic literatures. Martín Rodríguez[2] provides a thorough survey of the evolution of Chicano literature in relation to the use of Spanish. He argues that the choice of one language (or a mixture of the two) reveals aesthetic and ideological positions that in some way can help establish a history of Chicano literature. From his detailed analysis of that evolution, I will select two important moments. The first phase represents the initial impact of the Chicano movement from 1965 until the Seventies, when Chicano writers became very conscious of the use of Spanish in their writings. Spanish became a symbol of resistance, of confrontation with what they experienced as the oppressive American system. Editorial groups like Quinto Sol helped these authors in their bilingual cultural crusade. The Spanish language, which until then had been restricted in the United States to the domestic domain (as Martin Rodríguez explains),[3] acquired the prestige that literature confers. Studies of diglossic communities throughout history have revealed

---

This study is part of a research project funded by the Regional Ministry of Culture of the Autonomous Government of Castile and Leon (ref. number SA012A10-1).

[1] See Mary Louise Pratt, "Arts of the Contact Zone", in *Border Texts: Cultural Readings from Contemporary Writers*, ed. Randall Bass, Boston and New York: Houghton Mifflin, 1999, 367-78.

[2] Manuel M. Martín Rodríguez, "Lenguaje y poder: El español en la literatura chicana", in *El poder hispano*, eds Alberto Moncada Lorenzo *et al.*, Madrid: Universidad de Alcalá, 1994, 487-97. See also Ernst Rudin, *Tender Accents of Sound: Spanish in the Chicano Novel in English*, Tempe, AZ: Bilingual Press, 1996, 56.

[3] Rodríguez, "Lenguaje y poder", 489.

that this is a well known and effective means of changing the rigid functional distinction that gives prestige to the high and withholds it from the low.[4]

The second stage Martín Rodríguez presents in this evolution of Chicano literature, which I believe explains why English predominated over Spanish during that period, began in the Eighties, when Chicano editorial firms put more emphasis on reaching a mainstream readership than on linguistic assertion (that is, they emphasized economic rather than cultural or political benefit). The publication of works written in Spanish was displaced either to Mexico or to new publishing houses along the border. Moreover, the fact that Chicano literature began to enjoy widespread attention led to the republication of some representative novels by major publishing houses and even to the translation into English of those written in Spanish, which also underwent a process of transculturation.[5] These American publishing firms also began to offer good contracts to well-known authors such as Sandra Cisneros. In fact, after the editorial success of *The House on Mango Street*, Random House offered her a contract for *Woman Hollering Creek and Other Stories*,[6] making her the first Chicana writer to receive a contract from a major publishing house.

Sandra Cisneros and other acclaimed Chicano authors are aware of the need to reach a wide Anglo-American readership, so when they depict their geographical and cultural settings, they choose to become transcultural mediators[7] and mainly use the English language for their narrative voice. Is this a betrayal of the original Chicano movement, and of its aims to subvert the associations of the Spanish language with the low-prestige domains of the household and the neighborhood? Or is it a realization that in a society where English is the primary language, using English is a better way to represent Chicano identity and cultural roots as well as Chicanos' battle against discrimination? In order to explain Sandra Cisneros' predominant use of English, I will present an analysis profiting from insights from

---

[4] Harold Schiffman, "Diglossia as a Sociolinguistic Situation", in *Handbook of Sociolinguistics*, ed. Florian Coulmas, Oxford: Blackwell, 1997, 205-16.
[5] Cf. Rudin, *Tender Accents of Sound*, 59-75.
[6] Sandra Cisneros, *The House on Mango Street*, New York: Vintage Books, 1991; *Woman Hollering Creek and Other Stories*, New York: Vintage Books, 1992.
[7] Cf. Rudin, *Tender Accents of Sound*, 59-75.

several studies, ranging from linguistic anthropology to the social psychology of language. These linguistic disciplines show a constructionist view of language: they view language as a way of constituting realities, of constructing and performing the social dimension of identity. Literary-critical insights will be incorporated, too, in order to explore whether a more realistic and down-to-earth use of Spanish in the literary context of a short story is useful or, on the contrary, is just a hindrance, a communication barrier to a monolingual reader.

Linguistic anthropologists have shown a deep interest in the dynamics of alternating languages, or code-switching. The first studies were carried out in diglossic communities,[8] where two or more languages are used but there is a very neat and strict separation of linguistic functions and, as a consequence, each variety is spoken in different linguistic domains and the main distinction between them involves the idea of prestige. The high linguistic variety (with overt social prestige) is the norm in prestigious domains, such as religion, literature, administration and professional activity, and the low variety (lacking this prestige) is used in the home and neighborhood, in informal activities and in folk literature. The low linguistic variety is not used in a serious work of literature. A typical example is the Arabic situation, where the distribution of linguistic labor between classical Arabic and the various regional vernacular varieties is strict and clear. A diglossic analysis can be made in Hispanic communities in the United States where Spanish – or, rather, Spanglish, a mixture of Spanish and English – is the low language. It is the language of the inner sphere, that is, the expected language among intimates in the household and neighborhood, whereas English is the language used in the outer sphere (and usually the only one that is allowed, from a sense of linguistic order, especially with gatekeepers such as court officers, social workers and schoolteachers).

However, this is not as simple or neat as it seems, as can be deduced from some interesting insights in Hill's research.[9] In the intimacies of the inner sphere, "people who successfully negotiate

---

[8] The analytical construct of diglossia used to describe these communities is thoroughly analyzed by Schiffman, in "Diglossia as a Sociolinguistic Situation", 205-16.

[9] Jane Hill, "Language, Race, and White Public Space", in *Linguistic Anthropology: A Reader*, ed. Alessandro Duranti, Oxford: Blackwell, 2001, 450-65.

outer-sphere order are vulnerable to the accusation that they are 'acting white', betraying their friends and relatives".[10] However, in the outer sphere, even people who do not mix languages and always speak English feel anxious about their accents or worry about other uncultivated traces of their racialized identity. Thus, in the outer sphere, Hispanic people are always found wanting by this sphere's standards of linguistic orderliness. By contrast, whites allow themselves a considerable amount of disorder when they speak Spanish, intending to look congenial by sounding more colloquial, relaxed, funny, and so on. For them, heavy English accents in Spanish are perfectly acceptable; in fact, what would be somehow inappropriate for them is to try to sound "Spanish". And in the public written use of Spanish (in street names, advertising, public health messages) nonstandard and ungrammatical Spanish is allowed. Hill contends that this "linguistic disorder" is permitted for whites, while Hispanics are subject to monitoring efforts, ranging from individual judgments to Official English legislation. Their code-switching is condemned as disorderly, whereas whites feel free to incorporate Spanish words into their English so that they sound more cosmopolitan. Moreover, the whites' use of Spanish loans often has a jocular or pejorative semantic key (*hasty lumbago, el cheap-o, Fleas Navidad, mucho trouble-o*); to make sense of this middling style, which Hill calls "Mock Spanish",[11] one has to access very negative images of Chicanos and Latinos. Thus Mock Spanish functions as a covert racist discourse. Those negative racializing representations would never be acknowledged by speakers because they are activated through indirect indexicality (unlike the direct racism of "vulgar racist discourse"). The consequence is the construction of a white public space. Gloria Anzaldúa defines this situation as "linguistic terrorism".[12] She describes the situation vividly:

> We are your linguistic nightmare, your linguistic aberration, your linguistic *mestisaje*, the subject of your *burla*. Because we speak with tongues of fire we are culturally crucified. Racially, culturally and linguistically *somos huérfanos* – we speak an orphan tongue.[13]

---

[10] *Ibid.*, 452.

[11] *Ibid.*, 452-60.

[12] Gloria Anzaldúa, *Borderlands/La Frontera: The New Mestiza*, San Francisco: Aunt Lute Books, 1987, 58.

[13] *Ibid.*, 58.

Even more painful is the following quote, which highlights Chicanos' feeling of being somehow illegitimate:

> So, if you want to really hurt me, talk badly about my language. Ethnic identity is twin skin to linguistic identity – I am my language. Until I can take pride in my language, I cannot take pride in myself. Until I can accept as legitimate Chicano Texas Spanish, Tex-Mex and all the other languages I speak, I cannot accept the legitimacy of myself. Until I am free to write bilingually and to switch codes without having always to translate, while I still have to speak English or Spanish when I would rather speak Spanglish, and as long as I have to accommodate the English speakers rather than having them accommodate me, my tongue will be illegitimate.[14]

Against this discriminatory sociolinguistic background one finds the sociological pressure of the English Only movement, which advocates that English be the official and only language used in the United States. Crawford[15] summarizes this view as follows:

> For supporters, the case is obvious: English has always been our common language, a means of resolving conflicts in a nation of diverse racial, ethnic, and religious groups. Reaffirming the pre-eminence of English means reaffirming a unifying force in American life. Moreover, English is an essential tool of social mobility and economic advancement. The English Language Amendment would "send a message" to immigrants, encouraging them to join in rather than remain apart, and to government, cautioning against policies which could retard English acquisition.

This movement stems from the "subjective alert" that the Spanish language is gaining at the expense of English. English Only advocates often express fear that the traditional three-generation pattern of shift from immigrant languages to English no longer occurs, particularly among Spanish-speaking populations. However, evidence from research suggests that, despite the ethnic revival movements of the Seventies and Eighties, this traditional pattern of loss of immigrant languages continues even among Latin Americans. Schecter and Bayley provided "evidence that immigrants from Spanish-speaking

---

[14] *Ibid.*, 59.
[15] James Crawford, *Language Loyalties: A Source Book on the Official English Controversy*, Chicago: University of Chicago Press, 1992, 2-3.

countries were shifting to English at a very rapid rate".[16] This is offset, of course, by the constant flow of new Hispanic in-migrants.

So far I have presented a description of the "white public space" where English is required of a cultured Hispanic speaker. In the short stories under discussion here, Sandra Cisneros has to combine this expectation with her wish to portray Hispanic speakers in their daily life, in informal domains, where they use Spanish or Spanglish. And there is abundant sociolinguistic research on the dynamic nature of language practices in bilingual and multilingual communities. From the perspective of the interpretative or interactional paradigm, code-switching is a conversational strategy that has great communicative strength and conveys pragmatic meta-messages, such as showing some type of subjective assessment, changing the interpersonal connection with the interlocutor or contrasting a "we" code with a "they" code.[17]

Other scholars have highlighted other interesting dimensions. For example, in her well-known model Myers-Scotton analyzed the flexibility of these practices as devices for negotiating interpersonal relationships, with complex socio-psychological motivations.[18] Auer explored the sequentiality of code-switching, since it takes place within the conversational flow, and showed how its position is part of its communicative effect.[19] He has also paid attention to the degree of functionality these alternating practices may have: from completely functional code-switching, where each variety has an interactional role and transmits different social and psychological meanings, to a nonfunctional code-mixing whose significance is the mixing of codes itself, as a way for speakers to show their double identity.[20] This mixing behavior is the kind of code-switching we frequently find in

---

[16] Sandra R. Schecter and Robert Bayley, *Language as Cultural Practice: Mexicanos en el Norte*, London: Lawrence Erlbaum, 2002, 10.

[17] Cf. John J. Gumperz, *Discourse Strategies*, Cambridge: Cambridge University Press, 1982, 66, 73, 82-83, 85-86.

[18] Carol Myers-Scotton, *Social Motivations for Code-Switching: Evidence from Africa*, Oxford: Oxford University Press, 1993; *Multiple Voices: An Introduction to Bilingualism*, Oxford: Blackwell, 2006.

[19] Peter Auer, "The Pragmatics of Code-Switching: A Sequential Approach", in *One Speaker, Two Languages: Cross-disciplinary Perspectives on Code-Switching*, eds Lesley Milroy and Peter Muysken, Cambridge: Cambridge University Press, 1995, 115-35.

[20] *Code-Switching in Conversation*, ed. Peter Auer, London: Routledge, 1998.

Hispanic communities, though not to the exclusion of the others. And there are many other such studies in this field.[21]

In the fictional universe of Cisneros' *Woman Hollering Creek and Other Stories*, we do not come across the full range of these communicative dynamics. The writer's aim is not faithful realism or a mimetic depiction of conversational practices. Rather, the rich practices described by the sociolinguistic studies just mentioned point to what could be there but is not. Intensity and brevity, the key features of the short story style of narrative, characterize Cisneros' stylized depiction of speech as well as the stream of her narrative voice. Cisneros shows the finesse of a talented writer when she conveys so easily, unobtrusively and seemingly effortlessly, with just a few strokes, the Chicano or Mexican voices of her characters, when she intensifies the suffering that awaits her female characters through the ominous repetition of some words in the narratorial language, English, and in the emotional language, Spanish.

The sociolinguistic concept of audience design[22] is useful in looking at Cisneros' economical display of Spanish elements in her short stories. According to this theory, speakers design their style primarily for and in response to their audience. Audience design applies to all codes and repertoires within a speech community, including the switch from one complete language to another in bilingual situations, since the processes that make a monolingual person shift styles are the same as those that make a bilingual person switch languages. From this sociolinguistic perspective, linguistic design is a responsive phenomenon, but actively so, not passively. Cisneros' literary style can be interpreted as a responsive phenomenon. Though she needs to portray the Chicano community of speakers, her target readership is mainly mainstream Anglo-American. We should not forget that she was the first Chicana writer to receive a major publishing contract. Consequently, in this collection of short stories we cannot expect to find dynamic code-switching in realist contexts; rather, we should expect a stylized

---

[21] See *Code-Switching World Wide*, ed. Rodolfo Jacobson, Berlin: Mouton de Gruyter, 1998; *Code-Switching World Wide II*, ed. Rodolfo Jacobson, Berlin: Mouton de Gruyter, 2001.

[22] Allan Bell, "Language Style as Audience Design", in *Sociolinguistics: A Reader and Coursebook*, eds Nikolas Coupland and Adam Jaworski, London: Macmillan, 1997, 240-49.

approach. This stylized voice that Cisneros so wisely creates allows her stories to fall within the genre's parameters of brevity and intensity.[23] Yet she is also constrained by a more general convention found in Mexican American novels: that of avoiding sociolinguistic realism and instead using stylistic devices to reflect the non-English or bilingual background of their settings.

As I mentioned at the beginning of this essay, some earlier Chicano texts aimed to be realistic reflections of that society.[24] Literary critic Lipski distinguishes between texts that obey a literary canon and use only sporadic lexical items in Spanish, thrown in to add local color, and other types of bilingual literature where inter-sentential and intra-sentential code switches are used.[25] More generally, though (and despite that intense moment of resistance in Chicano literature mentioned above), code-switching in all Chicano prose fiction is rare, as Rudin concludes after a thorough analysis of a representative corpus of Chicano novels.[26] Even though some mimetic approaches are present, he expresses his doubts that the code-switches found in Chicano literature are a valid means of understanding Chicano language as it is really spoken.

In this corpus of Chicano novels analyzed by Rudin,[27] a dichotomous treatment of both languages is clearly observed: English as the language of business and Spanish as the language of love and romance. This clearly illustrates the diglossic separation of linguistic labor. In more general terms, what we find is a separation of broader functions: English is the public language, and Spanish the language

---

[23] Cf. Charles E. May, "Chekhov and the Modern Short Story", and "The Nature of Knowledge in Short Fiction"; and Norman Friedman, "What Makes the Short Story Short?", in *The New Story Theories*, ed. Charles E. May, Athens: Ohio University Press, 1994, 213-16, 138-43, and 131-46; Charles E. May, *The Short Story: The Reality of Artifice*, New York: Twayne, 1995, 119-21; Charles E. May, "Why Short Stories Are Essential and Why They Are Seldom Read", in *The Art of Brevity: Excursions in Short Story Fiction and Analysis*, eds Per Winther *et al*, Columbia: University of South Carolina Press, 2004, 14-25.

[24] See Gary D. Keller, "How Chicano Authors Use Bilingual Techniques for Literary Effect", in *Chicano Studies: A Multidisciplinary Approach*, eds Eugene E. García, Francisco A. Lomelí and Isidro D. Ortiz, New York: Teachers College, 1984, 171-92.

[25] John M. Lipski, *Linguistic Aspects of Spanish-English Language Switching*, Special Studies 25, Tempe: Arizona State University, Center for Latin American Studies, 1985, 78.

[26] Rudin, *Tender Accents of Sound*, 223-30.

[27] *Ibid.*, 254-56.

reserved for private domains. Sometimes we have a glimpse of this distinct diglossic functionality in Cisneros' collection of short stories – not in a very direct or explicit way, but through brief comments introduced in the narrative voice or through the voice of a character. For instance, near the end of the story "Woman Hollering Creek", we learn some key information about the female protagonist through a telephone conversation between two nurses:

> "This poor lady's got black and blue marks all over. I'm not kidding."
> "From her husband. Who else? Another one of those brides from across the border. And her family's all in Mexico .... This lady doesn't even speak English."[28]

The main strategy Rudin found in his extensive study is the use of isolated words or expressions that are evocative of some typical semantic field in the Mexican American culture. Cisneros' *Woman Hollering Creek* collection follows the same pattern, refined by the author's special narrative expertise and intuition. In these short stories, what predominates in Spanish are single words or short expressions. Long Spanish phrases or entire Spanish sentences are rare. As a whole, Spanish is used as a stylistic device, as a symbolic token of the Spanish-speaking community portrayed. The most remarkable strategy in this collection is the constant use of Spanish proper names, names of Virgins and saints, place-names, and a few terms of affection or insults, and a very few expressions of untranslatable cultural concepts. Throughout the story "Woman Hollering Creek" we encounter Spanish names. The story starts by describing "The day Don Serafín gave Juan Pedro Martínez Sánchez permission to take Cleófilas Enriqueta DeLeón Hernández as his bride, across her father's threshold", and very soon we learn the name of Cleófilas' friend (Chela), her son (Juan Pedrito), her neighbors (Soledad and *la señora* Dolores), and her husband's friends (Manolo, Beto, Efraín, el Perico, and Maximiliano).[29] Place-names also have a privileged indexical role. At the beginning, the reader is presented with a first reference to "a town *en el otro lado*" – on the other side – and very soon the name of that town is revealed, Seguín, Tejas:

---

[28] Cisneros, *Woman Hollering Creek and Other Stories*, 54.
[29] *Ibid.*, 43, 46, 52.

Seguín. She had liked the sound of it. Far away and lovely. Not like
Monclova. Coahuila. Ugly.[30]

The narrative flow is dotted with a few more Spanish place-names
after this one, Laredo, La Gritona, "the *arroyo* one crossed on the way
to San Antonio", until the protagonist feels herself stuck in that
remote place, with "no place to go".[31] Physically and psychologically
battered by her husband, she has no resort but to go to the creek that
she now renames La Llorona, the weeping woman:

> La Llorona calling to her. She is sure of it. Cleófilas sets the baby's
> Donald Duck blanket on the grass. Listens. The day sky turning to
> night. The baby pulling up fistfuls of grass and laughing. La Llorona.
> Wonders if something as quiet as this drives a woman to the darkness
> under the trees.[32]

At the end of the story, during her appointment to check on her
second pregnancy, some nurses take pity on her:

> This poor lady's got black-and-blue marks all over …. Another one of
> those brides from across the border. And her family's all in Mexico.

The nurses secretly drive her to San Antonio and compare her name to
"one of those Mexican saints. A martyr or something. Cleófilas. C-L-
E-O-F-I-L-A-S."[33]

Some Spanish expressions add up to this impact: *a head like a
burro*, for example, and *Qué vida, comadre.*[34] Key expressions in the
plot of the story include *la consentida* and expressions of affection,
such as *mi'jita* and *mi querida*, or insults: *grosero.*[35] Lexical items
reflecting key cultural concepts include watching the latest *telenovela*
episode, the *¡Alarma!* magazines, being without a television set and
without the *telenovelas*, and the episode of *María de Nadie.*[36] The
evocative strength of proper names and emotionally loaded words is

---

[30] *Ibid.*, 45.
[31] *Ibid.*, 52, 46, 51.
[32] *Ibid.*, 51.
[33] *Ibid.*, 54, 45.
[34] *Ibid.*, 44, 55.
[35] *Ibid.*, 47, 51, 52, 51.
[36] *Ibid.*, 44, 52.

reinforced through repetitions in English, embedded in either the narrative voice or the voice of a character or of the community: "*Tú o nadie.* You or No One";[37] "*La consentida*, the princess";[38] "*No es bueno para la salud. Mala suerte.* Bad luck. *Mal aire*";[39] "*Pues allá de los indios, quién sabe* – who knows, the townspeople shrugged."[40]

This subtle way of resorting to the function of reiteration at some key moments, and of concepts like *telenovelas* (representing her idealized vision of love), adds momentum to the drama of the female character. Her native language, Spanish, thus becomes a deep emotional code, the few words repeated in English and Spanish or just in Spanish (*telenovelas*, *La Gritona*, the *arroyo*, *La Llorona*) betokening the drama that is unfolding in her life.

One relevant observation from analyses on linguistic constructions of identity is that we have an instinctive capacity to construct identities based on minimal input.[41] Sociolinguistic analyses have also shown the significance of proper names as basic aspects of a person's identity.[42] These insights help us appreciate the skillful way Cisneros uses proper names as tokens or symbols to construct the characters in her fictional universe. But we also know that according to the Communication Theory of Identity,[43] the analysis of identity has moved away from self-conception and toward an understanding of how various layers of identity are constructed in interaction with others. Out of a framework of four types of identity (personal, enacted, relational and communal), I will highlight the notion of communal identity, which is not defined by an individual's conception of self but refers to the idea of identities in terms of collectivities. And this is also what we find in this collection of short stories. Cisneros' main aim is to offer a glimpse of the female micro-cosmos to which Chicano or Hispanic women belong. And full dialogues in Spanish or

---

[37] *Ibid.*, 44.

[38] *Ibid.*, 47-48.

[39] *Ibid.*, 51.

[40] *Ibid.*, 46.

[41] John Joseph, *Language and Identity*, Basingstoke: Palgrave Macmillan, 2004, 2.

[42] Joanna Thornborrow, "Language and Identity", in *Language, Society and Power*, eds Linda Thomas *et al.*, London: Routledge, 1999, 136-49.

[43] J.R. Baldwin and Michael L. Hecht, "The Layered Perspective on Cultural (In)tolerance(s): The Roots of a Multi-disciplinary Approach to (In)tolerance", in *Intercultural Communication Theory*, ed. R.L. Wiseman, Thousand Oaks, CA: Sage, 1995, 59-91.

Spanglish would not serve this purpose well; they would be burdensome. Spanish does not have the role of being an interactional language here, in this fictional medium; rather, its function is mainly evocative. For Cisneros, Spanish words or short phrases are like brushstrokes of paint in the hands of an artist – unobtrusive, but loaded with meaning.

Within the constraints of brevity and intensity of the genre, Sandra Cisneros shows great narrative ingenuity in her ability to depict Chicano communities and values through her sparing use of lexical items. It is indicative of her talent that most of these brief tokens are names. In the short story just discussed, "Woman Hollering Creek", and in the rest as well, the reader can follow the flow of the story with great ease, in the mainstream language of the Anglo-American society, but proper names, place-names, names of Virgins and saints, names of typical dishes and dances, and terms of endearments or insults are there like signposts in Spanish, linguistic anthropological ways of constructing the Other. In the story "Anguiano Religious Articles. Rosaries Statues Medals Incense Candles Talismans Perfumes Oils Herbs", which is only two pages long, the narrative flow is speckled with names: a religious store called "Soledad", Anguiano Religious Articles, a hospital called "Santa Rosa Hospital", a hotel called "the Cactus Hotel" and plenty of references to the "Virgen de Guadalupe", "La Virgen", or "San Martín Caballero, cutting his Roman cape in half with a sword and giving it to a beggar".[44] The story's plot is simple and minimal: the female protagonist needs to buy a Virgen de Guadalupe. This religious focus expands in the following short story, "Little Miracles, Kept Promises", which does not follow a conventional narrative pattern; rather, the story comprises a succession of paragraphs, each devoted to a saint, a Virgin, Christ, God, and so on, showing gratitude, asking for a favor, complying with the expected religious style, until the last plea to the Virgin begins, "Virgencita", which suddenly subverts the respectful tone and turns into a denunciation of the plight of these women:

> Virgencita de Guadalupe. For a long time I wouldn't let you in my house. I couldn't see you without seeing my ma each time my father

---

[44] Cisneros, *Woman Hollering Creek and Other Stories*, 114-15.

came home drunk and yelling, blaming everything that ever went
wrong in his life on her.

I couldn't look at your folded hands without seeing my *abuelita*
mumbling, "My son, my son, my son..." Couldn't look at you without
blaming you for the pain my mother and her mother and all our
mothers' mothers have put up with in the name of God .... Don't
think it was easy going without you .... Heretic. Atheist. *Malinchista.*
Hocicona. But I wouldn't shut my yap.[45]

We read on until she, the narrator, the writer herself speaking to us
from her heart, reaches a climax, a revelation for the reader, using
Virgin names as sources that connect with her inner strength, because
these names reside in her deepest Mexican roots, which will finally
empower women like her in their hard reality:

That you could have the power to rally a people when a country was
born, and again during civil war, and during a farmworkers' strike in
California made me think maybe there is power in my mother's
patience, strength in my grandmother's endurance .... When I learned
your real name is Coatlaxopeuh, She Who Has Dominion over
Serpents, when I recognized you as Tonantzín, and learned your
names as Teteoinnan, Toci, Xochiquetzal, Tlazolteotl, Coatlicue,
Chalchiuhtlicue, Coyolxauhqui, Huixtocihualt, Chicomecoatl,
Cihuacoatl, when I could see you as Nuestra Señora de la Soledad,
Nuestra Señora de los Remedios, Nuestra Señora del Perpetuo
Socorro, Nuestra Señora de San Juan de los Lagos. Our Lady of
Lourdes, Our Lady of Mount Carmel, Our Lady of the Rosary, Our
Lady of Sorrows, I wasn't ashamed, then, to be my mother's daughter,
my grandmother's granddaughter, my ancestor's child.[46]

Some literary critics consider Cisneros' previous work, *The House
on Mango Street*, a subversion of discourses that were predominant in
earlier Chicano production. Traditionally dominant categories of the
power struggle in the Chicano novel – social class and ethnic group –
are superseded here by a focus on gender.[47] As I have indicated, the
stories in *Woman Hollering Creek* follow the same path. Throughout
these short stories, she focuses on underprivileged, exploited and

---

[45] *Ibid.*, 124, 127.
[46] *Ibid.*, 128.
[47] Rudin, *Tender Accents of Sound*, 200. See Judith Butler, *Gender Trouble:
Feminism and the Subversion of Identity*, New York: Routledge, 1999.

poverty-stricken Mexican or Mexican American women and their men. After the success of *The House on Mango Street*, Cisneros' prestige as a talented contemporary writer enabled her to reach a wide audience of mainstream Anglo-American readers. In this collection, she has profited from this privileged position to speak of the poverty, suffering and resilience of her Chicano co-members of her Latino community, using the evocative and subtle linguistic strategies I have just presented. Cisneros uses code-switching as a clear strategy of brevity in the short story, which is the genre of brevity *par excellence*.

THE YELLOW HYBRIDS:
GENDER AND GENRE IN GILMAN'S WALLPAPER

CAROLINA NÚÑEZ-PUENTE

Born in the nineteenth century, Charlotte Perkins Gilman and Mikhail
M. Bakhtin became well-known thinkers toward the end of the
twentieth. Recently labeled the "leading theorist of 'first wave'
feminism",[1] Gilman also was a writer and one of the earliest
sociologists in the United States.[2] The Russian Bakhtin, most famous
as the promoter of dialogics, is also known as a philosopher who
theorized on the need for a sociological poetics of literature.[3] The
hybrid careers of Gilman and Bakhtin prompt both the study of other
hybrids and the combination of the two thinkers in a study. This
article approaches some of the many hybrids of Gilman's story "The
Yellow Wallpaper", which include gender and genre, such as the
hybrid femininity and sexuality of the protagonist in a text that is both
realist and gothic. Accordingly, I make use of a hybrid critical
perspective that is both feminist and dialogical.[4] Since the present

---

[1] Maggie Humm, *The Dictionary of Feminist Theory* (1989), rpt. London: Harvester
Wheatsheaf, 1999, 111.
[2] Mary Jo Deegan, "Introduction", in *With Her in Ourland: Sequel to Herland*, eds
Mary Jo Deegan and Michael R. Hill, Westport, CT: Greenwood Press, 1997, 1-57.
[3] For the purposes of this article, I shall say that dialogical thought stems from the
recognition of hybridity, a recognition that refuses the "either/or" opposition typical
of Western thought in favor of a more inclusive "both/and" way of thinking.
"Dialogics" comes from "dialogue" and uses dialogue as a form of ethics. Therefore,
dialogics promotes having many "voices/ideas", which form a vital "compound",
instead of a single one, and taking into account the others, whom we address and who
respond to us.
[4] Identified as a "new *school* of criticism", "dialogical feminism" (re)reads Bakhtin's
work in order to correct and expand on it (Lynne Pearce, *Reading Dialogics*, London:
Edward Arnold, 1994, 102). Some current works of dialogical feminism are
Feminism, Bakhtin and the Dialogic, eds Dale M. Bauer and Susan Jaret McKinstry,
Albany: State University of New York Press, 1991; *A Dialogue of Voices: Feminist*

volume is dedicated to the short story, I will start by clarifying my approach to the notion of "genre" with reference to Gilman and Bakhtin.[5]

Perhaps because "There is no single consistent use of the term 'genre'", scholars disagree on the genre status of Gilman's "The Yellow Wallpaper": diary (Michaels); autobiography (Rogers); and one could add "'literature of hysteria' hysteria" (Diamond), among others.[6] If we take into account all these views, "The Yellow Wallpaper" shares the generic "cannibalism" of the Bakhtinian novel. Its classification as "diary" enhances its prosaic and novelistic features, as one of the "units into which the novelistic whole usually breaks down ... [such as] everyday narration (the letter, the diary, etc)".[7] This kind of prosaic writing has been regarded as the starting point of "women's literature".[8] As a dialogical feminist, I find it disappointing that for Bakhtin, the preferred literary exponent of dialogics was not really the novel but only the novels of male authors.

Literary Theory and Bakhtin, eds Karen Hohne and Helen Wussow, Minneapolis: University of Minnesota Press, 1994; Patricia Yaeger, *Honey-Mad Women: Emancipatory Strategies in Women's Writing*, New York: Columbia University Press, 1988.

[5] Like genre, gender is in fact a complicated issue, which can be simplified only with reservations. As a critical category, gender has been defined as a "culturally shaped group of attributes and behaviors given to the female or to the male ... [in order] to distinguish between sex and gender" (Humm, *The Dictionary of Feminist Theory*, 106). When the feminist movement first came to examine gender, many of the supposed gender differences revealed themselves as inequalities, that is, as products of women's subordination in patriarchy. Therefore studying gender (questions) meant dealing with sexism in all its representations. Later there emerged a new concept of (gender) difference, which pointed out and celebrated women's different way(s) of relating to life, literature, etc. My own deployment of this analytic tool will be explained throughout.

[6] Walter B. Michaels, *The Gold Standard and the Logic of Naturalism*, Berkeley: University of California Press, 1987; Annie G. Rogers, "The 'I' of Madness: Shifting Subjectivities in Girls' and Women Psychological Development in 'The Yellow Wallpaper'", in *Analyzing the Different Voice: Feminist Psychological Theory and Literary Texts*, eds Jerilyn Fisher and Ellen S. Silber, Lanham, MD: Rowman and Littlefield, 1988, 45-65; and Elin Diamond, "Realism and Hysteria: Toward a Feminist Mimesis", *Discourse*, XXXIII/1 (Fall-Winter 1990), 59-92.

[7] Mikhail M. Bakhtin, "Discourse in the Novel" (1934-35), in *The Dialogic Imagination: Four Essays by M.M. Bakhtin*, trans. Caryl Emerson and Michael Holquist, ed. Michael Holquist, Austin: University of Texas Press, 2000, 262.

[8] Josephine Donovan, *Women and the Rise of the Novel, 1405-1726* (1999), rpt. New York: St Martin's, 2000.

In this article I attempt to expand Bakhtin's scope by examining the dialogics of a short story that was authored by a woman.

Bakhtin's obsession with the male-authored novel in the midpoint of his career prevented him from identifying in other genres the characteristics he attributed only to novels. Other thinkers such as Henry James or Virginia Woolf have celebrated the democratic, modern, experimental, and hybrid character of the short story.[9] Nowadays, the short story cycle has been labeled the clearest antecedent of the novel.[10] Furthermore, if Bakhtin's interest in the reader's role led him to focus on the novel, Poe assured us that the short story "needs an active reader",[11] and, for Charles E. May, the short story gives way to a more intimate form of communication between author and reader.[12] As I argue here, Gilman's short story demands an active responsive reader that is able to produce a dialogical reading. For instance, one of the features of Bakhtin's dialogic/novelistic hero is his ability not to coincide with himself.[13] In "The Yellow Wallpaper", the depressed female protagonist has already been altered by her illness and is susceptible to more alterations. Hence Gilman's text takes part in a dialogic criticism of the supposed stability of identity. Considering all this, and given that Gilman referred to "The Yellow Wallpaper" as her "little book",[14] one can strategically accept that it can still be a short story. Such a strategic definition allows me to study the possibility of dialogical short stories and to evaluate the (sub)genre of this one in particular: is it a realist short story, a gothic one, or both?[15] Interestingly, for

[9] Valerie Shaw, *The Short Story: A Critical Introduction* (1983), rpt. London: Longman, 1995, 16-22.
[10] James Nagel, *The Contemporary American Short-Story Cycle: The Ethnic Resonance of the Genre*, Baton Rouge: Louisiana State University Press, 2001.
[11] Pratt, "The Short Story: The Short and the Long of It", in *The New Short Story Theories*, ed. Charles E. May, Athens: Ohio University Press, 1994, 113.
[12] Charles May, "The Nature of Knowledge in Short Fiction", in *ibid.*, 131-43.
[13] Mikhail M. Bakhtin, "The *Bildungsroman* and Its Significance in the History of Realism (Toward a Historical Typology of the Novel)" (1936-38), in *Speech Genres and Other Late Essays*, trans. Vern W. McGee, eds Caryl Emerson and Michael Holquist, Austin: University of Texas Press, 1999, 10-59.
[14] Charlotte Perkins Gilman, "Why I Wrote 'The Yellow Wallpaper'" (1913), in *The Captive Imagination: A Case Book on "The Yellow Wallpaper"*, ed. Catherine J. Golden, New York: The Feminist Press, 1992, 53.
[15] As for these (sub)genre forms, most contemporary writers and critics see realism as conservative and find more emancipatory possibilities in the gothic (Leo Bersani, *A*

Bakhtin's circle, genres are epistemologies or forms of thought.[16] As ways of thinking, genres may contribute to reinforce the social system, as happens with the epic, or to destabilize and criticize it, as happens with the novel. Finally, if "The Yellow Wallpaper" were both dialogic and feminist enough, we would have to attribute Gilman the creation of a new genre or form of thought: the dialogical feminist short story.[17]

Among the hybrids examined in this article, I would like to start by listening to the voices of two narrators that, some critics think, might correspond with the author and the protagonist.[18] The main character of "The Yellow Wallpaper" is a woman writer and a mother whose name might be Jane and who tries to fight her postpartum depression by means of the nineteenth-century "rest cure". Such a cure consisted of being isolated in a bedroom and being "absolutely forbidden to 'work' until [she feels] well again".[19] Confined in an "atrocious"

Future for Astyarax: Character and Desire in Literature, Boston: Little, Brown, 1969, and Diamond, "Realism and Hysteria", 59-92). Bakhtin would disagree with such an "either/or" perspective, as he was able to appreciate the contesting spirit of the novel, even the realist one.

[16] Pavel N. Medveved and Mikhail M. Bakhtin, *The Formal Method in Literary Scholarship: A Critical Introduction to Sociological Poetics*, Baltimore: Johns Hopkins University Press, 1978.

[17] According to May, the most representative stories of Irving, Hawthorne, Poe, and Melville constitute a "'new' genre" given their "self-conscious combination of ... realistic and romance forms" ("Metaphoric Motivation in Short Story Fiction: 'In the Beginning Was the Story'", in *Short Story Theory at a Crossroads*, eds Susan Lohafer and Jo Ellyn Clarey, Baton Rouge: Louisiana State University Press, 1989, 65). I am suggesting that Gilman's "The Yellow Wallpaper" combines such forms – and does it in a feminist manner. This too helps me criticize the androcentric bias of some scholars and works.

[18] Richard Feldstein, "Reader, Text, and Ambiguous Referentiality in 'The Yellow Wall-paper'", in *The Captive Imagination*, 307-18; Paula Treichler, "Escaping the Sentence: Diagnosis and Discourse in 'The Yellow Wallpaper'", in *ibid.*, 191-210; and Jenny Weatherford, "Approaching the Ineffable: 'The Yellow Wallpaper' and Gilman's Problem with Language", *American Studies in Scandinavia*, XXXI/2 (1999), 58-75.

[19] Charlotte Perkins Gilman, "The Yellow Wallpaper" (1892), in *The Captive Imagination*, 25. Gilman herself suffered from both postpartum depression and the rest cure, which was prescribed to her by its inventor, Silas Weir Mitchell. The effects of this cure were very much against its purpose, leaving Gilman in a state similar to the one reached by her protagonist. In "Why I Wrote 'The Yellow Wallpaper'", she explained that her main purpose with the story was to reveal the dangers of the supposed cure in order "to save people from being driven crazy" (53).

bedroom, which looks like a "nursery",[20] she first spends her time
keeping a diary. Jane's act of writing is the reason many critics have
concluded that she narrates the whole story. Nevertheless, this
position loses credibility when one tries to explain the story's ending:
if there is only a protagonist-narrator and if, at the end, this
protagonist goes crazy – for example, as she goes crawling around the
room – who is narrating at that point?

   In his essay "Discourse in the Novel", Bakhtin defines narrative
hybridity as "a mixture of two social languages within the limits of a
single utterance".[21] Thus,

> The author manifests [her]self and h[er] point of view not only in
> h[er] effect on the narrator, on h[er] speech and h[er] language ... but
> also in h[er] effect on the subject of the story as a point of view that
> differs from the point of view of the narrator [for instance, that of a
> character]. Behind the narrator's story, we read a second story, the
> author's story; [s]he is the one who tells us how the narrator tells
> stories, and also tells us about the narrator h[er]self.[22]

Following Bakhtin's writings on hybridity, I argue that "The Yellow
Wallpaper" comprises two narrative voices: one that belongs to the
main character and another that coincides with Gilman's authorial
voice. Interestingly, at times the author's voice overlaps with the
protagonist's and contradicts her words. For example: "The wallpaper
[of my bedroom], as I said before, is torn off ... and it sticketh closer
than a brother – [the children] must have had perseverance as well as
hatred."[23] The clause "as I said before" belongs to the protagonist-
narrator; the comparison with a "brother", on the other hand, is deeply
ironic, as Jane's brother is also a medical doctor like John (her
husband) and Silas Weir Mitchell (the inventor of the famous "rest
cure"). Furthermore, Jane's narration is unreliable: as Monika
Fludernick suggests, how could she know that the paper is so sticky
without having tried to tear it off herself?[24] There are other reasons to

---

[20] Gilman, "The Yellow Wallpaper", 28, 26.
[21] Bakhtin, "Discourse in the Novel", 358.
[22] *Ibid.*, 313-14.
[23] Gilman, "The Yellow Wallpaper", 29-30.
[24] Monika Fludernik, "Defining (In)Sanity: The Narrator of *The Yellow Wallpaper*
and the Question of Unreliability", in *Grenzüberschreitungen: Narratologie im*

support Gilman's choice of a hybrid narrative model, such as the protagonist's sexuality and gender. The hybrid character of both the story and its protagonist may be represented in the wallpaper's pattern of Jane's bedroom.

The room's wallpaper is given anthropomorphic qualities: it has "expression" and seems to "kn[o]w" things.[25] Its pattern is described in the terms patriarchy uses to define the "feminine": it is "dull", "impertinen[t]", "absurd", and "silly"; it has "lame uncertain curves" and provokes "confusion". Lonely confined in her bedroom, Jane tries to examine the wallpaper's pattern, as if it really hid a secret meaning: "I … lay there … trying to decide whether that front pattern and the back pattern really did move together or separately." She is "determined … [to] find it out" and "spend[s] hours trying to analyze it". But the more Jane scrutinizes it, the more sick or patriarchally feminine she becomes. At a certain point, the protagonist feels, somewhat paranoically, that she is being pursued by the smell of the wallpaper, which "creeps all over the house …. I find it … lying in wait for me on the stairs …. Even when I go to ride, if I turn my head … there is that smell!" Having been well trained by patriarchy, Jane has a great ability to think in Western terms: that is, she either thinks most rationally (à la realist) or abandons herself to dreams (à la gothic). Her attitude supports the argument that both realism and the gothic are two (sub)genres to which Gilman's story belongs.[26] The author-narrator expresses an ironic attitude toward the main character's nondialogic "either/or" perspective by introducing

---

Kontext (*Transcending Boundaries: Narratology in Context*), eds Walter Grünzweig and Andreas Solbach, Tübingen: Gunter Narr, 1999, 75-95.

[25] Gilman, "The Yellow Wallpaper", 29.

[26] A quick look at Gilman's bibliography shows that she was an ardent practitioner of both realist and gothic forms. As a sociologist, Gilman writes essays intended to reflect and criticize contemporary social problems in the most faithful realist vein – see *Women and Economics: A Study of the Economic Relation between Women and Men* (1898), New York: Prometheus Books, 1994. Nevertheless, Gilman also finds emancipatory possibilities in the gothic, of which a couple of examples are "The Giant Wisteria" (1891) and "The Rocking-Chair" (1893). Thus Juliann E. Fleenor reads her autobiography, *The Living of Charlotte Perkins Gilman* (1835), as containing gothic features and her gothic stories as containing autobiographical details – see "The Gothic Prism: Charlotte Perkins Gilman's Gothic Stories and Her Autobiography", in *"The Yellow Wallpaper": Charlotte Perkins Gilman*, eds Thomas L. Erskine and Connie L. Richards, New Brunswick, NJ: Rutgers University Press, 1993, 139-58.

statements that seem comic to the reader, although Jane is unable to notice their hilarity. The intrusion of the author-narrator enables the feminist reader to occupy the position of the author or at least not to identify herself with the ill Jane. This parody is better appreciated through a dialogical reading of both the wallpaper and the portrayal of Jane's husband.

The wallpaper pattern features "interminable grotesques [that] seem to *form around a common center and rush off* in headlong plunges of equal distraction".[27] One can easily construct a dialogue between this story's fragment and an important theorization of Bakhtin. From a Bakhtinian stance, the stability of the linguistic system is created by "centripetal forces" that appear "to *form around a common center*".[28] Such forces coexist with the "centrifugal forces" that *rush off* from the center and make language susceptible to change. Since Bakhtin regards these "forces" as working within all literary genres, the epic is a "centripetal" genre, whereas the novel and, I would add, the short story are "centrifugal" ones. Gilman's wish to reform the system of patriarchy led her to fly away from established forms and hybridize her fiction.[29] The wallpaper's pattern is ultimately hybrid and contains a gothic or perhaps feminine "excess",[30] which can dismantle patriarchal meanings, since it "changes as the light changes".[31] The problem is that the main character decides to read the pattern in a simple realistic way: she is determined, she says, to "analyze ... the pointless pattern to some sort of conclusion". And a purely realistic approach is not enough: every day she finds "new shoots of fungus, new shades of yellow .... I cannot keep count of

---

[27] Gilman, "The Yellow Wallpaper", 31 (my italics).

[28] Mikhail M. Bakhtin, "Epic and the Novel" (1941), in *The Dialogic Imagination*, 3-40 (my italics).

[29] In other words: "There is a tension between the feminist writer's role as realist and her role as reformer. As a practitioner of realism ... the writer must respect the conventions ... accept[ed] as 'reality'. Yet if women's role is ... to [be] reform[ed], then those very conventions must be attacked" (Conrad Shumaker, "Realism, Reform, and the Audience: Charlotte Perkins Gilman's Unreadable Paper", *Arizona Quarterly*, XLVII/1 (Spring 1991), 87. As a result, Gilman both relies on and attacks established conventions.

[30] Luce Irigaray, "This Sex Which Is Not One", trans. Claudia Reeder, in *The Second Wave: A Reader in Feminist Theory*, ed. Linda Nicholson, New York: Routledge, 1997, 323-29.

[31] Gilman, "The Yellow Wallpaper", 34.

them".[32] Contemporary feminists, such as practitioners of *écriture feminine*, have argued for a dialogue between the symbolic and semiotic realms, which can be understood as a dialogue between the centripetal and the centrifugal or between the realist and the gothic. In "The Yellow Wallpaper", the author-narrator might be suggesting that the reader play with the lines in an attempt to reinvent patriarchal language, thus corroborating Gilman's play with gender/genres. Unsurprisingly, the story has been defined as an "attempt to write a new kind of story, one true to women's inner experience".[33] "The Yellow Wallpaper" can also be read as an attempt at a new way of thinking (of genre parameters) in order to let the voice(s) of a gender be listened to.[34] Curiously enough, *écriture feminine* has been described as that kind of hybrid realism, whether inner realism or feminist realism.[35]

In Gilman's text, the author-narrator's parody is more bittersweet when dealing with Jane's husband. Jane's desire to "reach the height of romantic felicity" reveals her belief that John is the kind of "rescuing prince" portrayed in the literary genres she has surely "read about".[36] In this way patriarchy has constructed gender(s) through genre(s), such as in the gothic: the brave male savior of the scared female victim. John's inaction, his inability to help his wife, is evident throughout: for example, "[John] is very careful and loving, and hardly lets me stir without special direction .... he takes all care from me, and so I feel basely ungrateful not to value it even more." The verb "stir" reifies the wife's condition, and the modifiers "all", "basely", and "even" enhance the scathing critique of the author-narrator.[37] Another example reads: "It is so hard to talk with John

---

[32] *Ibid.*, 35, 37, 31, 37.

[33] Weatherford, "Approaching the Ineffable", 73.

[34] Even if dealing only with the "feminine", we must be careful to use a label such as "genders" instead of "gender" so as not to homogenize the features attributed to women. For a reading of Gilman's story based on various levels of "gender", see Carolina Núñez-Puente, *Feminism and Dialogics: Charlotte Perkins Gilman, Meridel Le Sueur, Mikhail M. Bakhtin*, Valencia: Publicaciones Universidad de Valencia (Biblioteca Javier Coy de Estudios Norteamericanos), 2006, 19-40.

[35] Blanche H. Gelfant, *Women Writing in America: Voices in Collage*, Hanover, NH: University Press of New England, 1985, 74, 87, 187, 251, 260; *Spectacles of Realism: Body, Gender, Genre*, eds Margaret Cohen and Christopher Prendergast, Minneapolis: University of Minnesota Press, 1995, vii-xiii, 1-10.

[36] Gilman, "The Yellow Wallpaper", 24, 25.

[37] *Ibid.*, 26.

about my case, because he is so wise, and because he loves me so";
the lack of modifier here may indicate that he loves her "so" – that is,
as much as S. Weir Mitchell, in whose hands she does not want to be,
because "he is [a physician] just like John and [her] brother".[38] Her
husband's words make him sound foolish: "Your exercise depends on
your strength, my dear ... and your food somewhat on your appetite;
but air you can absorb all the time." Is this the prescription of a
medical doctor of "high standing"?[39] Here Gilman mocks the medical
genre and its reification of patients. Jane desperately needs to believe
that her husband really loves her and cares for her. However, no
perspicacious reader could share her opinion, given the subtle irony
displayed by the author-narrator.

Readers soon notice a marked difference between John's and
Jane's languages: as patriarchal husbands do, he "laughs at" her and
"scoffs openly at any talk of things not to be felt and seen and put
down in figures". Given Jane's "imaginative power and habit of story-
making", John mistrusts all her opinions: when she told him that she
felt "something strange about the house", "he said what [she] felt was
a *draught*, and shut the window". Gilman thus mocks the belief in a
stable reality that can be grasped through reason. Though Jane feels
almost bereft of hope, she tries to hold on to her beliefs: "Still I will
proudly declare that there is something queer about [the house]."[40] The
young Victorian wife experiences the ideological hybrid described as
the fight between the authoritative word and the inner persuasive
voice. According to Bakhtin, the authoritative voice "demands that we
acknowledge it ... [and] binds us quite independently of any power it
might have to persuade us internally; [since] we encounter ... its
authority already fused to it".[41] Therefore, the voice of authority, of
the Fathers, corresponds to the protagonist's husband and the inner
voice, which "is denied all privilege, backed up by no authority at all"
to herself. I suggest that her "inner personal voice" lets itself be heard
at times; for instance, like her brother, "John is a physician, and
perhaps ... *perhaps* that is one reason I do not get well faster ....
personally, I disagree with their ideas .... personally, I believe that

---

[38] *Ibid.*, 33, 30.
[39] *Ibid.*, 26, 24, 25.
[40] *Ibid.*, 24, 29, 25, 24 (italics in the original).
[41] Bakhtin, "Discourse in the Novel", 342.

congenial work ... would do me good."[42] Nevertheless, her "inner" language is still infected by John's authoritarian voice: "I sometimes fancy that in my condition if I had less opposition and more society and stimulus – but John says." Even in the last scene, when the protagonist is crawling around the room after having torn off the wallpaper, she might be alluding to herself in the third person: "I've got out at last ... in spite of you and Jane." That is one of John's habits that she probably acquires: for example, when talking to her, John says, "Bless her little heart! ... she shall be as sick as she pleases".[43] Fortunately, the author-narrator does not succumb to the gender pattern imprisoning the protagonist. In the same way, Gilman herself refused to accommodate herself to established genre/gender forms.

Jane's inability to refer to herself as "I" could thus stem from the fact that she is not seen as a "you" by John. This contrasts with the numerous times she mentions his name: four "Johns" in half a page of Golden's edition.[44] Feminist scholars have argued for a dialogical-like (non)ego who first moves toward the other not for the purpose of domination but to establish a relationship.[45] Also, for Bakhtin the dialogical subject "realize[s her]self initially through others".[46] This is related to Gilman's deployment of the gothic genre, which, scholars agree, accounts for a self that has relationships: "after all, gothic horror is domestic horror, family horror, and addresses precisely [the] gendered problems of everyday life."[47] In this story, it seems that John is not only bad at conversation but might also be bad at sex, which explains one of the sexual problems of his wife. William Veeder's allusion to *Gone with the Wind* is appropriate and suggestive. The protagonist-narrator tells us, "[And] dear John gathered me in his arms, and just carried me upstairs and laid me on the bed, and sat by me and read by me till it tired my head"; Veeder adds, "[But] Scarlett

---

[42] Gilman, "The Yellow Wallpaper", 25 (italics in the original).

[43] *Ibid.*, 42, 33.

[44] *Ibid.*, 28.

[45] Nancy Chodorow, *The Reproduction of Mothering: Psychoanalysis and the Sociology of Gender*, Berkeley: University of California Press, 1978; Patricia Waugh, *Feminine Fictions: Revisiting the Postmodern*, London: Routledge, 1989.

[46] Mikhail M. Bakhtin, "From Notes Made in 1970-71", in *Speech Genres and Other Late Essays*, 138.

[47] Susanne Becker, *Gothic Forms of Feminine Fictions*, Manchester: Manchester University Press, 1999, 11.

O'Hara encounters Book Man". The very imagery used to describe the wallpaper oozes with sexual connotations. Its color is "lurid", a "smoldering unclean yellow", which "makes [Jane] think [only] of ... old, foul, bad yellow things". Its design has a "vicious influence" on Jane, suggestive of an orgasm, like "a kind of 'debased Romanesque' with *delirium tremens*". Most critics have noticed its "smooch[es]", and some have suggested that they refer to masturbation.[48] One who masturbates is a subject and can be said to rebel against a society that imposes a heterosexual-reproductive regime. Surprisingly, many medical authorities of the 1920s still thought that "The habits of the ... homosexual or intersexual woman might take the form ... of masturbation".[49] Furthermore, the word "queer" appears three times in "The Yellow Wallpaper". This has prompted some readers to claim Gilman's story as a lesbian text.[50] As I suggested earlier, John does not consider Jane a subject with whom to establish a dialogical relationship, for instance, a sexual one. I would argue that, during her virtual imprisonment in the "yellow room", the protagonist reveals (maybe even discovers) something else about her own sexuality, something beyond John, perhaps about masturbation, lesbianism, or heterosexual non-satisfaction.

"The Yellow Wallpaper" goes on to examine the difficulties of such a dialogical although lonely subject. As a professional writer, Jane finds her lack of a listener, not to say an audience, very painful: "It is so discouraging not to have any advice and companionship about my work."[51] Jane's need to enter into a relationship is reflected in a text riddled with the pronoun "you": "I assure you", "you see", "I'll tell you why – privately – ". Her desperation is such that she begins to see others in her room's wallpaper – a "figure", "the same shape, only very numerous", of what appears to be a "woman", or even a "great many women". When Jane "finds out" that the crawling, "stooping down" woman of the wallpaper wants to be set free from its oppressive pattern, she decides to "help her .... I pulled and she

---

[48] *Ibid.*, 35, 40.
[49] Sheila Jeffreys, *The Spinster and Her Enemies: Feminism and Sexuality, 1880-1930*, London: Pandora, 1985, 170.
[50] Paula Smith Allen, *Metamorphosis and the Feminine: A Motif of "Difference" in Women's Writing*, New York: Peter Lang, 1999; Barbara A. White, untitled essay in *Charlotte Perkins Gilman: A Study of the Short Fiction*, ed. Denise D. Knight, Albuquerque: University of New Mexico Press, 1997, 197-209.
[51] Gilman, "The Yellow Wallpaper", 29.

shook, I shook and she pulled, and before morning we had peeled off yards of that paper". Hence, we face the problem of address once more: Jane never calls her companion "you" but refers to her, as John does with herself, in the third person. Moreover, she is in possession of a rope so that "If that woman does get out, and tries to get away, [she] can tie her!" – and ends up tying herself.[52] Traditionally, scholars have held that the mysterious figure is in fact Jane's own reflection, as if the "wallpaper" were a sort of mirror and its "pattern" a metaphor for patriarchal oppression.[53] By contrast, in Susan Lanser's postcolonial reading, Jane's "yellow" companion does represent another person.[54] In America, the turn of the twentieth century was a time of massive immigration, and many people during that era feared the "yellow peril". Lanser points out that the color yellow was associated with the immigrants, so the woman behind the yellow wallpaper might be one of them. Far from approaching her as an-other person in the Irigarayan manner,[55] Jane sees this woman as an inferior other with whom she can merge. Unfortunately, she is no more relationally adept than John, which contradicts the hypothesis that women are naturally more relationally adept than men. This complicates the issue of women's sisterhood – that is: women do not naturally get on well with each other; some women oppress other women, and so on. In what follows I will elaborate on this question of gender and the plurality of women.

Critics attribute much importance to the way a short story begins and the way it ends.[56] The first sentence of "The Yellow Wallpaper" reads: "It is very seldom that *mere ordinary people* like John and myself secure ancestral halls for the summer."[57] A couple who hire an estate, with an enormous mansion, a "private wharf", "servants", and

---

[52] *Ibid.*, 40, 41.
[53] Elaine Hedges, "'Out at Last?' *The Yellow Wallpaper* after Two Decades of Feminist Criticism", in *The Captive Imagination*, 319-33.
[54] Susan S. Lanser, "Feminist Criticism, 'The Yellow Wallpaper', and the Politics of Color in America", *Feminist Studies*, XV/3 (Fall 1989), 415-42.
[55] Luce Irigaray, "The Question of the Other", trans. Noah Guynn, *Yale French Studies*, LXXXVII (1995), 7-19.
[56] John Gerlach, *Toward the End: Closure and Structure in the American Short Story*, Tuscaloosa: University of Alabama Press, 1985. See also Susan Lohafer, "How Does a Story End?"; Austin M. Wright, "Recalcitrance in the Short Story"; and Thomas M. Leitch, "The Debunking Rhythm of the American Short Story", all in *Short Story Theory at a Crossroads*, 109-47.
[57] Gilman, "The Yellow Wallpaper", 24 (my italics).

so on, do not seem to be working-class.[58] Consequently, from the first section, we can glimpse the protagonist's unreliability in narrating the story – that is, it seems she has a disturbed perception of her class situation. Through her words, the satiric author could be saying: "It is very seldom that they would hire such a house; they would do so only if Jane needed to be put in a cage!" The question of class appears once more when she mentions that the estate has "lots of separate little houses for the gardeners and people", which reveals a latent class consciousness. She also confesses her liking for the rich and "pretty old-fashioned chintz hangings!".[59] Gilman herself had an austere taste and was very critical of decoration – hence her attempt to reform women's clothing.[60] Therefore, the protagonist-narrator's upper-class language and attitude would seem to be a subject of mockery to an author disdainful of what is considered to be old-fashioned. However, as an author she chose a wealthy woman as her main character. This leads to the conclusion that hysteria must be an upper-class woman's illness, since lower-class women have neither time nor occasion to become hysterical. It is pitiful and ironic that the main character uses her bedroom key to lock herself in.[61] It is ironic and pitiful that she does not look for help or escape when "[she] go[es] to ride".[62]

Continuing in this line, in the opening paragraph of "The Yellow Wallpaper", the protagonist-narrator says she and her husband had hired a "colonial mansion, a hereditary estate", as if the two adjectives were synonymous.[63] By her tendency to assimilate differences, Jane forgets that there were other women before her who might have suffered not only sexism but also racism and other multiple oppressions, such as the experience of being colonized. Furthermore, she would like to see the "yellow woman" of the wallpaper "out of all the windows at once".[64] This reveals a further splitting of the I/eye as well as anxiety for a limitless optical perspective – could she ever see/define all women from where she stands? This kind of gender approach has been criticized for erasing the differences among

---

[58] *Ibid.*, 28-29, 40.
[59] *Ibid.*, 25, 26.
[60] Charlotte Perkins Gilman, *The Dress of Women: A Critical Introduction to the Symbolism and Sociology of Clothing* (1915), Westport, CT: Greenwood Press, 2002.
[61] Gilman, "The Yellow Wallpaper", 40, 42.
[62] *Ibid.*, 37.
[63] *Ibid.*, 24.
[64] *Ibid.*, 38.

women. The protagonist's desire to capture the woman underneath the
wallpaper resembles that of first-wave feminism, which implicitly
defined woman mainly as white, middle-class, educated, and
heterosexual. I wish to encourage a dialogical reading of "The Yellow
Wallpaper" in order to avoid a merging of white feminist
consciousnesses that would simply repeat old mistakes. I am sure that
Gilman, who was keen on didacticism, would agree that the lessons of
the past can help us to lay the foundations for a better future. Whereas
"Wallpaper" starts with "It is very seldom", it ends with "time!".[65]
Related to this, temporal references are quite numerous throughout the
story: "night(s)" appears fourteen times, "time(s)" thirteen, "hour(s)"
and "week(s)" six times each, "daytime" four times, "month(s)" twice,
"years" and "the Fourth of July" once each, and so forth.[66] Susan
Lohafer has written that the clash of "The expected patterns of a man-
made *kronos* ... with *kairos* of individual moral or biological [or, I
would add, feminist] maturity ... is the essence of the ... American
short story".[67] Finally, in "The Yellow Wallpaper", Gilman might be
telling us, it is time to change genres (imaginary classifications, social
parameters) in order to change genders. But this might be only one of
its hybrid messages.

Given the hybridity of Gilman's story, it seems difficult for any
critic to sustain one single reading of it. Through the authorial
narrator-reader relationship, we learn that there are actually "many
women" in the wallpaper, whose color is not just yellow but also
"orange ... [and] sulphur".[68] All these colors point to women's
genders, races, ethnicities, national/clan origins, and political/religious
beliefs, among other differences. One can easily find an analogy
between "The Yellow Wallpaper" and the history of the feminist
movement. Thus, it has been noted that Gilman's "feminism was
inextricably rooted in the white supremacism of 'civilization'
[discourse]".[69] Recently, Gayatri Chakravorty Spivak has denounced

---

[65] *Ibid.*, 24, 42.

[66] *Ibid.*, 25, 30.

[67] Susan Lohafer, *Coming to Terms with the Short Story*, Baton Rouge: Louisiana
State University Press, 1983, 133.

[68] Gilman, "The Yellow Wallpaper", 38, 26.

[69] Louise Michele Newman, *White Women's Rights: The Racial Origins of Feminism
in the United States*, New York: Oxford University Press, 1999, 134. Actually, one
can learn about the xenophobic attitudes of first-wave feminism through Gilman's
own articles: "Is America Too Hospitable?" (1923), in *Charlotte Perkins Gilman: A*

the "inbuilt colonialism of First-World feminism toward the Third".[70] My feminist dialogic reading of the many colors of the women of Gilman's "The Yellow Wallpaper" sympathizes with contemporary feminists' critique of "the production of the 'third world woman' as a singular monolithic subject."[71] From Jane's mistaken way of reading, readers are to learn that, instead of scrutinizing the other, we have the ethical duty of listening to him or her. From a Third World perspective, the yellow woman appears literally more trapped than the white woman by the patriarchal (wall)paper. In all, "The Yellow Wallpaper" comprises more than one gender, one genre, one voice, one ending. Above all, the story encourages us to reinvent both genres and genders. It is the reader's feminist dialogical responsibility to read Gilman's dialogization of the short story as leading toward the hybridity and proliferation of genders.

Non-fiction Reader, ed. Larry Ceplair, New York: Columbia University Press, 1999, 288-95, and "A Suggestion on the Negro Problem", *American Journal of Sociology*, I/1 (July 1908), 78-85.

[70] Spivak cited in Julia Watson, "Unspeakable Differences: The Politics of Gender in Lesbian and Heterosexual Women's Autobiographies", in *De/Colonizing the Subject: The Politics of Gender in Women's Autobiography*, eds Sidonie Smith and Julia Watson, Minneapolis: University of Minnesota Press, 1992, 147.

[71] Chandra Talpade Mohanty, "Under Western Eyes. Feminist Scholarship and Colonial Discourses", in *Women, Culture and Society: A Reader*, eds Barbara J. Balliet and Susana Fried, Dubuque, IA: Kendall Hunt, 1992, 231.

SHORT NARRATIONS IN A LETTER FRAME: CASES OF GENRE HYBRIDITY IN POSTCOLONIAL LITERATURE IN PORTUGUESE

REBECA HERNÁNDEZ

Questions of definition and genre seem to be crucial elements in a great majority of the studies that deal with short story theory.[1] Other essential issues for debate include short stories' experimental and borderline functions within the field of literature and/or their social environment.[2] Also central to this point seems to be the subject of orality, which is often considered a predecessor to both traditional and modern short stories, closely linked to their actual development and change.[3] This essay takes these ideas one step further and argues that in certain literary contexts letters may operate as if they were short stories, understood in Vítor Manuel de Aguiar e Silva's terms as a brief narration mainly characterized by a high concentration of time and space.[4] Examples have been found in the work of three postcolonial authors from African Portuguese-speaking countries who opt for the conventional format of the letter to recount marginal experiences in an experimental way that is close to orality. These literary writings in letter form are the short story "Rosita até morrer" (1971) by the Mozambican writer Luís Bernardo Honwana; the poem

---

This study is part of a research project funded by the Regional Ministry of Culture of the Autonomous Government of Castile and Leon (ref. number SA012A10-1).
[1] Charles May, "Chekhov and the Modern Short Story", in *The New Short Stories,* ed. Charles May, Athens: Ohio University Press, 1994, 199-217; W.S. Penn, "The Tale as Genre in Short Fiction", in *ibid.*, 44-55.
[2] Norman Friedman, "Recent Short Story Theories: Problems in Definition", in *Short Story Theory at a Crossroads*, eds Susan Lohafer and Jo Ellyn Clarey, Baton Rouge: Louisiana State University Press, 1989, 13-31.
[3] Mary Louise Pratt, *Imperial Eyes: Travel Writing and Transculturation*, London: Routledge, 1992, 6.
[4] Vítor Manuel de Aguiar e Silva, *Teoría de la Literatura*, trans. Valentín García Yebra, Madrid: Gredos, 1986, 242.

"Carta de um contratado" (1961) by António Jacinto, from Angola; and a letter within the novel *Chiquinho* (1947) by Baltasar Lopes, from Cape Verde. I will show that, irrespective of the genre these letters adopt (narrative, lyric, etc.), they share a number of formal and functional conditions which in all the cases analyzed affect the reader in the same way the short story does. My argument supports Penn's claim that "the short story has genres of its own invention",[5] as well as the theories of other critics who see no strong boundaries between the short story and other presumably different genres, such as the prose poem, the lyric,[6] the essay,[7] and the letter.[8]

Postcolonial literature in Portuguese bears many of the characteristics that according to Mary Louise Pratt favor the production of short stories as an experimental form of narration.[9] As was generally the case with the literatures produced in the former colonies, postcolonial literature in Portuguese was one of the subversive artistic responses practiced and developed in the hybrid societies of the new evolving nations during the process of decolonization, when authors determinedly used their powerful inherited oral tradition as intellectual weaponry in combination with their acquired written literary practice of Portuguese and Western influence. Hybridity is an important factor in postcolonial literatures, as it results from the capacity of the new emergent cultures to integrate social, political, cultural, ideological, and even idiosyncratic features from the two communities that are in contact. The discourse these societies produce thus reflects the existing tension between the autochthonous and dominant cultures and the need to overcome it. Pratt talks of these dual realities as "contact zones" and sees in them "the space of colonial encounters, the space in which peoples geographically and historically separated come into contact with each other and establish ongoing relations, usually involving conditions of coercion, radical inequality, and intractable conflict".[10]

---

[5] Penn, "The Tale as Genre in Short Fiction", 44.

[6] John Gerlach, *Toward the End: Closure and Structure in the American Short Story*, Tuscaloosa: University of Alabama Press, 1985.

[7] Douglas Hesse, "A Boundary Zone: First-Person Short Stories and Narrative Essays", in *Short Story Theory at a Crossroads*, 85-105.

[8] Allan H. Pasco, "On Defining Short Stories", in *The New Short Stories*, 114-30.

[9] Mary Louise Pratt, "The Short Story: The Long and the Short of It", in *ibid.*, 104.

[10] Pratt, *Imperial Eyes*, 6.

Bhabha interprets the hybrid reality of postcolonial nations as a more autonomous third space where "new sites are always being opened up". He notes that these new sites are independent of the national and colonial cultures even if they draw from them, and says that "if you keep referring those new sites to old principles, then you are not able to participate in them fully and productively and creatively".[11] The emphasis Bhabha places on creativity and newness as characteristic of postcolonial hybrid cultures coincides with Pratt's remarks on the fact that in some parts of the world "the short story [is] being used to introduce new regions or groups into an established national literature, or into an emerging national literature in the process of decolonization". He is also in agreement with her general argument that the short story "is often the genre used to introduce new (and possibly stigmatized) subject matters into the literary arena".[12] In broad terms, both assertions are true of postcolonial literature in Portuguese, especially if we take into account the vast and extremely rich field of Portuguese-language short stories and look at their experimental quality.

As I have shown elsewhere, one of the main resources African writers have for constructing a social and literary identity and resisting the dominant colonial power pertains to decisions regarding language and linguistic choices.[13] As Loflin rightly points out, in colonized societies Africans are superior to their monolingual white oppressors because the Africans not only speak their own national languages but, as a rule, are also able to communicate in the European language of the colonists.[14] In this way, marks of orality associated with the autochthonous culture become an essential feature of postcolonial literary discourse, which is plurilingual in the great majority of cases, even when those works are highly normative and closer to the Western tradition. African writers frequently use monologue or

---

[11] Homi K. Bhabha, "The Third Space: Interview with Homi Bhabha", in *Identity, Community, Culture, Difference*, ed. Jonathan Rutherford, London: Lawrence and Wishart, 1990, 216.

[12] Pratt, "The Short Story", 104.

[13] Rebeca Hernández, *Traducción y postcolonialismo: Procesos culturales y lingüísticos en la narrativa postcolonial de lengua portuguesa*, Granada: Comares, 2007, 30-51.

[14] Christine Loflin, "Multiple Narrative Frames in R.R.R. Dhlomo's 'Juwawa'", in *The Postmodern Short Story: Forms and Issues*, eds Farhat Iftekharrudin *et al.*, Westport, CT: Praeger, 2003, 226.

dialogue and even narration to introduce representations of their more or less hybrid spoken language in their written texts, thus fusing orality and literacy in a way that Pratt again associates with the short story. She says: "The short story provides not just the 'small' place for experimentation, but also a genre where oral and nonstandard speech, popular and regional culture, and marginal experience, have some tradition of being at home, and the form best-suited to reproducing the length of most oral speech events."[15]

Within the framework that the short story (as the literary counterpart of traditional storytelling) opens up for experimentation, the letter emerges as a highly suitable narrative strategy to combine orality and literacy, as it has the capacity to convey a considerable amount of information formally enclosed in a distinctively separate text, and to present an action as a completed whole. The letter offers the reader all the information intended in a self-contained independent unit and concedes narrative autonomy to the character/speaker. As Silva remarks, the epistolary technique completely eliminates the narrative and descriptive part that corresponds to the novelist, for it is the characters themselves who narrate the action as it progresses, and they do so in their own voice and the first person.[16] In general, short story theoreticians include letters among the many variants that should be taken into account when stories, long or short, are considered.[17] However, the analysis of the letter as a narrative fictional entity in the postcolonial texts we are studying has shown that the letter, as an autonomous narrative unit, not only incorporates the specific properties of the genre – that is, orality, marginality, and short-storyness – but also helps to pass these properties on to other related genres, such as the novel and the lyrical poem.

Of the three cases mentioned above, Luís Bernardo Honwana's short story "Rosita, até morrer" is closest to the canonical expectations of the short story. Written between 1964 and 1967 while the author was a political prisoner in Mozambique, this story takes the form of a two-page letter that Rosita, the illiterate protagonist, dictates to someone named Chico Mandlate. The letter is intended for Manuel, a man who, wanting to become an *assimilado* (a status that allowed black men to enjoy the social and cultural benefits of the Portuguese

---

[15] Pratt, "The Short Story", 108.
[16] Aguiar e Silva, *Teoria de la Literatura*, 229.
[17] Randall Jarrell, "Stories", in *The New Short Stories*, 9.

nationality), left for the city with another woman and abandoned Rosita when she was expecting her baby girl. Unlike other, more conventional works by this author, "Rosita, até morrer" is written not in normative Portuguese, but in a pidginized version of Portuguese that incorporates syntactic structures, lexical items, and intonation patterns from Bantu languages, especially Ronga. This is a significant point for a writer, bilingual in Ronga and Portuguese, who defends translating his characters' national languages into standard Portuguese in order to preserve their psychological profile and their full expressive capacity.[18] Besides "Rosita", Honwana has published only a collection of short stories, *Nós matámos o Cão-Tinhoso*, a classic in Mozambican literature and a turning point in the narrative tradition of that country. *Nós matámos o Cão-Tinhoso* was the first prose work written by an African in Mozambique, and as Russel Hamilton observes, it was considered subversive at the time of publication in 1964, mainly because it was seen as a serious attempt to bring down social and cultural barriers.[19] The importance of Honwana's work in the Mozambican society of the moment is evidenced by the fact that it was soon translated into English and in 1969 was published in South Africa under the title *We Killed Mangy-Dog*. All of the stories in this collection are written in standard Portuguese, with limited use of other Mozambican national languages (Ronga, Swazi, Fangalô, Shangaan) to reflect the multilinguality underlying the social reality represented in this fiction.[20]

By choosing the letter format for "Rosita, até morrer", Honwana not only endorses some of the traits associated with short story writing but actually intensifies some of the features that make this narrative mode an experimental literary area. First, he succeeds in presenting the story as markedly oral. This is masterfully achieved by the fact that the letter is being dictated rather than written by the protagonist. This apparently insignificant detail nevertheless enables the introduction of what Pratt considers "another consistent trend in the short story, ranging from the incorporation of oral-colloquial speech

---

[18] Michel Laban, *Moçambique: Encontro com escritores*, Porto: Fundação Eng. António de Almeida, 1998, II, 675.

[19] Russel G. Hamilton, *Literatura africana, literatura necessária II – Moçambique, Cabo Verde, Guiné-Bissau, São Tomé e Príncipe*, Lisbon: Ed. 70, 1983, 50.

[20] João Ferreira, "O traço moçambicano na narrativa de Luís Bernardo Honwana", in *Les littératures africaines de langue portugaise: Actes du Colloque International*, Lisbon: Fundação Calouste Gulbenkian, 1984, 374.

forms in the language of narration … to instances where the whole
text takes the form of represented speech, often a first person narration
in an oral setting".[21] Thus, the language used in "Rosita" has marked
signs of phonological, morphological, lexical, and syntactic hybridity
that are effective and realistic representations of the character's
sociocultural condition, as can be seen in the examples below, all
taken from Saúte's edition of the story.[22] The translation provided is
by Richard Bartlett, done in collaboration with the author Luís
Bernardo Honwana and published in 2000 as part of a collection of
African stories edited by Stephen Gray.[23]

Examples 1 to 4 show the influence of the phonological system of
the national language Ronga on the phonological system of
Portuguese, which affects sibilants and aspects of nasality as well as
the length of vowels and diphthongs:

1. Eu não esquence mas eu já nem zanga nem nada.

[I not forget but I still not angry or anything.]

2. Mulher çimilado quema os cabelo, veste çapato com vestida bonita.

[Ssimilated woman burns the hair, puts shoes with beautiful dress.]

3. Não tem fiticero.

[There is no witchcraft.]

4. Depois você vai tembora quando não gosta ficar aqui fazer
machamba.

[Afterwards you go then when you don't like to stay here to make
machamba.]

There are also cases of morphological distortion, such as absence
of genre, number, and person agreement, as can be seen in examples 5
to 8 below:

---

[21] Pratt, "The Short Story", 107.
[22] Luís Bernardo Honwana, "Rosita, até morrer", in *As mãos dos pretos: Antologia do
conto moçambicano*, ed. Nelson Saúte, Lisbon: Dom Quixote, 2001, 171-73.
[23] Luís Bernardo Honwana, "Rosita, until Death", in *The Picador Book of African
Stories*, ed. Stephen Gray, London: Picador, 2000, 199-201.

5. Sorita com Matilda com as outra manda os cumprimento também, elas está boa obrigado.

[Sorita with Matilda with those other sends greeting too, she are good thankyou.]

6. Os homem é maluco.

[The mens is mad.]

7. Chegou um dia eu acordou contente, vendeu um saca de mandoinha, comprou vestida bonita com taralatana com çapato incarnado com chepéu para tua filha!

[There came one day I woke up happy, I sold a sack of peanut, bought beautiful clothe with taralatana petticoat, with red shoe with hat for your daughter!]

8. As vez eu pensa voce foste nos curandero ranjar remeido para eu gostar vocé.

[Sometime I thinks you went in the witchdoctors to get medicine so that I am liking you.]

Equally effective is the introduction of lexical elements from Bantu languages into the discourse in Portuguese. These lexical items serve to open a narrative metonymic space for the autochthonous culture in the colonizing culture represented by the dominant language,[24] as they contain direct references to aspects of the Mozambican way of life. Thus, *lobolo* (9) refers to the dowry the bridegroom gives the bride's family, *machamba* (10) to a labor field; *machimbomba* (12) is the Ronga word for bus; *ucanhi* (11) is a kind of drink; and *xingombela* (11) a dance:

9. Elas faz pôco, eu sabe é assim quando mulher tem disgraça, sai uma filha e homem não faz lobolo.

[They do littel, I know it is like that when a woman has disgrace, a child comes and the man doesn't make lobolo.]

---

[24] See Bill Ashcroft, Gareth Griffiths, and Helen Tiffin, *Post-Colonial Studies: The Key Concepts*, London: Routledge, 2000, 134.

10. Eu fez machamba grande de milho com fijão com mandoinha, com mapila.

[I made big machamba of mealie with beans with peanut, with mapila.]

11. Beber ucanhi ... dançar xingombela.

[Drink ucanhi ... dance the xingombela.]

12. Quando vocé quer vir vocé escreve carta, da chófer de machimbomba de Olivera.

[When you want to come you write letter, give the driver of Oliveira (*sic*) bus.]

The recourse to hybrid language in Rosita's dramatized monologue is a clear sign of orality, but it is also an indicator of marginality. Her pidginized Portuguese has the ability to put focus on the weakness of her social and cultural position, for the writer has chosen for his protagonist and narrator a formal mode that makes her illiteracy in the colonizing language even more visible. The emphasis is therefore put not only on the actual content of the letter she is dictating but also and most especially on the marginality of her situation.

Although "Rosita, até morrer" is quite short and takes the form of a letter, there is no doubt that it belongs in the short story genre. It was first published in the magazine *Vértice Coimbra* in 1971 and more recently appeared in Nelson Saúte's anthology of Mozambican short stories *As mãos dos pretos* (2000). In this sense, Rosita's letter perfectly suits Penn's basic criterion for genre classification. Following Jonathan Culler, Penn argues that the class or category to which literary works are assigned depends on the readers' expectations when first confronted with a given literary piece. Thus external issues such as "reviews, the dustjacket, previous knowledge of the particular author, or thumbing through the volume in the bookstore" are, according to Penn, defining factors for genre categorization.[25] With regard to its content, "Rosita, até morrer" also complies with May's conviction that the tendency in stories is to focus on "a single situation in which everyday reality is broken up by a

---

[25] Jonathan Culler cited in Penn, "The Tale as Genre in Short Fiction", 44-45.

crisis",[26] or with the opinion of Pasco, who affirms that "for a short story to succeed, the author must overcome the restraints of limited length and communicate not a segment, a tattered fragment, but a world".[27]

Less conventional is the letter encountered in Baltasar Lopes' work: this text cannot be considered a fully orthodox short story, for it is a letter contained within a novel. However, the effect it produces on readers, along with its formal and functional characteristics, are very similar to those found in Honwana's "Rosita". In his novel *Chiquinho*, Baltasar Lopes tells the story of a Cape Verdean boy whose childhood is spent in the small village of Caleijão on the island of São Nicolau. It portrays the poverty of the region, the tragic conditions of the peasants, and the protagonist's relation with his family. *Chiquinho*, published in 1947, is, like "Rosita", a key work in the literary development of Lopes' nation, as it is considered the first modern Cape Verdean novel. In relation to those questions of genre definition that are often at stake when short stories are discussed, it is quite significant that the chapters entitled "Bibia" and "Infância" were previously published in the literary magazine *Claridade*, which had been cofounded a few years earlier by Lopes and his friends. The novel is mostly written in normative Portuguese, like Honwana's collection of stories *Nós matámos o Cão-Tinhoso*, but midway through it, at the beginning of Chapter 29, there is a letter that shares some of the characteristics of Honwana's "Rosita, até morrer".

The letter, sent from America by a Cape Verdean emigrant, is addressed to a secondary character, the protagonist's aunt, Tudinha, who needs Chiquinho's assistance to read the missive because she, like Rosita, is illiterate. The letter informs Tudinha of the death of her son in a machinery-related accident at the factory where he worked. It gives details of the funeral, tells her that there was another boy from São Nicolau who died in the same accident, and mentions the impossibility of sending her son's belongings at the time. This is the complete text:

> Minha querida irmã do meu coração Gertrudes Ana Duarte, S. Nicolau, Caleijão

---

[26] May, "Chekhov and the Modern Short Story", 201.
[27] Pasco, "On Defining Short Stories", 127.

Eu peguei nesta pena para fazer estas duas regras e eu desejo que estas encontrarão você numa boa saúde na companhia dos meninos, *igualmente meu desejo* e eu graças a Deus estou bom. Tudinha você ponha consolança no seu coração e eu desejo você uma consolança e resignação na vontade de Deus. Tudinha *triste novidade* que eu tenho para *você é* teu filho Manuel que faleceu no dia 3 de Novembro, derivado de uma maquina que pegou ele e matou na fábrica. *Nós tudo ficou muito triste*, coitado de Manuel era um bom moço e *nós tudo tinha* com ele uma boa vivência. Tudinha, teu filho teve um *fanoral* bonito e *todos amigos* de Betfete *acompanhou* ele até *no* cemitério. Tudinha eu não mando você agora a mala do *falicido* porque *conse* disse que papel dele não está ainda tudo claro. Faleceu também *outrum* rapaz de S. Nicolau e ele não era da nossa ribeira. Tudinha eu não mando você uma lembrança porque agorinha assim não está *na jeito*. Tudinha eu tenho vontade de ir para Cabo Verde mas não estou na altura *porque serviço* está escasso. Abença que *eu manda* meus sobrinhos. Recomendação para todos aqueles que perguntar por mim. António Bia já está perto de ir para S. Nicolau. Uma boa consolança que *eu deseja* você no seu coração. Nada mais deste teu irmão

António João Duarte[28]

Chiquinho has not been translated into English. Following Richard Bartlett's model in his translation of Honwana's story, "Rosita, until Death", I will attempt here to translate Baltasar Lopes' letter into nonstandard English so as to preserve the linguistic identity of the original, with its nonstandard Portuguese. I follow the criteria of theoreticians like Lawrence Venuti, who defends "a theory and practice of translation that resists dominant target-language cultural values so as to signify the linguistic and cultural difference of the foreign text".[29] The point is to avoid, in Gayatri Chakravorty Spivak's words, "a betrayal of the democratic ideal into the law of the strongest". As she says, "This happens when all the literature in the Third World gets translated into a sort of with-it translatese, so that the literature by a woman in Palestine begins to resemble, in the feel of its prose, something by a man in Taiwan".[30] Within the linguistic

---

[28] Baltasar Lopes, *Chiquinho*, Lisbon: Prelo Editora, 1970, 104-5 (emphases added).
[29] Lawrence Venuti, *The Translator's Invisibility*, London: Routledge, 23.
[30] Gayatri Chakravorty Spivak, *Outside in the Teaching Machine*, London: Routledge, 1993, 182.

configuration of the novel, the letter sent by this Cape Verdean émigré to his uneducated sister is atypical:

> My dear sister of my heart Gertrudes Ana Duarte, S. Nicolau, Caleijão
>
> I have taken this pen to do these two lines and I wish you are in good health in the company of the children, equally my desire and I am well Thanks God.
>
> Tudinha you put relief into your heart and I wish you a relief and resignation in the will of God. Tudinha sad news I have for you are your son Manuel who died the third of November, due to a machine he took and killed him in the factory. Every of us became very sad, poor Manuel was a good boy and every of us had a good rapport with him. Tudinha, your son had a beautiful foneral and all friends from Betfete accompanied him onto the cementery. Tudinha I am not sending to you now the decesed's suitcase because conse said his paper is not clear yet. Anather boy from S. Nicolau died as well and he was not from our riverside. Tudinha I am not sending to you a reminder because now is not a good idea. Tudinha I want to go to Cape Verde but it is not the right time because service is sparse. A blessing that I sends my nephews and nieces. References to all those who may ask about me. António Bia is going to S. Nicolau soon. A good relief that I wishes in your heart. Nothing more from this your brother
>
> António João Duarte

In contrast to the rest of the novel, which, again, is written in standard Portuguese, the letter shows marks of hybrid oral language at grammatical and lexical levels. There are, for example, cases of subject/verb disagreement, as in "todos amigos de Betfete acompanhou", "eu manda", "eu deseja", "Nós tudo ficou muito triste", "nós tudo tinha"; the absence of determiners, as in "triste novidade", "todos amigos", "porque serviço"; the omission of connectors, as in "você é"; or nonstandard prepositions, as in "no cemitério" or "na jeito", which also shows genre disagreement. At the lexical level, there are inconsistencies in the spelling of the words "fanoral", "falicido", and "outrum", as well as the inclusion of a term, "conse", that does not belong to the Portuguese lexicon. Even at the pragmatic level, there is an inappropriate use of conventional formulas, as in "igualmente meu desejo e eu graças a Deus estou bom". These are all traces of orality that serve to differentiate the letter from the rest of the novel, giving it a high degree of narrative autonomy and converting it into an experimental literary zone, in true anticipation of the linguistically hybrid literature that would be produced later by other Cape Verdean authors who also wrote in Portuguese, but with much heavier use of dialectal forms and creole language.[31]

It can be said, therefore, that the letter in *Chiquinho* shares some of the basic characteristics that critics attribute to short stories in general, and more particularly to postcolonial short stories. And this is so not only with regard to its experimental use of the language, but also with regard to its content. The letter in Baltasar Lopes' novel informs us briefly and densely about a critical situation. It is presented as a self-contained episode, thematically distinct from the rest of the novel, and it is about the marginal experience of Cape Verdean emigrants in America. In this sense, the letter António João Duarte sends to his sister Tudinha may be described, to use Bal's narratological terms,[32] as a subtext: that is, an independent secondary text embedded within the larger text that carries additional information and explains aspects of the main story but is not central to it.

The capacity that the letter shows to acquire this condition of "storyness" may actually be explained using two complementary cognitive perspectives. Hunter Brown applies a discourse analysis approach to the investigation of short story comprehension and processing, and demonstrates with her analysis that genre categorization is firmly connected to readers' expectations. In this sense, she agrees with Penn, although she follows a totally different line of reasoning. Hunter Brown concentrates on readers' expectations in terms of framework activation and preexisting schematic structures. Drawing from the classic research done in the Sixties and Seventies on narrative schemata and story grammars, she says that "readers' uses of schematic structures are related to the primacy effect. Once people have activated a particular framework for meaning, they are more likely to apprehend following material if it is intelligible within

---

[31] See Manuel Ferreira, *Literaturas africanas de expressão portuguesa*, Lisbon: Instituto de Cultura Portuguesa, 1977.

[32] Mieke Bal, *Narratology: Introduction to the Theory of Narrative* (1985), trans. Christine van Boheemen, Toronto, Buffalo, and London: University of Toronto Press, 2009, 60.

the frame."[33] Accordingly, when the reader of Baltasar Lopes' *Chiquinho* encounters Duarte's letter within the novel, s/he activates a frame that does not necessarily have the same properties of the global narrative frame that functions for the rest of the narration. The letter schema, which the reader easily recognizes from previous personal and cultural experience, thus becomes embedded in the ongoing narrative plot, establishing a momentarily separate and self-directed frame. What is more, due to the formulaic conventions that encase the schematic structure of letters, the opening and closing markers, which are usually identified as fundamental criteria for triggering the sense of storyness in preclosure theory,[34] automatically turn into indicators of textual autonomy. In the case we are examining here, Lopes exploits these frame characteristics to introduce the experimental variations such as marks of orality through the use of hybrid language, specific account of a concrete marginal episode, and so on, which have been listed as defining features of postcolonial short stories. As Lohafer says, "Storying is a form of cognitive management. Closure is the proof that storying has happened".[35] Both issues may be said to be clearly at work when the letter frame is activated in the reader's mind, as the beginning automatically anticipates not only the telling of a certain story but also the end of it.

The coexistence of the novel and letter frames in *Chiquinho*, plus the linguistic and thematic autonomy of the latter with respect to the former, bring back into focus the old question of the fragility of boundaries in genre distinctions. A good example of this issue is provided by Brander Matthews, the first critic (after Poe) to discuss the short story in the North American theoretical context. In 1884, Matthews stated that "the short-story should not be void or without form, but its form may be whatever the author please", and Matthews claimed for the author "an absolute liberty of choice". Giving a quite

---

[33] Suzanne Hunter Brown, "Discourse Analysis and the Short Story", in *Short Story Theory at a Crossroads*, 219.

[34] See Susan Lohafer, *Coming to Terms with the Short Story*, Baton Rouge: Louisiana State University Press, 1983, 42-51; "Preclosure and Story Processing", in *Short Story Theory at a Crossroads*, 249-75; and Per Winther, "Closure and Preclosure as Narrative Grid in Short Story Analysis: Some Methodological Suggestions", in *The Art of Brevity: Excursions in Short Fiction Theory and Analysis*, eds Per Winther *et al.*, Columbia: University of South Carolina Press, 2004, 57-69.

[35] Susan Lohafer, *Reading for Storyness*, Baltimore: The John Hopkins University Press, 2003, 55.

exhaustive account of the many possible forms the short story might adopt, he said:

> It may be a personal narrative, like Poe's "Descent into the Maelstrom" or Mr. Hale's "My Double, and how he Undid me"; it may be impersonal, like Mr. Frederick B. Perkins's "Devil-Puzzlers" or Colonel J.W. De Forest's "Brigade Commander"; it may be a conundrum, like Mr. Stockton's insoluble query, the "Lady or the Tiger?" *it may be "A Bundle of Letters", like Mr. Henry James's story, or "A Letter and a Paragraph", like Mr. Bunner's (1994: 77); it may be a medley of letters and telegrams and narrative,* like Mr. Aldrich's "Margery Daw"; it may be cast in any one of these forms, or in a combination of all of them, or in a wholly new form, if haply such may yet be found by diligent search.[36]

Addressing the many formal variations that stories may exhibit, and founding his argument on a much more recent theoretical perspective, Randall Jarrell insists that "there are many more sorts of stories than there are sizes. Epics; ballads; historical or biographical or autobiographical narratives, letters, diaries; myths, fairy tales, fables; dreams, daydreams"; he also mentions "fiction in verse".[37] Penn, for his part, believes that "the short story has genres of its own invention" and states that "the terms we use to talk about it should be derived from the story form itself, not imported from other prose forms such as the novel or the novella".[38] Furthermore, in his article "The Margins of Narrative", John Gerlach poses "the question of whether stories can ever become poems", and after carefully considering a range of cases, he concludes that "the line between story and poem is … a rather thin one". He claims that "length and fictionality are not sufficient in themselves to imply story"; he argues that "stories, like all complete, satisfying forms such as essays and poems, exhibit point".[39] Silva agrees with the idea that tales and poems are closely related, since they both work within the field of suggestion.[40]

---

[36] Brander Matthews, "The Philosophy of the Short-Story", in *The New Short Story Theories*, 77 (emphases added).
[37] Jarrell, "Stories", 9.
[38] Penn, "The Tale as Genre in Short Fiction", 43.
[39] Gerlach, *Toward the End*, 80-84.
[40] Aguiar e Silva, *Teoría de la Literatura*, 243.

The proximity between short stories and poems is of relevance to my claim that letters work as experimental narrative units regardless of the genre they adopt. Such is the case with the third example from postcolonial literature in Portuguese that I want to explore: it too turns to the letter format to express the harshness and difficulties of the colonization experience, but this time the letter takes the form of a beautiful poem entitled "Carta de um contratado". Its author is António Jacinto, an Angolan poet who also wrote short stories under the pseudonym Orlando Távora. Jacinto shares with many other African writers – for example, Luís Bernardo Honwana – a life of creative literary subversion, political persecution, and active compromise with his country, Angola, where, after gaining independence from Portugal, he acted as Minister of Education and Secretary of State for Cultural Affairs. The poem is a love letter written by a "contratado", a man hired to work in the labor fields under extremely severe working conditions that were rather similar to slavery. In this case, and given the overriding formal characteristics of poems, the letter frame is perceived by the reader as physically secondary to that imposed by the poetic structure and has to be activated explicitly in the title and in the first line of the composition, which begins:

> Eu queria escrever-te uma carta
> Amor
>
> [I wanted to write you a letter
> my love]

As for its linguistic form, the poem is written in normative Portuguese except for the inclusion of some words in Kimbundu, the national language of Angola, a choice that at the time the poem was written could be considered subversive, because it functioned as an act of resistance and noncompliance.[41] For example, in these lines praising the beauty of the beloved through a series of comparisons describing her attributes, the second terms come from the autochthonous language and serve to anchor the poem in the hybrid reality of the two lovers:

---

[41] See Hernández, *Traducción y postcolonialismo*, 30.

> dos teus lábios vermelhos como *tacula*
> dos teus cabelos negros como *dilôa*
> dos teus olhos doces como *macongue*

> [of your lips red as henna
> of your hair black as mud
> of your eyes sweet as honey]

A similar effect of identity differentiation (at a time when the dominant culture was still that of the colonizer) is found in the verses that describe the environment:

> que recordasse nossos tempos na *capopa*
> nossas noites no capim
> que recordasse a sombra que nos caía dos *jambos*

> [that would recall the days in our haunts
> our nights lost in the long grass
> that would recall the shade falling on us from the plum trees]

The same phenomenon is present in the following stanza, where reference to the letter frame is again made explicit:

> uma carta que em todo o *Kilombo*
> outra a ela não tivesse merecimento ...

> [A letter to which in all Kilombo
> no other would stand comparison ...]

I have used the translation of the poem into English published in *The Penguin Book of Modern African Poetry* edited by Gerald Moore and Ulli Beier.

As in the texts by Luís Bernardo Honwana and Baltasar Lopes, the hybridity of the language António Jacinto uses in his poetic composition to represent the plurilingual and multicultural reality that surrounds him, in combination with his choice of the letter format, makes it possible for the poet to fuse orality and marginality with literacy and with the Western tradition, to which he brings new literary forms and meanings.

The last stanzas in Jacinto's poem once again deal with the subject of illiteracy:

Eu queria escrever-te uma carta ...
Mas ah meu amor, eu não sei compreender
por que é, por que é, por que é, meu bem
que tu não sabes ler
e eu – Oh! Desespero! – não sei escrever também.[42]

[I wanted to write you a letter ...
But oh my love, I cannot understand
why it is, why it is, why it is, my dear
that you cannot read
and I – Oh the hopelessness! – cannot write!]

In fact, this type of closure is a feature shared by all of the letters I have discussed here. Honwana's Rosita ends her letter to Manuel by saying:

Sou eu Rosa de teu coração que manda esta carta para teu coração. Chico Mandlate está escrever carta também manda os cumprimento. Chico não vai dizer ninguém coisa que escreveu para vocé.[43]

[In Bartlett's translation: It is me Rosa of your heart who sends this letter to your heart. Chico Mandlate is to write this letter also sends greeting. Chico not say to anyone things which written to you.]

And right beneath António João Duarte's letter, Tudinha rapidly sends for Chiquinho so that he can read to her what is said in the letter that arrived from America: "Nhá Tudinha mandou-me chamar a toda a pressa para lhe ler a carta que veio da América."[44] In view of this, it may be said that turning to the letter as a narrative choice among people who can neither read nor write ultimately reinforces Penn's observation that "with the presumption of communication, we may as well add the postulate that all genres of the short story communicate as if told or spoken".[45]

The emphasis put by all three writers on the characters' difficulties to express themselves in the language of the colonizer and to

---

[42] António Jacinto, "Carta de um contratado", in *Roteiro da literatura angolana*, ed. Carlos Ervedosa, Luanda: Edição da Sociedade Cultural de Angola, 1974, 74 (emphases added).
[43] Honwana, "Rosita, até morrer", 173.
[44] Lopes, *Chiquinho*, 105.
[45] Penn, "The Tale as Genre in Short Fiction", 47.

understand writing helps to accomplish some of the literary functions that have been recognized as central in postcolonial stories. The recourse to a pidginized sort of language proves an efficient means to denounce social marginality. It also serves to demonstrate the literary power of orality and the existence of a fully distinct national identity that emerges from the blend between the dominant and dominated cultures. In the texts analyzed here, the letter frame functions as a vehicle for the narration of a singular and yet common experience, in a way that may be considered innovative for Western-based theoretical approaches, as it bridges the gap between genres by fusing oral storytelling, written narration, and lyrical poetry into one single epistolary form. The corollary is a creative literary work of high quality in which hybridity of genres goes hand in hand with hybridity of discourse. This artistic combination works as a forceful manifestation of a hybrid space and language that resists colonialism and results in a vivid literary representation of a plurilingual and multicultural society.

SHORT-STORYNESS AND EYEWITNESSING

María Jesús Hernáez Lerena

> Speech is the twin of my vision, it is unequal
>   to measure itself,
> It provokes me forever, it says sarcastically,
> Walt, you contain enough, why don't you let
>   it out then?
>
> Come now I will not be tantalized, you
>   conceive too much of articulation.[1]
>
> Yet the knowledge, the explanation, never
> quite fits the sight.[2]

Is reality amenable to storytelling?

Does the short story speak to us about human limitations with regards to comprehension even before we read one? Do readers approach a story with the semiconscious premonition that the writer will show that our relationship with life involves more dumb amazement than understanding? Reading short stories has inscribed this expectation in readers' memory, and a certain amount of familiarity with short story theory makes us aware that the short story's only compromise with readers is to stun us with the impact of a situation whose nature upsets our customary attachment to sequential patterning.[3] This situation, which exemplifies a contact or, rather, a clash with reality, does not necessarily rest on a spectacular or out-of-the-ordinary event; instead, the story confronts us, as life occasionally does, with an occurrence

---

[1] Walt Whitman, "Song of Myself", in *Leaves of Grass*, eds S. Bradley and H. Blodgett, New York: W.W. Norton, 1973, 55.

[2] John Berger, *Ways of Seeing*, London: BBC and Penguin Books, 1972, 7.

[3] See Gabriel García Márquez, *La bendita manía de contar*, Madrid: Ollero y Ramos Editores, 1988, 16.

against which no system of thought can protect us. The impact derives from our looking at something as if we were still untrained by speech. Our helplessness derives from the gap between a sight and our previous learning, and it metaphorically defines us (the characters, the readers) as witnesses looking at a reality that our eyes unwillingly register and our mind absorbs, but without being able to decode it.

Looking into reality would be a more appropriate way of describing our engagement with the novel: we have internalized the novel as a bearer of the comprehensiveness of life, no matter how much it might have swerved from a nineteenth-century canonized model; in the novel, time keeps moving in whatever direction, but in the short story, the writer seems to create an atemporal dimension of time, and once we step aside, the vision gained from within that framed space will remain the main axis of the narrative, however much it might be disturbed by the continuum of life.

Walter Benjamin and Susan Buck-Morss described a mental state where the individual, by looking at something other than himself, lets this otherness, usually inhospitable, invade his senses.[4] As a result of this saturation of the senses, the powers of thought are paralysed. This understanding of reality as shock was explored by Benjamin to explain how modern society has created artistic mechanisms and commodities (phantasmagoria) that protect people from the excessive energies of external stimuli and from the harshness of industrial societies. The creation of cushioned spaces in the professions and in art is further developed by Buck-Morss, who located the threat of bewilderment and pain in the relationship between man and the image. According to her, we possess a synaesthetic system through which the images we store in our memory get connected with external stimuli, creating an internal language that cannot be grasped in conceptual terms.[5] This language threatens to betray the language of reason, endangering its philosophic sovereignty. What is absorbed

---

[4] Walter Benjamin, "The Work of Art in the Age of Mechanical Reproduction" (1936), in *Illuminations*, ed. Hannah Arendt, trans. Harry Zohn, London: Fontana Press, 1992, 211-43; Susan Buck-Morss, "Aesthetics and Anaesthetics: Walter Benjamin's Artwork Essay Reconsidered", *October: Art, Theory, Criticism, Politics*, LXII (Autumn 1992), 3-42.

[5] See Cetin Sarikartal, "Shock, mirada y mimesis: La posibilidad de un enfoque performativo sobre la visualidad", in *Estudios visuales: La epistemología de la visualidad en la era de la globalización*, ed. Jose Luis Brea, Madrid: Ediciones Akal, 2005, 106.

unintentionally resists intellectual comprehension. This idea is strikingly similar to recurrent theorizations of the short story as a genre that baffles notions of knowledge as comprehension and instead confers climactic status on states of bewilderment, focusing on a paradigmatic encounter with strangeness.

Critics and writers have often claimed that the short story is a form of fiction that challenges knowledge, a genre which posits that an intelligible explanation of our experience is impossible and perhaps not even desirable.[6] But does the short story really address life only as an irresolvable case? My hypothesis here will be that this feeling of impotence may come from our impression that what the genre does is paradoxical: it tries to convey through words an experience for the reader only to see, to look at, without reconciling this experience with the presumed comforts of narrative. The short story seems to deprive the story of its capacity to penetrate reality by weaving and then displaying a rational continuum of causally interlocked occurrences. We can usually find this kind of causal explanation in short stories, but this account often turns out to be expendable in the face of our awareness that the story claims no possibility of forwardness or fluidity, that we are forever at the beginning, trapped by the physicality of a situation in which the underlying motives are not definable. This situation remains visibly there as an obstacle, but also as the core of the story; it may be presented at the beginning, middle, or end of the narrative, but it stays in our reading and after-reading as the most valuable bond we have with that short story, or, to put it another way, the only possible source of knowledge or truth that we have been granted.

I would like to single out this notion of visual shock and subsequent paralysis of rational thinking that Benjamin and Buck-

---

[6] Many critics have described the potential of the short story as one of challenge to knowledge or synthesis: Julio Cortázar, "Del cuento breve y sus alrededores", in *La casilla de los Morelli*, Barcelona: Tusquets, 1973, 113; John Bayley, *The Short Story: From Henry James to Elizabeth Bowen*, Brighton: Harvester Press, 1988, 26; Thomas M. Leitch, "The Debunking Rhythm of the American Short Story", in *Short Story Theory at a Crossroads*, eds Susan Lohafer and Jo Ellyn Clarey, Baton Rouge: Louisiana State University Press, 1989, 133; Charles E. May, "The Nature of Knowledge in Short Fiction", in *The New Short Story Theories*, ed. Charles May, Athens: Ohio University Press, 1994, 133, 135, 141; Michael Trussler, "Suspended Narratives: The Short Story and Temporality", in *Studies in Short Fiction*, XXXIII/4 (Fall 1996), 560.

Morss examined and relate it to another kind of literature: testimony literature. However, I will emphasize Buck-Morss' idea of the creation of an internal visual language – regarded as a cognitive activity which, although at odds with a more rational mode of thinking (based on the articulation of language and on distance), can be legitimately considered an active performance and not a stagnant, nonprogressive mode of observation.[7]

In this essay I will deal with the short story through the prism of its heightened dependence on the visual as a mode of consciousness that affects the reading experience structurally: all fiction strives to make the reader visualize, but the short story engages in the visual as an index to reality, the image itself containing the drama that creates the story, the conflict that stirs our imagination. Our position as readers, or the position of the character within the story, will be defined, therefore, as that of an onlooker, a witness, rather than as interpreter or "knower". My proposal is to consider the short story as a mode of truth that offers the realm of the merely visible as a valid form of cognition. That is, the short story conceives of reality as visible in a physical sense and often stops short at that visibility, without an attempt to expand this quality into other modes of thinking more akin to the consolations often provided by novelistic, biographical, or historical narrative, with their sustained incursions into the characters' lives and their implicit reassurance that life is a journey that can be verbalized by the author.

From this perspective, the short story becomes akin to another kind of literature, witness or testimony literature, for in the act of bearing witness the relationship between seeing and understanding is also posed as an acute central problem. It is surprising how the epistemology of testimony literature echoes our own conceptions and preconceptions of the short story at every step. Many kinds of writings are testimonial in a sense, but testimony writing and testimonial literature address the specific problems stemming from the relationship between the eye (a horrible sight, a crisis, a trauma) and the creation of narrative as survival. It dramatizes the acute need to express through narrative that which obstructs any attempt at explanation or rationalization. Testimony projects in the impact of the

---

[7] See Rudolf Arnheim, *Visual Thinking*, Berkeley and Los Angeles: University of California Press, 1969, 116-34, 226-53, for a theorization of visual perception as a form of cognition, as a reasoning of the senses.

sight a truth that can hardly be narrativized into story. Against the belief that the essence of testimony literature is historical and political, its function to record and report certain events that enlarge a shared historical narrative with a healing goal, Shoshana Felman, Dori Laub, and other critics show that the act of bearing witness always points at the impracticability of speech: "The imperative to tell the story of the Holocaust is inhabited by the impossibility of the telling" because what is there to be witnessed is a "cognitively dissonant" situation, a "situation with no cure".[8] I will revise the epistemology of witness literature in conjunction with that of the short story in an attempt to expand the prisms through which the short story can be examined.

These two modes of fiction will be temporarily brought together for a brief consideration of four Canadian short stories: Douglas Glover's "Dog Attempts to Drown Man in Saskatoon", Guy Vanderhaeghe's "The Watcher", Katherine Govier's "The Immaculate Conception Photography Gallery", and Barbara Gowdy's "Body and Soul".[9] Although my views on the short story are obviously grounded in a restricted corpus that forms my experience as short story reader (stories mainly by American and Canadian authors from the

---

[8] Shoshana Felman and Dori Laub, *Testimony: Crises of Witnessing in Literature, Psychoanalysis, and History*, New York: Routledge, 1992, 4-5, 78.

[9] The four stories selected for analysis come from established Canadian writers who have published short story collections as well as novels. Douglas Glover is the recipient of a Governor General's Award for his novel *Elle*, Fredericton, NB: Goose Lane, 2003, and his short story "Dog Attempts to Drown Man in Saskatoon" belongs to the collection *Dog Attempts to Drown Man in Saskatoon*, Vancouver: Talon Books, 1985, which received the Literary Press Group Writers Choice Award. His stories are frequently anthologized in *The Best American Short Stories*, *The Best Canadian Stories*, and *The New Oxford Book of Canadian Stories*. The title story from *Dog Attempts to Drown Man in Saskatoon* was anthologized, together with Guy Vanderhaeghe's "The Watcher", in *The Best of Canadian Fiction Magazine: Silver Anniversary Anthology*, ed. Geoff Hancock, Kingston, Ont.: Quarry Press, 1997, 85-119. Vanderhaeghe's story is the first one in the collection *Man Descending* (1982). His collection won the Governor General's Award for fiction in 1982 and also the Geoffrey Faber Memorial Prize in England. Barbara Gowdy has been the recipient of the Marian Engel Award and has been a finalist for the Giller Prize and the Governor General's Award for fiction. "Body and Soul" is the first story in the collection *We So Seldom Look on Love: Stories*, Toronto: Somerville House, 1992, 1-42. Katherine Govier's title story from the short story collection *The Immaculate Conception Photography Gallery*, Toronto: Vintage Canada, 1994, was a prize winner in the Canadian Broadcasting Company literary contest.

nineteenth century onwards, and also classic French and Russian stories), it is the reading of recent Canadian short stories that has compelled me to try to articulate this perspective. The issues I wish to illustrate here are theorized in different degrees of explicitness within these four stories, so they offer a workable field of textual evidence within the limits of an article. The stories present narrators or characters for whom the act of looking at things, either as accidental witnesses to enigmatic or anomalous occurrences (and people) or as a vocation, is central. The characters are called upon to produce testimony of what they have seen, but they refuse to re-arrange the visual information they have collected into any form of story; they adamantly insist on possessing the object they have looked at as a pure icon, devoid of any plausible interpretation. A shocking image, or several such images, will become the only index to their lives; they will discard any narrative interpretation (or manipulation) and will consider these images either as the literal reflection of their own – often disoriented – subjectivities or as an incontestable motivation for their reactions. These four short stories are by no means the only ones that foreground the unnerving nature of the collision between a perceiving mind and an upsetting event, often identified as the main focus of the short story in general. Needless to say, not all short stories in the world highlight the issues that concern me here with the same obsessive pursuit as the ones I include in my analysis. However, an awareness of the lack of match between what we receive through the sense of sight and the elaborations of discourse is somehow always present in our experience of short-storyness.

Testimony writing and the short story brought together
The idea of testimony, particularly of Holocaust writing and the Gulag, as both a literary and a nonliterary genre, is the result of recent attempts to examine the constraints that the historical facts of outrage and pain on a grand scale impose on language's alleged remedial qualities, that is, on its capacity to represent and heal. Although it may be initially assumed that testimony writing on the Holocaust represents the effort to use narrative as healing, explanations of testimony writing instead establish the collapse of narrative (or the crisis of the telling) as definitive in the constitution of the genre because the witness harbors an experience that clashes with all normal

sense.[10] My main sources are Shoshana Felman and Dori Laub, Ernst van Alphen, and Horace Engdahl,[11] who they provide useful insights into the epistemology of this kind of writing.

There are at least four traits that characterize testimony: (1) it is a narrative that expresses the impossibility of narrative performance; (2) it focuses on events that exceed rationalization or meaning; (3) it defines the subject, the perceiver, as an accidental witness; and (4) it defines narrative as insufficient. These four stances will be briefly discussed below.

As implied by Felman and Engdahl, testimony writing presents an absolute lack of epistemology, since it achieves coherence as a distinct kind of narrative by showing that there are insurmountable obstacles hindering our capacity to comprehend. Paradoxically, the impossibility of communication justifies the very writing: "it becomes itself not a simple statement but a speech act which repeats, performs its own meaning in resisting our grasp, in resisting our replicating or recuperative witnessing. It thus performs its own solitude: it puts into effect what cannot be understood, transmitted, in the mission of transmission of the witness."[12] Felman claims that certain actions that happened historically "exceed any substantialized significance", that they cannot be turned into a "totalizable account".[13] Engdahl claims that the persona of a witness includes "a withdrawal from ideological struggles",[14] that testimony does not teach or build up beliefs, and that it retains alien and incomprehensive traits. Testimony destroys the semblance of necessity, logical end, and meaning. The solitary burden of the witness becomes the burden of the story itself. If this is so, it is because the experience that testimony mainly addresses is horror – situations of exposure and vulnerability, acts that undermine our capacity for explanation. Even if narratives are undertaken with a curative goal in mind, the event itself hampers any step forward; it

---

[10] Felman warns that the concept of testimony is estranging and that "it is not simply what we thought we knew it was" (*Testimony*, 7).

[11] Ernest Van Alphen, *Caught by History: Holocaust Effects in Contemporary Art, Literature, and Theory*, Stanford, CA: Stanford University Press, 1997; *Witness Literature: Proceedings of the Nobel Centennial Symposium*, ed. Horace Engdahl, Singapore: World Scientific, 2002.

[12] Felman, *Testimony*, 3.

[13] *Ibid.*, 5.

[14] Horace Engdahl, "Philomela's Tongue: Introductory Remarks on Witness Literature", in *Witness Literature*, 8-9.

completely monopolizes attention and keeps the witness emotionally engaged in a stage previous to narrativization: "As a relation to events, testimony seems to be composed of bits and pieces of memory that has been overwhelmed by occurrences that have not settled into understanding or remembrance, acts that cannot be constructed as knowledge nor assimilated into full cognition, events in excess of our frames of reference."[15]

The past is upheld as "enigma, as scandal, and as interpellation".[16] The experience of witnessing, as the experience of reading testimony, is described by Felman as "akin to a loss of language", "an experience of suspension", "a loss of human relatedness". The confrontation with this kind of text leaves readers "suddenly deprived of their bonding to the world and to one another", disoriented and uprooted.[17] Besides, Felman operates on the assumption that "life's horror gets noticed by people only on occasion".[18] The impact of the sight results from the fact that it happens accidentally, and the accident, defined from now on as the accidental encounter with the nondesirable, becomes the true source of insight because it creates a breach in previously acquired knowledge. Illustrating this idea with examples such as Freud's psychoanalysis or Mallarmé's theory of contemporary poetry, Felman poses that a new kind of intelligibility springs from the trivial, from the idiosyncratic nature of a particular case that unsettles predictability and expectations. Accidentally noticing formerly unseen or ill-understood relationships and comparing them with the perceived thing becomes the true source of insight, since the scope of the accident exceeds the seeming triviality of the single case.

The accident is defined as a dislocation, a breaking down, a disruption "whose origin cannot precisely be located but whose repercussions, in their very uncontrollable and unanticipated nature, still continue to evolve even in the very process of the testimony".[19] The accident is known only through its aftermath, its effects, its impact. It does not let the witness go; it is both incomprehensible and unforgettable. The witness does not possess the truth, but bears witness to a truth that continues to escape him. Although narrative is

---

[15] Felman, *Testimony*, 3.
[16] Quoted by Engdahl, *Witness Literature*, 10.
[17] Felman, *Testimony*, 48-50.
[18] *Ibid.*, 2.
[19] *Ibid.*, 21-22.

the medium of testimony, the only possible mould, the telling or the act of writing down – the literary act – "will be understood as a mode of truth's realization beyond what is available as statement".[20] The leitmotif of testimony seems to be the imperative to tell something which no telling ever can do justice to, "to articulate the story that cannot be fully captured in thought, memory and speech".[21] It is not only the crisis manifested in the event witnessed that becomes paradigmatic, but also the crisis of the telling. Felman notes that very often eyewitnesses are unable to absorb the historical dimension of their experience and fail to reconcile their experiences through testimony or narrative. This can also be found in literature, as in Albert Camus' *The Fall*,

> [where] the scene of witnessing has lost the amplifying resonance of its communality, the guarantee of a community of witnessing. It is no longer a collective, but a solitary scene. It does not carry the historical weight, the self-evident significance of a group limit-experience, but embodies rather the in-significance, the ineffectuality of a missed encounter with reality and of a non-encounter between two solitudes .... And yet, this very insignificance claims the narrative, since it decenters and defocalizes the significance of all the rest.[22]

Felman seems to define testimony mainly in view of those cases (both of eyewitnesses who are called upon to tell their experiences to an audience, and of writers who focused on historic outrage) in which telling, or writing, narrative does not offer an appropriate therapeutic outlet of experience. This is paradoxical, since testimony writing is produced precisely out of the necessity to retrieve the significance of the past and to recover and pay tribute to the already dead. Herta Müller insists that "speech does not cover our innermost realms", that "what has been lived couldn't care less about writing".[23] Alphen describes the events as occurring in a vacuum and their content as making impossible a total verbalization. The paradigmatic experience, according to him, is that of "speechlessness in the face of a

---

[20] *Ibid.*, 15-16.
[21] Laub, *Testimony*, 78.
[22] *Ibid.*, 171.
[23] Herta Müller, "When We Don't Speak, We Become Unbearable, and When We Do, We Make Fools of Ourselves. Can Literature Bear Witness?", in *Witness Literature*, 20.

metaphysical evil".[24] However, in the face of this crisis of language, language is continually tried out in an attempt to gain direction, in an attempt to penetrate reality and to pass through the state of being shocked or wounded by it.

This mode of relation to events establishes as primal reality the "woundedness" of the event.[25] "Woundedness" is a term that describes testimony's very ethos and reality's capacity to affect and hurt individuals. The state of being stricken comes about by the incomprehensible nature of certain realities, and it bears close resemblance to what some critics regard as the epistemology of the short story. Besides the unity of effect criteria and the mechanics of response, the generic message of the short story has been mainly located in its component of strangeness and of mystery, on its absence of plot connectivity, on the supremacy conferred to the instant, and on the trivial as signifier of deeper psychological predicaments.

Felman makes it clear at the beginning of her poetics on testimony writing that testimony cannot be subsumed by the familiar notion that texts simply report facts; rather, "in different ways, [the texts] encounter – make us encounter – strangeness".[26] The encounter with strangeness has been the stepping stone for short story critics to discuss the nature of the genre; mystery, amazement, and impenetrability have been considered from various angles by a number of critics.[27]

---

[24] Alphen, *Caught by History*, 59.

[25] Felman, *Testimony*, 28.

[26] *Ibid.*, 7.

[27] See Valerie Shaw, *The Short Story: A Critical Introduction*, London: Longman, 1983, 193; Bayley, *The Short Story*, 26; Robert Hampson, "Johnny Panic and the Pleasures of Disruption", in *Re-reading the Short Story*, ed. Clare Hanson, London: Macmillan, 1989, 85; John Gerlach, "The Margins of Narrative: The Very Short Story, the Prose Poem, and the Lyric", in *Short Story Theory at a Crossroads*, 80; Jose María Merino, "El cuento: narración pura", in *Del cuento y sus alrededores*, eds Carlos Pacheco and Luis Barrera Linares, Caracas: Monte Ávila Latinoamericana, 1993, 467; Charles E. May, "The Nature of Knowledge in Short Fiction", in *The New Short Story Theories*, 131-43; Charles E. May, *The Short Story: The Reality of Artifice*, New York: Twayne, 1995, 95, 98; Charles E. May, "Prolegomenon to a Generic Study of the Short Story", *Studies in Short Fiction*, XXXIII/ 4 (Fall 1996): 468-69; Mary Rohrberger, "Where Do We Go from Here? The Future of the Short Story", in *The Tales We Tell: Perspectives on the Short Story*, eds Barbara Lounsberry *et al.*, Westport, CT: Greenwood Press, 1998, 205; Mario Benedetti, "Cuento, *nouvelle* y novela: Tres géneros narrativos" (1953), in *Teorías del cuento:*

John Bayley, for example, developed the notion that the short story is committed to literature as enigma, in contrast to the novel, which is committed to literature as survey.[28] According to Walton Beacham, "short fiction is dealing with the *power* of the forces which act on us rather than the *nature* of the forces".[29] Suzanne Hunter Brown and Elizabeth Bowen also focus on the disturbing moments of wrongness, – on life gone askew or life on the edge – that the short story recurrently shows as being truer to the nature of our existence.[30] The idea of incongruence held in suspension has also been embraced by Italo Calvino, Lara Zavala, Thomas Leitch, Mario Lancelotti, and others, and has been further developed by Charles May (1994) and Michael Trussler (1996) in their respective studies on the short story's attitude towards knowledge and the short story's rejection of traditional understandings of relationship between time progression and event.[31]

Events are not seen as the fruits of time or as the culmination of a long process: "With short fiction, we are not so much amazed by the shift in character as we are by the power which a moment of perception has to change us."[32] Events and perceptions are embodied in images that come out of nothing, as in dreams.[33] As a result, the

---

Teorías de los cuentistas, ed. Lauro Zavala, México: Universidad Nacional Autónoma de México, 1995, 222.

[28] Bayley, *The Short Story*, 1-2, 9-10.

[29] Walton Beacham, "Short Fiction: Towards a Definition", in *Critical Survey of Short Fiction*, ed. Frank N. Magill, London: Methuen, 1981, 16 (emphases in the text).

[30] Suzanne Hunter Brown, "The Chronotope of the Short Story: Time, Character, and Brevity", in *Creative and Critical Approaches to the Short Story*, ed. Noel Harold Kaylor Jr., Lewiston, ME: Edwin Mellen Press, 1997, 197-98; Elizabeth Bowen, "The Faber Book of Modern Short Stories", in *The New Short Story Theories*, 261.

[31] Italo Calvino, "Rapidez", in *Teorías del cuento I. Teorías de los cuentistas*, 363; Hernán Lara Zavala, "Para una geometría del cuento", in *ibid.*, 374; Thomas M. Leitch, "The Debunking Rhythm of the American Short Story", in *Short Story Theory at a Crossroads*, 133; Mario A. Lancelotti, "El cuento como pasado activo", in *Del cuento y sus alrededores*, 178.

[32] Beacham, "Short Fiction", 14. See also Mariano Baquero Goyanes, *Qué es el cuento*, Buenos Aires: Editorial Columba, 1967, 67; Mary Doyle Springer, *Forms of the Modern Novella*, Chicago: University of Chicago Press, 1975, 11-12; Shaw, *The Short Story*, 194; Jean Pickering, "Time and the Short Story", in *Re-reading the Short Story*, 47; or Brown, "The Chronotope of the Short Story", 188.

[33] Clare Hanson, "'Things out of Words': Towards a Poetics of Short Fiction", in *Re-reading the Short Story*, 22-33.

presumed existence of inherent connections in the plot is questioned.[34]
The implication is that the short story operates on a logical emptiness
that Valerie Shaw, for example, has related to a sense of exile, a
dislocating sensation experienced by the reader when watching the
character cross a frontier, "a foreign state, unlike the one he normally
inhabits".[35]

Short-storyness seems to happen when a kind of hypnosis affects
either the character or the reader and puts continuity and sequence on
hold. As Clark Blaise remarks, the meaning of "then" is devastating:
"the purest part of a story, I think, is from its beginning to its 'then'".
Blaise understands the implications of the word "then" as ravaging
because "it conveys the explicit reassurance that things will continue
happening": "'Then' is the moment of the slightest tremor, the
moment when the author is satisfied that all the forces are deployed,
the unruffled surface perfectly cast, and the *insertion*, gross or
delicate, can now take place". The display of the forces that act on the
character or characters represents, for Blaise, a violation of the short-
storyness contained in any story: "It is the cracking of the perfect,
smug egg of possibility."[36] This invocation of the moment as
inexplicable, unaccountable, and persistent has prompted many critics
to define the short story by the impossibility of naming or verbalizing
its reality. Blaise says the story is a single example of something
much larger, "practically unnameable".[37] Charles May remarks that
the short story "thematizes the human dilemma of trying to say the
unsayable".[38] Valerie Shaw speaks of the "sense of unwriteable

---

[34] Austin M. Wright, "On Defining the Short Story: The Genre Question", in *Short
Story Theory at a Crossroads*, 51. According to Éjxenbaum and Shklovski, novels are
constructed on intertwined elements, short stories on "affixed" elements. Boris
Éjxenbaum, "La teoría del 'método formal'" (1925), in *Teoría de la literatura de los
formalistas rusos*, ed. Tzvetan Todorov, trans. Ana María Nethol, Buenos Aires:
Signos, 1970, 37; Boris Éjxenbaum, "Sobre la teoría de la prosa", in *ibid.*, 151; Viktor
Shklovski, "La construcción de la 'nouvelle' y de la novela", in *ibid.*, 128-29.
[35] Shaw, *The Short Story*, 193.
[36] Clark Blaise, "To Begin, To Begin", in *How Stories Mean*, eds John Metcalf and
J.R. (Tim) Struthers, Don Mills, Ont.: Porcupine Quills, 1993, 162 (emphasis added).
[37] Clark Blaise, "The Cast and the Mould", in *ibid.*, 163.
[38] Charles E. May, "Reality in the Modern Short Story", in *Style. The Short Story:
Theory and Practice*, XXVII/ 3 (Fall 1993), 369.

things".[39] "I personally read for dumbness", says short story writer Barry Hannah.[40]

There are many other intersecting points between testimony writing and the short story, such their insularity, the ahistoricity of their discourse, the alteration of criteria of relevance and triviality, the accidental encounter as paradigmatic of a crisis but also as the door for in-depth revelations, and so on. However, I wish to mainly focus on the idea that both acts of writing are characterized by a lack of narrativity, which is the result of a fixation on the "indelibility of a moment of a missed encounter with reality, an encounter whose elusiveness cannot be owned and yet whose impact can no longer be erased".[41] Both genres gravitate around the fight between discursive possibilities and experiential collapse. "In the revolt against explanations, testimony and literature are unified", Engdahl remarks,[42] and this is truest in the short story, a form that altered the novel's generous parameters for elaboration and comprehensiveness – "comprehensiveness" understood as both inclusive (large in scope) and amenable to understanding. We could even say that narrative discourse, in these genres, is seen as a betrayal, an attempt to endow the untamable inhospitality of reality with a "humanizing transactive process",[43] that is, with story: "The very form of narrative tempts us to tidy things up."[44] In fact, Theodor Adorno was against the representation of Holocaust experiences, because for him, art and fiction have an intrinsic alleviating power that cannot be tolerated in the context of the Holocaust;[45] and Primo Levi believed the true witness is the one who cannot testify.[46]

At this point we are caught in an apparent contradiction. On the one hand, as has been documented above, the generic proposal of both testimony writing and the short story is to regard narrative as an act against intelligibility. But, at the same time, the sight, the image, is regarded as a cherished fetish because in it resides that which cannot

---

[39] Shaw, *The Short Story*, 264.

[40] Barry Hannah, "Spies with Music", in *The Tales We Tell*, 208.

[41] Felman, *Testimony*, 167,

[42] Engdahl, "Philomela's Tongue", 10.

[43] Alphen, *Caught by History*, 152.

[44] Peter Englund, "The Bedazzled Gaze: On Perspective and Paradoxes in Witness Literature", in *Witness Literature*, 51.

[45] See Sue Vice, *Holocaust Fiction*, London: Routledge, 2000, 5.

[46] Primo Levi, *The Drowned and the Saved*, New York: Vintage Books, 1989, 83-84.

be discursively expressed. From this last statement, it follows that there is an option of considering those elements that cannot be connected at the level of the plot: that is, gestures, images, scenes, objects, as containers of meaning (however unarticulated). Many critics build short story theorizations and critical practice on the identification of seemingly trivial elements in the narrative because they convey the true significance of the story. These elements represent, for instance, a drama, a conflict, a mood, an injury that the reader can sense but that the writer has included in the narrative without making anything explicit. The reader has to infer meaning from "the available images", as Ewing Campbell[47] points out, because "meaning is communicated by the simplest of gestures and the most seemingly trivial of objects".[48] May finds this quality of short-storyness in Raymond Carver's story "Errand" – a tribute to Chekhov – in the fact that, at the end, we are made to watch a waiter picking up and hiding in his hand the cork that on the previous night, the night of Chekhov's death, had fallen to the ground after popping out of a bottle of champagne in his hotel room. H.E. Bates studies the gestures, the sights, the tiny moments that "stamp swiftly in the mind the impression of desolation, embarrassed love, or maternal despair".[49] The reader therefore has to face a system of great allusive potential,[50] since the implication is that the writer expresses inner reality by focusing on outer reality.[51] The spotlight is trained on events that call for an enquiry but whose nature prevents dissection, on situations whose function is to act as embodiment of a feeling without appealing to an examination by reason.[52]

This potentiality for indication, for signification, is perforce enhanced by the short story, a genre born after the amplifying tactics of the novel. The short story's brevity forcibly makes the selected materials metaphorical of a wider context, and it allows us to

---

[47] Ewing Campbell, "How Minimal Is Minimalism?", in *The Tales We Tell*, 18.

[48] May, *The Short Story*, 106.

[49] H.E. Bates, *The Modern Short Story from 1809 to 1953* (1941), rpt. London: Robert Hale, 1988, 21-22.

[50] Julio Peñate Ribero, "El cuento literario y la teoría de los sistemas: Propuestas para una posible articulación", in *Teoría e interpretación del cuento*, eds Peter Fröhlicher and Georges Güntert, Berlin: Editorial Científica Europea, Perspectivas Hispánicas, 1997, 46.

[51] May, "Reality in the Modern Short Story", 376.

[52] Bowen, "The Faber Book of Modern Short Stories", 256.

remember all of the details.[53] Thus, the short story and witness literature are narrative forms that exploit unintelligibility but at the same time offer situations amenable for unbounded meaning.[54] Perhaps it exists, in the genre, an implicit internal and deliberate dissociation of meaning from intelligibility, an epistemological claim to give significance autonomy from the requirements of intellect. Julio Cortázar said, "The short story does not inquire, it does not convey knowledge or carry a message".[55] Similarly, Engdahl states that "the witness produces no theory, teaches no doctrine".[56] Testimony and short story document the relationship with what is there but does not make sense.

Thus, we are looking at two genres which, by diminishing the representativity of story as narrating process and by discarding cognition – defined as causal, articulated thought – as a tool of comprehension, intensify the import of the irrational event as captured by the visual perception. The potential meaning that the images bear can be thought of as a substitute to conventional narrative emplotments. In this type of work, the kind of attachment that the witness has to certain images or scenes, and the ways in which the witness addresses those images internally, constitute the landmarks of a narrative that moves forward not by change or by the concatenation of events but by ocular bondage.[57]

---

[53] See Norman Friedman, "Recent Short Story Theories: Problems in Definition", in *Short Story Theory at a Crossroads*, 25-26, and Suzanne Hunter Brown, "Discourse Analysis and the Short Story", in *ibid.*, 248.

[54] We might recall here that Felman proposed to define witness writing as "the vehicle of an occurrence, a reality, a stance or a dimension *beyond himself*" (*Testimony*, 3, emphasis in the text). Similar definitions have been provided by short story critics such as Mary Rohrberger, "The Short Story: A Proposed Definition", in *Short Story Theories*, ed. Charles May, Athens: Ohio University Press, 1976, 80-82; and Luis Beltrán Almería, "El cuento como género literario", in *Teoría e interpretación del cuento*, 30-31.

[55] Julio Cortázar, "Del cuento breve y sus alrededores", in *La casilla de los Morelli*, 113 (my translation).

[56] Engdahl, "Philomela's Tongue", 8.

[57] The term "bondage" generally refers to the condition of being a slave or being controlled by something. In literature, the term "bondage" can be found in dictionaries of fantasy literature, and it means "the state of being contained or trapped by a particular place, time, physical shape or moral condition" (*The Encyclopedia of Fantasy*, eds John Clute and John Grant, London: Orbit, 1997, 339). Bondage implies the existence of an undefined something that keeps you immobile or under a spell, that turns you into a puppet. It refers to an illogical imposition or a burden from which

Some textual evidence

Douglas Glover's "Dog Attempts to Drown Man in Saskatoon" is constructed by a first-person narrator who concentrates on the time – spoken about in the present – he and his wife decide to separate. He offers us some intimations about his wife's past and about the little things they do on a daily basis, especially their visit to Saskatoon's art gallery, whose premises used to hold a slaughterhouse. He initially decides to tell its story, of their getting together and their separation, but is continually assailed by his conviction that the story is "buried, gone, lost – its action fragmented and distorted by inexact recollection. Directly it was completed, it had disappeared, gone with the past into that strange realm of suspended animation, that coatrack of despair, wherein all our completed acts await, gathering dust, until we come for them again." The story, for him, is unavailable from the start – dead, we could even say: on the second page of the narrative, he says, "Now I know the worst – that reasons are out of joint with actions".[58] From that moment on, the narrator occasionally repeats certain sentences as if they had been drilled into his monologue, like the one that opens the story: "My wife and I decide to separate, and then suddenly we are almost happy together."[59] As a result of this format, the narrative somehow threatens to become an analysis of how he tries to deal with emotional wreckage and how his story and his style are not faithful to things as they are or have been.

However, the story keeps moving, in terms of the forward progress of a narrative, because the narrator lingers on each small act performed between his wife and himself, and the story acquires structure through this series of recollections conveyed by the narrator. He creates a path of understanding that pins characters to a wall, as if he were framing them doing something revelatory. These pieces always appear in the form of a sight or a scene, as here:

> Watching Lucy shake her hair out and tuck it into her knitted hat, I suddenly feel close to tears. Behind her are the framed photographs of weathered prairie farmhouses .... This is an old song; there is no

characters try to escape. As the *Encyclopedia of Fantasy* explains, "Resistance could be called bondage, the process of change could be called story". Unlike the laws of causality, the laws of bondage make characters step aside, altering the habitual regime of their conscience.

[58] Glover, *Dog Attempts to Drown Man in Saskatoon*, 98.

[59] *Ibid.*, 97.

gesture of Lucy's that does not fill me instantly with pity, the child's hand held up to deflect the blow, the desperate attempts to conceal unworthiness.[60]

Soon the reader understands that the way the narrator handles the images in his head does not serve the customary purpose of "the frozen moment which reveals a life", because we will receive, in time, another image of the same character that will render this visual package futile and useless. Our expectations will be thwarted because we had already assumed that the image provided encapsulated the character's leading trait. However, a new sight will send our interpretation of the character in a totally different direction. For example, the helplessness embodied in the image of Lucy's tucking her hair into a woolen hat is invalidated by an astounding sight. When the couple come across a street puppet show, the narrator sees Lucy unconsciously spread her arms and start to dance: "it is a scene that brings a lump to my throat: the high, hot, summer sun, the children's faces like flowers in a sea of grass, the towering, swaying puppets, and Lucy lost in herself."[61] There has been a visual itinerary, somehow concealed by the *atrezzo* of the narrative, which leads the reader to interpret or reinterpret the character in a certain way. Paradoxically, this allegedly climatic point of watching Lucy spread out her arms in unconscious joy has the effect of putting the two selected images on hold forever because they cannot be reconciled: one will always discredit the other.

The same treatment is given to Lucy's mother, Celeste, a domineering and aggressive person who is described as the source of Lucy's psychological weaknesses. The sudden introduction of a surprising image makes her potentially active in a different way:

> Once, years later, Lucy and Celeste were riding on a bus together when Celeste pointed to a man sitting a few seats ahead and said, "that is the one I loved". That was all she ever said on the topic and the man himself was a balding, petty functionary type except in terms of the exaggerated passion Celeste had invested in him over the years.[62]

---

[60] *Ibid.*, 101.
[61] *Ibid.*, 109.
[62] *Ibid.*, 104.

This happens after the narrator has discussed with us the hatred Celeste felt for her daughter and after we had somehow lost track of this piece of Lucy's adulthood. Consequently, the sight of a man sitting before Celeste in the bus takes Celeste to another sphere of understanding, giving us a context that contradicts her son-in-law's explanations: Celeste can actually be seen as the victim of unreciprocated love. In this way, "Dog Attempts to Drown Man in Saskatoon", which is apparently designed as a psychoanalytic session with touches of postmodernist meditation, reverses itself and becomes parodic: the narrative itself, the events in the narrative, proves that the narrator finds truth only outside the rhetorical environment of psychoanalysis (by which I mean the familiar grammar of explanations and causes for trauma that are widely used in explaining behavior nowadays). If there is revelation, it takes the form of a character staring at an abrupt and unexpected image of something whose nature unarguably denies that one can possess a narratable or accountable self.

Thus, the story is framed within the style of psychotherapy and its compelling duty to think a way out of confusions, but it moves forward only "from sight to sight", so to speak, since the only plane of consistency, or, rather, evidence, is the image. Every character in the story does something because he or she has seen something or caught a glimpse of something: "Lucy and I were married because of her feet and because she glimpsed a man masturbating in a window as her bus took her home from work."[63] This sentence, which is repeated at least twice in the story, is elevated to the category of reliable explanation of why things happen in a certain way. Additionally, Lucy is considered an emotional wreck as an adult because she had seen her brother being run over by a car. We learn later that Lucy has only imagined seeing her brother being run over by a car – that she never saw the accident. However, this information does not contradict the ruling principle of the story: people do things only because (and just after) they have seen certain things. Lucy actually has been replaying this manipulated image over and over in her head for years. Her habit only shows how she creates herself imaginatively.

By this point in the story we know almost for certain that the real motivation to tell the story is that the narrator has had to bear witness to an amazing and unaccountable sight. He has seen a dog jumping

---

[63] *Ibid.*, 102.

into a hole in a frozen river on top of the bobbing body of a drowning man. We have been awaiting this image from the beginning of the story. The front page of the book of Glover's collection reproduces the newspaper headline and the article, together with a captioned photograph of the "scene of the near-fatal accident". This sight, which is the culmination of several unsettling visual climaxes offered earlier on in the story, is not only meant to satisfy our curiosity about the unusual occurrence named in the title. It is also the product of Glover's narrative method, which produces meaning by negating the narrative elements that usually make a story a story: continuity, coherence, and progression. Instead, we find a limited collection of images that decertify one another:

> I feel that in discussing these occurrences, these facts (our separation, the dog, the city, the weather, a trip to the art gallery) as constitutive of a non-system, I am peeling away some of the mystery of human life. I am also of the opinion that Mendel should have left the paintings in the slaughterhouse.[64]

This statement is the announcement that he is at the same time fabricating an assemblage (a system), no matter how unsystematic it is, and forever realizing that the only thing that really remains after the effort of expression is the inconsistency of what one accidentally happens to see. The image of the paintings in the slaughterhouse strengthens his belief that the absurdity of seeing certain things is paradigmatic of what experience is. About the gallery he had said before: "But whenever I go there I hear the panicky bellowing of the death-driven steers and see the streams of blood and the carcasses and smell the stench and imagine the poor beasts rolling their eyes at Gauguin's green and luscious leaves as the bolt enters their brains."[65]

"Dog Attempts to Drown Man in Saskatoon" shows a plot whose struggles occur at the level of the visual, not only because there are visually intense encounters but because of the way pictures or visual motifs are set in motion. They become unfixed and lead to wider reactions: as we have already said, things happen only because someone has seen something or has been looking at something. The core image of this mind-museum the narrator inhabits is the sight that

---

[64] *Ibid.*
[65] *Ibid.*, 101.

supremely denies the consistency of purpose. While descending the Idylwyld Bridge to take some pictures of the frozen river, he sees a dog running around the drifting body of a man where the crust is frozen and the water burbles up. When the narrator approaches the scene, he realizes the man is blind. The scene is only slightly disturbed by a symbol of rationality: after miraculously getting the man out of the water and undergoing an experience that did not enter any of the narrator's rational layers, a policeman takes out a notebook and "scribble[s] words against the void".[66]

This lunatic scene, the urgency of agony, the unexplained behavior of the dog, the alienness of the idea itself, expresses the hollowness between event and event, the numbing of thought, the impossibility of wrapping it up in story. The newspaper account is discarded by the narrator as utterly inadequate; rather, he likes to see himself fully committed to it in its total irrationality, in the impossibility of bearing witness to it:

> Perhaps man and dog chose together to walk through the pathless snows to the water's edge and throw themselves into uncertainty .... Or perhaps the dog accompanied the man only reluctantly, the man forcing the dog to lead him across the ice .... I saw the dog swim to him, saw the man fending the dog off. Whatever the case my allegiance is with the dog; the man is too human, too predictable. But man and dog together are emblematic – that is my impression at any rate – they are mind and spirit, the one blind, the other dumb; one defeated, the other naive and hopeful, both forever going out. And *I submit that* after all the simplified explanations and crude jokes about the blind man and his dog, the act is full of strange and terrible mystery, of beauty.[67]

The act of communication that the narrator of this story performs is identical to that of testimony literature: the core situation problematizes the telling of it through story. For the narrator, any step into narrative is seen as a betrayal of reality; he explicitly allies himself with that which cannot be shaken off. At the end of the story he says, "But my words are sad companions and sometimes I remember ... well ... the icy water up to my neck and I hear the ghost

---

[66] *Ibid.*, 112.

[67] *Ibid.*, 113 (emphasis added).

dog barking, she tried to warn me; yes, yes, I say, but I was blind".[68] This narrator decides to construct his past by endlessly replaying certain images,[69] and it seems that he is striving for a mode of narrative that depends not on actions but on acts, witnessed acts that we carry in our heads. What happens is presented in the story as devoid of agency, and the narrator concludes that there is no connective tissue that can make experiences mesh, that connection is only an invention of speech: the images are the proof that deny coherent contiguity. This story, through its narrator, openly declares the intention not to get over a traumatic event because words could only falsely convey it, because there is a desire not to eradicate the pain that absurdity irremediably causes. He refuses to make his wounds accessible to language.

My comments on the other three short stories will be less extensive: "Dog Attempts to Drown Man in Saskatoon" superbly represents how a certain rhetoric, a compelling ethos of inarticulateness, makes us think of ourselves as cut out from the presumed continuity and plausibility of our existence; it shows that totality and flow can be arrested by the impact of a traumatic image. The overwhelming impact of an image puts into question the limits of reality. "The Watcher" by Guy Vanderhaeghe also depends on the power that certain stored images have on our psychological routes; however, it shows a different method of pursuing "biographical meaning". In this story too we have a narrator who defines himself through seeing. He relishes looking at things, while his reality – he is a bedridden child – seems to be forever stagnated. But his life is not a realm of inaction: he decides what people are by using a selected image, and his talent is to catch them out when they would most desire not to be seen. If the narrator in "Dog Attempts to Drown Man in Saskatoon" had a need for story but was ashamed of it because he thought it was an anaesthetic, the boy in "The Watcher" is a story-intensifier: he looks for scandals in an adult world that, for the time being, he can only catch a glimpse of. From the angst of an accidental witness we move into the mind of a voyeur, a deliberate spectator, and one who will become trapped in the three subject positions that are

---

[68] *Ibid.*, 114.
[69] *Ibid.*, 141.

often seen as illustrative of Holocaust literature: perpetrator, victim, and bystander.[70]

Deprived of contact with other kids and unwanted by adults, he develops a vocation that will be critically tested when he is taken to his grandmother's farm for a long and boring summer. His grandma, a bossy and resolute woman who lives by herself, has to confront the unexpected visit of one of her daughters, Evelyn, who is in a state of complete emotional wreckage and is accompanied by her opinionated lover, Thompson, a man who passes himself off as a scholar. Before we actually see Evelyn crying and hear her lover's grotesque advice, the story has tied us visually (and emotionally) to the image of a farm animal, Stanley the rooster, singled out as a sad figure whose leg is forever fastened to a stake. The bird panics whenever the boy tries to approach it. Like the drowning dog in "Dog Attempts to Drown Man in Saskatoon", Stanley evokes a sense of captivity, isolation, and agony, but we know that his function in the story is not just to arouse a certain feeling, but to create the basis of the plot the boy will engender in his mind. We will experience in this story the performative effects of his "practices of the eye".

The lurid play of family misencounters that is displayed before the boy revolves mainly around two scenes that he witnesses and that leave him unbalanced because he cannot comprehend them. Once he sees Thompson and his aunt Evelyn strolling around the countryside; they are at a distance, and he cannot hear a sound, but he senses that they are having an argument. Suddenly:

> She snapped and twisted on the end of his arm like a fish on a line. Her head was flung back in an exaggerated, antique display of despair; the head rolled grotesquely from side to side as if her neck were broken.
>
> Suddenly Thompson began striking awkwardly at her exposed buttocks and thighs with the flat of his hand. The long gangly arm slashed like a frail as she scampered around him, the radius of her escape limited by the distance of their linked arms.

---

[70] Felman claims that testimony writing offers three cognitive positions: victims, perpetrators, and bystanders. According to her, these cognitive positions do not just imply a diversity of points of view or a variety of implications and emotional involvement; they signify three different performances of the act of seeing in the testimonial stance (*Testimony*, 207).

From where I knelt in the grass I could hear nothing. It was too far off. As far as I was concerned there were no cries and no pleading. The whole scene, as I remember it, was shorn of any of the personal idiosyncrasies which manifest themselves in violence. It appeared a simple case of karmic retribution.[71]

This scene powerfully evokes Stanley the rooster, the victim with a leg tied to a string. It is a silent scene with clear roles for everyone: victim, perpetrator, and bystander. This triad of roles will be internalized by the boy from then on; certainly his future behavior will be inscribed within this restricted scenario. Later he will become a participant motivated by the available roles that this image has activated in him. After watching this spectacle, the narrator accidentally witnesses sexual intercourse between Evelyn and Thompson. From this scene he will visually amplify a small slice, Thompson's face and a gesture that the boy takes for helplessness: "his mouth fell open and he looked stupider and weaker than any human being I had ever seen before in my life."[72] This string of images turns the watcher into a doer: the boy decides to again approach Stanley, the miserable rooster he has not been able to make friends with so far. Then, he is "intoxicated with power" and, when finally realizing that the animal will not ever allow any caress on his part (it even pecks his hand badly), he lets himself be carried away by the unreality of the situation: "Some strange images came to my head: the bruises on my aunt's legs; Thompson's face drained of life, lifted like an empty receptacle toward the ceiling, waiting to be filled, the tendons of his neck stark and rigid with anticipation."[73]

There seem to be a projection of physical characteristics from one figure to another (from Thompson's neck to Stanley's), and after several attempts, the narrator wrings Stanley's neck. He has become a perpetrator because the images that have had an impact on him in the past become models of action to follow; what he has absorbed through his eyes gives him compelling, almost unquestioning motivation to act. There will be an amount of mounting drama after this isolated event (that nobody sees): this time Thompson will become the victim of savage aggression on the part of the men grandma sends to beat

---

[71] Vanderhaeghe, "The Watcher", in *The Best of Canadian Fiction Magazine: Silver Anniversary Anthology*, 100-101.
[72] *Ibid.*, 104.
[73] *Ibid.*, 107.

him up. But even when the narrator is watching this brutal scene, he cannot get rid of what has already become an index to his machinery of reaction:

> Thompson, I saw, was weak. God, I remembered more than he dreamed. I remember how his lips had moved soundlessly, his face pleading with the ceiling, his face blotted of everything but abject urgency. Praying to a simpering, cross-eyed idol. His arm flashing as he struck my aunt's bare legs. Crawling in the dirt covered with blood.[74]

Three different sights are coming together here for a kind of unpleasant climax of the memory. And, just after that: "I thought of Stanley the rooster and how it had felt when the tendons separated, the gristle parted and the bones crunched under my twisting hands." The story is coming to a close. Earlier on, the boy, in the presence of the police, denies having seen anyone beating Thompson. In the last short scene of the story, Thompson, badly wounded and defeated, sees Evelyn in the window, and he believes she is calling him. Thompson is there, looking up, expectant, and the boy says: "But any damn fool could see she was only waving goodbye."[75]

In "The Watcher", looking at something does not numb one's will to act or to use words; on the contrary, it leads to an abusive use of the witness position for an empowerment of the self. The images in this story allow an unlawful exploration of privacy; they are created by a gaze that slowly approaches a few selected elements, a gaze that almost stalks its victim. Visual perception seemingly allows cognitive performance (seeing means knowing). However, in this case, the creation of an internal behavioral code is used by the speaking subject to justify cruelty to others. And the boy even refuses to bear witness to a crime. Is this a warning? Does this story illustrate how harmful unarticulated and private interpretations of the sheer physical world can be for an unattended individual? Whatever its ethical hold may be, we can say that, on the level of pure narrative tactics, the story possesses a clear trajectory mapped out by acts of seeing and that the sight is ultimately what permeates the character's reactions and the reader's involvement in the narrative.

---

[74] *Ibid.*, 118.
[75] *Ibid.*, 119.

If we turn our attention to Katherine Govier's "The Immaculate Conception Photography Gallery" and Barbara Gowdy's "Body and Soul" we find that the characters in these stories also regard the world as a visual display and find it impossible to reason in transitions. More specifically, the image is presented as a trope for a memory, one that can be deformed intentionally or may be faulty due to biological reasons. Both "The Immaculate Conception Photography Gallery" and "Body and Soul" play with the idea that people are sustained by retrospective images of themselves and others and that, if these images are corrupted or inassimilable, the individual's sense of self is erased and forever damaged. In "The Immaculate Conception Photography Gallery" we come across a photographer, Sandro, who sets up a small shop in Little Italy, in Toronto, which he calls the Immaculate Conception Photography Gallery. He specializes in wedding and family events. But one wedding goes awry because the bridegroom, Tony, seduces a bridesmaid named Alicia. He confesses six months later, and the bride's mother demands that Sandro erase Alicia's image from the wedding picture, which he does:

> "I'm like a plastic surgeon," he told his wife. "Take that patch of skin from the inner thigh and put it over the scar on the face. Then sand the edges. Isn't that what they do? Only that it isn't a face I'm fixing, it's a memory."[76]

Diora's mother is indescribably grateful to Sandro because he has rescued the image she wanted to keep forever.[77] But soon other members of that family are asking Sandro to take other people out of their pictures. The bride's father wants to have the groom's parents removed because he thinks they are bad people. Although Sandro feels almost nauseated to have to alter reality like that, he makes the erasure every time he is asked. And he is increasingly troubled by the consequences of what can be interpreted as a metaphysical issue. He talks about this with a wise friend:

> "Why do people care about photographs so much?" ….
> "You can put them on your mantel," said Becker. "They don't talk back."

---

[76] Katherine Govier, "The Immaculate Conception Photography Gallery", in *The Immaculate Conception Photography Gallery*, 250.
[77] *Ibid.*, 251.

"Don't people prefer life?" said Sandro.
"People prefer things," said Becker.
"Don't they want their memories to be true?"
"No," said Becker.
"Another thing. Are we here just to get our photographs taken? Do
we have a higher purpose?"

        ....

"I mean real people," said Sandro. "Have we no loyalty to the
natural?"[78]

Eventually Diora, the bride, who had lived with Tony since they
got married and had already raised several children by him, asks
Sandro to take Tony's picture out of the kids' birthday shots because
they have separated. "But Diora", said Sandro, "everyone knows he's
their father". "They have no father", said Diora flatly: "'It's
immaculate conception', said Becker gleefully."[79] The title of the
story and the name of the shop precisely point at the lack of
connection between two things we probably have accepted
unquestioningly. There is an absence of causality in the alleged
sequence of the Virgin Mary's conception, in which a child is
engendered without previous contact of the flesh. The biological
connection is extirpated in the Bible, as it is extirpated in the history
of this Italian immigrant family. But they need to rely on an image at
all costs if they want to preserve their mental sanity. Trauma has to be
dissected and burnt out, and Sandro is intensely aware that he is
"outplaying God at His own game", is not "just fooling around with
celluloid".[80]

This story, like "Body and Soul", shows the characters' attachment
to an image and also their belief that their life is not as told, but as
staged. They can only hold on to who they are through a picture. The
image, although initially conveying trauma, can be excised, so it can
create the moment that would sustain a life. Characters desire to
possess the frozen moment that summarizes their lives: the past, in
this frame of mind, is a thing to be viewed. The final erasing that
Sandro performs in his own shop through a photograph shows his
disagreement with this view: he thinks that the photograph should not
assure people of their existence, that we cannot understand reality

---

[78] *Ibid.*, 253-54.
[79] *Ibid.*, 258.
[80] *Ibid.*, 256.

even if we artificially arrange it in accommodating patterns. Sandro takes a picture of the street where his shop is, takes his shop out of the picture, and connects the buildings to the right and left as if the shop was not there. Then he displays this picture in his shop window and he leaves. He still believes that the image should reflect the intractability of life. The events his creations portray – weddings, birthdays, and so on – occur in a kind of artificial vacuum: he can pretend a person was alive when he was not, he can eliminate people's presences, but he is troubled by the idea that one should not mistake "these rituals of the image" for totality and flow. He is haunted "by the faces of those whose presence he had tampered with".[81] In this case, he is the traumatized victim who can no longer produce ready-made images because he does not want to encourage a too human desire to materialize certain moments in visual expression.

Finally, "Body and Soul" addresses the problem of faulty perception and the kind of bonding with the world that certain images, wrongly begotten, can create. An almost deaf elderly lady, Aunt Bea, volunteers to take care of disabled children until they are officially adopted. A blind and a mentally retarded girl live with her for the time being, and she tries to come to terms with the children's needs and fears. Terry has been deprived of sight from birth, and she awkwardly tries to attach images to the objects that are named by words. The other girl, Julie, has a different limitation when she tries to think of reality: she sticks to the image she thinks she remembers of the mother who abandoned her when she was little, and she projects this image onto every woman she sees or every voice she hears on the phone. These girls, who were shifted from home to home several times before they came to live with Aunt Bea, have picked up their various foster mothers' habits and expressions, although they do not really understand the attitudes they keep imitating. Their conversations are frustrating; Terry gets very poor answers from Julie when she asks her to describe something, because Julie collects only a limited number of possible situations in her mind.

As in "The Immaculate Conception Photography Gallery", in this story there is a hitch between reality and memory, an unbridgeable gap between what characters see and what they know. And the image does not correspond to what one believes reality is. Julie is an example of this, her moods forever sustained by the idea that every

---

[81] *Ibid.*

person that approaches her is her own mother or Terry's mother. For Terry, the referents are dispersed and private, and through her Gowdy invokes the visual moment that is "epistemologically innocent": Terry undergoes surgery on her eyes, and when she starts seeing things, she is unable to connect them to the concepts she had stored in her mind. She cannot recognize herself when she looks at the mirror. She had not even thought that people had different faces, and she is terribly disappointed to find that certain notions lack materiality: "'But where's the time?' she cries, distressed."[82] The speculations that sustained her so far are all gone, and she cannot comprehend the place she is in now. Whereas Terry tries to apprehend the world by storing concepts but not images, Julie takes the opposite tack, storing images but not concepts: for Julie every image is hard to interpret, and she finds it difficult to get hold of words, of names, that describe who or what she is seeing. She is continually dazed by sudden recollections of her past, and it takes her a while to return to the situation she was living before the memory of an image had upset her.

Aunt Bea becomes the main survivor in this domestic world of unconnected pieces of information (both visual and linguistic), which the girls try to make sense of. But despite her religiousness, she does not survive chaos by means of a plot that could be, for example, the plot of sacrifice followed by reward, nor by the goal-oriented narrative of finding a permanent home for the children. She finds her strength in an image of connection. The last paragraph of the story has Aunt Bea still accepting another child into her home, a child who is missing both arms and is in the process of being fitted for new prosthetic arms. This girl can actually dance, and she does so in front of Terry and Aunt Bea:

> Terry is enraptured. Aunt Bea is too, but not so much because of the dance – her daughter took tap-dancing lessons. What wins Aunt Bea's heart is the sight of those little wing-like arms flapping at one of her artificial arms (she insists on putting them on herself), flapping and failing to grasp it, flapping and failing, and at last lining it up, slipping the stump into the socket, and clicking it in.[83]

---

[82] Barbara Gowdy, "Body and Soul", in *We So Seldom Look on Love: Stories*, 32.
[83] *Ibid.*, 42.

Aunt Bea is sustained by this sight, the sight of artificial arms going into a stump, a sight that confirms the ultimate blend of different kinds of matter. On a more metaphysical level, this act brings about a confirmation of a possible degree of connectability (and of success) in a world forever interrupted by misunderstandings. A few pages previous to this reassuring image, the narrator says about Aunt Bea: "Sometimes she is happy just to be alive and a witness."[84]

Whereas the impossibility of happiness after having witnessed a traumatic image is the underlying philosophical nucleus of the first two stories, "Body and Soul" shows how, in fact, we can make a somehow disturbing image support ourselves psychologically. Each of the stories commented on here shares the same conspicuous hook on the image; this time, however, it is partially seen as a reassuring practice. For Aunt Bea, as for the other characters in the other stories, narrative is not plot, but instant perception.

The best known stories since the nineteenth century within the French, Russian, and English tradition have centered themselves around a character who eventually looks at something that overturns previous impressions of having led a satisfactory life. It would be almost impossible to name them all. All these moments bear a deep imprint in our memory as readers thanks to the canonization and accessibility of the stories that contain them: the sight of something that reduces everything else to insignificance is already a familiar narrative strategy that moves us deeply. These characters are seen normally as humble witnesses who tell about their cases and, in so doing, implicitly define the short story as a non-healing art form that somehow dispossesses narrative of its capacity to offer a survey of the world. According to Masaki Mori, what assures people of their relevance is precisely the extensive look – the possibility of assimilating totality and also the possibility of making the flux comprehensible.[85] Narrative, regarded as a soothing psychological practice, could be defined as a preparation for conscience.

But the short story represents a distinct form of invocation of reality that, although it can be present in all narrative forms (this is the reason we speak of "short-storyness"), achieves full consistency in

---

[84] *Ibid.*, 37.
[85] Masaki Mori, *Epic Grandeur: Toward a Comparative Poetics of the Epic*, New York: State University of New York Press, 1997, xii.

short texts, the only ones that can afford a high degree of vacuity
between events. By giving foremost importance to the image and by
presenting it as an obstacle to articulation, the short story is brought
very close to witness writing, where what the witness sees is
impossible to understand. Plots enable us to neutralize extreme events:
they can bridge transitions and can elaborate on the causes that
explain what may be otherwise senseless. But these two forms of
writing, the short story and testimony, both embody a refusal to think
about the change in a certain way. The awareness of the hollowness
between event and event is more powerful than any other generic
requirement.

The associations between these two forms of writing that have
been drawn out in this essay are not intended to reduce the short
story's potential to the problems of the transference of pain (facing
horror, trauma, illness, accidents) that testimony writing mainly
addresses; however, a considerable emphasis on the unexplainable
nature of these happenings in the short story makes their similarities
worthy of attention. The short story came to be shaped after the fine
and successful explorations of private and social life in the eighteenth-
century novel, and it implicitly counteracts any aspirations to enclose
the world. It shows that there are forms of accountability for the self
other than biography. Experience in the short story, as perforce also in
witness writing, is taken to a kind of interregnum where the only
condition is to feel the gap between perception and assimilation. As
Susan Buck-Morss explains:

> ... all of the senses can be acculturated .... But however strictly the
> senses are trained ... all of this is *a posteriori*. The senses maintain an
> uncivilized trace, a core resistance to cultural domestication .... they
> remain part of the biological apparatus.[86]

However, the power of the image either to contain unappeased
trauma or to give justification to one's decisions, should not only be
seen as a static pre- or postlinguistic encounter with the world, a
disarming tool that annuls all possibilities of continuance. The image,
however unnerving, manages, in these stories, to create a cognitive
style because it provides the stepping stones the reader has to tread on
to continue understanding the characters' lives. The image both arrests

---

[86] Buck-Morss, "Aesthetics and Anaesthetics", 6.

time and creates a narrative path. The selected images are devices by which the past is inscribed into oneself and also made available to oneself and to others. It is a progressive mode of observation; it develops a capacity towards narrative without having to shut out the experience of the inhospitable with conciliatory epilogues.

In Greek, the word "epic" meant "word", "speech", "song": the epic addressed the externality of life, and its grandeur expressed the joyful pleasure of violence. Perhaps we can oppose witness writing to the epic grasp of life and history. The susceptibility to suffering feeds witness literature, and also, like the short story, witness literature is fuelled by the commitment to reality that exists independently from words.

Margaret Atwood's Art of Brevity: Metaphorical Conceptualization and Short Story Writing

Teresa Gibert

A survey of the reception of Margaret Atwood's poetry clearly demonstrates that since the beginning of her literary career she has been commended for the originality of her metaphors. The strikingly innovative metaphorical usage in her early novels has also provided the basis for much speculative comment, particularly about her choice of a central metaphor as a technical device around which to structure *The Edible Woman* (1969) and about the clusters of metaphors emphasizing the themes of *Surfacing* (1972), *Lady Oracle* (1976) and *Bodily Harm* (1981). Furthermore, recent critical discussions of her later novels have underscored how Atwood displays a pervasive tendency to frame her basic insights in metaphorical terms. The majority of her short stories, however, have received little scholarly scrutiny in this respect, even though they contain excellent examples of her subversive use of metaphorical conceptualization.[1]

---

[1] I am using the terms "metaphorical conceptualization" and "metaphorical expression" to refer to simile, nonliteral analogy, extended comparison, and metaphor in the narrowest sense. I am taking a middle position between those who minimize and those who maximize formal differences, because I think such rhetorical distinctions are relatively unimportant. When one adopts a cognitive linguistic approach in order to focus on the essential meaning conveyed by these four tropes, they are conceived as figures of thought rather than simply figures of speech. In other words, I am bearing in mind the growing recognition that metaphor is much more than just a rhetorical device to embellish or enliven writing, and I am aware of how metaphor has moved from the ornamental fringes of discourse to a central position in the understanding of thought. See George Lakoff, *Women, Fire, and Dangerous Things: What Categories Reveal About the Mind*, Chicago: University of Chicago Press, 1987; George Lakoff and Mark Johnson, *Metaphors We Live By*, Chicago: University of Chicago Press, 1980; and George Lakoff and Mark Turner, *More Than Cool Reason: A Field Guide to Poetic Metaphor*, Chicago: University of Chicago Press, 1989. See also *Metaphor and*

Taking into account that Atwood's short fiction has already been studied from a variety of theoretical viewpoints, I will examine her collections *Dancing Girls* (1977), *Bluebeard's Egg* (1983), *Murder in the Dark: Short Fictions and Prose Poems* (1983), *Wilderness Tips* (1991), *Good Bones* (1992), *The Tent* (2006) and *Moral Disorder and Other Stories* (2006) to show how she has exploited the narrative potential of metaphorical expression while challenging the conventions of the short story genre.[2]

In her introduction to *The Oxford Book of Canadian Short Stories*, Atwood noted that several of the writers featured in the volume, including George Bowering and Matt Cohen, had "experimented with techniques that draw attention to the artificiality of art".[3] Although she did not add her name to the list, we can safely suppose that when she made this remark about their work, she also had in mind and was implicitly alluding to her own postmodernist methods of storytelling. Indeed, one of the most outstanding features of her short fiction is the use of easily noticeable procedures to expose the fictional illusion and underscore the overtly metafictional nature of her self-reflexive texts. Some of her devices, specifically designed to enhance the reader's awareness of literariness and to stimulate closer inspection of her short stories as artifacts, are related to the metaphorical strategies she deploys, not only by fashioning highly ingenious metaphors and similes but also by discussing figurative language in her fictional writings.

Atwood incorporates critical commentary on metaphor in the structure of many of her short stories, thus openly inviting her readers both to ponder on the trope from a theoretical perspective and to

---

Thought (1979), ed. Andrew Ortony, 2nd edn, Cambridge: Cambridge University Press, 1993.

[2] Margaret Atwood is probably the most frequently taught Canadian short fiction writer, and her short stories are included in anthologies worldwide. Scholars were at first much less drawn to her short stories than to her novels and poems, with the notable exception of Michelle Gadpaille's chapter "Margaret Atwood", in *The Canadian Short Story*, Toronto: Oxford University Press, 1988, 82-98. In her introduction to this book, Gadpaille hailed Atwood as one of "Canada's contemporary masters of the short story", together with Mavis Gallant and Alice Munro (viii). After a relatively long period of scholarly neglect, Atwood's short fiction has been subjected to a great deal of rhetorical and hermeneutical analysis by academic literary critics.

[3] Margaret Atwood, introduction to *The Oxford Book of Canadian Short Stories*, ed. Margaret Atwood and Robert Weaver, Toronto: Oxford University Press, 1986, xvi.

observe how it works in practice within her fictional discourse.[4] This kind of integrated commentary is expressed through occasional brief explanatory notes in her early short fiction, but becomes more frequent and elaborated in her later works, as the number of direct metafictional references increases.

One of the earliest examples of Atwood's use of the word "metaphor" or its cognates is to be found in "Polarities", initially published in 1971 and later collected in her first volume of short fiction, *Dancing Girls* (1977). Morrison, the male protagonist and focalizer of this narrative, reflects on the factors that have brought about Louise's nervous breakdown. While revising her notebooks, he concludes: "She's taken as real what the rest of us pretend is only metaphorical."[5] In an interview held thirty years after the publication of "Polarities", Atwood explained the characterization of Laura in her novel *The Blind Assassin* (2000) by pointing to a mental condition ("probably a mild form of autism") that makes it difficult for some people to handle metaphor, since they tend to be literalists.[6] Louise and Laura share the same type of disorder, which isolates them from external reality and causes them to dwell instead in a realm of fancy. This phenomenon has been identified by Charles May in his article "Metaphoric Motivation in Short Fiction" as an experience that Poe and Melville, respectively, wrote about in "The Fall of the House of Usher" and "Bartleby the Scrivener", two stories in which "characters have transformed themselves into aesthetic objects by means of metaphoric projection": both Usher and Bartleby "make the metaphoric mistake of projecting their own subjectivity onto the external world and then responding to it as if it were external".[7]

---

[4] I am aware that productive conclusions could be drawn if the metaphors of Atwood's short stories were examined in the light of her own extensive criticism on the subject in her essays, reviews and published lectures. However, given the limits on the length of this essay, I will focus exclusively on a selection of her statements on metaphor as expressed in her short narratives.

[5] Margaret Atwood, *Dancing Girls*, London: Virago, 1989, 69. The short stories in this volume were published individually between 1964 and 1977.

[6] Ann Heilmann and Debbie Taylor, "Interview with Margaret Atwood, Hay-on-Wye, 27 May 2001", *European Journal of American Culture*, XX/3 (November 2002), 140-41.

[7] Charles May, "Metaphoric Motivation in Short Fiction: 'In the Beginning Was the Story'", in *Short Story Theory at a Crossroads*, eds Susan Lohafer and Jo Ellyn Clarey, Baton Rouge: Louisiana State University Press, 1989, 67, 70.

In "Polarities" Morrison takes up a role antithetical to that of Louise; the two protagonists engage in an ill-fated relationship that leads to an irresolvable confrontation between them rather than to their finding completion in each other.[8] In this sense, the pattern of Atwood's story seems to correspond to the structure described by May as one that "depends on the interaction between a character metaphorically transformed by his obsession and a realistic character who unsuccessfully tries to recuperate the metaphoric figure".[9] On a first reading, Louise strikes us as a character so obsessed by her perception of the metaphor of the circle (a symbol of her wish to overcome divisions and find wholeness) that she becomes schizophrenic. She ends up in an asylum, whereas Morrison, who explicitly finds fault with Louise's inability to control metaphor, gives the impression of being more realistic and mentally stable. On a closer reading, however, we discover his obsessions and understand his "emotionally dysfunctional personality".[10] Actually, although he does not act in a way that would make his sanity suspect, he is equally divorced from reality, verging on neurotic. Morrison does not exhibit anything like Louise's severe psychotic symptoms, but a detailed analysis of the metaphorical strategies employed in the story helps us to ascertain what lies behind the appearances of his normal manners. The first simile applied to Louise is a clear sign of her position as a victim.[11] It foreshadows her unfortunate destiny, in which Morrison

---

[8] In "Margaret Atwood's Short Fiction" Charlotte Sturgess convincingly argues that "'Polarities' does not buy into the old myth of complementarity, of man and woman finding completion in each other's image, but is a critique of that dream" (*Margaret Atwood: Works and Impact*, ed. Reingard Nischik, Rochester, NY: Camden House, 2000, 88).

[9] May, "Metaphoric Motivation", 67.

[10] See Reingard Nischik, *Engendering Genre: The Works of Margaret Atwood*, Ottawa: University of Ottawa Press, 2009, 74-77. Nischik interprets "Polarities" in the light of Ronald D. Laing's popular psychiatric book *The Divided Self: An Existential Study in Sanity and Madness*, New York: Random House, 1960. For a more elaborate treatment of these issues, and in particular for an interpretation of Morrison as a schizoid character through the study of his verbal communication, see Reingard Nischik, "Speech Act Theory, Speech Acts, and the Analysis of Fiction", *Modern Language Review*, LXXXVIII/2 (April 1993), 297-306. On Laing's influence on Margaret Atwood's 1972 novel, published shortly after "Polarities", see also Catherine McLay, "The Divided Self: Theme and Pattern in *Surfacing*", in *The Canadian Novel: Here and Now*, ed. John Moss, Toronto: NC Press, 1983, 32-44.

[11] The author's victimization theory, expounded in a book dated one year after the publication of "Polarities", illuminates the treatment of this important aspect of her

would acknowledge playing a part yet refuse to assume full
responsibility for his deeds. Because the weather is very cold, Louise
is jumping up and down while Morrison gets his car ready. The
narrator/focalizer notices "her head coming out of the enormous
second-hand fur coat she wore like a gopher's out of its burrow", and
this humorous simile suddenly turns serious as it reminds Morrison of
the dead gophers he had seen "on the drive across, many of them
dead; one he had killed himself, an accident, it had dived practically
under the car wheels".[12]

Toward the end of the story, Morrison fantasizes about his special
infatuation with Louise, wonders about the possibility of taking care
of her, and envisions how "at night she would be there in the subzero
bedroom for him to sink into as into a swamp, warm and obliterating".
At last he confesses to himself that he would not have fallen in love
with Louise if she had been sane, for he can only be attracted to a
hopeless, mad woman. He describes their inequitable relationship by
means of a series of violent images that turn fictional characters into
two psychological archetypes:

> So this was his dream girl then, his ideal woman found at last: a
> disintegration, mind returning to its component shards of matter, a
> defeated formless creature on which he could inflict himself like a
> shovel on earth, axe on forest, use without being used, know without
> being known.[13]

This chain of thoughts is perhaps too contrived, but serves the main
function of establishing a visual schema in which two personalities are
set in diametrical contrast, situated at opposite poles, as the title of this
short story implies. Apart from their cognitive component, the similes
"like a shovel on earth" and "axe on forest" convey a sense of pain
and have a strong affective meaning that encourages readers to
sympathize with the victim and condemn the agent of her destruction.

---

fiction and is particularly relevant for interpreting how Louise is identified with an
animal victim. See Margaret Atwood, *Survival: A Thematic Guide to Canadian
Literature*, Toronto: Anansi, 1972, 80.

[12] Atwood, *Dancing Girls*, 52.

[13] *Ibid.*, 73. Morrison's previous mental associations concerning women reveal his
general attitude toward femaleness, as shown in the following observation: "the girls,
even the more slender ones, made him think of slabs of substance white and congealed,
like lard" (*ibid.*, 56).

The story offers an open ending whose meaning depends on whether the final scene of Morrison's body going numb and freezing to death is interpreted literally or metaphorically.

Another example of Atwood's use of the term "metaphor" occurs in "Giving Birth", also included in *Dancing Girls*. The first-person narrator of this metafictional work recalls an old picture of tar sands that may symbolize how she feels stuck with language, but she overcomes her anguish by reassuring herself that she is not actually trapped by lethal words, nor will she be sucked down by them. The painting in the Royal Ontario Museum need not represent her difficulties in articulating her ideas: "it's only a tableau after all, it's only a metaphor."[14] This statement indicates her determination to go on writing, avoiding "the metaphoric mistake of perceiving a metaphor as real" and thus averting the danger to which Louise succumbed in "Polarities".[15]

There is another explicit metafictional reference to metaphor in "Unearthing Suite", an overtly autobiographical story collected in *Bluebeard's Egg* (1983). The story's first-person narrator humorously remarks on her parents' courtship:

> My father first saw her … sliding down a banister … and resolved then and there to marry her; though it took him a while to track her down, stalking her from tree to tree, crouching behind bushes, butterfly net at the ready. This is a metaphor but not unjustified.[16]

The justification of this metaphor is an amusing allusion to the fact that Margaret Atwood's father, like Sylvia Plath's, was an entomologist.[17] This specific comment on metaphor occurs after

---

[14] *Ibid.*, 226.

[15] Charles May, "Why Short Stories Are Essential and Why They Are Seldom Read", in *The Art of Brevity: Excursions in Short Fiction Theory and Analysis*, ed. Per Winther *et al.*, Columbia: University of South Carolina Press, 2004, 20-21.

[16] Margaret Atwood, *Bluebeard's Egg*, London: Virago, 1989, 266.

[17] Carl Atwood, a Ph.D. in forest entomology and a professor of zoology at the University of Toronto, spent much of his life doing research in the woods of northern Ontario and Quebec. Otto Plath, a professor of entomology at the University of Boston, specialized in bees. Insects figure prominently in the works of Sylvia Plath and Margaret Atwood. In 1979, when Atwood reviewed Plath's *Johnny Panic and the Bible of Dreams* for the *New York Times*, she expressed her admiration for the story "Among the Bumblebees" (Margaret Atwood, *Second Words: Selected Critical Prose*, Toronto: Anansi, 1982, 319).

several uncommon instances that show how the narrator uses this trope to render some aspects of her parents' inner lives in graphic strokes, through comic nonliteral analogies such as the following:

> My parents' occasional dismay over me was not like the dismay of other parents. It was less dismay than perplexity, the bewilderment of two birds who have found a human child in their nest and have no idea what to do with it.[18]

Surprisingly, it is in the hybrid volume of very-short short stories and prose poems entitled *Murder in the Dark* (1983) that Atwood deals with metaphor in a comparatively more thorough manner than in the rest of her fiction, including her novels. "Metaphor can be dangerous", warns the narrator of "Raw Materials", standing before a Mexican carving that represents the decapitation of someone defeated in a sacred game: "the body of a man with a fountain in place of the head: the blessed loser, making it rain."[19] The speaker of the witty, satirical piece "Simmering" describes a society in which gender roles were reversed, so that cooking became an exclusively male activity. Language gradually reflected the way in which "sexual metaphor was changing", traditional mappings from cooking as a source domain were developed, and certain culinary words – such as "eggbeater, pressure cooker, and turkey baster" – became taboo for most women, who were not allowed access to kitchens.[20]

In "Women's Novels" Atwood teasingly contrasts the genre that is supposed to be favored by female readers with what is generally understood by "men's novels". She ends her satire with a section intended to ridicule the lack of precision with which certain popular writers use metaphorical language. This section begins by focusing on a hackneyed metaphorical expression, "She had the startled eyes of a wild bird", which becomes the target of Atwood's ironic banter:

> This is the kind of sentence I go mad for. I would like to be able to write such sentences without embarrassment. I would like to be able to read them without embarrassment. If I could only do these two

---

[18] *Ibid.*, 263.
[19] Margaret Atwood, *Murder in the Dark: Short Fictions and Prose Poems*, London: Jonathan Cape, 1984, 24.
[20] *Ibid.*, 32.

simple things, I feel, I would be able to pass my allotted time on this earth like a pearl wrapped in velvet.

The vagueness of the phrase "She had a feral gaze like that of an untamed animal" prompts a similarly sarcastic response on the part of this writer who is extremely conscious of the donor domains of her metaphors:

> Metaphor leads me by the nose, into the maze, and suddenly all Eden lies before me. Porcupines, weasels, warthogs and skunks, their feral gazes malicious or bland or stolid or piggy and sly .... *Which one?* I murmur to the unresponding air. *Which one?* [21]

The unnamed female protagonist of the second-person narrative "Him" finally gives up trying to understand her husband in metaphorical terms, as "a tree or a stone, one of those mute contained objects", putting an end to her longtime habit: "... but for once you avoid metaphors: there's nothing else you want to change him into. Your years of practice, that skill in metamorphosis, count for nothing here."[22]

The theme of metamorphosis in the Ovidian sense, which is central in Atwood's poetry, also has a prominent place in her fiction. Atwood has been fascinated by the phenomenon of metamorphosis since her childhood, an enthusiasm she herself has linked to her early interest in insects. In one of her interviews she remarked:

> The most transformative thing you can study is insects. They change from one thing into another, and the thing that they change into bears no relation to what they were before.[23]

Perhaps because Atwood's critics have so often emphasized the idea that the influence of entomology in her writings came from her father's research, she has deemed it necessary to remind them that "Ovid's father was not an entomologist".[24] This statement may be taken as an adequate

---

[21] *Ibid.*, 35-36.

[22] *Ibid.*, 56.

[23] Bonnie Lyons, "An Interview with Margaret Atwood", *Shenandoah*, XXXVII/2 (1987), 75.

[24] Linda Sandler, "Interview with Margaret Atwood", *Malahat Review*, XLI (January 1977), 14.

warning when examining Atwood's metaphorical expressions in search of sources, which are various and have been combined in quite an intricate manner.

The transformation of Atwood's characters into and out of the animal, vegetable and mineral states supplies a considerable number of metaphors in her novels and short stories, where the phenomenon of metamorphosis is often linked to dreams, visions and hallucinations. When Atwood seeks ways of integrating the fantastic worlds of desire with the world of material reality, she sometimes uses the typical devices of magical realism either in earnest or in jest. The transformation is presented as a funny game in "Happy Endings", where John is perceived by Mary's friends through three standard metaphors – as "a rat, a pig, a dog".[25] She believes that his better self will eventually come out, and imagines this transformation in metaphorical terms: "This other John will emerge like a butterfly from a cocoon, a Jack from a box, a pit from a prune, if the first John is only squeezed enough."[26] Again, Atwood uses three consecutive similes not only to further her point, but also to achieve a comic effect in a piece she regarded as unclassifiable:

> I did not know what sort of creature it was. It was not a poem, a short story, or a prose poem. It was not quite a condensation, a commentary, a questionnaire, and it missed being a parable, a proverb, a paradox. It was a mutation.[27]

Women are commonly depicted in floral terms both in literature and in everyday language. Atwood pokes fun at the sexist conceptualization of "women as plants" when she writes in "The Sunrise" that Yvonne is "like a plant – not a sickly one, everybody comments on how healthy she always is – but a rare one, which can flourish and even live only under certain conditions".[28]

Many of Atwood's metaphorical expressions involve an animal in the source domain and a human being in the target domain. Perhaps her most elaborated presentation of a character as a dog is in the short

[25] Atwood, *Murder in the Dark*, 37.
[26] *Ibid.*, 38.
[27] See Atwood's letter (5 September 1988) quoted in Robert Shapard and James Thomas, "Afternotes", in *Sudden Fiction International: Sixty Short-Short Stories*, eds Robert Shapard and James Thomas, New York: Norton, 1989, 298-99.
[28] Atwood, *Bluebeard's Egg*, 247.

story "Hurricane Hazel", where the protagonist recalls how she and her brother used to discuss her boyfriend:

> He spoke as if both he and I took it for granted that I would soon be getting rid of Buddy, as if Buddy were a stray dog it would be my duty to send to the Humane Society if the owner could not be found. Even Buddy's name, my brother said, was like a dog's. He said I should call Buddy "Pal" or "Sport" and teach him to fetch.
>   .... It was true that there was something dog-like about Buddy: the affability, the dumb faithfulness about the eyes, the dutiful way he plodded through the rituals of dating.[29]

Behavioral features predominate in the excerpt quoted above, but in subsequent passages some physical traits that reinforce the burlesque connection between Buddy and a "friendly Newfoundland dog" are also explicitly mentioned.[30] In this context, it should not come as a surprise that Buddy's new girlfriend has "bangs down over her forehead like a sheepdog's".[31]

Atwood often presents a simile, to make the comparison more explicit, and then a metaphor linked to it; on other occasions she reverses the order and starts with a metaphor, followed by a simile. The appearance of these closely related tropes in succession has a cumulative effect that is particularly striking in short fiction. Indeed, the author sometimes takes economy of expression to its limits, but now and then she lengthens her short narratives through extended metaphors, generally based on out-of-the-ordinary images that emphasize the artificial patterning of the genre and have a stunning impact on the readers. The powerful effects of this disruptive technique are intensified by the brevity of this genre, which conventionally demands compressed forms of characterization. These effects make us wonder in what ways short narratives amplify our perception of deliberately excessive metaphors, similes and other comparisons.

Some characters of Atwood's short stories are metaphorically conceptualized by themselves, by the narrator and by other characters,

---

[29] *Ibid.*, 37.
[30] "Buddy's mouth was soft, his body large and comforting" (*ibid.*, 41). "The skin of his back was soft and slightly loose over the muscles, like a sweater or a puppy's neck" (*ibid.*, 50).
[31] *Ibid.*, 58.

at times in such a highly wrought manner that certain readers may find her procedure too obtrusive. The protagonist and focalizer of "Loulou; or, the Domestic Life of the Language" (1983) is represented as a modern earth mother or mother goddess through an aesthetically coherent cluster of metaphors derived from the mineral kingdom. She is a professional potter whose vocation dates back to childhood, when her mother used to reprimand her for making mud pies, calling her by her first name "as if *Loulou* in itself meant mud".[32] Loulou constructs herself on purpose, and is also conscious about how she is being constructed by an improbable group of male poets (her husband, her ex-husband and three ex-lovers) who write about her in the collective poetry magazine they run. They consistently describe her as "marmoreal" (an adjective repeated on three different pages of this short story), "geomorphic", "telluric" and "earthy".[33] Loulou enjoys being their Muse and conforms to the role that is expected of a solicitous maternal figure, attending to the poets' material and emotional needs. Apart from her motherly function, which includes feeding the poets, she is or has been sexually related to all of them, as befits a genuine earth goddess. Although she has never considered her work with clay real art, she begins to get pleasure from being perceived as a creator by her accountant, and decides to incorporate this facet into her new conception of herself.[34] Linguistic creativity, however, seems to be reserved for men, since she feels that she must content herself with "the Domestic Life of the Language" mentioned in the subtitle of this short story. Still, despite her limited access to the world of letters, she both exerts her capacity as a terrestrial goddess and flaunts her practical personality by humorously defining two types of men as two different kinds of fruits of the earth: "The businessmen would be ... potatoes rather than, like the poets, slightly over-ripe avocadoes."[35]

Metaphor constitutes the main structural device of this piece of short fiction, which is closely connected to the folktale genre through both its unlikely plot and its intertextual references to "The Little Red Hen", a story that many years later would inspire Atwood's flash-fiction work "The Little Red Hen Tells All", another parody from a feminist perspective. Like the Red Hen of the old tale, Loulou toils

---

[32] *Ibid.*, 67.
[33] *Ibid.*, 61, 62, 66, 70.
[34] *Ibid.*, 75.
[35] *Ibid.*, 73.

alone, without the help of those who turn up when it is time to eat the loaves of home-baked bread just out of the oven.[36] In "Loulou; or, the Domestic Life of the Language" no attempt at verisimilitude is made, and realistic characterization is replaced by surrealist techniques of stereotyping precisely intended to subvert stereotypes when dealing with a number of topics, such as well-known categorizations of masculine/feminine speech, the portrayal of women in male-dominated literary discourse, male exploitation of women, and the supposedly inherent female tendency to nurture others.

The two protagonists of the short story "Isis in Darkness" characterize themselves and each other to a large extent by means of their divergent metaphorical styles. Richard, the character from whose point of view the story is told, is an untenured academic who gets a job teaching English literature courses and whose special interest in metaphor leads him to write a paper "on witchcraft as sexual metaphor".[37] Selena, a character partly inspired by the Canadian writer Gwendolyn MacEwen (1941-87), is a mysterious poet whose peculiar metaphors are similar to the ones that Atwood herself enjoys using whenever she wants to achieve grotesque effects in her own fiction, forcing her readers to take major associative leaps. The narrator refers to Selena as someone who "would love that intersection of the banal and the numinous" and illustrates this singular tendency with an example: "She once said that the universe was a doughnut."[38] Furthermore, Selena produced one of her most daring metaphors when she called the zero in the year 1960 "the white-hot luminous egg / from which everything hatches", whereas for Richard the same digit simply "signalled a dead end".[39] His metaphors are explicitly defined as "humbler" than Selena's.[40] When he notes that Selena's "darkly spiced" voice is "like cinnamon", that the irises of her turquoise eyes are "dark-ringed like a cat's", or that he may be "an open book", he confirms that his similes are conventional, trite expressions, worn-out after long years of service.[41]

---

[36] "If she wants the bread taken out when it's done but not overdone, and she does, she'll have to do it herself" (*ibid.*, 64); "Everyone depends on her, but when she needs help ... nobody's within call" (*ibid.*, 72).
[37] Margaret Atwood, *Wilderness Tips*, Toronto: McClelland and Stewart, 1991, 74.
[38] *Ibid.*, 60.
[39] *Ibid.*, 61.
[40] *Ibid.*, 82.
[41] *Ibid.*, 65, 66, 72.

While his writings are deemed "fatuously romantic", he admires her extraordinary capacity to transform ordinary objects, commonplace events and even ill-favored people into pure beauty. For instance, she is able to turn a group of strippers he derogatorily perceives as "a bunch of fat sluts with jiggling, dimpled flesh" into "surreal butterflies, emerging from cocoons of light".[42] She comes from the same unattractive social milieu as Richard but, unlike him, has managed "to construct her new, preferred identity".[43] Richard secretly craves her, as the epitome of femininity. However, since he intuits that this ideal woman is unattainable, he turns to practical Mary Jo so that the latter "might neutralize Selena, like an acid neutralizing an alkali; get her out of his head".[44] Richard marries Mary Jo not because he is in love with her, but because he thinks that "she would be good for him", "like corned beef, cottage cheese, cod-liver oil" or "milk".[45] Once this doomed-from-the-start marriage is over and Selena has died, the memory of her poem "Isis in Darkness" (from which the title of Atwood's short story is derived) spurs Richard to reverse the Isis-Osiris myth. He decides to conduct a literary research project on her work so as to gather her fragments in the hope that, by "fitting her broken pieces back together", "he will be created by her, he will have a place in her mythology after all".[46]

This short story exemplifies the "high degree of artistic stylization" that May wrote about when tracing the historical development of the genre from its mythic origins until recent times.[47] Atwood's "Isis in Darkness" as a whole, and in particular its appropriate metaphorical resolution, thematizes the interrelationship between the urge to depict everyday reality and the desire to construct a new mythology. The resulting tension is further complicated by the intrinsic brevity of the narrative form that the author has chosen to experiment with. Ancient myth and its postmodernist reversal are intricately intertwined with a true-to-life plot in a short story that plays with verisimilitude in a choice

---

[42] *Ibid.*, 80, 69-70.

[43] *Ibid.*, 60. Klaus Peter Müller singles out Selena as "one of the characters who most consistently and absolutely construct themselves in Atwood's work", in "Re-Constructions of Reality in Margaret Atwood's Literature: A Constructionist Approach", in Nischik, *Margaret Atwood*, 240.

[44] Atwood, *Wilderness Tips*, 69.

[45] *Ibid.*, 70.

[46] *Ibid.*, 82, 83.

[47] Charles May, *The Short Story: The Reality of Artifice*, New York: Twayne, 1995, 20.

of twentieth-century Toronto settings whose atmosphere is conjured up with scrupulous authenticity.[48] The extravagant metaphors of the doughnut and the white-hot egg draw attention to three specific years: 1960, 1970 and 1980. Additionally, the two metaphors produce a similar kind of conceptual shock and typify a technical device designed to parody the narrative strategies of writers who have carried metaphors to their extreme limits, such as Gwendolyn MacEwen, to whom Atwood has devoted critical attention.[49] This procedure serves a double purpose: on the one hand, she tries to make the abstract world understandable by casting it in concrete terms; on the other, she attempts to project the concrete details of our matter-of-fact existence in abstractions.

The portrayal of Selena and Richard exemplifies to what extent "the short story is an effective medium for the exploration of new versions of identity and character" even though "the form is not necessarily suited to character development".[50] The depiction of character in sudden or flash fiction is a much greater challenge, calling for a technical dexterity that Atwood evinces in her collections of short-shorts entitled *Good Bones* (1992) and *The Tent* (2006). Sharon Wilson has pointed out that "characters in *Good Bones* are mostly parodic versions of ones already familiar to us from popular culture, mythology, and literature".[51] This referential quality contributes to the success of the brilliantly compressed characterization embedded in these miniature masterpieces, most of which are plotless. For instance, "Unpopular Gals" is character-based instead of plot-driven, a feature underscored by the nameless protagonist of the third section when she claims, "I'm the plot".[52]

---

[48] "But what could be more realistic than the surfaces of some highly symbolic stories?" wondered Mary Rohrberger in her essay "Origins, Development, Substance, and Design of the Short Story", in *The Art of Brevity*, 5.

[49] There is a reference to the use of the Isis-Osiris myth in MacEwen's poem "Finally Left in the Landscape" in Margaret Atwood's essay "MacEwen's Muse", *Canadian Literature*, XLV (1970), 24-32; rpt. in Atwood, *Second Words*, 71.

[50] Paul March-Russell, *The Short Story: An Introduction*, Edinburgh: Edinburgh University Press, 2009, 122, 121.

[51] Sharon Rose Wilson, "Fiction Flashes: Genre and Intertexts in *Good Bones*", in *Margaret Atwood's Textual Assassinations: Recent Poetry and Fiction*, ed. Sharon Rose Wilson, Columbus: Ohio State University Press, 2003, 25. For a comprehensive analysis of Atwood's fairy-tale sources, see Sharon Rose Wilson, *Margaret Atwood's Fairy-Tale Sexual Politics*, Jackson: University Press of Mississippi, 1993.

[52] Margaret Atwood, *Good Bones*, London: Bloomsbury, 1992, 30.

"Unpopular Gals" comprises three monologues: the first is by the ugly stepsister, and the other two are spoken by composite characters that combine other fairy-tale archetypes of wicked women, including the witch and the evil stepmother. Although the five parts of the traditional plot arrangement (exposition, rising action, climax, falling action, and resolution) cannot be mapped out in the pattern of this brief fiction, it contains direct allusions to the plots of "Cinderella", "Rapunzel", and "Hansel and Gretel". Atwood subverts all of these tales by shifting conventional perspectives, so that readers are induced to revise standard interpretations and reappraise the events told in such stories from the point of view of the villains, instead of the heroes. Furthermore, she often gives a voice to those who had remained almost silent, as she does in "Gertrude Talks Back". Addressing Hamlet bluntly, Atwood's assertive Gertrude sums up with noteworthy verbal economy what she thinks of Ophelia and resorts to a scornful simile that evokes a vivid mental picture of the young virgin "all trussed up like a prize turkey in those touch-me-not corsets of hers", in contrast with Gertrude's self-acknowledged and self-affirmed lustful image.[53]

In *The Tent*, another miscellany of short texts that prove difficult to classify under conventional headings (prose poem, tall tale, parable, fable, diary note, recipe, essay-fiction, short dialogue, dramatic monologue, and parodies of all these generic forms), Atwood also presents narrators who characterize themselves very strongly through their use of metaphorical language. The ironic voice in "Encouraging the Young" is that of an elderly writer who, having achieved success, no longer sees those she labels with the "collective name" of "the young" as competitors: "Fish are not the rivals of stones." Therefore, she decides to "fling encouragement" to them "like rice at a wedding" and to stand cheering indiscriminately, "like a blind person at a football game".[54] Having abandoned her former severe standards, and posing as an old witch "at the edge of the dark woods", she announces that she will let the ambitious, inexperienced authors enter the "lavish

---

[53] *Ibid.*, 17. For a detailed analysis of this story, see Pilar Cuder, "Rewriting Canonical Portrayals of Women: Margaret Atwood's 'Gertrude Talks Back'" in *The Essentials of Literature in English, post-1914*, ed. Ian MacKean, London: Hodder Arnold, 2005, 186-93.
[54] Margaret Atwood, *The Tent*, New York: Nan A. Talese/Doubleday, 2006, 17.

gingerbread house" so that they may stuff their faces on "sugary fame".[55]

Nell, the incisive protagonist of *Moral Disorder* (2006), is identified by a similar ironic voice from the very beginning of the only short-story cycle that Atwood has published so far. The entire first paragraph of the opening story, "The Bad News", is written in a metaphorical mode that echoes the one prevailing in "Encouraging the Young".[56] Nell starts by imagining the arrival of bad news in customary terms (as the typically ominous bird of most mythologies), but then she abruptly astonishes the reader with an unexpected shift:

> I think of the bad news as a huge bird, with the wings of a crow and the face of my Grade Four schoolteacher, sparse bun, rancid teeth, wrinkly frown, pursed mouth and all, sailing around the world under cover of darkness, pleased to be the bearer of ill tidings, carrying a basket of rotten eggs, and knowing – as the sun comes up – exactly where to drop them. On me, for one.[57]

This quotation illustrates the ways in which Atwood capitalizes on the multiple possibilities of metaphorical expression throughout her wide range of short fiction, for this brief text contains the main features that distinguish the author's innovative handling of such cognitive and rhetorical devices. Despite their apparent casualness, these initial lines are carefully crafted to have a compelling visual impact, since they set before our eyes two poignant mental pictures audaciously set in contrast.[58] This amazing juxtaposition of disparate entities is related to Atwood's talent for blending realistic and fantastic elements in her

---

[55] *Ibid.*, 19.

[56] Margaret Atwood, *Moral Disorder and Other Stories*, New York: Nan A. Talese/ Doubleday, 2006. Four of the short stories of this volume were published individually between 2005 and 2006. Neither the much earlier "long short story" entitled "The Labrador Fiasco" (1996) nor the one that closes the volume, "The Boys at the Lab", features Nell, who alternates between the roles of first-person narrator and third-person center of consciousness. Robert Thacker refers to *Moral Disorder* as "a collection which almost becomes a story sequence though the last two personal stories disrupt that formal pattern", in "Quartet: Atwood, Gallant, Munro, Shields", in *The Cambridge History of Canadian Literature*, eds Coral Ann Howells and Eva-Marie Kröller, Cambridge: Cambridge University Press, 2009, 365.

[57] Atwood, *Moral Disorder*, 1.

[58] Atwood describes herself as "very visually oriented". See J.R. (Tim) Struthers, "An Interview with Margaret Atwood", *Essays on Canadian Writing*, VI (Spring 1977), 20.

writings. The bizarre clash between the familiar and the strange is a particularly appropriate way to conceptualize the delivery of evil news about an event that stems from a public, foreign sphere (the murder of the leader of the interim government council) and will threaten a private, domestic setting (Nell's home). The treatment of the image of the schoolteacher – a familiar figure provocatively made strange – constitutes a good instance of Atwood's defamiliarizing techniques.[59] Likewise, the mixture of the serious and the comic is deeply unsettling, because it enhances the menacing effect of this haunting paragraph, in which fear and anxiety are combined with the ability to laugh at danger and deride death. Dealing with the theme of mortality in such a playful manner proves that a sudden burst of eccentric humor, attained by means of a skillful manipulation of the grotesque, may help to capture the reader's attention more easily than if the same issue had been introduced in the usual earnest fashion. When the full meaning of this excerpt is unfolded in the following pages, the reader can discern to what extent blatant metaphors may become excellent tools for making sense of complex experiences.

The two visual images originally adopted to describe the bad news in *Moral Disorder* – the crow and the schoolteacher – are subsequently reinforced by other comparisons that equate such news, in succession, with diverse agents of destruction (for instance, burning heat, or illness). Again, the actual risk of having one's health affected by one's holding the bad news, rather than delivering it immediately, is evoked through a sequence of jocose analogies. The act of passing the news is likened to that of getting a "hot potato" off one's hands, whereas that of keeping the news inside one's body is hyperbolically rendered in medical terms, mocking a quote from a famous Hollywood film: if the bad news cannot be told right away, some gland or bladder may burst, and this may cause "peritonitis of the soul".[60] These utterances exemplify Atwood's habit of drawing her metaphorical language from a variety of sources, including everyday speech and popular culture (for example, cinema). The irreverent tone

---

[59] Gerd Bjørhovde analyzes the defamiliarization effects of Atwood's short story "A Travel Piece" in his essay "When Foreignness and Familiarity Become One: Defamiliarization in Some Canadian Short Stories", in *The Art of Brevity*, 128-37.

[60] Atwood, *Moral Disorder*, 2. "Half idealism is the peritonitis of the soul. America is full of it", says Hank Teagle (Wesley Addy) in Robert Aldrich's film noir *The Big Knife* (1955).

of these passages is sustained by other similes, such as one that describes the shock brought about by the terrorist attack, and its consequences on the frightened "leaders of the leading countries", who "aren't really leading any more" and whose eyes have become "white-rimmed like the eyes of panic-stricken cattle".[61] Once more, this simile evidences the author's favorite category crossings and her free play among disparate domains.

Atwood's increasingly experimental short fiction offers ample proof of her explorative work with new textual formats. She employs the subversive methods commonly identified with the discourses of postmodernism, particularly metafiction, self-conscious narration, intertextuality, magical realism, the mixing of literary genres, parody and irony. As a result, the metaphorical strategies displayed in her novels and short stories share the essential features of postmodernist fiction. Like many other postmodernist writers, Atwood exposes the rules that govern her metaphorical strategies by directing her readers' attention to them through various procedures. Sometimes she achieves this goal by questioning the adequacy of well-known metaphors, interpreting them in a nonconventional rather than straightforward manner, or by reversing the process of conventionalization through the device of "remetaphorization" or "resurrection" of dead metaphors.[62] If conceptual metaphors tend to be "automatic, effortless, and largely unconscious", Atwood frequently makes an effort to bring them to consciousness.[63] On other occasions she fashions wild metaphors whose extravagance cannot be overlooked. The deliberate contrivance of such eccentric metaphors has a defamiliarizing effect that highlights the artificial quality of her literary texts. Her playfulness and her clever sense of the absurd account for a number of grotesque metaphors, which reinforce many other elements of grotesquerie that Atwood herself has acknowledged when commenting on her writings.

A further issue to consider is whether it is possible to find any unique traits that set apart the metaphorical qualities ascribed to Atwood's short stories from those belonging to her novels. The main differences are related to the intensity of the effects produced within each narrative form, depending on length. In the context of short

---

[61] *Ibid.*, 3.
[62] Winfried Nöth, "Semiotic Aspects of Metaphor", in *The Ubiquity of Metaphor*, eds Wolf Paprotté and René Dirven, Amsterdam: John Benjamins, 1985, 6.
[63] Lakoff and Turner, *More Than Cool Reason*, 62.

fiction, the impact of a striking image can be stronger, a deliberately blatant metaphor may seem still more obtrusive, a series of elaborate similes is likely to be more conspicuous yet, and an extended comparison can be perceived as even more protracted. The basic difference is a matter of degree, but in literature this amounts to an extremely important difference. In contrast with her novels, Atwood's art of brevity illustrates the manifold ways in which metaphors and other related tropes may work creatively within a literary genre shaped by distinctive principles of concision, density and concentration of meaning.

BODY POLITICS: FEMALE DYNAMICS IN ISABEL ALLENDE'S *THE STORIES OF EVA LUNA*

FARHAT IFTEKHARUDDIN

It is probably dangerous to claim that the short story captures the feminine better than the novel does. Arguably, the novel, with its luxury of time and space, is an effective medium to enunciate the largesse that femininity encompasses, the time and space that Isabel Allende herself used in developing all her characters, including the females, particularly Clara, in her epic novel *The House of the Spirits*. However, as a larger form, in offering the magnitude of exposition where everything is laid bare and developed, an aesthetically pleasing experience in itself, the novel must logically forgo the other aesthetic experience that is central to the short story: enigma. Eileen Baldeshwiler assigns the short story to the domain of the "lyrical" by pointing to the short story's "concentrat[ion] on internal changes, moods, and feelings".[1] More than that, the enigmatic form of the genre and the structural compactness of the short story, which forces a near-complete reliance on symbolic and metaphoric vehicles to incorporate and convey meaning, creates avenues of multiplicity and a maze of variables at cognitive levels. It is this sense of multitudinous possibilities that the very form of the short story possesses in its composition that epistemologically complements the enigmatic nature of the feminine. The poetics of the short story potently captures the sublime within the female body and psyche. Also, through its symbolic and metaphoric dependency the short story, like the female, is dialogic, demanding the application of poetic sensibilities, making the short story an ideal form for incorporating the female body politics.

---

[1] Eileen Baldeshwiler, "The Lyrical Short Story: The Sketch of a History", in *Short Story Theories*, ed. Charles E. May, Athens: Ohio University Press, 1976, 202-13.

The open-ended aspect of the short story that sets into motion the idea of multiplicity readily accommodates the open-ended characteristic within the female/male duality that is a central focus in "Two Words", "Clarisa", "Wicked Girl", "Toad's Mouth", "Tosca", and "Simple Maria". In eschewing male dominance the females in these narratives re-establish the primal fact that the male is contained within the female – males are from and of females – and that the female/male duality is contained within the woman. This fundamental primacy of the female, which often occurs as an epiphanic realization in the male characters that helps mitigate subordination and diminution of women, reasserts the natural cyclicality embodied in the female. The critical organic feature of the short story – that by means of its physical linearity it promotes the concept of circularity – effectively serves to promote the cyclical within the female. The female *oeuvre* articulated, often in a tragicomic mode, in *The Stories of Eva Luna* elevate both the writer and the product beyond regional, national and even ethnic classification. Isabelle Allende uses the poetry of the short story as an effective form to incorporate feminine sensuality and explore the hermeneutics of the female condition. The female dynamics in her stories are not limited to a unique space, time or event. Through the delicacy of form that is inherent in the short story, Allende's stories illuminate intellectually pathogenic gender disparities and parody patriarchal notions, and ultimately repudiate male hegemony. The enigma of the female, the illusive sensuality of the feminine, the mystery of the eternal conflict between the genders, and the incomprehensibility that marks the persistent masculine desire to impose gender superiority, born primarily of assumed sexual superiority, to the extent of influencing socio-economic and political behavior detrimental to the female occupy the time and space within the narratives in *The Stories of Eva Luna*.

In *The Labyrinth of Solitude*, Octavio Paz observes that the "inferiority" of women "is constitutional and resides in their sex".[2] Although he laments that the diminutive placement of the woman in Mexican culture derives from the "anatomical openness"[3] of the

---

[2] Octavio Paz, *The Labyrinth of Solitude and The Other Mexico, Return to the Labyrinth of Solitude, Mexico and the United States, The Philanthropic Ogre*, trans. Lysander Kemp, Yara Milos and Rachel Phillips Belash, New York: Grove Weidenfeld, 1985, 9.

[3] *Ibid.*, 39.

female, which leads men to view women as entities to be possessed, Paz's observations capture a socially and psychologically demeaning condition of the female that crosses geopolitical borders and scales cultural boundaries. This solely male assignation of female inferiority has influenced and marked every aspect of the male/female dynamics, mostly masculine repression of women in terms of social equality, political and economic participation, and creativity. Tragically, this relegation of women to the category of possession is a common masculine attitude universally. Simone de Beauvoir in "Myths: Of Women in Five Authors", besides pointing to the "woman as *flesh*" attitude, notes that the placement of women in apparently elevated male prescribed roles is a self-serving masculine design. The female "represents to man the fertile soil ... the material beauty and the soul of the world". She is "*poetry*", "grace", "oracle", and has the ability to "bestow peace and harmony". She can even function as the "*mediatrix* between this world and the beyond". However, de Beauvoir is quick to identify the latent hypocrisy within this superficial patriarchal elevation: "If [the woman] declines this role, she is seen forthwith as a praying mantis, an ogress."[4] The end result of male-prescribed roles and the purely sexual classification of women is the economic and socio-political subjugation of women, conditions that continue to affect the male/female dynamics of contemporary society.

In defying patriarchal hegemony, Isabel Allende's female characters seem to exercise what Hélène Cixous demands in "The Laugh of the Medusa": through writing themselves into text, they interrogate their "erotogeneity". Cixous insists that women find "their meaning in history" and that through their "inevitable struggle against conventional man", they must emerge from the "enormity of ... repression that has kept them in the 'dark' – that dark which people have been trying to make them accept as their attribute".[5] Allende's female protagonists successfully renounce this attribute by re-establishing their natural primacy, which reverses the male/female order. There is no reciprocity in this reconfigured female/male dynamics. Domination of the male is not their objective; coexistence

---

[4] Simone de Beauvoir, "Myths: Of Women in Five Authors", in *The Critical Tradition: Classic Texts and Contemporary Trends*, 2nd edn, ed. David H. Richter, Boston: Bedford Books, 1998, 638 (emphasis in the text).
[5] Hélène Cixous, "The Laugh of the Medusa", in *ibid.*, 1454.

is. Allende's women create a language/body symbiosis to mediate gender balance.

In "Two Words" language is the essential weapon for the female protagonist, used to acquire both existential and transactional outcomes. Recognizing early on the power of words, she first names herself, an act counter to patriarchal authority. Belisa Crepusculario's name was not acquired through baptism: it was self-searched and invented out of the need to exist. Following the initial step of self-creation, Belisa becomes financially independent, "selling words", words with which she could invent "insults for irreconcilable enemies" if she so willed or even alter the subconscious, to improve "the quality of dreams".[6] Her facility with language, besides being her revenue stream, also serves as the mediatory catalyst that helps her maneuver through the web of political deceit that she encounters when asked to compose a speech for the illiterate and tyrannical colonel aspiring to be president. Belisa deliberates over the choice of words for the speech, discarding those that were nonproductive, evasive, dishonest, or lacked a sense of concern for the populace and ultimately settling on those words that had the potential to stir people's "intuition". The socio-political subtext of Belisa's contemplative perusal of appropriate words is the concentricity of the female that provides definition to the male and brings order to exponential masculine randomness. Subsequent to the formulation of an effective presidential speech, Belisa awards the colonel "two secret words ... for his exclusive use".[7] These two words produce a cataclysmic change in the colonel, whose notoriety was "ineradicably linked to devastation and calamity".[8]

Every time the colonel thought of those two words, it evoked thoughts of Belisa Crepusculario, the female with "firm wanderer's legs and virginal breast".[9] His masculinity is aroused by the memory of her "fiery heat" and "the "whisper of her hair".[10] The two words perpetually haunted his conscious and subconscious state of mind, turning him into a "sleepwalker", inducing a mental breakdown in the

---

[6] Isabel Allende, *Stories of Eva Luna*, trans. Margaret Sayers Peden, New York: Bantam Books, 1989, 9-10.
[7] *Ibid.*, 16-17.
[8] *Ibid.*, 13.
[9] *Ibid.*, 15.
[10] *Ibid.*, 18.

would-be president, and forcing him to confess to his El Mulato that his "befuddlement" stemmed from "those two words that were buried like two daggers in his gut". Belisa's two words, El Mulato realized, had placed the colonel in a "fog", and the "spell whispered into his ears had done what years of battle had not been able to do".[11] El Mulato arrests Belisa, hoping that the colonel can return the two words to Belisa and regain his "manhood". El Mulato's intentions fail as he watches the colonel's "voracious-puma eyes soften"[12] at the sight of Belisa. This complete dominance of the male is possible because words and the female body have merged to create this control; in this scenario, even keeping or losing malehood is not a male decision.

For a woman born into a "family so poor they did not even have names to give their children",[13] acquiring linguistic prowess can more than free Belisa from poverty: it can ensure a life free of male subjugation and offer supreme powers, since "words make their way in the world without a master". While men engaged in the destructive enterprises of war, corruption and wanton possession of women, Belisa empowered herself with the "honorable alternative", words with which she excelled in the world of economics that excluded women in general, but especially women born into poverty. She devours the dictionary "from A to Z" but discards it, refusing to offer her clients "packaged words";[14] instead, she decides to apply her cognitive abilities to appropriate words that best befitted the needs of her clientele, similar to her poetic abilities with which she had constructed her own name, Belisa Crepusculario, "beauty" and "twilight".[15] Her lexical dexterities give her the power of "infinite possibilities" that she uses as an essential expedient for her own success and as well as others'. Her lexicon is varied, magical. The words she sold were unique to each individual because using the same words for all, besides amounting to "collective deceit",[16] is contra to the limitless possibilities of words. Belisa Crepusculario is the Scheherazade of words in this story. With the insurmountable

---

[11] *Ibid.*, 19.
[12] *Ibid.*, 20.
[13] *Ibid.*, 10.
[14] *Ibid.*, 12.
[15] *Ibid.*, 9.
[16] *Ibid.*, 12.

combination of physical beauty and uncanny linguistic ability she transcends, challenges and averts danger from men such as El Mulato, whose "desire for her had turned into rage, and only the fear of her tongue prevented his cutting her to shreds with his whip",[17] a phallic extension. The suggestive tongue/whip positioning does not work out in El Mulato's favor; on the contrary, the fear of words flowing from Belisa's tongue leads to a metaphoric castration of the lust-stricken Mulato. Through adroit manipulation of language, Belisa Crepuscalario is reborn into a powerful woman who effects changes at the very top of the political process: she converts the colonel from a tyrannical male into a subdued partner. This resignification also advances the possibility that the colonel may become a responsible political leader as well. The metamorphosis on the part of the erratic male, the colonel, has the promise of permanency because the transformative powers of the female, Belisa, is now part of the psychosocial equation.

In "Clarisa" sexuality and language are inseparable forces that Clarisa employs for her own success, the security of her children and the "miracle[s]" she performs for the needy. To ensure long-term care for two retarded children, she is compelled to discard her husband, a judge, whose weak genes produced the handicap in favor of the genes from a fiery congressman. Clarisa's sexuality readily corrupts the "incorruptible"[18] politician and helps her apply her "theory of compensation" in order to "preserve the harmony of Creation".[19] Clarisa, by design, produced two boys from this illicit relationship, the children who would eventually acquire the responsibility of caring for their handicapped siblings. She was also born with the gift of "irrefutable logic".[20] Clarisa's power of persuasion is evident in her ability to acquire financial support for social causes from groups that logic would dictate are inherently opposed: German organizations supporting Hebrew enterprises, nuns aiding prostitutes, and the grape industry helping remedy alcoholism. The humorous but ironic juxtaposition of "young artists/Jesuits", "prostitutes/League of Catholic Dames", "Hebrew choir/German Institute", and "alcohol rehabilitation/viticulturists" point to Clarisa's sociopolitical astuteness

---

[17] *Ibid.*, 19.
[18] *Ibid.*, 42.
[19] *Ibid.*, 49.
[20] *Ibid.*, 48.

in bargaining diplomatically, not forcefully as typical males do, a positive outcome from improbable sources. As necessary, she shifts from sexual politics to social politics to achieve her goals, ensuring success in overcoming apparent oppositions. Even her infidelity, which may provoke the wrath of existing socio-religious orthodoxies, is part of Clarisa's logic. Her adultery is practical, devoid of emotion and free of base indulgence in sex; it is a measured response to a situation that needs immediate maternal solution, an internal calling that is greater than prescribed codes.

Economy of language, a predominant trait in the short story that assigns structural integrity to this collection, also contributes to the development of the theme in both "Two Words" and "Clarisa". The compact structure of these stories produces the thematic tension and advances feminist concepts of equity. The grace and poetry of the short story adorn the grace and poetry that Belisa Crepusculario and Clarisa embody as they eloquently strive to create an anthropological balance between the genders. The tension in these stories derives from the need to verbalize the female self. Belisa's linguistic exercise causes a synaptic imbalance, forcing the virile males to reconsider the female and adjusting their singular preoccupation with breasts and provocative thighs to include the cerebrum, thus elevating the female from the base to the profound. This reassessment also places the female in the subject position. Incapable of managing female-rendered vicissitudes, baser males like El Mulato adopt violent attitudes that promote the notion that intellectual enterprises on the part of females are deserving of scorn than appreciation. However, Belisa, in textualizing the female through erudition, countermands entrenched masculine assumptions and initiates the corrective balance in female/male dynamics. Clarisa's female politics accomplishes an economic security for both mother and children. Belisa Crepusculario and Clarisa achieve their objectives in these stories with greater intellectual prowess than the males without losing their femininity and their ability to arouse intense eroticism. In these stories a definition of "female" is elusive – as unusual as Clarisa's proclivity to create miracles and as enigmatic as Belisa's two words. The problem of definition that lends enchantment to the short story is the same problem that engenders mysticism in the female, making the short story and the female metaphorically identical.

Feminine sexuality is the language of interaction in "Wicked Girl" and "Toad's Mouth". These stories are a study, in effect, of the efficacy of the female body and the weakness within male virility. In one, this gender body politics reveals the male's realization of the mutability of unconsidered sex and in the other the achieved value in terms of economics and satisfaction derived from considered sex. In "Wicked Girl" a pubescent female named Elena learns early on, through watching her mother, the art of seduction and the power of the female body. Almost instinctively she uses this knowledge to seduce Juan José Bernal, her mother's lover. Although Bernal, the would-be famous singer and self-named Nightingale, thwarts the advances of Elena and marries the mother, it does not mitigate his problem: "… he thought of [Elena] constantly …. The child's image … stay[s] with him, intact, untouched by the years; she [remained] the passionate girl he had rejected."[21]

While the male preoccupation is physical possession only, female sexuality is more enduring, as it encapsulates the male at both the conscious and subconscious levels. In fact, the politics of the female body even as young and inexperienced as Elena's is sufficient to compel a perverse conversion in the male. Elena's body has so engraved itself in his memory, so altered his psyche, that Bernal can no longer make love to the "heavy body of his wife" without "meticulously invoking" the image of Elena in his mind. Only with Elena's pubescent body as a mental image can Bernal "awaken the … more diffuse impulse of pleasure". These etched memories of Elena's young body propel Bernal to the verge of pedophilia. Unable to involve religion to assist him in his pseudo-redemptive act, Bernal attempts redemption by burning the children's panties with which he masturbated. The overpowering quality of Elena's body keeps Bernal atrophied in a state of anguish and desire while Elena moves on. Years later, when he attempts to apologize to Elena for discarding her and calling her a "wicked girl", she stares at him, speechless, not knowing what to answer. What wicked girl was he talking about? She had left her childhood far behind; she did not remember any particular Thursday in her past.[22]

The female in this story does not suffer from hypocritical dichotomies, only the male does. The remorse is Bernal's alone, for

---

[21] *Ibid.*, 36-37.
[22] *Ibid.*, 38.

having initially failed to resist making love with an adolescent female, then to have rejected her, only to perpetually desire her. For Bernal, Elena is the intoxication; for Elena, Bernal is just a passing phase in her journey to womanhood.

In "Wicked Girl" the reduction of Bernal to a perverse pedophile is accomplished with the politics of female sexuality. In "Toad's Mouth" the same politics assists Hermelinda in establishing an affluent business on a "harsh land inhabited by rough men" who serve as drovers for Sheepbreeders, Ltd., run by the British, who, finding nothing on this desolate land to "carry away", decided to raise sheep. What the British could not physically remove, their sheep did. The large herds consumed all the "vegetation and trampled the last altars of the indigenous cultures".[23] The "English *patrones*" exercised their colonial atrocities by ignoring the plight of the drovers, who "survived in misery" in the cold, going for "months" without proper sustenance. Due to their neglect of both the drovers and the sheep, men and animals became identical in their suffering. The animals experienced the major brunt of this suffering. Seeking warmth and companionship and "impoverished for love", the drovers "lay with their sheep, even with a seal if they could get to the coast and catch one".[24] The iniquity associated with bestiality reveals the moral emptiness of the drovers and mirrors the emptiness of the land laid barren by nature, man and animal. This environment lacking moral parameters, social guidelines and political responsibilities ironically provides Hermelinda with an open field where she "reigns" like a "queen bee", the female in charge of creating in her own design and at her own will a "fantasy" world of "games" that reasserted discipline and promised intense pleasure.[25]

In the love-starved atmosphere of the sheepherders' camp, Hermelinda "made her fortune [lying] on a mattress".[26] Men traveled miles to enjoy her "horse-man's legs and breasts" that showed no "trace of wear .... On Fridays riders galloped frantically from far reaches [and] as they arrived their foaming mounts dropped beneath them."[27] Although the English *patrones* outlawed alcohol and

---

[23] *Ibid.*, 59.
[24] *Ibid.*, 60.
[25] *Ibid.*, 61, 60.
[26] *Ibid.*, 68.
[27] *Ibid.*, 60-61.

disapproved of Hermelinda's "illicit"[28] games, she flourished doing both, subverting colonial restrictions with her body and imposing her sexuality upon all the men in the pampas. The alcohol she brewed while raising the spirits and ruining the livers of her guests also "served to fuel the lamps at the hour of entertainment".[29] The merriments were her source of income. Hermelinda made her profit employing a myriad of games, the favorite and most anticipated being "Toad's Mouth", where

> Hermelinda [drew] a circle in which she [laid] … on her back, knees spread wide …. The dark center of her body … revealed as open as a fruit, as a merry toad's mouth …. The players took position behind the chalk line and tossed their coins toward the target.

The coins that landed within the encircling chalk mark belonged to Hermelinda. The ultimate prize for the men, however, was the right to physically posses Hermelinda by landing a coin inside her female cavity. The drovers willingly sacrificed a "month's pay" often "in fifteen minutes" in anticipation of the two hours alone with Hermelinda following a successful coin toss, the time alone that promised "absolute ecstasy" and the copulation that offered "consolation for all past wants and dreams of the pleasure of paradise". Her "golden" legs and firm body contained magical qualities, "ancient love secrets [that] could lead a man to the threshold of death and bring him back transformed into a wise man".[30] Hermelinda, as the proprietor of her trade, breaches all propriety as she uses her body to assume absolute control of her clients by exploiting the primal weakness of the male, the possession of the female. With the simple assumption that no male in the camp could possibly resist the opportunity to penetrate a female in one thrust as in the game of Swing, where she came swinging with her thighs open towards an aroused male, Hermelinda is able to posses far more than the males: she asserts herself as the illusive receptacle that dominates both the world of the real and the dream of these poverty-stricken drovers, whose "vigorous" bodies became "pliable in her hands".

---

[28] *Ibid.*, 60.
[29] *Ibid.*, 62.
[30] *Ibid.*, 63-64.

Raunchy sexual games are the artistic cloak for "Toad's Mouth".
By turning a child's game (*la rana*, where children attempt to toss
small objects in the open mouth of a toy frog) into an adult game
where males flip coins at an open vagina, the story ridicules the
breakdown of social order following political disengagement, a
breakdown that produces an economically and morally impoverished
population for whom relief comes through momentary, perverse
sexual release. The recipients of such socio-economic collapse at the
pampas are male. The body politics of the female brings order and
discipline to the chaos. Hermelinda has only the appearance of being a
prostitute. Her trade is not a direct transaction of sex for money. She
needs the coins to survive; however, she also provides "solace",[31]
hope and a path back to some semblance of morality for the drovers
by drawing them back from bestiality, the aberrant sexual behavior
that they were driven to as a result of human depravity at the hands of
the supposedly civilized British colonizers.

Ironically, Tierra del Fuego ("land of fire") carries hardly any
spark to sustain life of any form, human or animal – it is Hermelinda
who literally and metaphorically brings redemptive fire to this barren
land. The female is the regenerative agent. Rather than a pejorative
term, the "toad's mouth" reference to the "dark center" of
Hermelinda's body links it with toads' mythical connotations. Mayans
included the toad as one of the three animal entities that made up
Mother Earth: the other two were the alligator and the turtle.
Hermelinda lying on her back and in essence devouring men may very
well mimic an alligator and a turtle. In oriental mythology the toad
bears curative powers; it also symbolizes power and long life, similar
to what Hermelinda has to offer. "Toad's Mouth" is a socio-political
parody of "civilized" mores, moralities and behaviors. It also parodies
fairy tales, myths and restrictive religious dictates. The story contains
shades of the fairy tales *The Frog Prince* and *Cinderella* and a host of
creation myths. It recalls, with uncanny similarity, the Chinese myth
of Liu-Hai, a tenth-century alchemist whose best friend was a large
three-legged toad that often hid in a well and had to be enticed to the
surface with a gold coin. Images of Liu-Hai, the god of wealth and
prosperity, depict him grinning and standing on his toad and juggling
gold coins. This image is reversed in "Toad's Mouth" as Hermelinda

---

[31] *Ibid.*, 61.

grins and lies on her back, legs open, revealing her femininity while men flip coins at her "merry toad's mouth". Embodying perverse parodies of failed social structures, myths, everyday children's games, fairy tales and even religious beliefs such as the Liu-Hai myth, "Toad's Mouth" is a postmodern construct that ridicules the hypocrisies and deficiencies within social infrastructures and beliefs. Through its subversions, the story seeks to balance and remedy these flaws using the female body as the catalyst for change. The story shifts smoothly from social politics to female sexual politics. Here Hermelinda re-creates life on a desolate, unforgiving natural terrain through her femininity, by offering herself as the ultimate prize and through a combination of intense sexuality and "maternal tenderness". She dominates and re-establishes order to a failed community of sheepherders who approach her with the crude "illusory strength" of the phallus only to become "pliable" and "transformed"[32] by her female body politics.

The plasticity of the short story form aptly captures the metonymies of female sexual and interpersonal discourse in "Wicked Girl" and "Toad's Mouth". Male-oriented paradigms seek obfuscation of the feminine. Their perpetual existence challenges presumed masculine moral authority. Females like Elena and Hermelinda circumvent assumed phallic dominance not through denial or emasculation but through conscription, creating a holistic unity that includes the virility of the male and the potency of the female. This unification of the female/male in the feminine relegates the female to religious and mythic realms, goddess and omnipresent Mother who as both creator and destroyer can freely impose nuanced balances. In this ubiquitous form the female is greater than its individual components and more complex than its elemental physiological definitions, compelling the recognition of the female entity as a gestalt. The mythic form of the short story readily complements the mythic nature of the female, and the compact, yet elastic, form of the short story is an effective medium for incorporating the ubiquity of the female. The concept of the woman as a gestalt merges seamlessly into the short story as a gestalt form.

"Tosca" relates Maurizia Rugieri's story of failure and transformation. Patriarchal aspirations introduce Maurizia to the piano at the age of five and thrust her into her first recital at ten in front of a

---

[32] *Ibid.*, 61, 64.

"benevolent public" composed of Italians. Maurizia's embarrassing performance shatters the patriarchal desire to have produced "a new Mozart".[33] Maurizia's own dreams of becoming an opera singer meet the same embarrassing end as a result of her "small, birdlike voice barely strong enough to lull an infant in the cradle". Adhering to predetermined social customs and mores that apply more stringently to females, Maurizia at nineteen is "forced to exchange her dreams of being an operatic soprano for a more banal fate", marriage. Her husband, Ezio Longo, approaches marriage and love with the traditional expectations of the male as the family provider. His love for Maurizia bears the same marks of professionalism that architects bring to their projects. Ezio at thirty-five founded "an empire on cement". His "dedication to his work" makes it "possible for him to strew the capital with his buildings". Although Ezio provides Maurizia with a "mammoth mansion [where] … servants worked constantly merely to burnish the bronzes, polish the floors, clean the crystal teardrops of the chandeliers and … the gold-footed furniture", and even though he built her an amphitheater enabling Maurizia to entertain her guests with her "birdlike twittering", he failed to acquire an identical response from Maurizia of "affection with equal intensity" to his own.

The problem lies in the female/male polarity. This indefinable and, most frequently, unbridgeable rift results in oppositional gender assessments; consequently, the very "imagination" that "eternally fire[s]" and cognitively defines Maurizia registers as "imaginary ailments" in Ezio. Architecturally, Ezio is able to create grand edifices with the "confusion of styles … and profusion of adornment" that "disoriented the senses"; however, he lacked the "refinement of soul and a delicacy" that inhibited his ability to "translate deeds into words", which "made it impossible for him to express his feelings for Maurizia". He tries to obviate Maurizia's needs with materialism, "hoping to bridge the abyss between them".[34] Even the birth of a male child does not alleviate the angst born from the absence of passion and communication. Maurizia, whose subtleties embraced Verdi and Puccini, finds a seemingly kindred soul in Leonardo Gómez, whom she encounters in a streetcar. Although a medical student, Leonardo has an interest in the opera. During their initial encounter, Maurizia

---

[33] *Ibid.*, 123.
[34] *Ibid.*, 124-25.

joins Leonardo in a repertoire, he "whistling an aria from the third act" of Giacomo Puccini's *Tosca* and she singing "the words of the unfortunate Mario". Leonardo's "profile of a Roman statue" and his rendering of a segment from *Tosca* moisten "her bodice ... with sweet anticipation", and "between the two of lines of the score" that they exchange "the romance began".[35] Leonardo becomes Maurizia's "immortal passion"; she follows him to primitive locations where he serves as "camp doctor".[36]

The primal need that drives Maurizia's infidelity and abandonment of a child she loves deeply is beyond Ezio's comprehension. Part of the answer lies in Ezio's exasperated and "defeated" outburst: "'Dammit, I would like to know what it is that you don't have in this world; tell me, and I'll try to get it for you.'"[37] Ezio understands and controls a world of concrete and definable materialism, a world of easy substitution where one object from the real can be replaced by another object of the real of equal or greater value. Ezio's realm is transactional and linear. The nonlinear dynamics of Maurizia's world is alien to his perceptions, beyond his cognitive reaches. In fact, they are also beyond the harsh realities that encompass Leonardo's profession involving the poor and the sick. The connection of the spirit that takes place in a streetcar over a momentary operatic exchange leaves no transformational or indelible mark on Leonardo, who immerses himself completely in his profession, expends his inner being to the healing and caring of his patients and eventually dies of a body broken by exhaustion and tropical diseases. It is Maurizia's imagination, continuing inventions, and overactive sensibility that not only defines and redefines her but also, through her, assigns characteristics to Leonardo.

Despite the Mario/Tosca parallel, there is no shared tragedy in the lives of Maurizia and Leonardo that remotely reaches the brutality depicted in *Tosca*. Although Maurizia's intense desire to escape the circumscription resulting from patriarchal, phallocentric controls forces her from an affluent life into one of extreme strain, discomfort and hardship, Maurizia and Leonardo's lives are devoid of the intense suffering, political intrigue, greed and brutality that Mario Cavaradossi and Floria Tosca are subjected to in Puccini's *Tosca*,

---

[35] *Ibid.*, 126.
[36] *Ibid.*, 127, 132.
[37] *Ibid.*, 128.

where evil seems to prevail with Mario's murder and Floria's suicide. The abiding message of the opera is not the triumph of evil, but the sustaining power of love between Mario and Tosca. It is this intense passionate love, this romantic impossibility, that Maurizia seeks and around which she builds an inventive world where she is in "love in Italian, French, and German; she [is] Aida, Carmen, and Lucia di Lammermoor and, in every instance Leonardo Gómez [is] the object of her immortal passion".[38] Unwilling to capitulate to a banal life and unable to draw an entirely reciprocal passionate response from Leonardo, Maurizia must create herself and Leonardo in her own reality and simultaneously define herself through the conscious and the unconscious. Creating herself and Leonardo in her own image is a psychological imperative for Maurizia because she is determined to live "out her destiny in grandeur". To the surrounding masculine world, her excessive flights of imagination appear as aberrant behavior, "like a character escaped from some tale".[39]

In "Tosca", imagination and creativity is the real domain of the female that produces with simultaneity the creator/destroyer dyad in Maurizia. This duality instills the female with the prerogative not only to act as the catalyst to reach equity in the male/female imbalance within patriarchy, but also to reveal the natural superiority of the female gender in the male/female dialectics. The semiotic accommodation of the male in this dyad reverses the physical placement of words to appear as female/male, a physical corrective step necessary to accurately mirror the archetypal place of the female as the primary unit as a result of being the natural repository for both genders. This is the redefined role that Maurizia accomplishes through sheer determination and allows the inclusion of Leonardo into this reconfiguration, because unlike Ezio, who lacks "culture",[40] Leonardo appreciates opera and thus has a plasticity of character that Maurizia can use to remodel Leonardo in her imagination first and then transpose that as reality to his social surroundings. As a result, Leonardo becomes "Mario" and retains this romantic classification throughout the story: he is a "poet", a "hero of her personal opera" and finally "a saint dedicated to the services of mankind".[41] This

---

[38] *Ibid.*, 126-27.
[39] *Ibid.*, 130.
[40] *Ibid.*, 125.
[41] *Ibid.*, 127, 129, 130, 131.

creative process is not merely an amusement or an enforced arbitrary imposition, since Maurizia's re-creation of Leonardo involves considerable self-sacrifice. She devotes herself "to caring for him", accompanying Leonardo to "primitive hospitals" and acquiring the "duties of a nurse in order to assist him".[42] The female's natural inventive strength enables Maurizia to participate in the real while simultaneously employing the higher mental orders, imagination and creativity, as she imagines herself to be not just any nurse but the legendary "Florence Nightingale"[43] herself.

As in all births, where the male becomes secondary and unnecessary to the creation process, Leonardo's participation in his imaginatively reconstituted roles is inconsequential: "investing [Leonardo] with utopian virtues ... [Maurizia] never pause[s] to measure her lover's response, or gauge whether he was keeping pace with her in their grand passion."[44] As the dominant matriarch in charge of creation, all Maurizia requires to demonstrate "to the world that they [are] the protagonist[s] of an exceptional love" is to identify that the male (Leonardo through his medical service and connection to the "rusticity of the camp") like the female is in "contact with nature". Primal connection to nature allows Maurizia to vicariously function in the real and the imaginary and between the rigid gender demarcations born of the hegemony of heterosexual norms. As the female, the natural originator, Maurizia can at once be a lady with "veils" and "parasol[s]", a "Madame Butterfly", display "suicidal determination" or "timid coquetry", exist in conditions involving "mosquitoes, poisonous insects, iguanas [and] hellish heat", will into existence what others may view as illusionary or "hallucinatory", and survive "the animal pain"[45] arising from her memory of the son she had to leave behind. With this tenacity she forges a world for herself, all without abrogating her femininity or having the need to create a line between the real and the dream.

As the progenitor of her self-made opera, Maurizia's stoic realization that perhaps "the true hero of the drama" was always her husband, Ezio Longo, whom "she wanted to believe had continued to desire her", reveals the strain of the female to define herself into

---

[42] *Ibid.*, 136.
[43] *Ibid.*, 131.
[44] *Ibid.*, 130.
[45] *Ibid.*, 131-36 *passim*.

existence. The "persistent and impassioned love" that Ezio offered "was not in [Leonardo's] nature". Her grown son, in whom she sees a melding of the genders, has "her long bones and delicate skin" but bears the father's coarseness as well, "pound[ing] the table to emphasize his words". At the end of her opera, Maurizia stands alone observing from a distance the father/son interaction and realizes that even after having created "a new dimension" for herself, the "virile tenderness and staunch complicity" that exists in masculinity excludes Maurizia, the female. She steps back without intruding upon this masculine world of father/son; and, with the same "uncompromising sense of [self-]worth" that she notices in her son, Maurizia stands on the "borderline between reality and dream", leaves the tavern and walks home. The parrot circling above her head like a "bizarre archangel"[46] serves to connect her to nature and raise her experience beyond the material into the spiritual. In this configuration, Maurizia the female is complete in mind, body and spirit; she is the signifier providing the codes by which the signified can render themselves acceptable and the terms by which she must be recognized. However, the burden of transformation is a lonely one. In restructuring Leonardo in her own image in order to cherish him within her own parameters of refinement and sensibility, Maurizia transforms him into a project, the same approach that Ezio applied in his failed attempts at depicting his passion for her. In such an exercise, Leonardo becomes more an *objet d'art* than a reciprocal lover. The somber underpinning of Allende's "Tosca" is perhaps that in having to define the female into existence, the female/male dialectics renders the female nearly incomprehensible to the male.

Beginning with the adjectival qualifier "simple", the discursive nature of the female body politics is the playing field in the short story "Simple María". This is a story of total deconstruction and reconstruction of the female. The story begins with the death of María, "an old prostitute with the soul of a girl".[47] But this was not how it all began. Her life started in the traditional male-dominated world where circumscription applies primarily to the female. María is the "daughter" of a "proud" Spanish family. At twelve, at the onset of puberty, María is "struck by a freight train ... that transported [her] into a state of innocence". She forgets her "schooling ... piano lessons

---

[46] *Ibid.*, 136-37.
[47] *Ibid.*, 168.

[and] the use of her embroidery needle". Being struck into a complete "state of innocence" and with the loss of her hat, symbolically the shedding of tradition and propriety, María becomes relatively free of patriarchal taxonomies. Although she loses her ability to reason by traditional standards, what María retains, following the accident, is her "civility". Her impact with the train leaves her "devoid of animosity . . . and well equipped to be happy". At sixteen, her parents, considering her a burden, marries her off to a "groom many decades her senior". This grotesque union is more transactional than mutual: María serves as a commodity that erases the debt of the groom, Dr Guerra, to her family. Bearing the mentality of an innocent but the body of a woman, María enters the "marriage bed" with only observational knowledge of sex. She has seen "cold water [used] for separating dogs ... unable to disengage after coupling [and] ... the rooster fluff[ing] his feathers and crow[ing] when he wants to cover a hen". These were logistical matters for which "she had not found any useful purpose", nor did her experience with a "trembling old man with something unanticipated below his navel" introduce her to anything other than masculine incompetence and the pains of childbirth.[48]

With the death of her husband, María comes closer to breaking free of patriarchal control, though she is still tethered to tradition as she undergoes the ritual of mourning, during which others made "even the most minor decisions for her". After two years of this seemingly endless period of mourning predominantly assigned to females, María makes the final break from patriarchal control, "lift[s] her veil", "smile[s]" and answers the "unbearable" call of sexuality, that "sound of blood racing through her blood". It is on a ship bound for Spain where the family expected María to be sheltered by "solid traditions and [the] power of the Church" that she actually experiences phallic and vaginal powers as she allows a "dark-skinned man" to "remove her black veil" and seduce her.[49] Lying on a "coil of rope", a merged phallic/vaginal representation, María "learned in less than three minutes the difference between an aged husband stiffed by the fear of God and an insatiable Greek sailor afire from ... weeks of oceanic chastity".[50] On this transformative journey she loses both her baby boy to a freak accident and her relative virginity to a "dark shadow in

---

[48] *Ibid.*, 170-72.
[49] *Ibid.*, 173, 175.
[50] *Ibid.*, 173.

the moonlight".[51] Although in terms of the short duration of the copulative act the sailor and her old husband remain identical, the sailor's phallic vigor inflames María's sexuality. What awakens in her is not her awe of the phallus, but absolute *jouissance*. Bathed by the moonlight of Aphrodite, María discovers aphrodisia not simply in vaginal terms, but in terms of body and spirit as a whole. This symbiosis removes María's aphrodisia from the baseness traditionally associated with prurient behavior and elevates it to the quintessence that is inexplicably female.

The *jouissance* that María possesses is devoid of the discomfort that Jacques Lacan associates with intense sexual pleasure or the Freudian sense of regression of a deathlike experience induced by orgasmic pleasure. María's *jouissance* is pure life force, a continuously generative process that is holistic and that depolarizes historical male/female tensions, resulting in a convergence of the genders through sexual epiphany. Her *jouissance* merges readily with her belief that this pleasure is "the blessing from heaven that the nuns in her school had promised good girls in the Beyond".[52] Absent parochial controls, freed from being a sexual commodity and propelled into innocence through a violent impact with a locomotive (in essence a phallus), María's merged sexuality and spirituality defines her body politics, the new language of communication that can transport her *jouissance* to those who share in her quintessence, leading to the entropic decay of social codes marked by male unilateralism. The sailor who is a "brawler and a drunk" and who can only "practice … the acrobatics that he learned in whore houses from Singapore to Valparaiso"[53] is limited to raw phallic energy and, unable to respond to María's *jouissance*, flees from her as though she were a black widow, "a perverse spider who would devour him like a defenseless fly in the tumult of their bed".[54]

What is merely biogenic for María manifests itself as a metaphysical experience for every male she encounters. After the Greek sailor departs, the first "stranger" to experience María's *jouissance* approaches the sexual encounter with the typical virile attitude of the superiority of manhood, thinking "he would divert

---

[51] *Ibid.*, 175.
[52] *Ibid.*, 177.
[53] *Ibid.*, 176.
[54] *Ibid.*, 177-78.

himself with her for ten minutes ... never suspecting ... he would find himself in the whirlpool of a sincere passion". He spreads the news that María has the power to sell "the illusion of love". Her satisfaction rate soared, making her the "most famous prostitute in the port". Her clients transformed her into an icon, tattooing "her name on their arm" and telling "her story on other seas, until the legend ... circled the globe". The innate masculine drive to possess the female changes for her partners following their experience with María, making them the receiving object of this prurient deity.

With her body, her enthusiasm and her elegant manners, María alters the semiotics of sociopolitical codes that traditionally places the male in the dominant position. With her *jouissance*, she emerges as the subject, continuously altering this assumption of masculine dominance. Even as age reduced her to a "tiny grasshopper", a "pile of pathetic bones", a "little nobody" who turned away many clients in sadness, when one of those clients stayed out of "pity [he] received an unexpected prize" leaving "stunned ... carrying with him the image of a mythic girl, not the pitiful old whore he thought he had seen when he arrived". There is no emotional equanimity in this experience with María. The males leave with the dissolution of their phallocentricism. Recognizing María's *oeuvre* but unable to locate the language that can define her *jouissance*, they resort to deifying both her and the experience. María's *jouissance* is disciplined, fluid and all-encompassing, eliminating the distinctions between male-imposed propriety, moral dissonance, and religious irrationalities. To each client she "gave herself" with "the same uncompromising love, anticipating, like a daring bride, the other's desires". María "never saw them as anonymous objects, only the reflection of herself in the arms of her imaginary lover".[55] The unhindered assignation of individuality to herself and her male partners and the harmony and purpose of thought with which she expended her passion are the center points of her *jouissance* with which she mediates the discursive terrain of female/male dynamics, expiating, along the way, male-engendered inequities and the discord that is associated with such inequities, and ultimately revealing the need for homogeneity to solve male-generated female predicaments on equitable terms.

"Simple María" is a magical-realist story that is an indictment of accepted myopic patriarchal views of society, morality, religion and

---

[55] *Ibid.*, 178-79.

myths that place women in a recidivist position. The story changes this long-established and continuously perpetuated diminution of the female with a swift violent action that places María in a permanent state of innocence, a cognitive state that allows her the creative distance required to manufacture modalities of behavior that challenge the norm. With this construct, she incorporates her body to re-create the male-dominated social codes, becoming the aphrodisiac that elevates her to the realm of deity, the goddess that can transform phallocentric social, moral, religious and mythical thoughts and practices. The almost blasphemous depiction of her death, lying like Virgin Mary holding her dead, near-miracle child in her arms, demonstrates María's defiance of patriarchy to attain personal power for the female. Her "simple" mind allows her to identify sex as a heavenly gift and therefore renders it free of sin, leaving her spiritual virginity intact. Her decrepit husband takes her with the fear of God in his heart and it is, in fact, a miracle that he is able to impregnate María, who like the Virgin Mary is unaware of her impregnation.

She defies ancestral codes and takes to drinking chocolate, the aphrodisiac of Mayan and Aztec gods and forbidden to women, following nearly the same ritual that the Meso-American gods followed: consuming large quantities of this magical brew considered to endow the consumer with wisdom and power. María's baptism by moonlight on the coil of rope elevates her to mirror the trinity of the Moon goddess, maiden, mother and crone, providing her the potency to maintain her *jouissance* at mythic proportions. The obvious parody involved in this story deconstructs the phallocentric world that women are subject to, thus forcing shifts in the semiotic game of signs and signals in society that currently impose a male-dictated code on female behavior. María as the agent of this deconstruction modifies established role codes between men and women that eventually forces transformations in her clients, who operate within the established social, moral and religious codes, making them the recipients of María's semiosis.

"Tosca" and "Simple Maria" reveal, through dark humor and religious and social parody, the flawed basic principles of patriarchy that often threaten to alter the core architecture of femininity. The female protagonists in these stories defy patriarchal control and achieve individuality through self-sacrifice and immutable obstinacy. The mutability of the short story form parallels the mutability of female body politics, the shifting and mythical nature of the feminine that often appear to the male psyche to be opaque. This partnership of form and content accelerates the pace within the stories and significantly magnifies intergender tensions, thereby drawing attention to gender inequities, specifically the subordination of the female. Although the males in these stories remain impervious to the sensibilities of the feminine, as in "Tosca", or are incapable of fully grasping the mysticism within female sexuality, as articulated in "Simple Maria", the resulting conclusion in these stories is not insurmountable male/female polarization but a convergence of genders in a female/male recodification evident in "Tosca" and the coalescence of the semiotics inherent in male/female tensions through sexual epiphany delineated in "Simple Maria". Unlike the male counterparts, the females in these narratives are in a constant state of evolution. The desire to define themselves and also to accommodate the male within that definition requires the simultaneity of deconstruction and reconstruction, a cyclical inventive process that, reflecting the magnanimity of the female, embraces infinite adjustments and offers a myriad of outcomes. The female, like the natural form of the short story, is circular and thus open to multitudinous beginnings and endings. Consequently, defining the female, much like defining the short story form, is a protracted and mythic affair. This is the sublime interconnectedness that the genre and the female gender share.

Like the stories themselves, the female characters in *The Stories of Eva Luna* are constructs. Females like Belisa Crepusculario, Hermelinda, Elena, Clarisa, Maurizia and María are self-created individuals and entrepreneurs. Their ultimate power lies in the politics of language and body, in methodically directing the males linguistically and physically to a point of resurrection where the males must cognitively, not physically, rediscover the females they encounter. The female characters are presence not through absence but by virtue of being the primary. They achieve their desired effect through primordial authority and alter existing arbitrary masculine prescriptions without prejudice. Belisa Crepusculario, Clarisa, Elena, Hermelinda, Maurizia and María are well-rounded protagonists who without holding any high office or designations such as colonel or *patrones* are capable of commanding a situation with just their being. They are successful in their politics because they incorporate passion and reasoning into a single insurmountable force. The political superiority of these females comes by virtue of their genetic construct. Language, sexuality and intuition are the unified signature of that genetic pattern, a gestalt. In the males, intuition is difficult to come by, sexuality is a possessive, sadistically violent act and language is a theoretical construct. Thus, what the female can accomplish by simple acclamation, the male struggles to separate, decipher, compile and then act, but by then the political game has already been lost.

"Two Words", "Clarisa", "Wicked Girl", "Toad's Mouth", "Tosca" and "Simple Maria" are not mere polemics, narratives set forth to win an argument. On the contrary, taking advantage of the enigmatic aesthetics of the short story form along with the open-endedness of this genre that allows for the inclusion of inexhaustible possibilities in form and meaning, the stories explore the enigma of the feminine and the epidemiology of masculine control. Along with the recognition of established conflicts demarcated along gender lines, these stories suggest the multitudinous possibilities of balanced coexistence. Compelled to textualize the feminine into existence, to establish the female on equitable terms in a predominantly counterintuitive masculine world, the females in these stories, while firmly establishing their presence apply intuitive processes that uphold the generative permanence of both genders. The structural open-endedness of the short story form complements both the thematic inconclusiveness within the female/male dynamics and the enigmatic openness in the concept of the female. At the very least, the content of these stories reveal the need for measured reassessments of socio-economic, political, and religious orthodoxies while recognizing that the female and gender-related issues, with their continuously irregular patterns that defy clear definition, are akin to fractals, infinitely complex.

INTERTEXTUALITY AND COLLAGE IN BARTHELME'S SHORT FICTION

LUISA MARÍA GONZÁLEZ RODRÍGUEZ

Donald Barthelme belongs to the category of disruptive, innovative American writers who have not only abandoned the mimetic narrative modes, but have also engaged in formal experiments that have revitalized the short story genre. In "The State of the Short Story", Susan Mernit[1] lists Barthelme as one of the writers who helped to define the modern short story and suggests that he promoted the popular revival of the genre. In the same vein, Charles May[2] has placed Barthelme among the most influential postmodernist short story writers who focus attention on the fiction-making process. His short fictions are also acclaimed for promoting new and inventive approaches and for addressing the problems of the postmodern age. As Miriam Clark aptly remarks, his short fiction, distinguished by its "depthlessness, incoherence and ephemerality", falls under the category of the postmodern because it calls into question "metanarratives of self-knowledge and insight".[3] Moreover, Barthelme's stories display all the characteristics that Lauro Zavala[4] has attributed to the postmodern short story: they are not only rhizomatic, intertextual and anti-mimetic, but also seem to be under construction, such that their different components can be assembled

---

This study is part of a research project funded by the Regional Ministry of Culture of the Autonomous Government of Castile and Leon (ref. number SA012A10-1).
[1] Susan Mernit, "The State of the Short Story", *Virginia Quarterly Review*, LXII/2 (Spring 1986), 303.
[2] Charles E. May, *The Short Story: The Reality of Artifice*, New York: Routledge, 2002.
[3] Miriam Marty Clark, "Contemporary Short Fiction and the Postmodern Condition", *Studies in Short Fiction*, XXXII/ 2 (Spring 1995), 148, 153.
[4] Lauro Zavala, "De la teoría literaria a la minificción posmoderna", *Ciências Sociais Unisinos*, XLIII/1 (January-April 2007), 91.

and reassembled *ad infinitum*. Furthermore, Barthelme's original
experiments with narrative structure seem to corroborate Noel Harold
Kaylor's opinion that "the innovations through which postmodernism
finally gained its success in the United States were in form and
structure rather than content and in the postmodernist's inventive
alternative to realist representation of the 'world outside the work'".[5]

Although Barthelme also produced longer fiction, he has been
particularly praised for his short stories, which can be described as
original collages that explore the textures of postmodern experience.
His sense of cultural fragmentation made him resort to the short story
genre as the best means of conveying the incoherence of a
kaleidoscopic reality. For this reason, his short fiction is
representative of the postmodern crisis of perception, the waning of
subjectivity, and the shallowness and unreality of postmodern
ordinary experience. Furthermore, Barthelme's short fiction is marked
by a creative interest in exploring the possibilities of fiction beyond its
own limitations. Disenchantment with conventional narrative forms
led him to explore new techniques in order to deconstruct traditional
forms of representation; and in challenging the ordinary practices of
meaning production, Barthelme's fiction points to the essence of the
postmodern mode. He experiments with narrative form in such a way
as to emphasize the supremacy of form over content and to make it
the very subject of his fiction.

Barthelme resorts to collage and intertextuality as powerful
techniques that enable him to insist on the story as artifice and also to
privilege the artistic process at the expense of the finished work. Carl
Malmgren cleverly draws attention to the relationship collage
established between the artwork and reality when he points out that
collage not only challenges mimetic aesthetics, but also represents an
arbitrary, open system with crumbling boundaries.[6] This description
of collage is linked to Graham Allen's ideas about intertextuality. This
critic claims that postmodern fiction resorts to intertextual practices in
order to highlight and control the tension between fiction and reality.[7]

[5] Noel Harold Kaylor, "Postmodernism in the American Short Story: Some General
Observations and Some Specific Cases", in *The Postmodern Short Story: Forms and
Issues*, eds Farhat Iftekharrudin *et al.*, Westport, CT: Praeger, 2003, 247.
[6] Carl D. Malmgren, *Fictional Space in the Modernist and Postmodernist American
Novel*, Cranbury, NJ: Associated University Presses, 1985, 129.
[7] Graham Allen, *Intertextuality*, London: Routledge, 2000, 193.

It seems obvious that Barthelme uses both techniques in an attempt to emphasize the notion of literary texts as constructed artifacts pointing to the dynamics of artistic creation. Thus, he conceives his short stories as complex intertextual spaces where collage and intertextuality work on the metafictional paradox between the construction of a fictional reality and the laying bare of that illusion.

Barthelme has published about eight collections of short stories. This article focuses on several works excerpted from *Sixty Stories,*[8] a 1981 compilation of works that were published between 1964 and 1974. Using stories from this collection, which offers a broad perspective on Barthelme's development as a story writer, I will explore the author's use of collage and intertextuality. He recycles texts and intertexts, which results in a textualization of space and foregrounds the materiality of the printed text. I am especially interested in pointing out the use of collage and intertextuality as self-conscious techniques challenging social, political and aesthetic modes and structures. However, I also focus on the way both strategies can blur the distinction between fiction and reality and create a radically open text in order to increase the reader's involvement in fiction and mirror the fragmentation of contemporary experience.

Barthelme's poetics of fragmentation is a radical challenge to power structures and totalizing perspectives. In his short fiction "provisionality and heterogeneity contaminate any neat attempts at unifying coherence – formal or thematic".[9] One story that exhibits Barthelme's lack of commitment to coherent, complete plots or to a controlling, realist point of view is "Eugénie Grandet". This verbal collage, consisting of twenty-five disconnected sections, is a revision of Balzac's novel by the same title. The borrowed text focuses on Eugénie Grandet, a rich miser's daughter, who is courted by two rival suitors but falls in love with her cousin Charles, to whom she remains faithful. Barthelme's version begins with a summary of Balzac's text excerpted from *The Thesaurus of Book Digests.*[10] This trivial summary, focused on a few sequentially arranged events of Eugénie's life, satirizes the importance that traditional literature has given to well-structured plots and suggests that plots can be irrelevant or

---

[8] Donald Barthelme, *Sixty Stories*, New York: G.P. Putnam's Sons, 1981.
[9] Linda Hutcheon, "Beginning to Theorize Postmodernism", *Textual Practice*, I/1 (1987), 17.
[10] Barthelme, *Sixty Stories*, 236.

misleading. Although Barthelme evokes Balzac's work intertextually, his story will be different intentionally, for he is not going to focus on the plot. Rather, he is going to play with form and structure in order to subvert traditional modes of representing experience.

While Balzac, through careful attention to detail, attempts to depict and interpret French society, Barthelme's text avoids any insight into the lives of his characters. Accordingly, Barthelme's story subverts the notion of the author as a coherent, omniscient subjectivity and stresses the intertextual nature of fiction. Barthelme refrains from offering a complete picture of reality: rather than making logical transitions between events, he displays the story's various textual components in all their fragmentary glory, delighting in the process of composition and mocking the traditional rules governing the construction of meaning in fiction. Thus, his radical rewriting of Balzac's novel is not a coherent whole, but a chaotic collage of drawings, photographs, letters, dialogues, lists of words, slogans and clichés seeking to deconstruct and reorganize the original composition. In this short story Barthelme resorts to fragmentation in order to destabilize all notions of coherence and completeness. And this aesthetic collage of fragments illustrates the artificiality of the creative process.

Barthelme constructs his story around arbitrary situations and details that do not seem to contribute to a particular line of narrative or character development. Examples of this fragmented vision of reality are four very short sections that introduce three of the story's characters. The first section introduces Charles, Eugénie's cousin and the man she is in love with: "'It looks as though I'm going to be quite successful here in Saumur', thought Charles, unbuttoning his coat." The next section has no logical connection to the previous one and focuses on possibilities of marriage for Eugénie: "A great many people are interested in the question: Who will obtain Eugénie Grandet's hand?" In the third section we can see a drawing of Eugénie's hand. And the last section is about one of Eugénie's wealthy suitors: "Judge Bonfons arrives carrying flowers."[11] The gaps between these fragments deliberately contribute to disrupting linearity, causality and temporality in the story. These gaps open up the textual space and induce the reader to supply the structure and search for connections between the materials provided by the writer.

---

[11] *Ibid.*, 237.

In fact, Barthelme understands that collage is more a process of appropriation and arrangement than a product: these fragments he presents can be assembled and reassembled, an activity that turns the reader into a co-creator of his text. One example of this sketchy representation of reality achieved by merely providing the reader with raw materials is the section describing Charles' adventures in the Indies:

> Charles in the Indies. He sold:
> Chinese
> Negroes
> swallows' nests
> children
> artists[12]

This section also includes a photograph of Charles in the Indies in an ironic attempt to offer as much information as possible about the vicissitudes of Eugénie's cousin in the West Indies. In Balzac's novel Charles, whose father has gone bankrupt, goes to the West Indies, where he becomes wealthy. However, far from offering a coherent and complete description of the facts, Barthelme delights in providing irrelevant details while omitting important information about the plot. In Barthelme's story the plot of the original novel seems to be refracted through the prism of a postmodern consciousness and thus becomes a heterogeneous mosaic of fragments. Here the gaps between the fragments are underlined, for there are no conventionally logical transitions between the events. In fact, the result is that the pieces, which were imperceptibly knitted together in the original text, are now separated and given autonomy to be rearranged by the reader.

Through his formal experiments Barthelme acknowledges that old forms and structures cannot be used to represent the postmodern experience. He seeks to challenge old-fashioned value systems and modes of thought. As a consequence, his short stories are shapeless fictions marked by disruption, incoherence and shallowness. He underlines the artificiality of the assemblage not only to challenge conventional forms of representation, but also to draw the reader's attention to the process by which meaning comes into being. Collage

---

[12] *Ibid.*, 242.

and intertextuality can thus be considered the most powerful strategies he uses to attack narrative structures:

> For Barthelme it is narrative structures themselves which have the most unclear status. Is the narrative structure, in the eyes of the postmodern artist, the quintessential piece of junk, since so often these structures rest on assumptions about individual psychology, linear time, and social order that are by and large hopelessly out of date?[13]

In "Eugénie Grandet", the use of collage and intertextuality allows the writer to accumulate heaps of trivial content, thus avoiding any teleological commitment and drawing attention to mere textuality. Consequently, drawings, photographs, letters, profuse information about ancient coins, and lists of repeated words are haphazardly juxtaposed to make the reader focus on the surface of the text. In other words, the use of collage in this short fiction is a powerful tool for foregrounding the materiality of the printed text, the text as an artificial assemblage. In addition, the absence of a defined, coherent structure frees Barthelme from any commitment to plot or narrative development and allows him to recontextualize Balzac's text in a polyphonic space. The sections of this story are randomly assembled, contributing to what has been called the "textualization of space", which opens the text to a multiplicity of possibilities and meanings. And this spatialization of form serves as "an alternative to the old novel's sequential organization in plot and narrative", since, in Ronald Sukenick's view, "through such techniques as juxtaposition and manipulation ... the novelist can create a structure that communicates by means of patterns rather than sequence in a manner approaching that of the plastic arts".[14]

In this short story, collage and intertextuality also enable Barthelme to highlight the problematics of authorship. "Eugénie Grandet" seems to corroborate the postmodern decentering of the subject and the absence of a center of consciousness that controls narrative discourse. The absence of a totalizing perspective around which narrative is structured brings about a freedom of composition that, by contradicting the parameters of logic and reality, allows

---

[13] Charles Molesworth, *Donald Barthelme's Fiction: The Ironist Saved from Drowning*, Columbia: University of Missouri Press, 1982, 78.

[14] Ronald Sukenick, "The New Tradition in Fiction", in *Surfiction: Fiction Now and Tomorrow*, ed. Raymond Federman, Chicago: Swallow Press, 1975, 38.

Barthelme to flee from restrictive structures and to explore the limits of the fictional worlds he constructs. In this sense, the story is very anti-Balzacian, for it is an assemblage of intertextual borrowings in which ruptures proliferate in order to prevent the reader from reaching coherent meanings or universal truths. The text emphasizes the heteroglossic, dynamic nature of fiction and meaning construction. Moreover, the lack of a central point of view defies the traditional omniscience and challenges the idea of the author as the source of meaning. Thus, Barthelme's "Eugénie Grandet" makes it impossible for us to attribute the fragmented utterances to a single, univocal originating consciousness. An example of this is the incomplete letter extracted in one of the sections:

> ... And now he's ruined a
> friends will desert him, and
> humiliation. Oh, I wish I ha
> straight to heaven, where his
> but this is madness ... I re
> that of Charles.
> I have sent him to you so
> News of my death to him and
> In store for him. Be a father to[15]

This fragmented letter, in which gaps of space or time are almost as important as the information given, seems to accomplish the radical function of collage, since the blocks of meaning have been separated in order to challenge the naturalness of ordinary language and narrative development. Once again, Barthelme has refused to provide a structure that makes the fragments cohere into a meaningful whole. In this way, it could be argued that both the fragmented letter and the complete short story in which the letter is excerpted are examples of a reversible space responding to the polyphonic principle of collage.

The narrator of Barthelme's short stories is the ventriloquist who disembodies himself so that other discourses and voices can be heard. More often than not, his depersonalized prose consists of a collage of fragments and disconnected borrowings in which the organizing consciousness has been replaced by an intertextual web of appropriations. This is clearly illustrated in "The Rise of Capitalism",

---

[15] Barthelme, *Sixty Stories*, 238.

a nine-paragraph collage of prose fragments made up of unconnected materials and recycled clichés from contemporary culture, which acknowledges the plural identity of the postmodern narrator. Rupert, the voice narrating this story, far from being a fixed unified entity, is a fragmented consciousness that constructs reality in a discontinuous, sketchy and chaotic fashion. The intertextual allusion to Balzac's *La Comédie humaine*, in which Balzac described the rise of French capitalism, makes us think that the narrator is trying to emulate Balzac and, accordingly, will provide a coherent description of the rise of American capitalism. However, Rupert's kaleidoscopic picture is an amalgam of recycled materials and cultural debris that confront us with the heterogeneous mosaic of contemporary society. In this short story the components speak with disparate, disrupted voices, turning the text into a polyphonic space bereft of a controlling perspective. The narrator himself acknowledges, ironically, that he has no objective vantage point, since he is integrated into bourgeois society. Indeed, the unconnected ideas and paragraphs contribute to the impression that the narrating voice is being disintegrated and reduced to fragments:

> Always mindful that the critic must *"studiare da un punto di vista formalistico e semiologico il raporto fra lingua di un testo e codificazione di un"* – But here a big thumb smudges the text – the thumb of capitalism.[16]

"The Rise of Capitalism" is a sketchy mosaic of cultural clichés and ready-made concepts illustrating how pop-cultural irrelevance has colonized postmodern experience. This story attempts to be a critique of the fascinations and dissatisfactions offered by capitalism. Whereas for Martha, the narrator's wife, the capitalist system "has given us everything we have – the streets, the parks, the great avenues and boulevards, the promenades and malls – and other things", for Rupert, the narrator, capitalism appears to be connected to abulia and pointlessness, which makes his neighbor continue "to commit suicide, once a fortnight". And for Azalea, the narrator's mistress, it seems to be the reason why "Roger has lost his job (replaced by an electric eye)" or why "Gigi's children are in the hospital being detoxified, all three". These glimpses of different aspects of capitalism are

---

[16] *Ibid.*, 204 (italics in the original).

juxtaposed and interspersed with political and religious messages. For Rupert's description of capitalism is an accumulation of clichés, aphorisms and verbal detritus taken from politics, religion, philosophy, the media and other discourses representing official culture. Examples of this randomly assembled cultural debris are certain political remarks – for example, "Capitalism places every man in competition with his fellows for a share of the available wealth"[17] – juxtaposed with ecological opinions complaining about the strands of hair floating on the surface of the Ganges, and other religious messages, such as "He who desires true rest and happiness must raise his hope from things that perish and pass away and place it in the Word of God".[18] Far from privileging any of these recycled materials, the narrator simply allows these messages to become ironic glimpses into contemporary culture.

Thus, collage and intertextuality are the techniques used to provide the manifold aspects of the situations depicted. In "The Rise of Capitalism", each paragraph seems to offer a new perspective to be added to the previous one, rather than a progression or development of the preceding sections. In fact, the story consists of a centrifugal collection of independent pieces that neutralize each other, thus denying a coherent interpretation of the text. This effect of presenting the text as a composed surface by providing shifting or alternating points of view is one of the hallmarks of Barthelme's short fiction, and it compels the reader to move across the surface of the text. The reader is never allowed to get into the text at any depth, since the postmodern short story seeks to undermine the very concepts of insight and self-knowledge in fiction. Copeland persuasively argues that "collage abandons the illusion of depth we associate with single-point perspective .... In collage, the eye of the spectator tends to fluctuate freely between disparate points on the same shallow plane."[19]

In "The Rise of Capitalism" Barthelme appropriates generic frames of reference in order to parody the means of representation that have been used to construct meaning. This short story is conceived as a mosaic of appropriated fragments from master narratives projecting

---

[17] *Ibid.*, 204, 205.
[18] *Ibid.*, 208.
[19] Roger Copeland, "Merce Cunningham and the Aesthetic of Collage", *TDR / The Drama Review*, XLVI/1 (Spring 2002), 21.

the cultural myths of capitalism. The repetition and recycling of intertextual borrowings from different discourses within high culture and mass media is an attempt to suggest ironically that language has become meaningless in contemporary culture. The narrator can only reproduce packaged messages that seem to be filtered and degraded by mass media. Rupert's repetition of what he has heard seems to highlight the notion that master narratives have degenerated into clichés. And that is the effect we get when we read

> 'Capitalism sure is sunny!' cried the unemployed Laredo toolmaker, as I was out walking, in the streets of Laredo. 'None of that noxious Central European miserabilism for us!'

When the narrator makes similar statements, such as "Laredo is doing very well now, thanks to application of the brilliant principles of the 'new capitalism'", the reader experiences a sense of *déjà vu*. For Barthelme, appropriation and rearrangement are strategies of subversion that point to the meaninglessness of this disposable rhetoric. His contingent juxtaposition of cultural clichés and ready-made concepts turns them into verbal waste and thereby undermines and degrades some of the master narratives sustaining Western civilization. Dominant cultural discourses are set right next to banal reflections: a few Marxist chunks, such as "Cultural underdevelopment of the worker, as a technique of domination, is found everywhere under late capitalism",[20] are recycled and assembled with some irrelevant opinions about the strands of hair floating on the Ganges as a result of the refusal of wig factories to install sieves. Consequently, in Paul Maltby's words, "even a discourse as uncompromisingly and sharply critical as Marxism has been neutralized, incorporated into the bourgeois social order".[21]

Religious messages are also degraded and deconstructed by Barthelme's technique of stripping conflicting elements from their original contexts and forcing them into bizarre relationships. For example, a quotation from I Corinthians 6, "It is better to marry than to burn", is used to end a section that jumbles political commentaries about capitalism, absurd information about the King of Jordan, and a

---

[20] Barthelme, *Sixty Stories*, 206-207.
[21] Paul Maltby, *Dissident Postmodernists: Barthelme, Coover, Pynchon*, Philadelphia: University of Pennsylvania Press, 1991, 65.

description of the narrator's dialogue with his mistress. The narrator himself, acknowledging that ideology is what supports our perception of reality, argues that "St. Paul is largely discredited now, for the toughness of his views does not accord with the experience of advanced industrial societies".[22] It seems clear that for Barthelme "no pattern of interpretation, whether it be provided by the novel, science, history, or psychology, can hope to 'mirror reality' or 'tell the truth' because 'reality' and 'truth' are themselves fictional abstractions whose validity has become increasingly suspect".[23] Thus, in this story the different frames of reference presented draw attention not only to authority structures, but also to the dialogically constructed nature of meaning.

This intertextual collage dealing with sociopolitical issues reveals the way in which dominant discourses or master narratives have conditioned our perception of reality. As Mary Orr points out "postmodern intertextuality claims to break with the old sureties, especially about meaning as mythical and metaphysical or atheistic, agnostic, or anti-metaphysical".[24] And this contingent arrangement of cultural debris serves not only to foreground the fact that any representation of reality is always clearly ideological, but also to highlight the postmodern crisis in perception. Thus, when Rupert's wife tells him that "the embourgeoisment of all classes of men has reached a disgusting nadir in your case",[25] the narrator is forced to acknowledge that he cannot give a coherent picture of the rise of capitalism, since he is in fact an integral part of this bourgeois society. Ironically, a fiction apparently conceived as an ambitious chronicle of modern society has turned out to be a multifarious arrangement of contradictory discourses that eventually render the narrator's task impossible. Indeed, we could argue that Barthelme constructs fragmented spaces that enable him to explore multiple perspectives "without promoting completeness, wholeness, or closure".[26] Accordingly, the final section is constructed as a dialogic, open space

---

[22] Barthelme, *Sixty Stories*, 205.

[23] Larry McCaffery, "Donald Barthelme and the Metafictional Muse", *Sub-Stance*, IX/2 (Issue 27 1980), 76.

[24] Mary Orr, *Intertextuality. Debates and Contexts*, Cambridge: Polity Press, 2003, 15.

[25] Barthelme, *Sixty Stories*, 208.

[26] Nicholas Sloboda, "American Postmodern Extensions: Donald Barthelme's Picture/ Text Mosaic", *New Novel Review*, III/ 2 (Spring 1996), 98.

where the reader is invited to explore the topic and develop his or her own view about capitalism:

> Smoke, rain, abulia. What can the concerned citizen do to fight the rise of capitalism? Study the tides of conflict and power in a system in which there is structural inequality is an important task. A knowledge of European intellectual history since 1789 provides a useful background. Information theory offers interesting new possibilities. Passion is helpful, especially those types of passion which are nonlicit. Doubt is a necessary precondition to meaningful action. Fear is the great mover, in the end.[27]

"The Party" is another verbal collage presenting unconnected glimpses of experience and filtering reflections of the deconstruction of postmodern society through a fragmented consciousness. The sketches that comprise the story mirror the narrator's disrupted sense of self and his perception of superficiality and unreality in social relationships. Once again, this story avoids any straightforward development of plot or character in favor of the arrangement of heterogeneous elements that contributes to a collage effect.

The transformation of plot into pattern may be considered one of the hallmarks of the postmodern short story; Rohrberger and Burns aptly remark that "as pattern begins to replace plot, intrarreferential motifs (which form static patterns) become increasingly important to the communication of meaning in short fiction".[28] The pattern of "The Party" is that of a broken mosaic in which the images, noises, characters and events observed at a party are randomly arranged by the narrator in order to reflect the banality, confusion, and meaningless of modern life. Here, the assemblage of disparate, repetitive elements and characters serves not only to draw attention to the surface of the text, but also to project a fictional reality. The collage composition enables Barthelme to juxtapose heterogeneous bits of experience as a means of blurring the distance between reality and representation.

The story depicts a world of fantasy in which everything is possible: an adjunct professor dressed as King Kong enters through the window, two nuns watch TV and take showers, a man complains

---

[27] Barthelme, *Sixty Stories*, 208.
[28] Mary Rohrberger and Dan Burns, "Short Fiction and the Numinous Realm: Another Attempt at Definition", *Modern Fiction Studies*, XXVIII/1 (Spring 1982), 6.

about the music, a woman combs King Kong's dark thick fur and a child swallows twenty aspirin tablets. However, what generates more confusion between appearance and reality is not the juxtaposition of absurd events but the absence of space-time or cause-and-effect transition between the fragmented glimpses of playful irrationality provided.

"The Party" is also concerned with the process of simulation, characterized by a blending of reality and representation. This story reflects the way society is dominated and colonized by the mass media and pop culture, so it is only natural that Barthelme should use advertising as a discourse for making sense of contemporary existence. The narrator suggests that the media, especially TV commercials, are so integrated into daily experience that we cannot distinguish the unmediated from the mediated, the real from the imagined. For him modern society, represented by this bizarre party, is a realm of hyperreality and simulation in which the boundaries between the real and the imaginary are blurred. "The Party" embodies the postmodern view that the world can be interpreted only by means of a fictionalized reality. This is illustrated by the narrator's acknowledgment that our desires are now defined by commercials and media images:

> A number of young people standing in a meadow, holding hands, singing. Can the life of the time be caught in an advertisement? Is that how it is, really, in the meadows of the world?[29]

The voice narrating "The Party" depicts a world dominated by images, signs and simulacra imposed on individuals by the mass media. He seems to agree with Jean Baudrillard that simulacra are the signs of culture and media that create the perceived reality and that society has become so dependent on simulacra that it has lost contact with the real world.[30] In Barthelme's party we see that the guests' experience is of a simulation of reality rather than reality itself. All of the partygoers seem to be trying to escape from their banal existence by imitating social rites. The narrator attempts to comply with social expectations; consequently, he praises a painting by Bonnard that is a

---

[29] Barthelme, *Sixty Stories*, 234.
[30] Jean Baudrillard, *Simulacra and Simulation*, Ann Arbor: University of Michigan Press, 2006.

reproduction, and he feels awkward. Similarly, the other guests seek to slide into an unreal world that helps them escape from meaninglessness: Francesca, the narrator's partner, wanders off "into another room, testing the effect on members of the audience of your ruffled blouse, your magenta skirt".[31] Another guest, an adjunct professor of art at Rutgers, enters through the window disguised as King Kong, "simply trying to make himself interesting". The narrator himself claims that modern society subsists in appearance:

> When one has spoken a lot one has already used up all of the ideas one has. You must change the people you are speaking to so that you appear, to yourself, to be still alive.[32]

However, he observes that language more often than not keeps us from accessing reality and that recycling and repetition has contributed not only to the loss of meaning, but also to the loss of communication. Acknowledging, like Baudrillard, that "socialization is measured by the exposure to media messages",[33] the narrator is aware that he is "desocialized" or "asocial", therefore he complains about social expectations: "Why am I called upon to make them happier, when it is so obviously beyond my competence?"[34] Indeed, the narrator is an outsider observing the deconstruction of the social and criticizing the guests' perception of the world as appearance and simulation. Thus, he finally recognizes that social rituals and simulation cannot conceal the collapse of our social organization: "What made us think that we could escape things like bankruptcy, alcoholism, being disappointed, having children?"[35]

Most of Barthelme's short stories are open-ended mosaics reflecting the uncertainty and chaos of the postmodern experience. They are also assemblages that recycle the waste and junk of the hyperconsumer capitalist society and depict the alienation and abulia in which individuals are mired. "Critique de la Vie Quotidienne", for instance, criticizes the contemporary ideals of family life and quotidian experience. Barthelme becomes a bricoleur who playfully and randomly combines the junk and debris of modern family life in

[31] Barthelme, *Sixty Stories*, 231.
[32] *Ibid.*, 232, 234.
[33] Baudrillard, *Simulacra and Simulation*, 80.
[34] Barthelme, *Sixty Stories*, 234.
[35] *Ibid.*, 235.

order to explore and deconstruct the myths of contemporary society. This short story is constructed as a fragmentary mirror of domestic life: the incoherence of its pieces reflects the monotony and disintegration of the protagonist's married life. Here the narrator constructs a vivid collage of clichés, ready-made expressions, routines, and other heterogeneous narrative fragments describing the chaos and tedium of his own life. The narrator himself reads the *Journal of Sensory Deprivation* in an attempt to become immersed in a culture dominated by simulacra. All too conscious of the wide gap between his real life and the ideals of family life imposed by the mass media, the narrator resorts to alcohol to mitigate frustration. For him "the world in the evenings seems fraught with the absence of promise, if you are a married man. There is nothing to do but go home and drink your nine drinks and forget about it."[36] The narrator collects trivial aspects from daily life, such as the day his child urinated in bed or asked for a horse just like his friend Otto had, and juxtaposes them in order to bring to the foreground his discontent with a tedious, banal existence. Indeed, the story is an amalgam of domestic quarrels, absurd situations and various banalities depicting the collapse of a middle-class family.

The story's title, "Critique de la Vie Quotidienne", is an intertextual reference to Henri Lefebvre, a French author who wrote a book by the same title on alienation in the modern world. The allusion to Lefebvre's work underlines the palimpsestic nature of Barthelme's writing, suggesting that, as Genette pointed out, literature exists "in the second degree", that is, texts are "derived from preexistent texts".[37] For Barthelme the act of writing gives way to a process of rewriting characterized by intertextual self-reflexivity. This short story recycles Lefebvre's ideas about ordinary life and the passivity of the bourgeois subject. However, Barthelme's revision focuses on the fragmentation of postmodern subjectivity and on how the mass media and pop culture have contributed to the homogenization of individuals. Dialogues and emotions seem to be borrowed utterances and clichés recycled from cultural trash. Thus, when Wanda, his former wife, complains that their marriage "was not the happiest of marriages", the narrator replies that "there has been a sixty percent

[36] *Ibid.*, 183.
[37] Gérard Genette, *Palimpsests: Literature in the Second Degree*, Lincoln: University of Nebraska Press, 1997, 5.

increase in single-person households in the last ten years, according to the Bureau of the Census" and concludes, "Perhaps we are part of a trend".[38] Here, personal opinion appears to be stripped of all emotions as it is interspersed with statistics and objective opinions, and individuality seems to have dissolved into collective consciousness. As Maltby argues, "what emerges is an image of an attenuated subjectivity: a consciousness, in the final stage of alienation, characterized by inertia; a consciousness at times 'flipping' into a post-alienated state, ecstatically immersed in the instantaneous present".[39]

Furthermore, there are continuous references to magazines, newspapers and other media that induce characters to perceive reality according to models of the real that have become part of their lives. Consequently, the composition process recycles the trash produced by society and culture and demonstrates the enormous power that the media and popular culture have in establishing stereotypes. The character of Wanda, for example, is a two-dimensional collage of clichés excerpted from the magazine *Elle*. The narrator ironically describes her as an addicted reader of *Elle* and states:

> Wanda empathized with the magazine. "*Femmes enceintes, ne mangez pas de bifteck cru!*" *Elle* once proclaimed, and Wanda complied. Not a shred of *bifteck cru* passed her lips during the whole period of pregnancy.[40]

The conception of postmodern identity as a collage of intertexts is linked to Barthes' definition of the self as "a plurality of other texts, of codes which are infinite", and to his notion of subjectivity as having "ultimately the generality of stereotypes".[41] This fading away of subjectivity as if cancelled out by media messages is best illustrated by the narrator's descriptions of his wife: "She cultivated, as *Elle* instructed, *un petit air naïf*, or the schoolgirl look", or "During this period *Elle* ran something like four thousand separate *actualité* pieces on Anna Karina, the film star, and Wanda actually came to resemble her somewhat".[42] The sketchy description of Wanda as an amalgam of

---

[38] Barthelme, *Sixty Stories*, 189.
[39] Maltby, *Dissident Postmodernists*, 56.
[40] Barthelme, *Sixty Stories*, 183 (italics in the original).
[41] Roland Barthes, *S/Z*, New York: Hill and Wang, 1974, 10.
[42] Barthelme, *Sixty Stories*, 183.

images and simulacra draws attention to the homogenization brought about by mass media saturation. At the end, after their divorce, his former wife starts studying Marxist sociology with Lefebvre, and the narrator ironically suggests that this new discourse has become another cultural consumer object: "Wanda is happier now, I think. She has taken herself off to Nanterre, where she is studying Marxist sociology with Lefebvre."[43] Even critical discourses are reduced to meaninglessness as they are consumed and integrated into the bourgeois lifestyle. This underlines the idea that the individual is so saturated by information and media messages, consumed in the form of commodities, that postmodern experience has become a simulacrum.

Barthelme's constant process of recycling makes him turn to genres such as the fairy tale in order to deconstruct their elements and motifs. One example of this appropriation of generic material is "The Glass Mountain", a postmodern piece of fiction that depicts a reality apparently reflected through a shattered glass. This short story narrates the vicissitudes of a modern knight's ascent to the top of a glass mountain in order to rescue a beautiful princess. "The Glass Mountain" intertextually evokes a Scandinavian fairy tale and literally quotes the conventional means of attaining the castle from the earlier version included in *The Yellow Fairy Book*.[44] However, Barthelme's experimental rewriting of the story abandons the traditional structure of fairy tales and mocks the generic conventions evoked by constructing a collage of decontextualized literary and extraliterary fragments. The relevance of intertextuality in this fiction is deeply connected to Borges' idea that everything has been said, which has given way to the postmodern realization that "it is only as part of prior discourses that any text derives meaning and significance".[45]

This postmodern fairy tale consists of one hundred incoherent and disconnected sentences, most of which are quotations from different sources. The numbered sentences suggest a randomness of arrangement, since these numbers seem to be arbitrary ways of organizing experience. Accordingly, after quoting part of the fairy tale evoked in sentence 80, he proceeds to disrupt conscious surface coherence with an unconscious form that cannot be conveyed in

---

[43] *Ibid.*, 190.
[44] *Ibid.*, 181-82.
[45] Linda Hutcheon, *A Poetics of Postmodernism*, London: Routledge, 1988, 126.

rational terms. The technique Barthelme uses consists in separating the blocks of signification into a series of unconnected sentences that shatter the flow of narrative. Therefore, the subsequent sentences, from sentences 88 to 96, are repetitions of the previous quotation, with little variation. The process of cutting the ancient tale into chunks serves to subvert both the content and the structure of traditional modes of narrative. The disjointed sentences depict not a coherent, teleological world, but a fragmented reality with no transitions between the events narrated. An example of this is the way the main character interrupts his narration of his approach to the castle in order to express his fear:

> 81. I was afraid.
> 82. I had forgotten the Band-Aids.
> 83. When the eagle dug its sharp claws into my tender flesh–
> 84. Should I go back for the Band-Aids?
> 85. But if I went back for the Band-Aids I would have to endure the contempt of my acquaintances.
> 86. I resolved to proceed without the Band-Aids.

These sentences not only disrupt the narration of the story, but also challenge the content and formal conventions of the fairy tale. The hero's fear of being hurt by the eagle clearly deconstructs his traditional role as the valiant rescuer of the princess. Furthermore, the hero's narration of his vicissitudes seems to hint that postmodern reality can no longer believe in a hero-character and in the happy ending of the typical fairy tale. Barthelme deconstructs the process of myth-making and meaning construction: refusing to marry the princess, the hero tells us, "I threw the beautiful princess headfirst down the mountain to my acquaintances".[46] The ancient tale seems to be filtered through a postmodern sensibility, for one needs new parameters to make sense of contemporary experience.

Moreover, collage and intertextuality allow Barthelme to directly express the fiction/reality dichotomy by underlining the artificial element in art. He resorts to both strategies in an attempt to challenge mimetic representations in art. Postmodern short stories, as Cristina Bacchilega remarks, "hold mirrors to the magic mirror of the fairy tale, playing with its framed images out of a desire to multiply its

---

[46] Barthelme, *Sixty Stories*, 182.

refractions and to expose its artifices".[47] Barthelme collects and borrows scattered materials and rearranges them into a pattern that makes clear that these elements come from other contexts. "The Glass Mountain" becomes an assemblage of cultural materials, suggesting a parallel to Marcel Duchamp's ready-made objects. This manipulation of the collected fragments and appropriated messages contribute to producing an alienating or estrangement effect. That is, by inserting the borrowed elements into new contexts, the artist turns them into rare, artificial objects. The juxtaposition of appropriated elements in different interpretative frameworks serves to problematize the constructed worlds. "The Glass Mountain", for example, underlines the gaps existing between the fragments that form it in order to highlight the process of composition. The collage points to its own seams, which reveal that its pattern is the result of pasting together a series of heterogeneous materials. As Charles May persuasively observes: "Rather than presenting itself 'as if' it were real – a mimetic mirroring of external reality – postmodernist short fiction often makes its own artistic conventions and devices the subjects of the story as well as its theme."[48]

This seems to be obvious in this short story, presented as a provisional arrangement of borrowed literary conventions that self-consciously lays bare its fictionality. Self-conscious reflections such as "Do today's stronger egos still *need* symbols?"[49] prevent the reader from believing that s/he is contemplating a truthful picture of reality. This question also focuses attention on the role of the postmodern author, who, being aware that postmodern society has replaced reality and meaning with symbols and signs, undertakes the difficult task of disenchanting symbols. The narrator therefore wonders: "Does one climb a glass mountain, at a considerable personal discomfort, simply to disenchant a symbol?"

Barthelme challenges the idea that signs and symbols can represent reality and reveal transcendental truths. Thus, he constructs a narcissistic text where collage and intertextuality are strategies used for turning the story into an assemblage of empty signs arranged not according to their meanings but according to their signifiers. "I

---

[47] Cristina Bacchilega, *Postmodern Fairy Tales: Gender and Narrative Strategies*, Philadelphia: University of Pennsylvania Press, 1997, 23.
[48] May, *The Short Story*, 84.
[49] Barthelme, *Sixty Stories*, 180.

approached the symbol, with its layers of meaning, but when I touched it, it changed into only a beautiful princess",[50] says the narrator, in an attempt to highlight the limitations of language as a means of representing reality. Furthermore, "the absence of a transcendental signified extends the domain and interplay of signification *ad infinitum*".[51] That is, in "The Glass Mountain" Barthelme recognizes the signifier's limited capacity to attach itself to a definite signified in postmodern culture. Thus, he constructs a polyphonic space prone to meaning proliferation. By underlining the unreliability of the written text as a mimetic description of reality, the author not only frustrates the reader's expectations of finding a final coherent meaning, but also reinforces the idea that what really matters is the meaning-construction process itself. In its resistance to being read as a coherent picture of the world, this short story becomes a postmodern experimental collage drawing attention to the structures that delimit meaning.

Moreover, these techniques of recycling and rearranging the appropriated fragments endow the short story with a freedom that allows Barthelme to incorporate elements from other genres and discourses, thus contributing to the short story's hybridity. Quotations are inserted in the narrative not only to break the continuity of the plot, but also to reinvigorate the short story with borrowings from other genres. For instance, sentence 56, "A weakening of the libidinous interest in reality has recently come to a close",[52] is a quotation from *The Hidden Order of Art* by Anton Ehrenzweig.[53] The quotation interrupts the hero's story of his ascent to the top of the mountain and turns the fairy tale into a self-reflexive critical text about the process of artistic creation. The sentences following Ehrenzweig's intertext are self-conscious reflections on the role of the artist in contemporary society. Thus, the mythical quest of the knight has turned into the modern artist's search for symbols that can appeal to the modern reader. The fragmented intertexts avoid the possibility of reaching a *Gestalt* or a coherent configuration of the story. Rather,

---

[50] *Ibid.*, 180, 182.
[51] Jacques Derrida, "Structure, Sign, and Play in the Discourse of the Human Sciences", in *The Structuralist Controversy*, eds Richard Macksey and Eugenio Donato, Baltimore, MD: John Hopkins University Press, 2007, 249.
[52] Barthelme, *Sixty Stories*, 180.
[53] Anton Ehrenzweig, *The Hidden Order of Art*, Berkeley and Los Angeles: University of California Press, 1967, 141.

they contribute to producing a kaleidoscopic arrangement that enables us to distinguish as many patterns as fragments. This is a radical and intertextual collage where the superficial fragmentation attacks the *Gestalt* principle in favour of a new mobile space. As Charles May aptly remarks: "One of the implications of this collage process is a radical shift from the usual temporal, cause-and-effect process of fiction to the more spatial and metaphoric process of poetry."[54]

Barthelme's short stories are intertextual collages exhibiting dynamic patterns designed to challenge old fictional forms, stale notions of subjectivity and realistic expectations about authorship, causality and closure. In all of his stories, collage and intertextuality are used to assert these works of fiction as simulacra projecting images not of external reality, but of the writer's creative manipulation of reality. Barthelme's contribution to the postmodern short story is manifold: he has not only appropriated and recycled traditional narrative structures and demanded new ways of reading but has also endowed the short story with a freedom of form and content that has resulted in a renaissance of the genre. His short fiction represents the positive achievements of postmodernism by drawing the reader to a central position. He tries to overcome the loss of meaning and narrative exhaustion by filtering stale clichés and materials through a postmodern prism in order to suggest new possibilities. Moreover, he manipulates traditional narrative modes, creating kaleidoscopic stories and opening up fictional space to the reader's intense collaboration and creativity.

---

[54] May, *The Short Story*, 87.

REALISM AND NARRATORS IN
TOBIAS WOLFF'S SHORT STORIES

SANTIAGO RODRÍGUEZ GUERRERO-STRACHAN

Literary minimalism is considered a critical realist reaction to the excesses of postmodernism. It began in the United States in the Eighties and received critical sanction with the 1983 *Granta* issue in which some of the minimalist authors were published and which enjoyed a wide array of critical response.[1] In both positive and negative ways, minimalism has been associated with a smallness of vision and smallness of execution[2] and with the "reflection of the fragmentary and alienated condition of the twentieth-century self". It focuses on defining a small literary world.[3]

Minimalism was a reaction against postmodernism, since after the postmodernist trend a return to nineteenth-century realism was inconceivable. As Stefan Colibaba, one of the most important scholars in the field, points out, "The Minimalists grew up in a world that already had a postmodern sensibility".[4] They never regarded literature as a mere recount of contemporary life. They moved away from postmodernism because of their contrasting sensibility and understanding of life.[5] However, the imprint of postmodernism cannot be totally eliminated. Ann-Marie Karlsson describes minimalism as a subversion of representational realism, a point on which most critics

This study is part of a research project funded by the Regional Ministry of Culture of the Autonomous Government of Castile and Leon (ref. number SA012A10-1).
[1] Myles Weber, "Revisiting Minimalism", *Northwest Review*, XXXVII/3 (1999), 118-19.
[2] Ewing Campbell, "How Minimal Is Minimalism?", in *The Tales We Tell*, eds Barbara Lounsberry *et al.*, Westport, CT: Greenwood Press, 1998, 15.
[3] Stefan Colibaba, "Raymond Carver's Minimalism", *British and American Studies*, I (1997), 126-27.
[4] *Ibid.*, 120.
[5] *Ibid.*, 124.

agree. Her starting point is Frederick Barthelme's article "On Being Wrong: Convicted Minimalist Spills Bean", published in the *New York Times Book Review*. She observes that minimalist realism suggests the "film-like quality of this fiction".[6] For Karlsson, "its extreme verisimilitude creates an 'over-realism'". Minimalism is hyper-realistic because of form, content and ideology. The shift from "traditional" realism makes minimalism "partly an experimental avant-garde fiction, which is attempting to find new means of expression beyond traditional realism and postmodern fiction".[7] Critics generally assume that minimalism is a development of postmodernist fiction and that minimalist writers have acquired postmodernist techniques and have been affected by the postmodern frame of mind.

The minimalist writers' attack on realism has fostered a fiction that presents affinities with hyperrealism or the grotesque and the uncanny. Their assault subverts representational realism without losing sight of verisimilitude. As W.M. Verhoeven argues, minimalism's gimmicks are not "a wilful departure from formal realism and mimetic rendition of truth, but rather an act of discovery – discovery, that is, in the process of composing their stories".[8]

At present there is not a large body of critical writings on late twentieth-century realism. The aim of this essay is to help to fill the void in this field of study. Although I am well aware that this investigation has to be limited in scope and constitutes only a preliminary approach to the much broader research of minimalism, the purpose of this essay is to explore the nature of realism in late twentieth-century American short stories. Centering on three short stories – "The Night in Question", "Sanity" and "The Other Miller" from *The Night in Question*[9] – this essay focuses on the role of the narrators in Tobias Wolff's short stories and on his use of narrative

---

[6] Ann-Marie Karlsson, "The Hyperrealistic Short Story: A Postmodern Twilight Zone", in *Criticism in the Twilight Zone: Postmodern Perspectives on Literature and Politics*, eds Danuta Zadworna-Fjellestad and Lennart Björk, Stockholm: Almquist and Wiksell International, 1990, 150.

[7] *Ibid.*, 153.

[8] W.M. Verhoeven, "What We Talk About When We Talk About Raymond Carver: Or, Much Ado About Minimalism", in *Narrative Turns and Minor Genres in Postmodernism*, eds Theo D'haen and Hans Bertens, Amsterdam: Rodopi and New York, 1995, 55.

[9] Tobias Wolff, *The Night in Question*, New York: Vintage, 1996.

voice, which reveals the minimalist use of narrative strategies. As a minimalist writer, Tobias Wolff is concerned with reducing the literary world to its most concise form. His universe, much like that of Raymond Carver's stories, is stripped of heroism and grandeur.[10]

The author's use of narrators is indicative of his conception of the relationship between reality and literature. It is through the narrator's point of view that readers perceive the reality of the literary space created by the short story. Narrative voices are keys to the dynamics of a short fiction's literary world. They represent the author's tools for presenting a realist depiction of society. However, this new type of realism has been strongly influenced by modernist and postmodernist conventions.

As Stefan Colibaba remarks:

> ... minimalist art does not require moral involvement .... The key precept of minimalism appears to be precisely this requirement that the work be stripped of judgment and invite no judgment; it deletes any visible sign of the work's having an intention upon the reader .... The minimalist short story writer leaves things unsaid, unexplained because he may choose to convey a view of life in which things felt but left unstated have value.[11]

An absence of judgment, the refusal to give explanations, and the adoption of an elliptical style are certainly the main features of minimalism, which must be taken into account when analyzing minimalist short stories. Occasionally the author can be judgmental, but more often than not, his opinions are voiced by the narrator. In fact, the narrator acts as the authorized speaker in the narration, and it is through his point of view that readers see the world and come to terms with the final meaning of the story. The minimalist writer's strategy is to leave things unstated. Thus, the narrator may subtly refer to or hint at something that is not openly stated in the story but may have a decisive meaning in its overall structure. The narrator does not act as the author's mask and is not invested with authorial responsibility. Consequently, his role becomes problematic. He holds narratorial authority, but his view of the surrounding world is not comprehensive. His point of view is partial and fragmentary. In

---

[10] Colibaba, "Raymond Carver's Minimalism", 126-31.
[11] *Ibid.*, 127.

consonance with the nature of the short story, the narrator does not attempt to give a full picture of the world. And he does not assume that existence is meaningful.

Tobias Wolff has reflected on the nature and the origins of fiction. In an interview by J.H.E. Paine he explained:

> That distance between the supposition of why you are doing what you are doing and the shadowy reality of it is the loam of fiction. That terrain, that's exactly where fiction writers work.[12]

Wolff seems to place fiction in the uncertain terrain between reality and desire, somewhere between fantasy and reality, very close to Nathaniel Hawthorne's theorization of the neutral ground of fiction. As such, the short story writer must consider both reality and imagination. If the narration gravitates excessively towards one of these poles, it is bound to lose some of its features. If too realistic, it can give the impression of being a documentary; if too fantastic, it can miss the sense of reality. In the latter case the "as-if-real" function that became prominent in late Romanticism in Herman Melville's short stories does not play a role anymore. The narrative contract between the writer and the reader is thus maintained with the illusion of reality that is created in the story. In this interview Wolff insists on the liminal nature of short fiction:

> I think the besetting vice of most writers is a programmatic intention, making a story like an algebra equation with a solution at the end. Chekhov gives another model of conclusiveness – that conclusiveness inhabits the whole body of the story, not just the ending. That every good story expresses inevitability in all its parts, and yet is not foreclosed, shut down, at the last word. A good story somehow continues in a shimmer of possibility.[13]

The reader must supplement what the narrator silences. His omissions indicate or hint at some aspects of the story that the reader must solve for himself. This lack of resolution obliges the reader to seek the missing links and forces him to provide the story's ending.

---

[12] J.H.E. Paine, "Tobias Wolff", *Les Cahiers de la nouvelle – Journal of the Short Story in English*, XLI (Autumn 2003), 369.
[13] Jack Livings, "Tobias Wolff, The Art of Fiction No. 183", *The Paris Review*, CLXXI (Fall 2004), 16.

Thus the narrator must carefully balance what he says and what he omits.

In his Introduction to *The Vintage Book of Contemporary American Short Stories* (1994), Wolff declares his interest in stories that are not postmodern – that is, stories that are not "concerned with exploring [their] own fictional nature and indifferent if not hostile to the short story's traditional interests in character and dramatic development and social context". He expresses his preference for

> ... stories about people who led lives neither admirable nor depraved, but so convincing in their portrayal that the reader has to acknowledge kinship.
>
> That sense of kinship is what makes stories important to us. The pleasure we take in cleverness and technical virtuosity soon exhausts itself in the absence of any recognizable human landscape. We need to feel ourselves acted upon by a story, outraged, exposed, in danger of heartbreak and change. Those are the stories that endure in our memories, to the point where they take on the nature of memory itself.[14]

Wolff is more concerned with the meaning and moral of the story than with its technical aspects, and it is no wonder that he has been classified as a moral writer.[15] In Brian Hanley's opinion, "Tobias Wolff sees his fiction as 'inquisitive' rather than didactic".[16] For Wolff the short story is not a matter of abstract philosophy embodied in an array of virtuous narrative techniques. Fiction must have recognizable characters and a plot that deals with human experience. Wolff is interested in short stories that have a moral purpose and that deal with human experience lived by common people under normal circumstances. Based on these interests, Wolff writes a type of fiction that may be relevant to the contemporary reader who has to face the challenges of modern society. He believes that the artistic experience of the short story can have a transformative power: "I think we are changed by the experience of beauty, by the experience of a profound

---

[14] Tobias Wolff, Introduction to *The Vintage Book of Contemporary American Short Stories*, New York: Vintage, 1994, xiii.
[15] Paine, "Tobias Wolff", 372-73.
[16] Brian Hanley, "Modernity's 'Mr. Rambler': Tobias Wolff's Exploration of Vanity and Self-Deception in *The Night in Question*", *Papers on Language and Literature*, XXXIX/2 (Spring 2003), 147.

emotion so artistically formed that it becomes an experience of the generosity of life."[17]

In order to make his fiction credible, Wolf resorts to a series of narrative techniques, among which narrative voice and point of view hold a prominent role. Narrators create the standpoint from which the story is told, providing selected information about themselves, the story and the characters, and establishing the emotional distance between the reader and the characters. The narrator shares with the reader his emotional relationship with the characters of the story. Wolff's basic strategy is to resort to a narrator who is independent of the action of the story and who recounts a moment in the characters' lives. As the story progresses, one of the characters takes on the role of the narrator and carries on with the story. This is the case of short stories such as "Sanity", "The Other Miller" and "The Night in Question", which illustrate this narratorial frame.

"Sanity" is the story of an unnamed insane man in the hospital who is visited by his daughter April, accompanied by his second wife, Claire. The reader is offered a glimpse into the difficult relationship between his daughter by his first marriage and her stepmother. After their visit, while waiting to take the bus, the two women reminisce about particular moments of their past. Both remember April's initial rejection of her stepmother and ponder on their subsequent mutual understanding and cooperation. There is little action in the story. Wolff prefers to render the events of the story through the subjectivity of his characters. He creates a narratorial frame in which he alternates the characters' point of view with the narrator's.

The story is elliptically told by a third-person narrator who does not play any active role in the story. However, the narrator provides the reader with all the information on the two women's life. As soon as the reader becomes familiar with the characters and their lives, the narrator's report is dropped. His account is replaced by a dialogue between Claire and April, followed by Claire's remembrance of her life with her first husband. Claire's story will be expanded in turn by the anonymous narrator. It is important to note that the shift in the voice is not abrupt: first there is a transition from the third-person narrator to the dialogue between the two characters, and then there is a second, fluent transition towards Claire's own account of her first marriage. The last intervention of the third-person narrator is not

---

[17] Paine, "Tobias Wolff", 380.

innocent. This time the narrator knows more about Claire's thoughts and feelings, and gives more information about them. The narrator comments on Claire's relationship with her first husband and on April's love affair with a young man, who is regarded with suspicion by her stepmother. Given their mutual distrust, April cannot communicate with her stepmother. At the end of the story, the third-person narrator experiences an emotional transformation and gives up his initial detachment for an involvement with his character's innermost feelings.

The last shift from Claire's free indirect style to the narrator's account parallels the latter's increasing involvement in the story. The transition from the direct style to a free indirect style turns the narrator into the character's spokesman. Although this seems to be a minimal change in narrative style, the effect is very powerful in terms of the narrator's emotional involvement, since he seems to be closer to the characters and the readers. His emotional involvement is greater at the end of the story than at the beginning. Moreover, the use of the free indirect style allows Wolff a closure that is not complete. The narrator does not have the last word; instead he opens up a wide range of interpretive possibilities. Wolff himself corroborates his conscious purpose in resorting to this literary strategy: "One of the things that I am at home with in Chekhov is the degree to which he trusts his reader to travel beyond the given, to collaborate with him in the making of his stories."[18]

"The Other Miller" is an interesting example of the importance the narrator's voice holds for Wolff in the construction of short stories. Miller is a soldier who, upon receiving a letter announcing his mother's death, is given leave to go home for bereavement. Yet in the same battalion there is another soldier who bears the same name and has the same initials. The irony of the story consists in the fact that Miller thinks that the first sergeant has by mistake handed him the letter that was intended for "the other Miller".

Miller does not say anything about the confusion he believes the sergeant made when he gave him the letter; instead, he ponders on his mother. They had been on bad terms since she married Miller's high school biology teacher. Disappointed, Miller decided to join the army, knowing his mother would disapprove of his decision. During the first

---

[18] *Ibid.*, 371.

months she used to send him letters on a weekly basis, which she would receive back unopened. In the end she gave up any kind of communication with her son. When Miller arrives home he realizes that the first sergeant did not make any mistake in handing him the letter. His mother had actually died, and he was able to arrive in time for her funeral.

Wolff's story is told in the present tense, a strategy that gives the impression that the story is located in a timeless present, which confers a certain air of detachment and impersonality. The narratorial voice and the narrative tense create an atmosphere of estrangement that adequately render Miller's situation. At first the story seems to belong to the genre of the fantastic tale of the *Doppelgänger*. But as the story unfolds the reader is aware that there is no fantasy in the story. In fact, the main concern of the story is Miller's rejection of reality.

Miller's emotional coldness is well reflected by the third-person narrator who tells the story. The narrator observes the events from a distanced and probably superior standpoint. At the end of the story, when Miller goes back home, there is a covert change in the narratorial strategy: the reader becomes gradually aware that the story is now being told not by the third-person narrator, but by Miller himself, who records his own thoughts:

> You could be going along just fine and then one day, through no fault of your own, something could get loose in your bloodstream and knock out part of your brain. Leave you like that. And if it didn't happen now, all at once, it was sure to happen slowly later on. That was the end you were bound for.[19]

This narratorial shift does not last long. In the following paragraph, a new turn of the narratorial voice brings the third-person narrator back. This brief lapse has been sufficient enough to provide a direct glimpse into Miller's thoughts. Miller's psychological detachment makes the narratorial voice problematic. If Miller had accepted from the beginning that the letter was directed to him and not to the other Miller, and that the news of the death referred to his own mother and not to his companion's mother, there would have been no need for Wolff to introduce two narrative voices, Miller's and the narrator's.

---

[19] Wolff, *Night in Question*, 99.

To the reader's great surprise (and this is also the climax of the story), it turns out that the narrator's voice and Miller's voice are one and the same. The use of these two different narrative voices corresponds to Wolff's intention to stage by means of narrative technique the psychological processes of a mind close to schizophrenia.

The variations in the narrative voice imply, firstly, an alienation from the persona and, secondly, a lack of emotional involvement. Both narrative voices, third- and second-person, indicate that the narrator does not participate in the story, yet the great irony of the story is that the narrator turns out to be Miller himself, and the former detachment translates into the latter's mental estrangement and inner dissociation.

Wolff's third story, "The Night in Question", presents a more complex narrative strategy, which relies heavily on shifts in narrative voices. It is composed of two interrelated stories. The first is the story of Frances and Frank, two siblings, whose lives were ruined by their father, and the second is the story of Mike Bollingen, a friend of Frank's, whom Frank turns into the hero of an extremely sad life. In this first narration the past returns obsessively. Frank's father, a violent and arbitrary man, used to physically abuse his son, while his daughter, Frances, actively protected him against their father's aggressive behavior. Subdued by his father's personality, Frank used to repeat his father's story about a father's decision to sacrifice the life of his own son in order to save a trainload of strangers. Frances pressures her brother to reject this unloving moral. She makes him say he would choose to save a person he cares for instead an anonymous crowd, which is an indirect reference to what she has done over the years for her brother.

The story of Frances and Frank's childhood is told by an external anonymous narrator who is not directly involved in the recounted events, whereas Mike Bollingen's story is told by Frank. Since Frank acts as narrator, there are certain differences between the frame story and Mike's. Although both stories are told by an external narrator, in the first there is little moral and sentimental involvement: Frank and Frances' lives are narrated in free indirect speech reflecting Frances' thoughts. In Mike's story, however, the narrator is not involved in the story. The narrator's emotional involvement emerges not from his narrative point of view but from the narrator's biased selection of events. Frank highlights those details he believes to be more effective in causing pity in the reader. In the end, the narrator's emotional involvement is a matter of selection and presentation of events. The narrator singles out some events of Mike's life and discards others. Even his sister Frances objects to his subjective selection. In this case, the narrator, though external to the story, is not objective, since he tends to sentimentalize Mike's life.

The reader perceives the different degree of narrative involvement in both stories. The reader tends to have more trust in Frances and Frank's story, which, although retold by an anonymous narrator, seems to be more reliable because it is more objective. The anonymous external narrator makes use of free indirect speech, creating the impression that he is close to the characters and that he is privy to their thoughts. Conversely, in Mike's story, the reader knows the narrator, and this seems to favor his credibility as storyteller. However, the narrator's overt emotional involvement prevents the reader from knowing the protagonist's real thoughts. Consequently, the reader is suspicious of the narrator's account.

In conclusion, the narrators of these three stories play a fundamental role in Wolff's narrative strategies. The narrative voice opens or closes the narrative focus, which in turn has a bearing on the selected events and the dynamics of point of view. The narrators' reliability depends on the union of narrative voice and point of view. Realism is based on the narrators' reliability, which in turn is sustained by a narrative voice that must be as unobtrusive and impersonal as possible. Wolff's stories resort mainly to impersonal narrative voices.

In cases where the narrator is too involved in the events he is narrating, his reliability and the realist genre are compromised. Wolff's subtle manipulations of point of view and narratorial voice create a realistic short story, which encompasses both the external reality of events and the subjective internal reality of the characters' innermost thoughts. Wolff's new realism is no longer the plain realism of the nineteenth century, but a more nuanced mode filtered by modern and postmodern aesthetics.

THE BOUNDARIES OF SERIAL NARRATIVE

LAURO ZAVALA

Genre and reading in serial fiction

The study of short story cycles – that is, of series of stories united by theme, genre, or style – belongs in borderline writing: in terms of length and internal structure, these textual series are halfway between novel and short story, so analyzing them allows us to reframe some fundamental problems of theory and literary criticism concerning the existing boundaries between writing, editing and reading. Furthermore, their very existence points toward the need to formulate a new normative theory of literary genres.

In other words, the study of short story cycles is an opportunity to reframe the persistent problem of defining literary genres: what is a short story? What is a novel? And, more recently, what is a minifiction? What are the boundaries between these genres? And, even more important in the case of minifiction series, how can the differences between prose, essay and prose poem be produced by the context of each reading?

Insofar as the writer is the first editor of the text he is writing, writing may be a strategy that advances modes of reading, not only of a specific text, but also of former texts.

Short story cycles and other forms of serial narrative

In Anglo-American literature there are a number of studies of short story cycles; however, Spanish-American literature lacks analyses of such works, even though there are magnificent serial and fragmentary narrative compositions which deserve theoretical attention. The abundance of minifictions (ironic, hybrid texts of less than four-hundred words), minifictional series and novels consisting exclusively of this type of text represent literary contributions specific to this region. At present, we need to distinguish between different forms of minifiction, since this term can refer both to short-short stories[1] (which are primarily narrative and have a traditional structure) and to microfictions (which are of a hybrid nature and have an unconventional structure).

A field of literary studies that has seldom received theoretical attention is that of generic literary norms and the reading processes they involve. The tradition of genre experimentation in Spanish-language literature poses specific problems linked to the concept of fragmentation, which goes back to avant-garde movements of the early twentieth century. Furthermore, if, as some critics have affirmed, the lingua franca of the novel (in its purest realistic form) was French during the second half of nineteenth century, and the lingua franca of the short story (in its most canonical form) was English during the first half of the twentieth, then perhaps the lingua franca of minifiction (as a protean genre, distinct from the tradition of short-short story) has been Spanish, especially Latin American Spanish, during the second half of the twentieth century.

At the same time, the study of short story cycles and other genres of a hybrid, fragmentary and serial nature reveals the gradual relativization of the genre's canonical forms. Perhaps today a really experimental task would be to write a novel or a short story completely free of fragmentation and generic hybridity. Thus, the mandatory generic references are no longer the novel (in its most traditional form, subject to rules of realism and verisimilitude), nor the short story (in its classic and epiphanic variety, characterized by its surprise ending), but rather minifiction, a literary genre practiced throughout the twentieth century that in turn prefigures the birth of hypertextual writing.

In this article I explore various strategies for writing, editing and reading serial narratives that can relativize the generic conventional boundaries of textual unity (particularly those of the novel) and of generic diversity, that is, the identity of each short story or minifiction. Studying short story cycles and other forms of serial and fragmentary narrative obliges us to rewrite the norms of generic definitions.

Studying short text series can sharpen one's awareness of various possibilities of reading offered by textual manifestations of the one and the many and by shifting the boundaries between the whole and

---

[1] The "short-short story" is a term generally used as an equivalent to very-short story.

its parts. These strategies help us understand the existing differences between short story cycles, fragmentary novels, sequential minifictions, minifiction cycles and dispersed short stories.[2] In some cases these different forms of writing coexist within a single work. Readers are forced to make choices, to reformulate their strategies of interpretation. The text offers diverse generic possibilities, so that a work can be read, simultaneously or alternatively, as a novel, as a series of short stories or as a minifiction cycle. This simultaneity of genres contrasts with the generic orthodoxy that ruled in the early twentieth century, although a century later this same orthodoxy has coexisted with other textual strategies. Conventional normative theorizations on the novel and the short story have omitted texts that were considered anomalous.

Studying these forms of writing prompts us not only to reformulate the distinctions between traditional literary genres, but also to reconsider our reading strategies. For instance, why do we think of Carlos Fuentes' *Aura* as a novel, but of Julio Cortázar's "El perseguidor" as a short story? The differences between one genre and another are not restricted to the adoption of one literary norm over another; these formulations have only established general distinctions between the canonical and experimental forms of the novel and the short story and set up clear differences between narrative, essay and poetry.

When the exception becomes the rule (or, more precisely, when rupture turns into a tradition of rupture), it is necessary to reformulate the very concept of the canon and to recognize the strategies of

---

[2] These strategies do not limit the diversity of reading possibilities or the writing of short story series, since electronic technologies make it possible for a reader to also participate in the creation of a text through her interaction with the screen. I will call these texts "minifiction cycles" and "sequential minifiction". Specialists of electronic forms of creative writing simply call these new genres "hypertexts". The study of these new literary possibilities has already begun in Spanish-language criticism: Jaime Alejandro Rodríguez, *Hipertexto y literatura: Una batalla por el signo en tiempos posmodernos*, Bogotá: Ediciones de la Pontificia Universidad Javeriana, 1999, and Núria Voiullamoz, *Literatura e hipermedia: La irrupción de la literatura interactiva: Precedentes y crítica*, Barcelona: Paidós, 2000. Also, a number of important translations already exist, such as Janet H. Murray, *Hamlet en la holocubierta: El futuro de la narrativa en el ciberespacio*, Barcelona: Paidós, 1999, and the important work by George P. Landow, *Hipertexto: La convergencia de la teoría crítica contemporánea y la tecnología*, Barcelona: Paidós, 1995.

reading and interpretation that are made possible by the composition of texts that seem exceptional merely from the perspective of prevailing literary norms.

Fragmentary reading as a productive act

The act of reading can have many different consequences for the reader. In some cases it can involve a momentary suspension of what the reader already knows. In particular, reading narrative series (including short story cycles) can involve a suspension of what the reader knows about literary genres.

Parallel to the recognition of this more and more frequent phenomenon, it is necessary to reformulate the traditional theory of genres in order to allow for all the forms of writing (and reading) that have proliferated throughout the twentieth century. What we now call minifiction has developed through new forms of reading and writing that announce the onset of new forms of reading and writing the world; minifiction's rise has coincided with the emergence of a new sensibility. Acknowledgment of these forms of writing requires more flexible strategies of interpretation than traditional literary norms – that is, strategies that remain open to the contingencies of each interpretive context.

A first attempt to come to terms with the diversity of textual forms that surpass the traditional literary norms consisted in the erratic use of the term "tale" rather than "short story". (Similarly, in French the word *nouvelle* was used rather than the more traditional *récit* and *conte*.) In Spanish, "tale" (*relato*) has been used to refer either to something more than a short story (an experimental short story), something less than a short story (a story without literary value) or something different from a story (whether a hybrid text, a long story or even a prose poem).

The use of the term "minifiction" is a direct consequence of this new context of reading, in which the possibilities of textual interpretation demand a reformulation of traditional literary norms and a redefinition of the genre in terms of interpretive contexts within which readers are willing to invest their reading experience (memory), their ideological competencies (worldview) and their literary appetite (those texts that they are willing to bear in mind and that challenge their worldview).

Throughout the twentieth century we find minifictions that can be read alternatively as prose poems, essays, chronicles, allegories or short stories. Quite often, the same text is included in anthologies dedicated to different genres, which reveals the insufficiency of traditional generic norms to account for texts that cannot be classified within a specific canonical genre. This is the case with the parodic fables of Augusto Monterroso, the allegorical vignettes of Juan José Arreola, the ironic prose of Julio Torri and the textual games of Guillermo Samperio, to mention a few names within the canon of contemporary Mexican narrative. Minifictions from the Southern Cone (Argentina, Chile, Uruguay and Paraguay) include the *espantapájaros* of Oliverio Girondo, the *archiprólogos* of Macedonio Fernández and the still unclassifiable texts of Felisberto Hernández.

In contrast to this great diversity of Spanish-American short fiction, what prevails in the tradition of Anglo-American literature is the "mini-short story", that is, the conventional short-short story.[3] If we consider the series of sequential short stories as an extreme case of short story cycles, we observe that in English and other non-Spanish languages, there is a striking absence of genuine minifictions (hybrid, protean and subject to the aleatory rigor of literary serialization); and with the notable exception of France, the prose poem tradition outside Latin America has not yet reached the same level of sophistication that it has in Latin America.

At the moment of composition, writers of story cycles were conscious of the existing relations among stories, which accounts for their clear structural unity. For this reason, some scholars have called them *cuentos enlazados* ("interwoven stories", Enrique Anderson Imbert) or "molecular stories" (Slawomir Dölezel).[4] Generally, when the unity between stories in the same book is obvious, we are dealing

---

[3] By "conventional" (also called "classical") short-short stories I mean short-short stories with traditional literary features, namely, a linear structure, exclusively narrative contents, moral development of the main character, and a surprise ending. These classical short-short stories (in Spanish, *minicuentos*) are clearly distinguished from modern short-short stories (*microrrelatos*), and postmodern short-short stories (*minificciones*). Modern short-short stories are the opposite of classical short-short stories (fragmentary structure, poetic contents, allegoric characters, open ending), whereas postmodern short-short stories have a simultaneous and paradoxical juxtaposition of both classical and modern literary features.

[4] Enrique Anderson Imbert, "Cuentos enlazados", in *Teoría y práctica del cuento*, Barcelona: Ariel, 1992, 115-19.

with a "short story cycle" (Forrest Ingram) or a "short story sequence" (Gerald Kennedy). This modality has been intensively studied in the English-language tradition. Maggie Dunn and Ann Morris (1995), in a study covering more than 250 titles, do not hesitate to call this form a "composite novel". However, this denomination is problematic, since we need to differentiate between a series of short stories and a fragmentary novel.[5] Moreover, in Mexican literature of the second half of the twentieth century it is possible to mention more than fifty titles that fit this category,[6] while the tradition of short story cycles is still alive in many contemporary authors.[7]

---

[5] For example, Russell Cluff emphasizes that "la secuencia cuentística, antes de formar un total coherente, es una colección de cuentos. Y no es, ni será nunca, una novela donde los apartados internos – tanto por tradición como por función práctica – sean totalmente interdependientes" ("the short story sequence, before conforming to a coherent whole, is above all a collection of short stories. And it is not, nor will it ever be, a novel whose internal sections are totally interdependent in virtue of tradition or literary practice"). Cluff, "Doce peregrinajes maravillosos", in *Si cuento lejos de ti: La ficción en México*, Tlaxcala: Universidad Autónoma de Tlaxcala, 1998, 66.

[6] The thematic unity of these series of short stories can be established by characters' inhabiting a common setting, as in *El llano en llamas* (1953) by Juan Rulfo, or *Benzulul* (1959) by Eraclio Zepeda, or on some occasions by the presence of a common narrator, as in Hernán Lara Zavala's *De Zitilchén* (1981) or Mauricio Magdaleno's *El ardiente verano* (1954). Generic unity can be defined by a clearly recognized tradition, as in the case of detective fiction in *La obligación de asesinar* (1957) by Antonio Helú or in the fantastic fiction in *Una violeta de más* (1968) by Francisco Tario. Stylistic unity can be produced by a common thread in a series of short stories – for example, the search for personal truth in *Río subterráneo* (1979) by Inés Arredondo, or in *El gato* (1984) by Juan García Ponce. See, among others, Russell Cluff, "Los Ferri: La saga familiar de Sergio Pitol", in *El cuento mexicano: Homenaje a Luis Leal*, ed. Sara Poot Herrera, México: Universidad Nacional Autónoma de México, 1996, 379-406, and "Colonizadores y colonizados en Zitilchén: La secuencia de cuentos de Hernán Lara Zavala", in *Revista de Literatura Mexicana Contemporánea*, III, 1996, 56-66.

[7] Without going beyond the field of Mexican narrative we can mention some short story cycles in which a group of characters inhabits a common setting. Well-known examples of stories set in Mexico's northern border region include *Los viernes de Lautaro* (1979) by Jesús Gardea, *Registro de causantes* (1992) by Daniel Sada, *Tijuanenses* (1989) by Federico Campbell and *La frontera de cristal* (1995) by Carlos Fuentes. Stories set in Mexico City include *Cerca del fuego* (1975) by José Agustín. Detective or fantastic short story cycles with a strong common thread include *El regreso de la verdadera araña* (1988) by Paco Ignacio Taibo II and *Escenas de la realidad virtual* (1991) by Mauricio José Schwartz. For short story cycles whose unity is determined by tone, see the gallery of sarcastic portraits of sentimental daily life scenes in *Amores de segunda mano* (1991) by Enrique Serna, or the medley of

The relevance of short story cycles in theorizing literary genres and their boundaries is evident. The problems of generic definition raised by their existence can be recognized in other narrative cycles. In what follows, I will compare short story cycles with other types of textual series that correspond to and differ from them in important ways. In the final section I use certain concepts that can prove useful to the systematic study of these various textual series and of other creative forms in contemporary culture, such as musical, lyric and audiovisual minifiction (for example, songs, ballads, poems, video clips, spots, trailers and film title sequences).

The fragmentary novel: a nonsequential narrative series
There is a complex relationship between the whole and its parts in some narrative cycles – for example, in novels whose structure does not necessarily maintain a sequential logic. This form of writing was very common throughout the nineteenth century in what Umberto Eco calls the "serialized novel", which preserves a sequential order that cannot be easily altered by the internal structure of each chapter. We also find this structure in soap operas or in melodramatic films, fictionalized by Manuel Puig in the novelistic series he started writing in 1968 as *La tradición de Rita Hayworth*. On the other hand, when we talk about the "fragmented novel",[8] we deal with a text that is formed by fragments of considerable extension, and whose separations may be marked typographically or signaled by a conventional division into chapters. Each fragment can include many types of extra-narrative material.

Strictly speaking, every novel is necessarily fragmentary. However, the fragmentation of "fragmented novels" *per se* involves the simultaneous fragmentation of logical and chronological sequences, and the presence within each fragment of genre elements or themes that establish the formal consistency of the narrative project. This literary tradition has prestigious antecedents, such as *Al filo del agua* (1947) by Agustín Yañez, *La sombra del caudillo* (1929) by Martín Luis Guzmán and *Los de abajo* (1915) by Mariano Azuela. In contemporary Mexican literature the best such narratives include

---

eroticism, science and humor in *Dios sí juega a los dados* (2000) by Oscar de la Borbolla.
[8] Carol D'Lugo, *The Fragmented Novel in Mexico*, Austin: University of Texas Press, 1997.

288   *Lauro Zavala*

La región más transparente (1958), *La muerte de Artemio Cruz* (1962) and *Cambio de piel* (1967) by Carlos Fuentes, *Morirás lejos* (1967) by José Emilio Pacheco and *Farabeuf o la crónica de un instante* (1965) by Salvador Elizondo. In each of these books, the reader is forced to reconstruct the narrative sequence and to simultaneously recognize the existing ideological interrelation between narrative events. For this reason, it may seem paradoxical to use the term "fragment" when referring to this type of novel, since in strict terms each narrative unity is a detail that forms part of a pre-existing whole, without which it would make no sense.

That the unity of the whole is given precedence over the fragment is a consequence of the romantic tradition, which concedes all the weight of meaning to the author's editorial process. On the other hand, the frequency with which a reader decides to reread, comment on or even memorize some of the fragments as autonomous units confirms the thesis of reader response criticism, according to which literary history is being written by successive generations of readers by their own recognition of what is meaningful in the context of their reading. This occurs, for example, in the poetic erotic language of Chapter 68 of *Rayuela* (*Hopscotch*, 1963) by Julio Cortázar, in the splendid chapter on the varieties of secret language in *La muerte de Artemio Cruz* (1962) by Carlos Fuentes, in the baroque monologues about power in *Yo el Supremo* (1974) by Augusto Roa Bastos or in the erotic adventures told by an ironic narrator in *La Habana para un Infante difunto* (1980) by Guillermo Cabrera Infante.

Thus the nonsequential form of the fragmented novel brings into play reading mechanisms that are similar to those we experience while watching a film. Time is being spatialized when we reconstruct the sequential order of those fragments that occurred simultaneously and when we remember the fragments that metonymically recall others in the same series. The reading of fragmentary texts (where internal monologues prevail) demonstrates the fragility of traditional genres, since everyday experience is, by definition, a fragmentary experience. Genre conventions are most evident precisely when we are aware of their absence.

Sequential minifictions: the novel of minimal fragments
Novels formed by minifictional series – that is, extremely short literary texts – form a borderline genre, since they are the site at which

diverse genre conventions and limits are brought into play and treated with irony. This challenges the notion that a text needs a certain minimal length to acquire sufficient literary value, and it also challenges the concept of unity of effect that is implied by the novel and the traditional short story. Minifictional series constitute a textual genre whose identity is defined by its very borderline placement. That is to say, it situates itself in uncertainty, in the liminal, paradoxical, indeterminate and productive space of possibility where all limiting interpretations become irrelevant. The surprising literary possibilities offered by extremely short compositions have been systematically explored during the twentieth century, most notably in the Spanish-American context.

Minifiction cycles that form novels erase established hierarchies. The critical reading of these texts poses fundamental questions to literary theory and to the practice of composition, because they are at once fragmentary novels, short story cycles and minifiction series. They tacitly make us raise questions concerning their original generic definitions: are they novels? Are they short stories? Are they literature? The answers to these and other questions depend on the angle from which we frame each inquiry, and it is this protean ambiguity that defines the generic, structural and semantic nature of serial minifictions.

In short, sequential minifictions are literary borderline texts in many ways. First, they are generic borderline texts in their structure, as each tends to incorporate simultaneous or alternative elements of narrative, poetry or essay. By incorporating elements from diverse literary genres, each of these texts situates itself on the boundaries between narration and essay, between narration and poetry or between essay and poetry. Furthermore, minifictions are borderline texts because they resort to parody and incorporate diverse extra-literary genres: urban vignette, travel chronicle, epistolary writing, taxonomic description and virtually any other kind of writing. By integrating these elements of extra-literary genres, these texts straddle the boundary distinguishing forms of composition that have traditionally been considered literary from forms that have been considered nonliterary.[9] All of these forms of itinerancy – or generic hybridism –

---

[9] The hybrid nature of minifiction has already been pointed out by numerous scholars. See Adriana Berchenko, "Proposiciones para una estética del cuento brevísimo: ¿Un género híbrido?", in *América*, XVIII/1: *Formes breves de l'expression culturelle en*

are made possible by the use of irony. In these texts, irony (generally in the form of puns or parody) functions as a type of rhetorical acid that dissolves the borders between literary genres and between literary and nonliterary writing. Finally, minifictions are borderline texts in that they are nomads between modernist forms of writing (defined by strategies of stable irony) and postmodernist ones (defined by unfixed, unstable irony).[10]

In minifiction series and textual cycles by Spanish-American and Chicano writers, then, the writing may lie between narration, poetry and essay; between literary genres and extra-literary forms; between pretextuality and architextuality. However, since these series are formed by extremely short texts, we must define the existing limits between the whole and its parts, which entails the simultaneous relationship of each short text to a larger, more complex, serial unit (a novel) or to a specific narrative cycle (a short story) without losing, in the process, its autonomy as a textual unit (a minifiction). This also means that, besides being borderline texts in the ways previously mentioned, minifictions remain borderline genres when they form part of a larger series, since each text may be read either as an autonomous text or as part of a larger serial unity. Hence, minifiction narrative cycles can be read, alternatively, as extremely fragmentary novels (novels formed by very short fragments) or as series of sequential short stories.

Amérique Latine de 1850 a nous jours: Poétique de la forme breve. Conte, Nouvelle, París: Centre de Recherches Interuniversitarire sur les Champs Culturelles en Amérique Latine, Presses de la Sorbonne Nouvelle, 1997, 25-44, and others. For example, Violeta Rojo affirms: "Aunque los minicuentos tienen algunas características de los cuentos tradicionales y siguen perfectamente los rasgos diferenciales del género, también tienen otro tipo de características. Así, entre los minicuentos podemos encontrar desde fábulas hasta ensayos, pasando por todas las variaciones posibles de las formas simples y de los escritos no literarios. Es por esta razón que se habla del cáracter proteico de los minicuentos, ya que su forma, como la de Proteo, es cambiante" ("Although minifictions share some characteristics with traditional short stories, and follow perfectly well the characteristic features of the genre, they also present a different set of characteristics. Thus in minifiction we can find fables and essays, passing through all possible variations of the simple forms and non-literary writing. It is for this reason that we refer to their protean nature, since their form, like that of Proteus, is mutable"). Violeta Rojo, "Características del minicuento", in *Breve manual para reconocer minicuentos*, México: Universidad Autónoma Metropolitana – Azcapotzalco, 1997, 93.
[10] For the distinction between stable and unstable irony, see Wayne Booth's *A Rhetoric of Irony*, Chicago: University of Chicago Press, 1974, 233-77.

The surprising literary possibilities offered by extremely short texts
have been explored throughout the twentieth century, and the most
notable developments in this genre have taken place in Latin America.
The canonical antecedents of cycles of very short sequential
minifictions in Mexican literature include *Cartucho* (1920) by Nellie
Campobello and *La feria* (1963) by Juan José Arreola. Many of the
recent novels in this tradition are metafictional.[11] There are several
remarkable South American novels formed of minifictions, and many
of these are heavily intertextual.[12]

The field of sequential minifictions is still in need of further study.
Special attention must be paid to their generic nature, since they
represent a form of writing that is different from short story cycles,
fragmentary novels and other types of minifiction series.

Minifiction cycles: series of different inventions
Minifiction cycles are series that lack the extension and the structure
of a novel yet comprise parodies and generic pastiche; they display
diverse structural, intertextual and linguistic variations. In Latin
America there is a rich tradition of minifiction cycles, which go back
to famous antecedents such as *De fusilamientos* (Mexico, 1940) by
Julio Torri and *El hacedor* (Argentina, 1960) by Jorge Luis Borges. In
this genre it is possible to distinguish between cycles of cycles, which
have the extension of an autonomous volume, and brief cycles that do

---

[11] This is the case with *Los juegos* (1967) by René Avilés Fabila; *¿ABCDErio o
AbeCeDamo?* (1975) by Daniel Leyva; *Fantasmas aztecas* (1979), *Muchacho en
llamas* (1987) and *A la salud de la serpiente* (1988) by Gustavo Sainz; *Héroes
convocados* (1982) by Paco Ignacio Taibo II; and *Cuadernos de Gofa* (1981) by Hugo
Hiriart. In the last decade of the twentieth century this mode of writing prevailed and
presented a marked tendency toward self-referentiality, as can be seen in *La luna
siempre será un amor difícil* (1994) and *Estrella de la calle sexta* (2000) by Luis
Humberto Crosthwaite, *La señora Rodríguez y otros mundos* (1990) by Martha Cerda
and *Remedios infalibles contra el hipo* (1998) by José Ramón Ruisánchez.
[12] *La guaracha del Macho Camacho* (1976) and *La importancia de llamarse Daniel
Santos* (Puerto Rico, 1989) by Luis Rafael Sánchez are written in the form of a
musical chronicle; *Luisa en el país de la realidad* (México, 1994) by the Salvadorean-
Nicaraguan Claribel Alegría is written as a poetic chronicle; *Pero sigo siendo el rey*
(Colombia, 1983) by David Sánchez Juliao is a textual homage to Mexican *ranchera*
music; *Tierra de Nadia* (Ecuador, 2000) by Marcelo Báez is written as a diary on the
Internet; and the Chicano novels *Klail City* (1976) by Rolando Hinojosa and *The
House on Mango Street* by Sandra Cisneros are autobiographical tales that depict a
specific linguistic and cultural community.

not reach the extension of a single volume and generally are part of a larger work.

Among the many "cycles of cycles",[13] *Varia invención* (1949) and *Palíndroma* (1971) by Juan José Arreola are outstanding titles. Each of these volumes presents a wide diversity of themes, tones and genres, yet each also achieves a remarkable literary unity thanks to the author's conscious stylistic intentions.

The "brief cycles" find an obligatory reference in the minifiction series contained in the *Material plástico* section in Julio Cortázar's *Historias de cronopios y de famas* (Argentina, 1974). In this kind of protean minifiction we find generic games in the manner of a pastiche, as in the *Cosas* series in *Disertación sobre las telarañas* (Mexico, 1980), or in the *Rarezas* series in *Discutibles fantasmas* (Mexico, 2001), both by Hugo Hiriart.

Minifiction cycles usually adopt a ludic style and are often explicitly intertextual, as in *Falsificaciones* (Argentina, 1966) by Marco Denevi, *La oveja negra y demás fábulas* (Mexico, 1969) by Augusto Monterroso, *Caja de herramientas* (México, 1989) by Fabio Morábito and *Adivinanzas* (México, 1989) by the Peruvian writer Manuel Mejía Valera. These books involve the generic rules of diverse extra-literary traditions such as myths, fables, allegories, catalogues and children's games.

Other minifiction cycles are structured as series of linguistic games. This is the case with *Exorcismos de esti(l)o* (1976) by Guillermo Cabrera Infante, in which each brief cycle of minifictions has different rules.[14] In Spanish-American literature a common variant

---

[13] Worth mentioning are the humorous series *Me río del mundo* (Venezuela, 1984) by Luis Britto García, as well as *Despistes* (Uruguay, 1989) by Mario Benedetti; *La Musa y el Garabato* (Mexico, 1992) by Felipe Garrido; *Textos extraños* (Mexico, 1981) and *Cuaderno imaginario* (Mexico, 1990) by Guillermo Samperio; *La felicidad y otras complicaciones* (Mexico, 1988) by the Chilean Hernán Lavín Cerda; *La sueñera* (1984), *Casa de geishas* (1992) and *Botánica del caos* (2000) by the Argentinian Ana María Shua; and *Retazos* (Mexico, 1995) by Mónica Lavín.

[14] Other notable examples are *Léérere* (México, 1986) by Dante Medina, in which syntactic rules are broken for humorous purposes, and *Sea breve* (Guatemala, 1999) by Otto-Raúl González, which presents a full range of language games. One extreme case of structural play is to be found in *Infundios ejemplares* (México, 1969) by Sergio Golwarz, in which each text is shorter than the preceding one, producing a structure that the author has called *infundibuliforme*, that is to say, a structure that has the form of an *infundio* or *embudo* ("funnel").

of minifiction cycles is the collection of vignettes and of extremely short journalistic chronicles.[15]

A special case: fantastic bestiaries

As a special kind of minifiction cycle, bestiaries require a separate treatment, since the bestiary genre in the Spanish-American literary tradition differs from that in the European. In the millennial European tradition, human features are beastified (that is to say, they acquire animal form) in a process of moral degradation that has produced vampires, gargoyles, goblins, homunculi and werewolves. In the Spanish-American tradition, however, bestiaries appear when the Spanish chroniclers of the Indies (Gonzalo Fernández de Oviedo and many others) describe the fauna and the flora of the New World with a wondrous gaze, projecting human features upon natural phenomena.

In the tradition of Latin American bestiaries we find two fundamental trends, both of them of an anthropomorphic nature. The first, rooted in the pre-Columbian Mesoamerican culture and known as "fantastic zoology", produces sacred and ominous beasts that have a special intimacy with death. During the colonial period this tradition gradually incorporated a rich apocalyptic and extemporaneously millennialist iconography, revitalized at the turn of the twentieth century by a generation of young writers. The second, a more recent trend that goes back to the 1950s, has produced allegorical beasts, at times parodic, on occasion hyperbolic, and quite often lyrical. In this recent tradition, the bestiaries are steeped in humor and irony so as to signify the paradoxical nature of beings that, without being completely human, exhibit in the style of moral-less fables the contradictions of the human condition.

About a dozen essential bestiaries in the Spanish-American tradition published in the second half of the twentieth century illustrate both bestiary trends. The primary texts of fantastic zoology go back to *Manual de zoología fantástica* by Jorge Luis Borges and Margarita Guerrero (Argentina, 1954). A few years later, Juan José

---

[15] Examples in Mexican literature include *Gente de la ciudad* (México, 1986) by Guillermo Samperio, *Ciudad por entregas* (México, 1996) by Norberto de la Torre and *Crónicas romanas* (México, 1997) by Ignacio Trejo Fuentes. A variant of this modality is the series of extremely short journalistic *chronicles* like *Patas arriba* (Uruguay, 1998) by Eduardo Galeano and *Objetos reconstruidos* (Argentina, 1979) by Noé Jitrik.

Arreola published his *Bestiario*, one of the most important prose poems written in Spanish (Mexico, 1959). José Emilio Pacheco's *Álbum de zoología* (Mexico, 1985), inscribed in a clearly poetic tradition, deserves special attention. Branda Domecq's short story series *Bestiario doméstico* (Mexico) can also be considered here, although it is not composed of minifictions.

Other interesting Mexican contributions to the tradition of minifiction bestiaries include *El recinto de animalia* by Rafael Junquera (1999) and the apocryphal *Bestiario de Indias* (followed shortly after by *Herbario de Indias*) by the Muy Reverendo Fray Rodrigo de Macuspana, the pseudonym of Marco Antonio de Urdapilleta (1995). In Guadalajara, Raúl Aceves published a *Diccionario de bestias mágicas y seres sobrenaturales de América* (1995).

Regarding the tradition of ironic parables, in 1951 Julio Cortázar published his *Bestiario*, which, comprising short stories of a conventional length, has much more in common with Kafka's bestiary than with the Chronicles of the Indies. In 1969, Augusto Monterroso, who was born in Honduras of Guatemalan nationality and later established himself in Mexico, published *La oveja negra y demás fábulas*. And in 1989 in Chile, Ricardo Cantalapiedra published *Bestiario urbano*. In Mexico there are several writers who continue in this tradition, such as René Avilés Fábila, known for the allegorical mini-chronicles of human stupidity in his *Los animales prodigiosos* (1989). In 1991, Pedro Ángel Palou published his tender and sarcastic parodies, *Amores enormes*. In 1999, Ediciones El Ermitaño published two collections: the minipoems of *Bichario* by Saúl Ibargoyen (an Uruguayan writer living in Mexico) and a collective volume titled *Bestiaro fantástico* that came out of a workshop organized by Bernardo Ruiz and comprises minifictions springing from all of the traditions mentioned here, ranging from the ominous to the apocalyptic, and ironic allegories of the paradoxes of everyday life.

Generally, texts written in the apocalyptic or fabulist tradition tend to adopt a hieratic tone – at times poetic, almost urgent, sometimes oracular, as if portending something irrevocable and definitive. Texts that inscribe themselves in the ironic tradition are fantastic stories in the form of allegories of reading, of time's passing, or of human weakness. In these stories, the narrator takes a day-to-day situation and transforms it into a kind of crystal ball where, as with an aleph, another equally common situation (the reader's own) can be observed. Such stories are anamorphic mirrors that reflect back to their readers an image that is at once both strange and familiar. They seem to answer questions about the characters' identity, highlighting our own animal nature, which is both finite and complex.

Dispersed short stories: waiting for a rereading

Another strategy of articulation of the whole and its parts can be found in chapters of novels that are self-contained enough to be considered short stories: in other words, "dispersed short stories", which can be found either in different novels (such as those by Fernando del Paso)[16] or within a single novel.[17]

The same thing happens during the act of reading performed by a specialized reader who is able to establish formal or generic affinities between texts written by one or more authors. Furthermore, the specialized reader can propose different ways of reading these texts when he brings them together, compiling separate stories, minifictions, chapters or fragments into a single whole: for example, anthologies with a peculiar structure of chapters, or the anthologies elaborated by Borges and Adolfo Bioy Casares (Argentina, *Cuentos breves y extraordinarios*, 1953), and later by Edmundo Valadés (Mexico, *El libro de la imaginación*, 1976). These writers/readers selected extremely short fragments from very long works, and in this way, through a process of reading and editing, they created numerous minifictions. Another example of dispersed short stories would be a collection of "complete stories" by a canonical writer: that is, the types of annotated series produced by publishers such as Cátedra and Castalia, and the equally popular collections by Aguilar and Alfaguara. Worth mentioning here are the various compilations of stories organized by the same author at different moments in time, as in the case of Sergio Pitol, whose editorial reorganization of his own stories has resulted in many versions.

Another variation on this genre involves the recompilation of various short texts by the same author. For example, *Cuentos en miniatura* (Argentina, 1976), by Enrique Anderson Imbert, gathers *casos* (incidents) written by him and dispersed throughout several

---

[16] Fernando del Paso, *Cuentos dispersos*, selección y prólogo de Alejandro Toledo, México: Universidad Nacional Autónoma de México, Serie Confabuladores, 1999.
[17] An example from Spain is *El desorden de tu nombre* by Juan José Millás.

books, especially the fantastic and playful mini-stories that he placed at the end of each section of more conventional short stories.[18] The collection of texts that in another context could be considered ancillary writing bestows more relevance on the collected material: in the new compilation the common elements shared by these pieces are more evident, and they seem to articulate a more unitary literary project.

In one type of dispersed short stories, the texts belong to a particular generic (or subgeneric) tradition and are published in a series that also contains other generic traditions. For example, in *Confabulario* by Juan José Arreola we find various science fiction stories ("El guardagujas", "Anuncio", "En verdad os digo" and "Baby H.P.") mixed with fantastic, allegorical and realistic stories.

A conclusion for a new beginning: fragments, details and fractals

The discussion of the structural relationships between the whole and its parts took as point of departure the distinction between the fragment (the breaking of a totality in elements that conserve a relative textual autonomy) and the detail (the provisional segmentation of a global, indivisible and integral unity). One particular type of detail is the fractal, which refers to those texts that contain generic, stylistic or thematic features that are shared with others in the same series. The detail, or fractal, is a narrative unit that makes sense only in relation to the series to which it belongs.[19] The fragment is a narrative unit that retains its literary or linguistic autonomy within the structural totality of the novel to which it belongs.[20] The fragment is the opposite of the fractal: the former is

---

[18] Anderson Imbert called *casos* (incidents) the very short stories he used to place at the end of his other stories of conventional extension. After a group of five short stories he placed five very short narrative texts and introduced them as *casos*, even though each of them had a title.

[19] This is the case with each of the sections of novels whose structure is based on the logic of music, such as *La creación* (1959) by Agustín Yáñez, *¿Quién desapareció al Comandante Hall? Sinfonía metropolitana para cinco voces* (1998) by Julia Rodríguez or *Bolero* (1997) by Pedro Ángel Palou. In the first two, each chapter adopts a rhythm of composition that corresponds to the tone of a musical score. In the last example, each chapter adopts the title of a bolero and indicates also the length of the song.

[20] This is the case with Chapter 62 of Cortázar's *Rayuela* (which later served as inspiration for his novel *62 / Modelo para armar*) or Chapter 68, already mentioned, of this same novel (written in *glíglico*, an idiolect specific to this text).

autonomous, while the latter conserves the features of the series. But while the detail is the result of an authorial decision, the fractal is the product of the reading process. All such elements further a decline in the integrity of traditional genres.

Studying textual series involves acknowledging the intensive use of literary resources such as ellipsis, implication, semantic ambiguity, narrative cataphora (the announcing of a narrative continuation in another textual segment) and an extreme economy of style. Such textual strategies are characteristic of literary minifiction.

Each of the titles mentioned above can be analyzed in terms of the structural organization of each series, which would enable one to examine the existing boundaries between the whole and its parts. We could name these mechanisms of unity and fragmentation "serial strategies", either hypotactic (a series of subordinate narrative units linked in syntactic order) or paratactic (a series of coordinated narrative units that are relatively autonomous and can be recombined during the reading process). These dynamics include other strategies as well: anaphoric (in which a narrative unit resumes an earlier event), cataphoric (which announces an event that is about to occur), elliptic (which suppresses an event that has already happened), analeptic (that is, flashback) and proleptic (that is, flashforward). At different moments of the short story, these strategies can affect fundamental narrative elements such as characters, time, setting, genre or style. How relations between the whole and fragment are articulated in each series depends on various elements, such as irony (either stable or unstable), which dissolves generic unity; extra-literary genres; and intertextuality, especially that which fuses various literary genres.

The notion of boundaries helps define concepts, establish limits, legislate exclusions, regulate identities, implant beginnings and establish properties. Short text series demand a reformulation not only of the borders between the whole and its parts and the limits between diverse canonical genres, but also of the most important border in the literary space: the one between the act of creation and the act of reading.

THE AMERICAN SHORT STORY IN THE TWENTY-FIRST CENTURY

CHARLES MAY

Although the short story, pioneered by Poe in the early nineteenth century, is often said to be a uniquely American invention, few American writers have ever been able to make a decent living from the form. The most obvious fact about the short story in American publishing is that agents and editors are seldom enthusiastic about taking on a collection of short stories – unless the author is a name with a novel to his or her credit, or unless the author is promising and will promise a novel in the near future. Most people would rather not read short stories. As the popularity of "reality" television in America makes clear, most people prefer the real to the fictional. The ratio of nonfiction to fiction in popular periodicals is about 99.9 to 1.

If readers do not want to read short stories, publishers certainly will not publish collections of them, and periodicals that have to make a profit will stick to pictures and celebrity-oriented nonfiction. The fairly large-circulation magazines that pay well for short fiction are few: *The New Yorker*, *Esquire*, *Playboy* and *Harper's Magazine*. Back in the Fifties, the *New Yorker* published between 100 and 150 stories a year; now it is only about 50. With the other three publishing one story an issue or fewer, the total number of stories in wide-circulation magazines per year in America is less than a hundred. Many hundreds more appear in such reviews and journals as *Agni*, *Cimarron*, *Cottonwood*, *Descant*, *Gulf Stream*, *High Plains*, *Kalliope*, *Nimrod*, *River Styx*, *Rosebud*, *Salmagundi*, *Thin Air* and *ZYZZYVA*, but their subscription lists are largely limited to university and college libraries, so they often go unread.

Most of those who do read fiction would rather read novels than stories. This has always been the case. Readers like to believe that characters have a life of their own, and they have to live with fictional figures for a while in order to believe that. Once you get started with a novel, you become friends, get familiar, take up residence. With a short story, you are no sooner introduced to a character than the story is over, leaving you a bit dazed. With a collection of stories, you have to do this over and over again. Unlike chapters in a novel, which tease you with the illusion of continuity, short stories are always ending. And often those conclusions – one of the form's most important aspects – are frustrating in their inconclusiveness. When readers finish novels, they close the book with a satisfied thump and a sense of a big job well done. Afterward they can talk about their experience with others – at the Xerox machine or at a cocktail party. Readers often finish short stories with a puzzled "Huh?" Few people open a conversation with "Have you read that story in the *New Yorker* this month?"

Occasionally a short story writer will arrive on the scene at just the right time, with just the right voice and vision, to reignite interest in the form. This happened in the late Seventies and early Eighties with the appearance of Raymond Carver, who, along with others such as Bobbie Ann Mason, Ann Beattie, Jayne Anne Phillips, Richard Ford and Tobias Wolff, wrote short stories of such hallucinatory realism that reviewers and critics had to create a name for it – "minimalism" or "hyper-realism"– a critical affectation that marked the end of the trend almost as soon as it had begun. However, for a time there was such a resurgence of interest in the short story that critics claimed that the form had experienced a "renaissance". But after the death of Carver and the denigration of minimalism by critics, the short story once more languished in the shadow of the novel. The following twenty major American short story collections published in the first six years of the twenty-first century, divided into characteristic categories, are fairly representative of the form today. After a brief discussion of new stories by some of those writers who participated in the minimalist boom of the Eighties, I discuss stories by young writers trained in America's burgeoning MFA programs, stories that primarily depend on narrative tricks and games, stories that are linked together novelistically and, finally, stories that, by their individual stylistic and thematic complexity, transcend any such categories.

The return of minimalist masters

After Carver, Ann Beattie was the most highly respected short story writer of the Eighties renaissance. Often labeled the spokesperson of the yuppie generation of the Seventies, Beattie has been alternately praised for her satiric view of that era's notorious passivity and criticized for presenting sophisticated *New Yorker* magazine versions of characters unable to understand themselves and unwilling to understand others. In the collection *Follies*, Beattie departs from her famous minimalism and plays with a variety of literary parodies and comic voices. Instead of being tightlipped, she is downright voluble. Instead of writing in an impassive monotone, she skips about her characters with self-conscious authorial glee.[1]

The longest story in the book is a novella called "Fléchette Follies".[2] The title is a sly joke about the tone and structure of the story itself, for "fléchette" is a type of ammunition used in cluster bombs, and "follies" is a kind of slapstick comic romp: both terms describe the story's narrative style very well. The main characters are a man named George Wissone and a woman named Nancy Gregerson in Charlottesville, Virginia. One morning Wissone gets in a minor traffic accident with Gregerson. Because Gregerson is worried about her son, Nick, who has disappeared in London, a victim, she supposes, of drug traffic and street life, she is curt and rude to Wissone, accusing him of having had too much to drink. Later she regrets her behavior, and when she runs into him at a coffee shop, she apologizes and they have a chat together. Puzzled by his reluctance to talk about his own life, she jokes that he is probably a CIA agent and asks if he would go to London and try to find her son. As it turns out – in true follies fashion, almost a slapstick twist – Wissone is indeed a CIA agent. Furthermore, since he is not involved in a serious assignment at the time, he is quite happy to search for Gregerson's son, not because he is attracted to Gregerson or eager to do a good turn for her, but because he just wants to see if he can be a responsive human being willing to do someone a favor when the goal is not money, sex or danger. He just wants to do something he thinks a normal person with a normal life would do.

However, again in true follies fashion, Wissone's task is anything but normal, and Beattie's story is anything but realistic or

---

[1] Ann Beattie, *Follies: New Stories*, New York: Scribner, 2005.
[2] *Ibid.*, 1-109.

minimalistic. When Wissone gets to England, he makes inquiries, and then abruptly, as if Beattie has no other purpose than to get him out of the way so she can hurry on to the end of the story, George Wissone steps out into the street and is run down by a cab rushing a pregnant woman to a doctor's appointment. He dies immediately, trapped under the cab. The remainder of the novella deals with Wissone's best friend and colleague trying to find out what happened to him, pursuing an investigation that includes an annoying interview with Nancy Gregerson, who finally orders him and his wife out of her house. "Fléchette Follies" is a curious, heavily plotted piece of work for the previously laconic Beattie. Although it is a pleasure to read because of Beattie's clever narrative style, it is mostly a *tour de force* of writerly fun, a playful parody combining light comedy and intrigue.

Although a multitude of sins may underlie it – indifference, insincerity, self-centeredness, fear of commitment – the single social sin that obsesses Richard Ford in the ten stories in his collection *A Multitude of Sins* is adultery.[3] It is such a hackneyed theme –hard to handle without becoming predictable, banal, and trivialized – that a writer must be especially wise or eminently polished to bring it off with insight and style. Ford won the Pulitzer and the Pen/Faulkner in 1995 for his novel *Independence Day*; sadly, however, in these stories Ford is often neither wise nor polished. The weakest are the three long, novelistic stories – "Crèche", "Charity" and "Abyss". They go on endlessly, padded with pondering, pontificating, philosophizing – all of which a writer may be able to get away with in a novel, but not in a short story, where such self-indulgences serve simply to tediously postpone a predictable end.

"Abyss", about an adulterous couple who leave a sales conference in Phoenix to go see the Grand Canyon, will probably get the most attention, both because it is the longest and – according to a common prejudice about contemporary narrative – must therefore be the most important, and also because it ends with a bit of a shock. The family trip in the midst of an illicit affair convinces the man that although the woman is a "tough, sexy little package" with "strong little bullet breasts" who is "screwing the daylights out of him",[4] she is intelligent only in bed. With writing this bad and a premise that adultery is an act that erases itself once the performance is over, the reader may guess

[3] Richard Ford, *A Multitude of Sins*, New York: Alfred A. Knopf, 2002.
[4] *Ibid.*, 236.

how the story ends as the woman peers over the edge of the abyss. The longer Ford goes on in his stories, the more he gives in to a penchant for playing the wise old novelist who knows about such things as love, betrayal, gender differences, what holds people together and what tears them apart. The trouble is, what he seems to know is often an uncomfortable mix of Hemingway-esque macho rubbish and *Redbook* pop psychology. The result is too much self-indulgence, too much self-analysis, too much self-absorption: in short, but unfortunately not in short enough, just too much self.

It has been twenty years since Amy Hempel published her first book, *Reasons to Live*, a collection of stories that prompted Madison Smartt Bell to complain in a controversial article in *Harper's* that, like most modish minimalists, Hempel just did not have much to say. In this, her fourth book, *The Dog of the Marriage*, Hempel is as tight-lipped as ever.[5] The question is not, however, whether Hempel has little to say, but whether the few words she chooses to explore the huge subjects in this book – love, loss, divorce, death, grief, betrayal, rape, heartbreak – are the right words to express their inexplicable essence. The stories are about finding a way to live when life is unlivable and language seems inadequate. For example, in one story, the reader rides with a woman who, having lost a solid center, stays constantly in motion by putting fifty-thousand miles on her car. Feeling she has no place to go, she just drives, listening to a tape of the Reverend Al Green repeating the theme "Jesus is waiting".[6] It is the "geographic cure" for her suffering, a search for symptoms; her only comfort is the old reassurance that "wherever you go, there you are".[7]

In another story, a fifty-year-old woman who thinks she may be pregnant but does not know who to blame – the husband she no longer lives with or the rapist she did not report – is fascinated by the spooky 1944 Ray Milland/Ruth Hussey film *The Uninvited*. She lives a haunted life in which fiction and reality, dream and waking, the real and the more-than-real are bound together so closely that the story ends in a scene of almost pathological pathos. In the title story, a woman facing the breakup of her marriage pretrains dogs who will then be further trained to be guides for blind partners. Although she is

[5] Amy Hempel, *The Dog of the Marriage*, New York: Scribner, 2005.
[6] *Ibid.*, 11.
[7] *Ibid.*, 15.

often asked how she can bear always to part with animals she has lived with, the woman struggles with the hard truth that all relationships are weighted with the threat of loss. A casual first reading of these stories may make one feel short-changed and cheated, but short stories are seldom meant to be read rapidly and once only. The challenge is to try to become the attentive, sympathetic reader they demand. Hempel's compulsion, like that of many short story writers, is similar to that of the poet – to struggle with human complexities that psychologists, sociologists, historians, novelists and other dispensers of explanatory discourse never quite account for.

When Bobbie Ann Mason's first book, *Shiloh and Other Stories*, was published, critics called it "K-mart chic" and raved about its introduction of "unremarkable" working-class Kentuckians who watched daytime television and shopped at chain stores while coping with the transition from life on the farm to a new world of strip malls and subdivisions. Mason then did what any short story writer must do to satisfy her publishers: she wrote some novels. Early admirers, who had seen no short fiction from Mason since her second collection, *Love Life* (1989), have wondered when she would return to the form at which she was best. With *Zigzagging Down a Wild Trail* Mason reasserted her position as one of the most important short story writers in the last quarter of the twentieth century.[8]

The stories in *Zigzagging* do not depend on brand names, pop culture, rural Kentucky folkways and cultural transitions – all characteristics that made Mason's early stories new and intriguing. However, because those surface characteristics at first attracted so much interest, little attention was paid to what ultimately will assure Mason's fiction a place in the short story canon in the future: her profound understanding of the secrets of her characters and her unerring ability to transform the mere stuff of experience into significance. Overall these stories are hopeful, not because something wonderful happens in them, but because nothing tragic does. The woman in "With Jazz", for example, is full of joy at the end of that story simply because there is no reason not to be. This is also true in the story "Tobrah" for a forty-four-year-old woman who has divorced two husbands and has no children. When her father, who deserted her as a child, names her as godparent to her five-year-old half-sister in

[8] Bobbie Ann Mason, *Zigzagging Down a Wild Trail*, New York: Random House, 2001.

his will, it is not the same as having a child of her own, but it is good enough to fill her with blissful abandon.

In "The Funeral Side", Sandra McCain returns home from Alaska to a small Kentucky town after her funeral director father has suffered a stroke. With light but significant touches, Mason leads the woman to an understanding of her father and an appreciation of – in what may be a description of the driving force of most of the characters in this collection – how people carry on, "out of necessity, and with startling zest, at the worst of times".[9] Even those who cannot come to a full acceptance of their past reach a point at which they understand what they have to do. For example, in "Three-Wheeler", when a woman living alone hires two boys and they begin to play dangerously on her old three-wheel lawn mower, she hops on the mower herself and takes off down the road, remembering a time with a young man on a motorcycle when she was in love. Still riding that Harley in her imagination, she is now "looking for road signs".[10] When it comes to the short story, Bobbie Ann Mason always knows exactly what she is doing. Lovers of that frequently neglected form and early admirers of Mason will be glad to know she is doing it again.

Tricks and games

T.C. Boyle has always wanted to be famous. Almost twenty-five years ago, he told an interviewer, "I would like to have about four or five times the audience Michael Jackson has for his records – and out dance him publicly".[11] Recently, the FAQ file at tcboyle.com quotes him as saying that if he had the choice of having a million people read his books or making a million dollars, he would take the first without qualification. Coming after his best-selling *Drop City* and his National Book Award nominee *The Inner Circle*, his collection *Tooth and Claw* may bring him closer to the goal expressed by one of his characters – attaining "mythic status".[12]

In print and in person, Boyle is always the showman. Tall and lean, with shaggy hair and scraggly beard, he looks like a hippie Ichabod Crane. Boyle says that in his readings he wants to give the audience a

---

[9] *Ibid.*, 138.
[10] *Ibid.*, 113.
[11] Garry Adams, "T.C. Boyle Would Be Famous", *Los Angeles Times*, 7 October 1987, C13.
[12] T.C. Boyle, *Tooth and Claw*, New York: Viking, 2005, 166.

good show, that he likes the power of being able to cast a spell. No
doubt about it, Boyle is a manipulative writer. You know this when
you hear or read one of his stories. But whether he is breaking your
heart or making you laugh, you just do not care because he is so
darned good at it. A classic example of his comic ability, "Swept
Away", takes place on the Shetland Islands, on the north coast of
Scotland, where the winds blow with such gale force that when
visiting American Junie Ooley steps off the ferry, she gets hit by a
flying twelve-pound tomcat. The result, irresistible enough to be
included in the 2003 *O. Henry Prize Stories*, is a whimsical folktale
with a love-struck hero and heroine doomed to be swept away from
each other, like Pecos Bill and Calamity Jane.

The two themes of *Tooth and Claw* – animals and losers – are
united in the title piece, which, Boyle says in his contributor's note to
the 2004 *Best American Short Stories*, returns to the Darwinian
conundrum of his first collection, *Descent of Man*. Taking its title
from Tennyson's *In Memoriam*, which warns of "Nature, red in tooth
and claw",[13] the story is about a lonely loser who wins a wild cat in a
barroom dice roll. Although he hopes the cat will heat up a sexual
relationship with the waitress who gives him advice on how to care
for it, like all wild things – women, relationships, sex – the creature
cannot be tamed or controlled. "Dogology", which echoes earlier
Boyle pieces about humans reverting to animal life, alternates two
complementary stories – one about a modern woman who so identifies
with dogs that she runs in a pack, and another about two young girls
raised by wolves in India.

Boyle's "loser" theme is most obvious in the significantly titled
"When I Woke Up This Morning, Everything I Had Was Gone" and
"All the Wrecks I've Crawled Out Of". In the former, men do stupid
things and risk losing all that is important to them in "a moment of
aberration".[14] In the latter, a Boyle-sounding character who says that
all he ever wanted was to achieve the larger-than-life status of James
Dean, Brom Bones or Paul Bunyan stumbles through alcohol, drugs,
sexual games and other land mines of the Sixties. In "Up against the
Wall", a Vietnam-era story (and perhaps autobiographical), a young
man who escapes the war by teaching eighth-grade English in a ghetto

---

[13] Alfred, Lord Tennyson, *In Memoriam*, 2nd edn, ed. Erik Gray, New York: W.W.
Norton, 2003, Canto 56, 41.
[14] Boyle, *Tooth and Claw*, 19.

school gets involved with bad company and heroin. Even though you may have heard these folktales and down-and-out fables before, Boyle has the voice to make you smile, make you care and make you hate yourself in the morning for being taken in by such a slick storyteller.

When George Saunders' first collection of stories, *CivilWarLand in Bad Decline*, appeared in 1996, he was hailed as a brilliant new satirist, and *The New Yorker* named him one of the twenty best American fiction writers under forty. Three stories in his well-received second collection, *Pastoralia* (2000), garnered O. Henry Awards. But it is hard nowadays for a satirist. No matter what fantastic concept one invents to mock commercialism and pop culture, it seems marketing has got there already. The story "My Flamboyant Grandson" in his third collection, *In Persuasion Nation*,[15] features a man who gets in trouble for removing the Everly Strips from his shoes, thus disabling omnipresent advertising images that target him with opportunities to "Celebrate His Preferences". But how distant is this from current Internet and credit card databases that allow corporations to anticipate the things we obviously want and need?

Variously called "cool",[16] "savage"[17] and "searing"[18] as a satirist, Saunders says he always starts off earnestly toward a target. However, "like the hunting dog who trots out to get the pheasant", he says, he usually comes back with "the lower half of a Barbie doll".[19] And indeed, this Saunders collection is chockfull of detritus and dreck. The title story, arguably the most experimental and challenging in the book, takes marketing to the ultimate cartoon extreme of bringing products to life. A Doritos bag decapitates a young man with a huge sword, and a torn green corner of a Slap-of-Wack candy bar morphs into an omniscient symbol that becomes demandingly godlike. When a polar bear preaches to penguins that a gentler god exists within us if we look for it, their response is to lay eggs that look like Skittles. "Bohemians" is a story Saunders admits he was stalled on for several

[15] George Saunders, *In Persuasion Nation*, New York: Riverhead, 2006.
[16] Jay McInerney in a review of *CivilWarLand in Bad Decline*, *The New York Times*, 4 February 1996, section 7, 7.
[17] Michiko Kakutani in a review of *CivilWarLand in Bad Decline*, *The New York Times*, 2 February 1996, C27.
[18] Michael Rezendes in a review of *Pastoralia*, *Boston Globe*, 14 May 2000, 1.
[19] Saunders in an interview with Kristen Tillotson, "Bookmarks", *Star Tribune* (Minneapolis, MN), 7 May 2000, F16.

years. Originally, he thought it would show how a person who had
suffered greatly could be a kinder person than one who suffered less,
but the story kept sounding like "Isaac Babel on stupid pills" until he
suddenly discovered that it was about something entirely different
than what he had thought. Even though the story ends, Saunders-like,
with a piece of dog dung rolled up in a Twinkie wrapper, it creates a
complex epiphany about a young man's discovery of the implications
of anguish.

A magical metaphor, a transforming trope – that is what initiates
and energizes the short stories of Rick Bass collected in *The Hermit's
Story*.[20] When the title story appeared in the 1999 *Best American
Short Stories* collection, Bass said that as soon as he heard about a
frozen lake with no water in it, he knew he wanted to write a story
about that.[21] In that story a female dog trainer and the Canadian man
who has hired her get caught in a freezing storm, then fall into the
fairy-tale wonderland created when a shallow lake freezes over and
the water under the ice percolates down into the soil. The result, says
Bass, is a realm in which the air is a thing of its own and reality takes
on the feeling of dream – a zone in which appearances disappear and
the essence of things is revealed. Such an alternate reality is an
appropriate metaphor for the kind of story that fascinates Bass.

Bass has said that "The Fireman", which appeared in the 2001 *Best
American Short Stories*, began with the image of a lost fireman
puncturing a tiny hole in a hose to create an umbrella-like protective
mist, a temporary "tiny refuge or brief harbor from duress".[22] "The
Fireman" is a kind of awe-inspired paean to the passion of a fireman,
a passion that Bass says takes on a rhythm of its own, like a living
thing. And indeed it is not plot but poetry that makes this story
fascinating. In another metaphor for the kind of story that Bass cannot
resist, he describes the moment of fire as one in which the importance
of a second is magnified almost to eternity. The trick of such stories is
to catch the reader up in the poetry of place or the magic of the
moment in which ordinary people are miraculously transformed and
mere things are illuminated with significance. "The Cave" is perhaps

---

[20] Rick Bass, *The Hermit's Story*, New York: Houghton Mifflin, 2002.
[21] Bass, Contributors' Notes, *Best American Short Stories*, ed. Amy Tan, Boston:
Houghton Mifflin, 1999, 377-78.
[22] Bass, Contributors' Notes, *Best American Short Stories*, ed. Barbara Kingsolver,
Boston: Houghton Mifflin, 2001, 346.

the purest example of Bass' fascination with creating magical worlds. An ex–coal miner goes naked into a narrow mineshaft with his equally naked girlfriend. They get separated, find each other, make love, board a small boxcar for an underground rail ride, make love, get lost, make love, come full circle around the little mountain under which they have wandered, come out into the light and are ready to "rejoin the unaltered flow of things".[23] Summarized, the story sounds absurd, but by the sheer power of imaginative projection and narrative drive, Bass makes it work. About half the stories in this collection are either trivial sleight-of-hand exercises or works where the illusion is not sustained, but the other half are genuine magical transformations that leave the reader smiling with wonder and wondering how the magician managed to pull it off.

MFA short fiction

Music through the Floor, a debut collection of nine stories by Eric Puchner,[24] a University of Arizona MFA recipient, now teaching in the creative writing program at Claremont McKenna College, is a classic example of short fiction consciously created within academia. Instead of erupting with originality out of powerful compulsions, as great stories must, Puchner's stories seem largely learned – skillful but, in both style and substance, imitative of so many other stories developed in MFA programs proliferating across the country. First, there is a story about a loner aimlessly searching for significance. In "The Children of God", a transient young man who says he cannot take care of himself gets a job caring for two developmentally disabled men whom he admires because they can be freely and openly themselves. This provides an opportunity for some sly social scorn. Then there is a story about a young woman looking for love. "Essay #3: Leda and the Swan" is in the form of a particularly long essay by a not particularly bright female student about the poem by William Butler Yeats, whom she calls a mentally ill person who knows nothing about the mating habits of swans. Her malapropisms and misunderstandings about literature and life provide an opportunity for some sophomoric humor.

Next there is a story about bullying children preying on weak outcasts. "Child's Play" is about a group of young boys who come together cruelly and dangerously on Halloween with a gun, a shampoo

---

[23] *Ibid.*, 89.
[24] Eric Puchner, *Music through the Floor*, New York: Scribner, 2005.

enema, and a bald mother with cancer. The meaningful metaphor is that after this grotesque reality they can come out later that night as startling creatures, such as animals, or monsters, or men. And naturally there must be one or two multicultural stories about the plight of the immigrant. "Diablo" is about an illegal laborer who sends money to his wife and children in Mexico. Reaching a breaking point, he gets in a fight, threatens his boss with a length of rebar, and loses his job. His one solace is the dignity of a Chinese woman in a neighboring apartment who has lost her husband. "Mission" is about an ESL teacher in San Francisco who experiences a mysterious animosity from one of his students. At a potluck party he throws, a game of charades provides an opportunity for some comic dialogue about the differences between cultures. Once again, there is a final display of dignity as the student makes a poetic presentation to the class about her childhood in Mexico.

Of all these well-made stories, the most academically rigged with symbolic significance and thematic unity is "Legends", a textbook piece self-consciously held together by the relentlessly repeated theme of death. A man with a "lazy heart"[25] takes his wife to Mexico to try to revive their marriage, where a stereotypical con artist accompanies them to a museum to see mummies and to a semi-comatose woman who performs miracles. Naturally the young man ends up losing everything. If you do not read lots of short stories, you will probably like these; they are intelligent, well written, and fairly typical of the form as it is taught in the schools these days. If you do read lots of stories, you will probably find them a bit too well wrought and too typical of stories taught in the schools these days.

To be the winner of the 2003 John Simmons Short Fiction Award given by the University of Iowa, *Bring Me Your Saddest Arizona* is a remarkably ordinary collection of stories.[26] One of the many graduates of the Iowa Writers' Workshop, Ryan Harty has neither a distinctive voice nor a compelling vision that would transform his shallow people into meaningful and memorable fictional characters. In two coming-of-age stories, a first-person narrator tells about ostensibly life-changing experiences with an older brother. In "Crossroads", the brother takes the narrator to a Led Zeppelin concert, where he teaches

---

[25] *Ibid.*, 106.

[26] Ryan Harty, *Bring Me Your Saddest Arizona*, Iowa City: University of Iowa Press, 2003.

him how to shotgun a can of beer, spit tobacco juice and pick up a young married woman for impromptu sex. In "What Can I Tell You about My Brother?" the narrator's older brother kills someone's German Shepherd with a Phillips screwdriver because the guy stole his girl. Perhaps the young narrator in these stories talks much the way someone of his age, education and social class might actually talk, but that is hardly enough to make the reader care about him.

Harty does better when he shifts to a third-person point of view, as he does in "Sarah at the Palace", about a man who comes to Las Vegas to clear out his sister's apartment after her death, for which he feels some guilt, and "Don't Call It Christmas", in which an assistant teacher in San Francisco gets involved with a homeless girl he supposedly is trying to help but with whom he really wants to have sex. Although these men are hardly more sympathetic than Harty's adolescent boys trying to come of age, at least they do not stumble through telling their own stories.

Because Julie Orringer seems so typical of today's young MFA-mill writers (graduate of the Iowa Writer's Workshop, Stegner Fellow in creative writing at Stanford, Pushcart Prize winner), one might be prepared to encounter a batch of cookie-cutter stories in her first collection, *How to Breathe Underwater*.[27] And, to tell the truth, there is some predictability in these well-made fictions, as if they spring as much from stories Orringer has studied as from emotions she has felt. There is no question that Orringer's teachers – Thom Jones, Frank Conroy and James Alan McPherson – have taught her well the art of the short story. However, despite the "not-another-Iowa-graduate" sigh the book jacket bio may prompt, these stories will often elicit a sharp shock of profound recognition and a begrudging nod of sincere admiration. For example, "Stations of the Cross", one of the many stories here about the sometimes-violent world of children, moves to an inevitable brutal climax: however, the fact that you know it is coming does not lessen the horror it provokes. And although "Pilgrims", the best-known and most celebrated story in the collection, seems almost a parody of running-wild children and New Age adults, when a terrible accident occurs that seems easily covered up by youthful viciousness and parental preoccupation, you cannot help but be shocked. Although some of the stories seem too much like

[27] Julie Orringer, *How to Breathe Underwater*, New York: Alfred A. Knopf, 2003.

312 *Charles May*

assignments for an MFA creative-writing class, they will jolt you. Artificial though they may be, you will not easily forget them.

When a thirty-four-year-old man becomes obsessed with an eighteen-month-old girl for whom he is babysitting, the reader, accustomed to shock stories "ripped from the headlines",[28] may initially feel uneasy. However, Kevin Brockmeier's "These Hands", the opening story of his debut collection, *Things That Fall from the Sky*,[29] has no such horrors lurking in its lyrical language. If the man were the girl's father and the word "love" were used instead of "obsession", the reader would smile approvingly. So why cannot a man, even though he is not the parent, idealistically love a little girl for her grace and beauty and innocence? It is one of the questions Brockmeier – a dreamer, a writer of fairy tales and a fabulist – poses in this engaging collection of eleven stories. Not yet thirty, still another prodigy of the University of Iowa writing program, Brockmeier has already won the *Chicago Tribune*'s Nelson Algren Award, the Italo Calvino Short Fiction Award, *Glimmer Train*'s New Writers Award and an O. Henry Prize Stories Award for four of these short fictions.

In the title story, an aging librarian gets in trouble with her supervisor when she answers a smart-aleck kid's question about where the pornography is. However, an elderly man fascinated with wonderful "things that fall from the sky" artfully rescues her by reminding her that the "world is a strange place".[30] "Space" is a lyrical meditation about a man who holds on to the memory of his dead wife while he and his son try to cope with the fact that electricity has gone out all over the city. The story ends with his recalling his wife's childhood practice of pointing a flashlight at a starless spot in the heavens and leaving it on until she fell asleep, hoping the beam would eventually reach a dark planet. He fantasizes wistfully that one day it will arrive at such a world and there will be feasting and celebration. Although he will inevitably be compared to T.C. Boyle, Steven Millhauser and George Saunders, Brockmeier's work is sweeter than theirs; there are no smirking satires here, no intellectual puzzles, no

---

[28] This phrase was used in commercial announcements for the long-running American television show *Law and Order* (2000-2010) to suggest stories that were of topical interest.
[29] Kevin Brockmeier, *Things That Fall from the Sky*, New York: Pantheon, 2002.
[30] *Ibid.*, 45.

metafictional mysteries. Instead, Brockmeier's stories explore an adult nostalgia for the fantasies of childhood, whether they came from the Bible or the Brothers Grimm.

Each year hundreds of earnest, hard-working graduates of the nation's MFA programs send their stories off to well-paying, wide-circulation magazines such as *The New Yorker* and *Harper's*, hoping to get a sale or two, which they can parlay into a six-figure book contract, followed by talk-show interviews and photo spreads in the big entertainment magazines. It seldom happens. However, when it does, as it did with ZZ Packer, it is worth speculating about how it happens. It is not enough that one is a good writer, although that certainly helps; the good writer must arrive at just the right time to fulfill the culture's need with just the right persona and just the right voice. ZZ Packer is a young African American woman whose rise to big-city buzz and momentary media stardom began with the summer 2000 special Debut Fiction issue of *The New Yorker*. Accompanying her story, "Drinking Coffee Elsewhere", was a full-page photo of Packer sitting on some rough city steps beside a cracked, graffiti-covered wall. Dressed simply in black slacks and a white top, her hair in cornrows, she stares at the camera with a sullen, even angry, look. Given this projected persona, it is not surprising that reviewers of her first book of short stories, of which *The New Yorker* story is the title piece, called her a fresh voice of the outsider and the disenfranchised. However, ZZ Packer is no child of the ghetto who has risen up shaking her fist in righteous anger at white economic oppression. Her parents were a middle-class small business owner and a schoolteacher. She is a Yale graduate who has also attended the prestigious Writing Seminar at Johns Hopkins University as well as the influential Iowa Writers Workshop.

After *The New Yorker* story appeared, Packer's recognition gathered speed at a fast pace. In the same year, *Harper's* published her story "Brownies", which was later chosen for the 2000 edition of *Best American Short Stories*. The buzz picked up when Riverhead Books, part of Penguin Putnam, won a bidding war for her first book, paying her an advance of approximately $250,000. Packer then won several prestigious awards, was given a Wallace Stegner Fellowship to teach in the Stanford University creative writing program, and was asked to teach at one of her alma maters, the famed Iowa Workshop. When her first book, *Drinking Coffee Elsewhere*, was published in early 2003,[31] Packer went on a whirlwind thirteen-city book tour, with picture spreads in *Vogue* and *O* magazine. In May 2003, John Updike picked her book for the *Today* Book Club, and she was interviewed by a gushing Katie Couric.

So what's the buzz all about? What Packer has succeeded in doing is to create African American characters who are not defined solely by their race or economic status or whose assertion of race is a relatively harmless result of the uncertainty of well-meaning whites. For example, "Brownies", whose narrator is a young African American girl at summer camp with her Brownie troop, begins as a typical race prejudice story, with her friends vowing to kick the butts of a troop of little white girls who have come to camp with complexions like a blend of strawberry and vanilla ice cream, packing Disney character sleeping bags. The African American girls are tough-talkers who laugh that the white girls smell like wet Chihuahuas and who scornfully call everything dumb or distasteful "Caucasian". The immediate cause of the conflict develops when one of the African American girls hears a white girl use the hated "N" word. Although the talk of retaliation is tough, it comes from the mouths of very young children who are not quite sure what would be the appropriate revenge, except maybe putting daddy longlegs in the white girls' sleeping bags and then beating them as flat as frying pans when they wake up. By the time the black girls decide to corner the white kids in the bathroom, the narrator says that the revenge was no longer about one of them being called a derogatory name, for the word that started it all now seems to have turned into something deeper and unnamable.

When the little white girls are actually confronted, the black girls discover that they are mentally handicapped, evoking the derogatory name "retarded" and suggesting an easy sort of turning-the-tables discrimination. Furthermore, the black girls are told that the white children are echolalic, which means they say whatever they hear, like an echo. The story thus ends as a sort of cautionary fable about prejudice and about how older generations pass down racial intolerance. Although the young African Americans are hard to resist, with their little-girl streetwise talk, they are really middle-class kids, posturing the way they have seen others do. Like the white girls, they are small children who say things they have heard others say. The story succeeds because it allows African American girls to make fun

[31] ZZ Packer, *Drinking Coffee Elsewhere*, New York: Riverhead, 2003.

of white girls and talk tough about beating them up for using the "N" word, but since they are only small children at summer camp, it is all within a harmless, comic context. It pleases readers that the discrimination tables get an O. Henry turn and that the story ends with a simple moralistic message about prejudice. ZZ Packer's stories are less about people who have been disenfranchised because of race or economic status than they are about a new generation of middle-class African Americans who have previously been ignored because all the attention has gone to the children of the ghetto.

Linked stories
There is a certain pleasure involved when you read a story in a collection and run across a character you have met in a previous story. Such character reappearances create amusing little shocks of recognition for the reader, a sort of "wow" factor that suggests that these characters actually live outside the fictions in which they exist and have been hanging around just waiting for another story in which to pop up. Called a "short story sequence", a "short story cycle", a "composite novel" or a "novel-in-stories", collections of stories that focus on the same characters or the same locale have been a staple of American fiction at least since Sherwood Anderson's *Winesburg, Ohio* (1919). However, such collections experienced a resurgence of interest in the first decade of the twenty-first century, partially as an organizing device by writers to hold the reader's interest throughout an entire book, and partially as a sales incentive by publishers to capitalize on the reading public's preference for a long continuous story over several short elliptical ones.

Joan Silber's tactic in her collection *Ideas of Heaven*,[32] signaled by her subtitle, "A Ring of Stories", is to make a minor character in one story a central character in a subsequent one, and thus to bring these six stories full circle by making the central character in the first story reappear as a secondary but important character in the final story. Although the linkages between the stories vary from the significant to the trivial, it cannot be determined whether Silber wrote these stories specifically to link them in this fashion or whether she wrote them individually and then later invented ways to link them to create this book. Perhaps more important than the somewhat artificial device of

---

[32] Joan Silber, *Ideas of Heaven: A Ring of Stories*, New York: W.W. Norton, 2004.

making secondary characters primary in a subsequent story is the way that the stories are unified by a central theme. All of the stories focus on some aspect of the relationship between romantic and religious passion, for all the characters find themselves caught in a fervor of love that exceeds any attempt at control. For this reason, the central or emblematic story in the collection is the third one, entitled "Gaspara Stampa", about an actual sixteenth-century Italian poet who, at age twenty-six, meets and becomes passionately obsessed with Collaltino di Collato, about whom she writes a series of love sonnets in the manner of Petrarch's passionate religious/romantic love poems for Laura. This thematic heart is more important, for example, than the somewhat peripheral introduction of Gaspara Stampa in the second story in the collection, "The High Road". Another method Silber uses to move from one story to another is illustrated in the segue from "Gaspara Stampa", which ends with Stampa dying of a fever, recalling how her poems were about "burning" for her lovers and feeling she has now set herself on fire and smoldering all night, to the subsequent story, significantly entitled "Ashes of Love", which begins with a quotation from Rainer Maria Rilke about Gaspara Stampa's soaring, objectless love. Whereas it may be mildly motivating to try to identify the connections as one reads, it is more interesting to respond to the stories as individual variations on the theme of religious and romantic passion. Short stories should be tight, unified literary forms that stand alone, not interdependent chapters in a longer work.

Although Stuart Dybek's first book after *The Coast of Chicago* (1990) was promoted by his publisher as a "novel-in-stories", the only thing novelistic about *I Sailed with Magellan* is that some of the same characters appear in all the stories.[33] In an interview from the year the collection was published, Dybek said that the overall narrative line of such linked story collections as Sherwood Anderson's *Winesburg, Ohio* and James Joyce's *Dubliners* does not even begin to suggest what they are about, for a successful story sequence refuses to believe that the design of life is a neat pattern of cause and effect. Thus, to call *I Sailed with Magellan* an ethnic "coming-of-age novel" about a young Polish American named Perry Katzek growing up on the South Side of Chicago in the Nineteen-Fifties and -Sixties is to minimize the universal power of the eleven individual stories, for each one is a self-

---

[33] Stuart Dybek, *I Sailed with Magellan*, New York: Farrar, Straus and Giroux, 2003.

contained, lyrical and powerful literary experience. In "Live from Dreamsville", an irresistible story about escape and fantasy, Perry tells his younger brother Mick that he has a secret trapdoor in his bed going down to a clubhouse full of sodas, malts and candy. They play a radio game, in which Mick sings a song he made up entitled "I Sailed with Magellan". However, the real world hovers near them: the story ends with the sound of a dog softly whimpering in the next apartment because its owner beats it.

Even the pieces with the kind of polished professionalism that has often given the short story a bad name are redeemed by Dybek's lyrical style and his refusal to rush to a neat final twist. And though the best-known story in the collection, "We Didn't" (picked for both *Best American Short Stories* and the *O. Henry Awards* in 1994), is primarily a clever *tour de force*, Dybek makes it into an evocative piece of music. There is an unforced, memoir-like quality to Dybek's stories, but do not be deceived, for they only seem to have memory's laxity, until they slowly tighten and – without any forced epiphanies – transport the reader to a different realm of reality. These eleven pieces are powerful not because they are novelistically linked but because they are compelling individual short stories.

Beth Lordan, professor of creative writing at Southern Illinois University, had just returned from a spring semester in Ireland when she wrote "The Man with the Lapdog", the first story in *But Come Ye Back*, a "novel-in-stories" about an American man and his Irish-born wife retiring to her homeland.[34] Although each story in the collection is a perfectly formed independent fiction, the separate parts create an even greater whole. And the reason is the reader's gradual discovery of, and growing concern for, the central characters. As you read each story, you experience shifting allegiances. At one point Lyle seems like a gruff curmudgeon and his wife long-suffering; at another, Mary seems shrewishly sharp-tongued and Lyle quietly self-sacrificing. Like most couples who have lived together for many years, Lyle and Mary chafe against each other, find it difficult to say how they really feel and occasionally fantasize about being with someone else. For Lyle, it occurs when he meets an American couple on holiday and discovers that the husband is dying of cancer; he imagines meeting the wife again later, but, unlike in famous Chekhov story of illicit love from which "The Man with the Lapdog" gets its name, he quietly

---

[34] Beth Lordan, *But Come Ye Back*, New York: William Morrow, 2004.

values his own relationship. For Mary, it is an Irish man about whom she can momentarily pretend a quite different story than her marriage to this American who sometimes seems so much an ungrateful stranger in a strange land. *But Come Ye Back* concludes with a novella in which Mary gets her wish to be buried among her own people and in which Lyle, now in his seventies, comes gruffly together with his two grown sons and must decide whether to return to America or to stay where Mary seems most alive. Lordan is a wise and honest writer of great skill and delicacy who knows the short story form well.

Masters that transcend categories

The Secret Goldfish is David Means' third book,[35] and it goes against good economic sense, not to mention the probable pleas of his agent and publishers, that it is, once again, a book of short stories. Although his previous collection, *Assorted Fire Events* (2000), won the *Los Angeles Times* Book Prize for fiction, was short-listed for the National Book Critics Circle Award, and received rave reviews both in America and England, still it was just a collection of short stories. Like José Luis Borges and Adolfo Bioy Casares, who once said that a short story may be, for all purposes, "essential",[36] or Andre Dubus, who said he loved short stories because "they are the way we live",[37] or Alice Munro,[38] who once told an interviewer that she does not write novels because she sees her material in a short story way, David Means sees the world in a short story way. To understand that "short story way", pick up *The Secret Goldfish*. But do not rush through its fifteen stories. Read one, put the book aside and meditate on the mystery of the human condition the story explores. Then wait a while before reading another.

The short story is often misunderstood and underrated because readers read it the same way they do sections of novels. One should not go to David Means for plot that rushes to its inevitable end or for easily recognizable character, like the folks you meet every day. One should go to Means for some scary, sacred sense that what happens is

---

[35] David Means, *The Secret Goldfish*, New York: Fourth Estate, 2004.

[36] José Luis Borges and Adolfo Bioy Casares, Preliminary Note, *Cuentos breves y extraordinarios* (1953), eds José Luis Borges and Adolfo Bioy Casares, Buenos Aires: Santiago Rueda, 1970, 7.

[37] Andre Dubus, "Marketing", in *Broken Vessels*, Jaffrey, NH: Godine, 1991, 104.

[38] Rothstein Mervyn, "Canada's Alice Munro Finds Excitement in Short Story Form", *The New York Times*, 10 November 1986, C17.

not as important as what it signifies and for the shock of recognition that those you thought you knew you do not really know at all. One goes to Means for mystery and the paradox understood by the great short story writers from Poe to Chekhov to Carver – that if you remove everything extraneous from a scene, an object, a person, its meaning is revealed, stark and astonishing. The first paragraph of the first story, "Lightning Man", makes clear that the realm of reality that matters for Means is sacramental, ritualistic, miraculous – a world in which the old reassurances, such as "Lightning never strikes twice in the same place", are shown to be nonsense. Here a man is struck seven times throughout his life by a powerful revelatory energy until he becomes a mythic creature, waiting for the inevitable eighth. In the short story world of David Means, a mundane tale of infidelity and divorce gets transformed by the metaphoric stillness of a neglected goldfish in a mucked-up tank, surviving despite the stagnation around it.

Means' short stories are seldom satisfied with linear plot and thus often become lists of connected mysteries. "Notable Dustman Appearances to Date" is a series of hallucinatory manifestations of famous faces in swirling dust kicked up by wind or smoke: Nixon, Hemingway, Gogol, Jesus. "Michigan Death Trips" is a catalog of catastrophic disruptions, as people abruptly disappear beneath the ice of a frozen lake, are suddenly struck on the highway, or are hit by a stray bullet from nowhere. "Elyria Man" lays bare mummified bodies found lying beneath the soil, as if patiently waiting to embody some basic human fear or need. In each of these stories, Means reveals the truth of our lives the way great art always has – by making us see the world as it painfully is, not as our comfortable habits hide it from us. He is a brilliant new master of the short story who fully understands and respects the form's power.

Since reading her first collection, *Taking Care*, in 1982, I have been of two minds about the stories of Joy Williams. On the one hand, I think she is one of the very best short story writers in America, uncannily able to create pearls of revelation with seemingly inconsequential irritants of insight and language. On the other hand, some of her stories just grate on my ear and consciousness with quirky and flippant bits of cultural grit. *Honored Guest*,[39] her third collection (her second, *Escapes*, was published in 1990), reaffirms that dual

---

[39] Joy Williams, *Honored Guest*, New York: Alfred A. Knopf, 2004.

reaction. Most of the twelve stories in *Honored Guest* are brilliant and beautiful: "Congress", in which a woman develops a loving companionship with a lamp made out of four cured deer feet and decides to take over a small taxidermy museum; "Visiting Privilege", in which a woman, after befriending an older lady in a hospital, takes care of her dog after her death – one of those irritating toys that mechanically barks when someone comes near; "Substance", in which a man wills various possessions to his friends, which they cannot wait to get rid of; "Charity", in which a woman leaves her husband on the highway to go back to help some people in trouble and cannot escape them; "Hammer", in which a sixteen-year-old girl picks up a destitute man at a bus station and brings him home to aggravate her mother, whom she abhors.

Trust me, these stories are nowhere near as silly as some of them sound. Williams is a master at making us giggle at the ghastly. The title story, which was included in *Best American Short Stories, 1995*, is a beautiful signature piece for Williams, not only because it deals with the last few months of her ill mother's life but also because it tenaciously explores what she says all art should be about – our apprehension at the approach of nothingness. To live, the central character in this story understands, is to be like an "honored guest" in a Japanese aboriginal ritual, in which a bear cub is captured and treated royally for some time, until an inevitable day when everyone in the village drags it out, tortures it and kills it. These six stories make us laugh at the things we do to cope with what beleaguers us on the way to the inevitable. Joy Williams' characters do silly things. They buy Grecian Formula for their dog when he starts going gray. They get an inflatable Safe-T-Man as a protective companion, and then become afraid of it. Such absurd nonsense. Such painful truth. As Williams once said, a writer "loves the dark ... cherishes the mystery .... Oh, it's silly, dangerous work indeed."[40]

What makes Charles D'Ambrosio a great short story writer is his sympathy for the frailty of the self, his respect for the delicacy of story structure, and his reverence for the precision of language. However, in an age in which the majority believe that reality television is real and that "hip-hop" is as precise as language can get, these are, unfortunately, the very qualities that will make his stories appreciated

---

[40] Joy Williams, "Why I Write", in *Ill Nature: Rants and Reflections on Humanity and Other Animals*, New York: Lyons Press, 2001, 207.

only by a minority. Read some of D'Ambrosio's contributor's notes in *Best American Short Stories* and *The O. Henry Prize Stories*, where three of the stories in his collection *The Dead Fish Museum* (2006)[41] appeared over the past few years, and you will understand his respect for his characters and his work – how he struggled with sympathy for the two drifters in "The Scheme of Things", how "Screenwriter" developed slowly over the years from his experience with several wounded people, and how the sentences of "The High Divide" finally became "healthy and true" only after 116 drafts.

Two stories here – "The High Divide" and "Drummond & Son"– are about the delicate division between fathers and sons – the first about two boys trying to come to terms with the inexplicability of fathers, and the second about a man trying to care for a son suffering from a neurological disorder brought on by the drugs he takes for schizophrenia. Rigorously unsentimental, yet absolutely heart wrenching in their consummately controlled language, the stories will leave you stunned with love and marveling at the concluding images of echoes reverberating out of darkness and reflections staring back out of mist. "Screenwriter" is a combination of the comic coping language of a skilled writer suffering on a psychic ward with suicidal obsessions and his frighteningly beautiful images of a ballerina who burns herself. From the first time she ignites her paper gown and seems to levitate phoenix-like in flames to the final excruciating assault she makes on her body with a cigarette, the screenwriter narrator is unable to take his eyes off her. When he tells her he wants to crawl into her mouth and die, she says her mouth is full of dead boys and blows him a kiss that elevates the moment out of space and time.

The title story is also about a man energized by his desire to kill himself. Supervising carpentry on the filming of a porno movie in the desert, he becomes involved with his Hispanic crew and the film's female star, all of whom perhaps, or perhaps not, manage to save him, at least for a time. The title comes from a Spanish woman's inability to pronounce "refrigerator", calling it instead "the dead fish museum". It is a sardonic name for a book filled with painfully alive characters. D'Ambrosio is a great short story writer because he compellingly confronts the inexplicable mysteries of what it means to be a human being – mysteries that cannot be solved, only gaped at with awe. He is

---

[41] Charles D'Ambrosio, *The Dead Fish Museum*, New York: Alfred A. Knopf, 2006.

a great short story writer because he honestly struggles with the way
language tries to capture those mysteries. There are few writers today
who should be read so carefully that your lips move: D'Ambrosio is
one of them.

Andrea Barrett once told an interviewer that after doing graduate
work, first in zoology in the late Seventies and then in history in the
early Eighties, she began to see a way to weave science and history
together with her love of fiction. The resulting elegant tapestry was
her collection *Ship Fever and Other Stories*, a surprise winner of the
National Book Award in 1996. After the success of her Conradian
adventure novel of ideas, *The Voyage of the Narwhal*, in 1998, Barrett
returned to short fiction in *Servants of the Map*[42] to explore
connections between science, history and storytelling in a collection
of eight exquisite narratives.

The title story – a carefully constructed novella about a nineteenth-
century surveyor who is part of an exploration party to the Himalayas
– has already been twice honored: selected for *The Best American
Short Stories: 2001* and *Prize Stories 2001: The O. Henry Awards*. In
a series of letters to his wife Clara back in England, Max Vigne
discovers the power of writing to construct reality and thus the ability
to go beyond mapping and recording to actually seeing, thereby
creating a map not only of the physical world but of the human mind.
The many admirers of *Ship Fever* will recognize recurring characters
in *Servants*. Rose and Bianca, competitive siblings in the earlier "The
Marburg Sisters", reappear here in "The Forest" and "The Mysteries
of Ubiquitin". In the former, Bianca, doomed to languish in the
brighter light of her successful scientist sister, takes an elderly visiting
scientist to a magical sighting of deer in a forest clearing, in the
process establishing a sense of conjunction between cultures,
individuals, and the past and present. The latter is a traditional story of
Rose's idolization at age eight of a young zoologist. When she has a
brief affair with him when she is thirty-one and he is fifty-one, she
discovers only an aging man whose scientific approach is old-
fashioned and who is unable to understand her own complex study of
the mysteries of ubiquitin, a protein that binds to other molecules and
marks them for degradation.

Although these character reappearances create pleasurable little
shocks of recognition for the reader, they are not just narrative

---

[42] Andrea Barrett, *Servants of the Map*, New York: W.W. Norton, 2002.

gimmicks, but rather indications of Barrett's conviction of the basic similarities between science, history and storytelling. She knows that all three construct narratives – whether they are called scientific theories, historical accounts or fiction – reveal connections, relationships, the interdependence of all things: all are human efforts to understand, or perhaps construct, what makes life meaningful. Barrett's obsession with connections sometimes goes too far and results in a self-conscious concern with structure and parallelism, but her stories are always fascinating because they brilliantly explore the central driving force of the human imagination.

The short story's lack of room to ruminate about big sociopolitical issues is one reason the form is not popular with serious critics who prefer genres that generalize. The kind of complexity that fascinates masters of the short story is captured not by using more and more words but by using just the right ones. The best stories in Deborah Eisenberg's *Twilight of the Superheroes*[43] reflect her continuing conscientious effort to provide a structure and a syntax for feelings unspeakable until just the right rhythm makes what was loose and lying around inside clench and cluster into a meaningful pattern. For example, in "Some Other, Better Otto", the central character is so self-negating, so full of doubt and dubiousness, that you just want to smack him. But you know he cannot help it, that of all his possible selves he cannot quite seem to find that other, better one that would make his life full and complete. What great short story writers like Eisenberg know is that there is no unified self, only rare moments of recognition, evanescent contacts of communication.

In "Like It or Not", a divorced midwestern high school biology teacher visits a sophisticated friend in Italy and is expertly guided about by a polished and knowledgeable European man. As in a delicate Jamesian romance, nothing much happens, but much is immanent. It is not just that the man feels he is getting older or that the woman feels insecurely empty, but rather, as the man tells a young woman they encounter in a hotel: "It's quite mysterious, what attracts one human being to another."[44] This is the kind of mystery that great short story writers, such as Chekhov, have always struggled with.

---

[43] Deborah Eisenberg, *Twilight of the Superheroes*, New York: Farrar, Straus and Giroux, 2006.
[44] *Ibid.*, 119.

However, when Eisenberg veers away from the inexplicable motivations that the short story captures so delicately and moves toward the sociopolitical generality of the novel, she lapses into generalities. In the title story, four young people live in a kind of "holding pattern" in a luxurious apartment in New York City. One of them draws a comic strip entitled *Passivityman* about a superhero indifferent to "Captain Corporation who tightens his Net of Evil around The Planet Earth".[45] Having lost the superpowers of their youth, they witness the terrorist attack on the Twin Towers, and somehow their private lives are absorbed by the "arid wasteland of policy and strategy"[46] and the story evaporates into abstraction and rumination. Eisenberg, a master of the short story, succeeds much more often than she fails because she brilliantly exploits what the form does best. It is only when she seems to be seduced by the public demand for the novelistic that she breaks faith with the great masters who have preceded her.

Because American readers are more interested in nonfiction and the occasional novel than the short story, the form is currently in the literary doldrums in the United States. The fact that no one short story writer has been able to capture the imagination of both popular readers and academic critics the way Raymond Carver did in the late Seventies and early Eighties has not helped matters. This does not mean that excellent short stories are no longer written, published or read in America, just that, with few exceptions, they have not received the attention that they did in the minimalist renaissance. When readers get tired of the careless long-windedness of the current novel and long for carefully crafted prose about complex human experience, the short story, which has always been the pride of American literature, will regain its lost respect.

---

[45] *Ibid.*, 22.
[46] *Ibid.*, 36.

NOTES ON CONTRIBUTORS

Pilar Alonso is Associate Professor of English Linguistics in the English Department at the University of Salamanca, Spain. Her main fields of research are discourse analysis and cognitive linguistics, with a special interest in literary discourse analysis. She has published numerous articles on semantic, pragmatic and cognitive aspects of literary works by North American and British authors; among them are "The Conceptual Integration Network Model as a Paradigm for Analysis of Complex Narrative Discourse" (2004), "Conceptual Integration as a Source of Discourse Coherence: A Theoretical Approach with Some Examples from William Boyd's 'My Girl in Skin-Tight Jeans'" (2003), and "Grammatical Conceptualization as a Poetic Strategy in e.e. cummings' '*yes is a pleasant country*'" (2003). She is the author of *Semantics: A Discourse Perspective* (2005) and has coedited *Aspects of Discourse Analysis* (2002) and translated and edited I.B. Singer's book *Un amigo de Kafka y otros relatos* (1990). She is currently working on a research project on creative patterns of coherence in literary discourse.

María Teresa Gibert is Professor of English at the Spanish National University of Distance Education (UNED) in Madrid, Spain, where she is head of the Department of Foreign Languages and teaches courses on American and Canadian literature. A well-known T.S. Eliot scholar (a contributor to *T.S. Eliot at the Turn of the Century*, ed. Marianne Thormählen, 1994, and *T.S. Eliot and Our Turning World*, ed. Jewel Spears Brooker, 2000), she has written extensively on British, American and Canadian literature. She is the author of *American Literature to 1900* (2001; 2nd edn, 2009) and contributed the chapter "'Ghost Stories': Fictions of History and Myth" to the volume *The Cambridge History of Canadian Literature* (2009). She has published numerous articles on short fiction in journals and essay collections and has participated in the international conferences of the Society for the

Study of the Short Story. She is currently an editorial consultant for the *Journal of the Short Story in English*.

Peter Gibian is Associate Professor of American Literature in the English Department at McGill University in Montréal, Canada. His publications include an edited essay collection, *Mass Culture and Everyday Life* (1997), as well as essays on Whitman, Melville, Poe, Hawthorne, Twain, Edward Everett Hale, Bayard Taylor, Wharton and James, Doctor Holmes and Justice Holmes, Michael Snow and shopping mall spectacle, the experience of nineteenth-century shopping arcades, and cosmopolitanism in nineteenth-century American literature. His study *Oliver Wendell Holmes and the Culture of Conversation* (2001) was awarded Best Book Prize in 2001 and 2002 by the New England American Studies Association. Gibian is just completing a new book, *Talking in Circles*, that explores the mid-century American "culture of conversation" as it shaped the writings of a wide range of authors. He is also working on an ongoing book project on the relation of a line of nineteenth-century American writers and artists to the cosmopolitan vision of a "traveling culture".

Luisa Mª González Rodríguez is currently teaching at the University of Salamanca, Spain. Her main fields of interest are postmodernism, reception theory and the American postmodern short story. She has published articles on postmodern writers such as John Fowles, John Barth and Donald Barthelme and is also the author of *Documentos históricos de los EE.UU: Introducción y comentarios* (1998), a compilation of documents of American history. Her latest research is on the intertextual manipulation of the Gothic in the novels of John Fowles, published as part of a book by the University of Salamanca Press. She has also written a book on Fowles and the role of the reader (in press). She has participated in various research projects on American poetry and American short stories.

María Jesús Hernáez Lerena is Associate Professor at the University of La Rioja (Spain), where she teaches American and Canadian literatures. Her main field of research for a number of years was short story theory, and she has written three books on the short story: *Exploración de un género literario: Los relatos breves de Alice Munro* (1998), *Story Time: Exercises in the Study of American*

Literature for Advanced Students of English (1999), and *Short Story World: The Nineteenth-Century American Masters* (2003). She has published articles on Sara Orne Jewett, Wyndham Lewis, Carol Shields, Alice Munro, Barbara Gowdy, Katherine Govier, Douglas Glover and others in Spanish, English and Canadian journals. She has been editor of the *Journal of English Studies* (University of La Rioja). She coedited the book *Canon Disorders: Gendered Perspectives on Literature and Film in Canada and the United States* (2007). She is now doing research on the literature and culture of Newfoundland.

Rebeca Hernández holds a PhD in Portuguese studies from the University of Salamanca and is Assistant Professor in the Department of Modern Languages. Her main research interests are postcolonial literature in Portuguese, literary translation, translation of postcolonial literary texts in Portuguese, translation ethics, cognitive linguistics, discourse coherence and the translation of multilingual literary texts. She is the author of the book *Traducción y postcolonialismo: Procesos culturales y lingüísticos en la narrativa postcolonial de lengua portuguesa* (2007) and has published articles in various scholarly journals. She is a member of the editorial board of the research journal *Estudios portugueses: Revista de filología portuguesa* from the University of Salamanca. She is also a literary translator and has translated into Spanish works by João de Melo, Luís Bernardo Honwana, Manuel Alegre and Hugo Milhanas Machado.

Farhat Iftekharuddin is Professor of English at the University of Texas at Brownsville. After serving for several years as the Dean of the College of Liberal Arts, he is currently the Special Assistant to the Provost for International Programs. Along with his teaching, he also assists the university in its efforts to develop cooperative relationships with international institutions. His academic area of specialization is twentieth-century American literature, with an emphasis on postmodernism. He has written on a variety of authors, including Salman Rushdie, Carlos Fuentes, Isabel Allende, Sandra Cisneros, Richard Brautigan, Bharati Mukherjee and Rudolfo Anaya. He is also the editor of *The Postmodern Short Story: Forms and Issues* (2003) and *Post Modern Approaches to the Short Story* (2003).

Antonio López Santos is Associate Professor of English Literature at the University of Salamanca (Spain) and Chair of the English Department, where he teaches medieval and Renaissance English literature. He has published books and articles on Shakespeare and on medieval and modern drama. His published books include a bilingual poetic anthology titled *Wordsworth, Coleridge, Keats, Shelley* (1978), a study and edition of *Bernard Shaw's "Saint Joan"* (1982), and various coedited collections of essays. He is also the author of a book on the theater of the avant-garde, *Bernard Shaw y el teatro de vanguardia* (1989). Together with Rubén Tostado, he has coauthored a study on Spanish drama, *Interludio de Calisto y Melibea* (2001). He has just finished a book-length study titled *The Origins of the Theatre in England*.

Charles May is Emeritus Professor at California State University, Long Beach. He is the best-known and most frequently quoted expert on the short story genre. He has published a number of scholarly books on the topic: *Edgar Allan Poe: A Study of the Short Fiction* (1991), *The Short Story: The Reality of Artifice* (2002) and *Twentieth Century European Short Story* (1989). He is editor of *Short Story Theories* (1977), New *Short Story Theories* (1994) and *Fiction's Many Worlds* (1992). He has published over two hundred articles in journals such as *Studies in Short Fiction*, *Style* and the *Minnesota Review*. He has also developed a software program, HyperStory.

Consuelo Montes-Granado is Associate Professor at the University of Salamanca, where she teaches English pragmatics and sociolinguistics. Her main fields of interest are politeness phenomena, feminist pragmatics and critical pedagogy. She has published books and articles on sociolinguistic stylistics and on the sociolinguistic dimension of teaching language and content subjects. Her published books include *D.H. Lawrence: El dialecto en sus novelas* (1990) and *Sons and Lovers y las tres versiones de Lady Chatterley's Lover: Interpretación sociolingüística* (1993). She is coeditor of *Multidisciplinary Studies in Language and Literature: English, American and Canadian* (2008).

Carolina Núñez-Puente holds an MA in Women's and Gender Studies from Rutgers University and a PhD from the University of La

Coruña, where she teaches courses on English and feminist studies. She is the author of a book titled *Feminism and Dialogics: Charlotte Perkins Gilman, Meridel Le Sueur, Mikhail M. Bakhtin* (2006). She is currently preparing a second book that reads nominally ethnic literature from a Bakhtinian-feminist perspective. More concretely, her current research deals with the works of Sandra Cisneros, Zora Neale Hurston, Bharati Mukherjee and Leslie Marmon Silko and the way in which they reconfigure US literature.

Viorica Patea is Associate Professor of American Literature at the University of Salamanca, where she teaches American and English literature. Her published books include *Entre el mito y la realidad: Aproximación a la obra poética de Sylvia Plath* (1989); a study on Whitman, *La apología de Whitman a favor de la épica de la modernidad: El Prefacio de 1855 de Hojas de hierba* (1999) and a study of T.S. Eliot's *The Waste Land* (2005). She has edited various collections of essays, such as *Critical Essays on the Myth of the American Adam* (2001) and, together with Paul Derrick, *Modernism Revisited: Transgressing Boundaries and Strategies of Renewal in American Poetry* (2007). In addition to poetry, her research interests include witness literature. In collaboration with Fernando Sánchez Miret, she has translated from Romanian into Spanish the annotated edition of *El diario de la felicidad* by Nicolae Steinhardt (2007) and *Proyectos de Pasado* and *Las Cuatro estaciones* by Ana Blandiana (2008, 2011). Currently she is working on a book project on the relationship between poetry and visual arts. At present she is translating the poems of Ana Blandiana into Spanish and English in collaboration with the poets Antonio Colinas and Paul Derrick.

Santiago Rodríguez Guerrero-Strachan is Associate Professor at the University of Valladolid (Spain), where he teaches American literature. His field of research is the American short story and postcolonial literature. He has published extensively on American short fiction. He is also interested in the cultural and literary relations between America and Spain. His publications include *Presencia de Edgar Allan Poe en la literatura española del siglo XIX* (1999) and the coedition of *Cuentos insólitos* (2000). He has also edited and translated Henry James' stories for a volume titled *Daisy Miller, Otra vuelta de tuerca y otras historias* (2005) and recently published *En* *torno a los márgenes: Ensayos de literatura poscolonial* (2008). He is the editor of an anthology of grotesque short stories, *Antología del cuento grotesco* (2007), and of an anthology of nineteenth-century American short fiction, *Pioneros* (2011). His articles focus on Romantic short fiction, twentieth-century American short fiction and poetry, and the reception of British Romanticism in Spain.

Erik Van Achter is Associate Professor English at the K.U. Leuven Association (Belgium). His PhD at the University of Utrecht concerned short story theory, with a focus on Portuguese short fiction. His main fields of interest are Anglo-American and postwar German short story theory. He has published various essays on the genre. He has just finished a book in this domain, *A Poetics of Intimacy, on the Nature of the (Portuguese Short)*, and he is currently working on a book project on the history of short fiction theory. He has participated in various research projects on Portuguese and American short stories.

Per Winther (1947-2012) was Professor of American Literature at the University of Oslo. His publications include *The Art of John Gardner: Instruction and Exploration* (1992), *The Art of Brevity: Excursions in Short Fiction Theory and Analysis* (2004) and articles on Emily Dickinson, Ernest Hemingway, Robert Lowell, Ralph Ellison, Alice Walker and Canadian short fiction. From 2004 to 2007 he was editor of the biannual journal *American Studies in Scandinavia*. He was president of the American Studies Association of Norway and head of the Norwegian chapter of the Nordic Association for Canadian Studies and chair of the Department of Literature, Area Studies, and European Languages at the University of Oslo.

Lauro Zavala is Professor at the Universidad Autónoma Metropolitana – Xochimilco, Mexico City, where he is head of intertextual semiotics. He is known for his work on literary theory, semiotics and film, especially in relation to irony, metafiction and micro-narratives. He is author of a dozen books and has published over a hundred-and-fifty articles in books and journals in the US, UK, France, Spain, and fifteen other countries. Chair of the Permanent Seminar on Film Analysis (SEPANCINE) since 2005, he organizes a National Conference on Film Analysis. He is the director of *El cuento* *en red: Estudios sobre la ficción breve*, http://cuentoenred.xoc.uam. mx, a journal of research theory and literary analysis created in 2000 at UAM – Xochimilco in collaboration with Humboldt State University. His most recent books are *Manual de análisis narrativo* (2007), *La minificción bajo el microscopio* (2006), *La precisión de la incertidumbre* (2006), *Cartografías del cuento y la minificción* (2004), *Paseos por el cuento mexicano* (2004), *Cómo estudiar el cuento* (2003) and *Elementos del discurso cinematográfico* (2003). His book *Relatos vertiginosos: Antología de cuentos mínimos* (2000) has already sold 58,000 copies.

INDEX

CPSIA information can be obtained at www.ICGtesting.com
Printed in the USA
LVOW06*1423031013

355308LV00023B/79/P